Revitalizing Endangered Languages

Of the approximately 7,000 languages in the world, at least half may no longer be spoken by the end of the twenty-first century. Languages are endangered by a number of factors, including globalization, education policies, and the political, economic, and cultural marginalization of minority groups. This guidebook provides ideas and strategies, as well as some background, to help with the effective revitalization of endangered languages. It covers a broad scope of themes including effective planning, benefits, well-being, economic aspects, attitudes, and ideologies. The chapter authors have hands-on experience of language revitalization in many countries around the world, and each chapter includes a wealth of examples, such as case studies from specific languages and language areas. Clearly and accessibly written, it is suitable for nonspecialists as well as for academic researchers and students interested in language revitalization. This book is also available as Open Access on Cambridge Core.

JUSTYNA OLKO, director of the Center for Research and Practice in Cultural Continuity at the University of Warsaw, is engaged in revitalizing the Nahuatl language in Mexico and works with activists supporting other endangered languages, especially in the area of Poland. Her current research focuses on the relationship between heritage language use, health, and well-being. She is the author of *Insignia of Rank in the Nahua World* (2014) and coeditor of *Integral Strategies for Language Revitalization* (2016).

JULIA SALLABANK'S language revitalization work started with her heritage language, Guernesiais, in 2000, and spread worldwide. She teaches documentation and revitalization at the School of Oriental and African Studies (SOAS), University of London. She has written *Attitudes to Endangered Languages* (2013) and, with Peter Austin, *Endangered Languages: Beliefs and Ideologies* (2014) and the *Cambridge Handbook of Endangered Languages* (2011).

Revitalizing Endangered Languages
A Practical Guide

Edited by

Justyna Olko
University of Warsaw

Julia Sallabank
SOAS, University of London

CAMBRIDGE
UNIVERSITY PRESS

University Printing House, Cambridge CB2 8BS, United Kingdom

One Liberty Plaza, 20th Floor, New York, NY 10006, USA

477 Williamstown Road, Port Melbourne, VIC 3207, Australia

314–321, 3rd Floor, Plot 3, Splendor Forum, Jasola District Centre, New Delhi – 110025, India

79 Anson Road, #06–04/06, Singapore 079906

Cambridge University Press is part of the University of Cambridge.

It furthers the University's mission by disseminating knowledge in the pursuit of education, learning, and research at the highest international levels of excellence.

www.cambridge.org
Information on this title: www.cambridge.org/9781108485753
DOI: 10.1017/9781108641142

© Justyna Olko and Julia Sallabank 2021

This work is in copyright. It is subject to statutory exceptions
and to the provisions of relevant licensing agreements;
with the exception of the Creative Commons version the link for
which is provided below, no reproduction of any part of this work
may take place without the written permission of Cambridge University Press.

An online version of this work is published at doi.org/10.1017/9781108641142 under a Creative Commons Open Access license CC-BY-NC-ND 4.0 which permits reuse, distribution, and reproduction in any medium for noncommercial purposes providing appropriate credit to the original work is given. You may not distribute derivative works without permission. To view a copy of this license, visit https://creativecommons.org/licenses/by-nc-nd/4.0

All versions of this work may contain content reproduced under license from third parties.

Permission to reproduce this third-party content must be obtained from these third-parties directly.

When citing this work, please include a reference to the DOI 10.1017/9781108641142

First published 2021

A catalogue record for this publication is available from the British Library.

Library of Congress Cataloging-in-Publication Data
Names: Olko, Justyna, editor. | Sallabank, Julia, editor.
Title: Revitalizing endangered languages : a practical guide / edited by Justyna Olko, University of Warsaw ; Julia Sallabank. School of Oriental and African Studies, University of London.
Description: Cambridge ; New York : Cambridge University Press, 2021. | Includes bibliographical references and index.
Identifiers: LCCN 2020027565 (print) | LCCN 2020027566 (ebook) | ISBN 9781108485753 (hardback) | ISBN 9781108724500 (paperback) | ISBN 9781108641142 (epub)
Subjects: LCSH: Language revival. | Language maintenance. | Language policy. | Language revival–Case studies. | Endangered languages–Case studies.
Classification: LCC P40.5.L357 R48 2021 (print) | LCC P40.5.L357 (ebook) | DDC 306.44–dc23
LC record available at https://lccn.loc.gov/2020027565
LC ebook record available at https://lccn.loc.gov/2020027566

ISBN 978-1-108-48575-3 Hardback

Cambridge University Press has no responsibility for the persistence or accuracy of URLs for external or third-party internet websites referred to in this publication and does not guarantee that any content on such websites is, or will remain, accurate or appropriate.

Contents

List of Figures	page x
List of Contributors	xiii
Acknowledgments	xvii

Welcome!   1
JUSTYNA OLKO AND JULIA SALLABANK

Part I Planning to Revitalize   7

1 Why Revitalize?   9
LENORE A. GRENOBLE
    1.1 Endangered Languages and Well-being   23
    PATRICK HEINRICH
    1.2 Benefits for Communities: The Case of the Black Tai Community in Thailand   24
    SUMITTRA SURARATDECHA
    1.3 Language Revitalization Benefits in Wilamowice   27
    JUSTYNA MAJERSKA-SZNAJDER
    1.4 Reading Ancestral Texts in the Heritage Language   30
    JUSTYNA OLKO

2 What Do We Revitalise?   33
JULIA SALLABANK AND JEANETTE KING
    2.1 Wymysiöeryś   46
    TYMOTEUSZ KRÓL
    2.2 Language Purism in Nahua Communities   47
    JUSTYNA OLKO

3 Ethical Aspects and Cultural Sensitivity in Language Revitalization   49
JOANNA MARYNIAK, JUSTYNA MAJERSKA-SZNAJDER, AND TYMOTEUSZ KRÓL
    3.1 Being a Helper: A Few Ethical Considerations for Conducting Research with Indigenous Communities   60
    ALEKSANDRA BERGIER

4 Planning a Language Revitalization Project   62
SUSAN D. PENFIELD
    4.1 Doing Things with Little Money   69
        WERNER HERNÁNDEZ GONZÁLEZ

5 Getting Funding and Support   72
NICHOLAS Q. EMLEN
    5.1 Attitudes of NGOs in Guatemala toward the Inclusion of Indigenous Languages in the Workplace   80
        EBANY DOHLE

Part II Practical Issues   83

6 Types of Communities and Speakers in Language Revitalization   85
JOSÉ ANTONIO FLORES FARFÁN AND JUSTYNA OLKO
    6.1 The Community of Wymysoü   99
        TYMOTEUSZ KRÓL
    6.2 What Is Community? Perspectives from the Mixtec Diaspora in California   100
        GRISELDA REYES BASURTO,
        CARMEN HERNÁNDEZ MARTÍNEZ, AND ERIC W. CAMPBELL
    6.3 An Introspective Analysis of One Year of Revitalization Activities: The Greko Community of Practice   102
        MARIA OLIMPIA SQUILLACI

7 Attitudes and Ideologies in Language Revitalisation   104
NICOLE DOŁOWY-RYBIŃSKA AND MICHAEL HORNSBY
    7.1 Language Ideologies in an Endangered Language Context: A Case Study from Zadar Arbanasi in Croatia   117
        KLARA BILIĆ MEŠTRIĆ AND LUCIJA ŠIMIČIĆ
    7.2 Attitudes towards Guernesiais   119
        JULIA SALLABANK
    7.3 What's the Point of Manx?   120
        ADRIAN CAIN
    7.4 Emotions and Relationships in Language Revitalisation and Maintenance   123
        SOUNG-U KIM
    7.5 Nahuatl Language Ideologies and Attitudes   124
        JUSTYNA OLKO

8 Some Considerations about Empowerment and Attitudes in Language Revitalization   127
WERNER HERNÁNDEZ GONZÁLEZ
    8.1 Empowerment and Motivation in the Revitalization of Wymysiöeryś   133
        TYMOTEUSZ KRÓL
    8.2 Language Activism   135
        NICOLE DOŁOWY-RYBIŃSKA

	8.3 'I'm Revitalizing Myself!'	136
	JEANETTE KING	
	8.4 'It's Good for Your Heart': Three Motivational Steps for Language Revitalization	137
	MARIA OLIMPIA SQUILLACI	
	8.5 Monolingual Space	139
	JOHN SULLIVAN	
9	Economic Benefits: Marketing and Commercializing Language Revitalization	140
	JUSTYNA OLKO	
10	Local Power Relationships, Community Dynamics, and Stakeholders	156
	WESLEY Y. LEONARD	
	10.1 Power Relationships and Stakeholders: How to Orient Yourself in Complex Situations	163
	GREGORY HAIMOVICH	
11	Dealing with Institutions and Policy Makers	165
	TOMASZ WICHERKIEWICZ	
	11.1 Language Revitalization and Academic Institutions: Refocusing Linguistic Field Methods Courses	176
	ERIC W. CAMPBELL, GRISELDA REYES BASURTO, AND CARMEN HERNÁNDEZ MARTÍNEZ	
12	Making Links: Learning from the Experience of Others in Language Revitalisation	178
	BEÑAT GARAIO MENDIZABAL AND ROBBIE FELIX PENMAN	
	12.1 Networking and Collaboration between Speakers	191
	JOHN SULLIVAN	
	12.2 The Engaged Humanities Project and Networking for Language Revitalisation	192
	JUSTYNA OLKO	

Part III Tools and Materials — 197

13	Language Documentation and Language Revitalization	199
	PETER K. AUSTIN	
	13.1 Technical Questions in Language Documentation	212
	JOANNA MARYNIAK	
	13.2 MILPA (Mexican Indigenous Language Promotion and Advocacy): A Community-Centered Linguistic Collaboration Supporting Indigenous Mexican Languages in California	216
	CARMEN HERNÁNDEZ MARTÍNEZ, ERIC W. CAMPBELL, AND GRISELDA REYES BASURTO	

viii   Contents

    13.3 Developing Innovative Models for Fieldwork and Linguistic Documentation: ENGHUM Experience in Hałcnów, Poland   217
          BARTŁOMIEJ CHROMIK

14 Writing Our Language   220
    SHEENA SHAH AND MATTHIAS BRENZINGER
    14.1 Orthographies and Ideologies   228
          TOMASZ WICHERKIEWICZ
    14.2 Writing Your Language: The Case of Wymysiöeryś   232
          TYMOTEUSZ KRÓL
    14.3 Indigenous Research, Methodology and Writing   233
          JOHN SULLIVAN

15 Teaching Strategies for Language Revitalization and Maintenance   235
    JANNE UNDERRINER, LINDSAY MAREAN, PIGGA KESKITALO,
    ZALMAI ZAHIR, PYUWA BOMMELYN, AND RUBY TUTTLE
    15.1 Ka Hoʻōla ʻŌlelo Hawaiʻi I O Nā Kula: Hawaiian Language Revitalization through Schooling   256
          LARRY L. KIMURA
    15.2 Kristang Language Revitalization in Singapore under the Kodrah Kristang Initiative, 2016–Present   258
          KEVIN MARTENS WONG
    15.3 Teaching and Learning of Wymysiöeryś   260
          TYMOTEUSZ KRÓL
    15.4 Immersive Łemko Ethnophilology   261
          OŁENA DUĆ-FAJFER (TRANSLATED BY
          JOANNA MARYNIAK)
    15.5 Culture Place-Based Language Basketry Curriculum at the Confederated Tribes of the Grand Ronde Community   263
          JANNE UNDERRINER
    15.6 Sámi School Education and Cultural Environmentally Based Curriculum   266
          PIGGA KESKITALO
    15.7 'Use It, Don't Lose It'   269
          MICAH SWIMMER
    15.8 We Stand Strong in Our Knowledge: Learning Anishinaabemowin One Word Bundle at a Time   271
          ALEKSANDRA BERGIER, KIM ANDERSON,
          AND RENE MESHAKE

16 Art, Music and Cultural Activities   273
    GENNER LLANES ORTIZ
    16.1 Art, Music and Cultural Activities in the Revitalisation of Wymysiöeryś   284
          JUSTYNA MAJERSKA-SZNAJDER
    16.2 *Fest-noz* and Revitalisation of the Breton Language   287
          NICOLE DOŁOWY-RYBIŃSKA

16.3	Modern Music Genres for Language Revitalisation	289
	JOSEP CRU	
16.4	The Jersey Song Project	289
	KIT ASHTON	
16.5	One Song, Many Voices: Revitalising Ainu through Music	291
	GEORGETTE NUMMELIN	
16.6	The Revitalisation, Maintenance and Linguistic Development Project	293
	JOSÉ ANTONIO FLORES FARFÁN	

17 Technology in Language Revitalization 297
ROBERT ELLIOTT

17.1 How about Just Shifting Back? How One Passamaquoddy Speaker Led Her Community to Language Documentation and Revitalization 312
BEN LEVINE

17.2 Online Language Learning Materials Development 314
JENNIFER NEEDS

17.3 Rising Voices 315
EDDIE AVILA

Afterword 317
JULIA SALLABANK AND JUSTYNA OLKO

Index 319

Figures

1.1	Traditional healing knowledge transmitted in Nahuatl. Engaged Humanities project field school, San Miguel Xaltipan, Mexico. Photo by Justyna Olko	page 17
1.2	Indigenous communities that lose their languages often face a youth suicide problem. Suicide prevention program, Shoshone Reservation, Fort Hall, Idaho. Photo by Justyna Olko	19
1.2.1	Revitalization workshop with young people. Photo by Sumittra Suraratdecha	26
1.2.2	Linguistic and cultural revitalization program for all generations: Raising silkworm. Photo by Sumittra Suraratdecha	27
1.3.1	Performance by the Wilamowianie Dance Group. Photo by Robert Jaworski, Polish Theatre in Warsaw	28
1.4.1	Participatory workshop on reading Nahuatl historical texts in modern Nahuatl, Archivo General de la Nación, Mexico. Photo by Justyna Olko	30
1.4.2	Participatory workshop in the community of San Miguel Xaltipan, Mexico. Reading a colonial document from the region. Photo by Justyna Olko	31
2.1.1	Speaking Wymysiöeryś: Tymoteusz Król, the revitaliser of the language. Photo by Justyna Olko	47
7.3.1	Language materials in Manx. Photo by Justyna Olko	121
7.3.2	Manx for children. Photo by Justyna Olko	122
8.1.1	Performance in Wymysiöeryś, *Der Hobbit*, Polish Theatre in Warsaw. Photo by Robert Jaworski, Polish Theatre in Warsaw	134
9.1	The performance and agency of Indigenous communities. The group of Zohuameh Citlalimeh, San Francisco Tetlanohcan, Mexico. Photo by Justyna Olko	148
9.2	Local products sold during the Mother Tongue Day in Wilamowice. Photo by Piotr Strojnowski, © Engaged Humanities Project, University of Warsaw	150

List of Figures   xi

9.3	A local store with some names and announcements in Nahuatl, San Miguel Tenango, Mexico. Photo by Justyna Olko	150
12.2.1	Mixtec, Ayuuk, and Nahua activists at the field school of the Engaged Humanities project, Mexico. © Engaged Humanities Project, University of Warsaw	193
12.2.2	Justyna Majerska-Sznajder and Tymoteusz Król, revitalisers of Wymysiöeryś, greeted by a speaker of Nahuatl. San Miguel Tenango, Mexico. © Engaged Humanities Project, University of Warsaw	194
14.1	A Nahua boy reading an ancient creation story written in his variant. Chicontepec, Mexico. Photo by Justyna Olko	222
14.2	Katrina Esau and Sheena Shah introduce the newly developed N|uu alphabet charts. Photo by Matthias Brenzinger	225
14.3	A postcard written by a young student of Manx. Photo by Justyna Olko	226
14.4	An exercise book for (writing) the Lemko language (*Робочий зошыт до лемківского языка*), Barbara Duć/Варвара Дуць. © Engaged Humanities Project, University of Warsaw	227
15.1	A Manx picture dictionary. Photo by Justyna Olko	239
15.2	A Manx language class taught by Jonathan Ayres, Arbory School, Isle of Man. Photo by Justyna Olko	243
15.3	Nahua children reading a pictorial dictionary. Chicontepec, Mexico. Photo by Justyna Olko	243
15.4.1	A presentation of Lemko books by Olena Duć-Fajfer, the founder of the Lemko philology, and Petro Murianka, a Lemko poet, writer, and teacher. Photo by Jarosław Mazur	262
15.6.1	A girl in a *gákti* (traditional Sámi dress). Photo by Ibbá Lauhamaa	267
15.6.2	Reindeer meat will be smoked in a *lávvu* (lean-to-shelter). Photo by Pigga Keskitalo	268
16.1.1	Performance in Wymysiöeryś, Uf jer welt, Polish Theatre in Warsaw. © Engaged Humanities Project, University of Warsaw	286
16.1.2	Performance in Wymysiöeryś, *Ymertihła*, Polish Theatre in Warsaw. Photo by Krzysztof Kędracki, Polish Theatre in Warsaw	286
16.1.3	Concert in Wymysiöeryś, the Majerski family. Photo by Marcin Musiał	287
16.5.1	Concert poster	292
16.6.1	*Los sueños del tlacuache*. © PRMDLC Project	294

16.6.2	'Carrusel'. *Los sueños del tlacuache*. © PRMDLC Project	294
17.1	The Wide World of Apps. A possible sea of uncharted 'Apps' relevant to language revitalization workers. Developing expertise in all areas is daunting, perhaps even an impossible task	300
17.2	Islands of Competence. Rather than feel overwhelmed by the vast number of areas that need to be learned, users can start small, building 'islands of competence' in a few specific skill sets	301
17.3	Expanding Islands of Competence. Over time, a user can expand their islands of competence, forming larger islands, chains of islands or even turning islands into entire continents	301
17.1.1	Ben Levine and Julia Schulz documenting Passamaquoddy-Maliseet natural conversation as developed with Margaret (Dolly) Apt. Photo by Ian Larson	313

Contributors

KIM ANDERSON
University of Guelph

KIT ASHTON
Goldsmiths College, University of London

PETER K. AUSTIN
SOAS, University of London

EDDIE AVILA
Global Voices

ALEKSANDRA BERGIER
University of Guelph

KLARA BILIĆ MEŠTRIĆ
University of Zagreb

PYUWA BOMMELYN
Tolowa Dee-ni' Language Revitalist

MATTHIAS BRENZINGER
University of the Free State

ADRIAN CAIN
Manx Language Development Officer, Culture Vannin

ERIC W. CAMPBELL
University of California, Santa Barbara

BARTŁOMIEJ CHROMIK
University of Warsaw

JOSEP CRU
Newcastle University

EBANY DOHLE
SOAS, University of London

NICOLE DOŁOWY-RYBIŃSKA
Polish Academy of Sciences

OŁENA DUĆ-FAJFER
Jagiellonian University in Krakow

ROBERT ELLIOTT
University of Oregon

NICHOLAS Q. EMLEN
University of Tübingen & Leiden University

JOSÉ ANTONIO FLORES FARFÁN
CIESAS Mexico

BEÑAT GARAIO MENDIZABAL
University of the Basque Country

LENORE A. GRENOBLE
University of Chicago

GREGORY HAIMOVICH
University of Warsaw

PATRICK HEINRICH
Università Ca' Foscari Venezia

WERNER HERNÁNDEZ GONZÁLEZ
Psychiatrist and Nawat language activist in Colectivo Tzunhejekat

CARMEN HERNÁNDEZ MARTÍNEZ
Mixteco/Indígena Community Organizing Project (MICOP) & University of California, Santa Barbara

MICHAEL HORNSBY
Adam Mickiewicz University

PIGGA KESKITALO
University of Lapland, University of Helsinki & Sámi University of Applied Sciences

SOUNG-U KIM
SOAS, University of London

LARRY L. KIMURA
University of Hawai'i, Hilo

JEANETTE KING
University of Canterbury

TYMOTEUSZ KRÓL
Association Wilamowianie & Polish Academy of Sciences

WESLEY Y. LEONARD
University of California, Riverside

BEN LEVINE
Speaking Place, Universidad Autónoma Benito Juárez de Oaxaca-TAVICO

GENNER LLANES ORTIZ
Leiden University

JUSTYNA MAJERSKA-SZNAJDER
Association Wilamowianie & University of Warsaw

LINDSAY MAREAN
University of Oregon

JOANNA MARYNIAK
University of Warsaw

RENE MESHAKE
Anishinaabe Elder, visual artist and storyteller living and working in Guelph

JENNIFER NEEDS
Swansea University

GEORGETTE NUMMELIN
SOAS, University of London

JUSTYNA OLKO
University of Warsaw

SUSAN D. PENFIELD
University of Arizona & University of Montana

ROBBIE FELIX PENMAN
Department of Anthropology, University of Montreal

GRISELDA REYES BASURTO
Mixteco/Indígena Community Organizing Project (MICOP), University of California, Santa Barbara

JULIA SALLABANK
SOAS, University of London

SHEENA SHAH
University of Hamburg and University of the Free State

LUCIJA ŠIMIČIĆ
University of Zadar

MARIA OLIMPIA SQUILLACI
University of Naples 'L'Orientale'

JOHN SULLIVAN
IDIEZ & University of Warsaw

SUMITTRA SURARATDECHA
Research Institute for Languages and Cultures of Asia, Mahidol University

MICAH SWIMMER
Cherokee Adult Language Education Coordinator, Cherokee Adult Language Learners (CALL), Eastern Band Cherokee Nation

RUBY TUTTLE
Yurok, Yuki, Maidu

JANNE UNDERRINER
Northwest Indian Language Institute, University of Oregon

TOMASZ WICHERKIEWICZ
Adam Mickiewicz University in Poznań

KEVIN MARTENS WONG
Kodrah Kristang

ZALMAI ZAHIR
Northwest Indian Language Institute, University of Oregon

Acknowledgments

This book would not have been possible without the help and support of many people. It is an outcome of the project *Engaged Humanities in Europe: Capacity building for participatory research in linguistic-cultural heritage*, a Twinning programme coordinated by the Faculty of 'Artes Liberales' of the University of Warsaw and carried out jointly with the Department of Linguistics at SOAS, University of London and Leiden University's Faculties of Linguistics and Archaeology. The project was funded by the European Union's Horizon 2020 research and innovation programme under grant agreement number 692199. This grant sponsored much of the preparation of the book, including editorial assistance, and also fully funded the free Gold Open Access online edition. We would also like to thank SOAS University of London's Publication Fund for financing the preparation of the Index.

The Engaged Humanities project (ENGHUM) also enabled us to get to know many of the authors of this book, and to learn about many of the things that the book includes. We would like to thank all of the contributors to the book, and everyone who participated in the project workshops, field schools and visits, and all the community members who hosted our visits and research, without whom nothing would be possible and who have taught us so much.

Individuals have given their time and effort well beyond contractual obligations. They are too many to name all of them, but we would particularly like to thank (in alphabetical order) Willem Adelaar, Peter Austin, Bartłomiej Chromik, Ebany Dohle, Maarten Jansen, Stanisław Kordasiewicz, Tymoteusz Król, Genner Llanes Ortiz, Justyna Majerska-Sznajder, Zuzanna Rosłaniec and Anna Styczeń-Kawałek. We are particularly grateful to Ellen Foote for her excellent stylistic revision of the book, to Mary Chambers for preparing the Index, and to Joanna Maryniak for her technical support during our work on this complex publication.

Welcome!

Justyna Olko and Julia Sallabank

Who This Book Is For

Local languages have been falling into disuse and becoming forgotten in an increasingly accelerating pace over the last century or so: media and scientific reports keep reminding us, with quite alarming statistics. However, the last few decades have also witnessed another steadily growing trend: initiatives, both grassroots and top-down, to counteract the devastating loss of linguistic diversity and to promote multilingualism and the use of local languages. There have been programs and activities that can be considered real success stories or at least important steps toward them, even if revitalizing and supporting endangered languages is a never-ending task. But it is a task that can be planned, implemented, evaluated, and brought into a next stage thanks to this growing body of individual and collective experience and generated knowledge.

This book is meant for anyone who feels concern or even pain because of the loss they and their communities might face; it is for people who experience joy when speaking their languages and want to have them heard, spoken, and strong. It is for people who learned their languages, or who wish to learn them, from their parents, grandparents, community members, or on their own. It is also for people who want to pass their ways of speaking to children and peers. As an Indigenous teacher in the Navajo reservations recently shared with one of us, the most committed parents wanting their children to learn the ancestral Diné language were those who grew up in borderland towns and lost it themselves. Loss can be an empowering stimulus to act. It can also lead to a profound joy of reclaiming a language, learning, speaking, and passing the language to other people, to experiencing the world through its unique perspective, to accessing the knowledge generated and transmitted by the ancestors. But language revitalization is not about going back to the past; it is about acting in the present and heading toward the future, recognizing that the past provides an important foundation and stimulus to achieve it.

This book emerges from the results of the collaborative *Engaged Humanities* project[1] and reflects the philosophy of this collaborative initiative. It has been created jointly by community members and language activists, as well as by educators, students, and academics interested in developing fair and nonpatronizing ways of working with local communities and in response to communities' initiatives and needs. All the contributors generously share their perspectives, thoughts, and practical experience, in the hope of inspiring others. Our project has shown the potential and utility of learning from other contexts, even geographically or culturally remote ones. We also learned that mutual empowerment is possible. The profound respect we have developed for different knowledge systems and approaches can not only decolonize our research and practices, but also help to develop more effective language revitalization strategies.

What This Book Does

The aim of this guidebook is to provide practical help and guidance on how to approach and plan language revitalization. We want to stress from the outset that there is no 'one-size-fits-all,' lock-step solution to language endangerment. Just as each language is different, the contexts in which each language is used are different, and the reasons why its use is declining might also be different. While the case studies are intended to help readers learn from each other, perceived similarities between communities can lead to underestimating or ignoring differences that may seriously influence revitalization efforts, as it is risky to assume that a specific approach implemented in one case will bring similar impact and results in another community. It is important to understand each context in order to address its unique features, even if the experience of others can be very useful; this book will provide insights into how to go about this in a principled manner.

Our intention is also to fill the dearth in available literature on the topic. Most of the relevant existing works are specialized, academic publications that reflect more the views of researchers than the perspectives, goals, and interests of communities and their members interested in revitalizing their own languages. We want this book to be affordable and accessible to local people. The guidebook provides members of language communities and other readers with concrete ideas and real examples of actual experiences and strategies, as well as essential background knowledge that they will need in order to launch successful grass-root initiatives.

---

[1] Twinning Programme of the European Commission, Horizon 2020 coordinated by the University of Warsaw along with the School of Languages, Cultures and Linguistics at SOAS, University of London, Leiden University's Center for Linguistics (Faculty of Humanities) and Department of Archaeological Heritage (Faculty of Archaeology).

What This Book Is Like

For this reason, our aim for this book has been to create readable content presenting a broad range of options and voices. We are convinced that accessible and understandable style, free of academic jargon, does not result in simplification, nor does it make the publication unfit for students or researchers. The organization of the book is intended to help readers conceptualize and plan practically oriented projects. The chapters are written by contributors with a wealth of practical and research experience in language revitalization that is being carried out in many countries around the world. Each chapter includes 'Capsules' that share insights from the direct experience of contributors.

The final result covers language revitalization seen as a holistic, multilevel, multiphase, and long-term process, as completely as possible without resorting to a 500-page monograph or a 1,000-page encyclopedia.

It is primarily **practitioner-oriented**. The fact that our book is designed first and foremost as a practical guide implies that it is as 'hands-on' as possible (e.g. the capsules relate to the real-life experiences of various revitalizers), backed up by reliable research (the chapters are for the most part written or cowritten by recognized scholars who engage in revitalization activities). Therefore, the book is intended to present only as much theory as needed to support the practical guidance, as well as many relevant, hands-on examples. We avoid the one-size-fits-all approach by not presenting any single possibility as the best or the only one. The guidebook shares good practices, different approaches previously applied in specific cases, and new possibilities currently being explored or put into practice. We discuss, for example, planning aims and objectives, understanding and addressing language attitudes, the advantages and disadvantages of writing or standardizing your language, policies and fundraising, and suggestions for practical activities including music, arts, and teaching and learning endangered languages. We also want to draw our readers' attention to the economic value of local languages and possible marketing strategies for language revitalization.

Where We're Coming From

What are our ideological background and motivations? In the first place we wish to stress we aren't imposing a particular party line – the point of presenting options is to provide tools and share knowledge to facilitate making informed decisions and undertaking specific steps toward language revitalization. We also think that it is important not to 'exoticize' Indigenous viewpoints – many endangered language community members live in cities and/or have been acculturated to majority lifestyles.

In nearly every part of the world, smaller or less powerful languages are being used less and less, while the use of larger, more dominant languages is growing. Some people do not see this as a problem; indeed, some even welcome it, saying that it is more useful for children to learn regional, national, or international languages of wider communication. We believe it is important for language revitalizers to understand their own motivations, and to develop arguments to counter critics and gather support. The authors and editors of this book see language endangerment and loss as linked to the marginalization of Indigenous and minoritized peoples and their cultures. For us language revitalization is therefore a key component of empowerment, reclaiming identities, and challenging colonialist attitudes.

In fact, the majority of people in the world speak more than one language, using different languages and styles of speaking for different purposes in their daily lives. Multilingualism is beneficial, both for personal intellectual development and for social integration. We need to get across the message that engaging with wider societies and learning major languages does not mean that people need to abandon their own linguistic identities and cultural heritage.

A Note on Terminology

Many concepts, terms, and approaches have been developed in the area of language revitalization, including language maintenance, language revival, or language reclamation. We should keep in mind, however, that these are ideas created and promoted by researchers and often not the conceptualizations of communities themselves. These concepts are also strongly influenced by biological metaphors of Western science and not necessarily seen that way by language communities. Therefore while referring to the broad and open meaning of 'language revitalization' this book avoids making strict conceptual distinctions and definitions, leaving decisions on how the process should be defined to the people involved.

The Need for Reflection

There are many different ways of reacting to language endangerment. As mentioned, some people see it as a sign of progress. Some are in denial, especially if they feel partly responsible for not passing their languages to their children. Others feel nostalgic for a view of the past that, for them, is linked to their heritage language. But there are some who feel motivated to do something. Quite often, they feel a sense of urgency, because they can literally see their language dying – in Guernsey or Wilamowice, for example, most speakers are now very old and we're losing some every month or two. So it is not uncommon for language activists to rush into the first activities that come to mind; however, this might not be the best use of their time or energy.

This is why we want to encourage critical discussions about other ideas and real situations. For example, people often assume that because children seem to learn languages easily, and because schools are effective at killing minority languages, they need to get their languages taught in schools. But if our languages are not part of the mainstream curriculum, and have no materials or trained teachers, they often end up being taught for half an hour a week, after school or at weekends, by people who are passionate about their language but don't know how to teach it. Very few children will become fluent from this kind of teaching, and some will be put off the language for good; they may also absorb the implicit message that the minority language is not good enough for 'proper' school. And the language activists have no time for other activities that might be more effective, such as conversing with other adults to maintain or increase their fluency. It is important to take time to find out more about the language situation and to reflect on potential courses of action and their outcomes, in light of the resources available – human, financial, and in terms of language teaching and reference materials. This book discusses aims and objectives: short-term, medium-term, and long-term. We believe that spending a bit of time to undertake a survey of language attitudes, and who speaks the language, and how well, will repay the time and effort by providing a sound basis for planning other activities.

This book aims to share the richness of multiple perspectives and examples as well as a coherent, logical sequence of complementary topics to consider while planning language revitalization or struggling in the midst of this process. It is intended not only to provide revitalizers with coherent knowledge and a strong point of departure, but also to encourage, inspire, and empower them. And, as we have already said but wish to emphasize again, we avoid a 'one-size-fits-all' approach by presenting concrete examples and **providing readers with the tools they need to make their own decisions.**

Examples of language revitalization in this book (see map on page 6)

1. Ainu
2. Alznerish
3. Anishinaabemowin
4. Arbanasi
5. Euskara | Basque
6. Black Tai | Lao Song
7. Breton
8. Catalan
9. Cherokee
10. Chinuk Wawa
11. Diné | Navajo
12. Scottish Gaelic
13. Irish Gaelic | Irish
14. Greko
15. Guernesiais
16. Hawaiian
17. Inuktituk
18. Jejudommal | Jejuan, Jejueo or Jejubangeon
19. Jèrriais
20. Kaqchikel
21. Kashubian
22. Khwe
23. Kristang
24. Lemko
25. Lushootseed
26. Makushi
27. Manx | Manx Gaelic
28. Northern Māori
29. Southern Māori known as Kai Tahu
30. Mapudungun
31. Yucatec Maya, maaya t'aan
32. myaamia | Miami-Illinois
33. Nahuatl
34. Nawat | Pipil
35. Okinawan
36. Pahka'anil
37. Passamaquoddy | Maliseet | Wolastoqi
38. Potawatomi
39. Ryūkyūan
40. Sámi
41. Tolowa Dee-ni'
42. San Martín Peras Mixtec | Tu'un Savi (Mixtec)
43. Welsh
44. Wymysiöeryś | Vilamovian

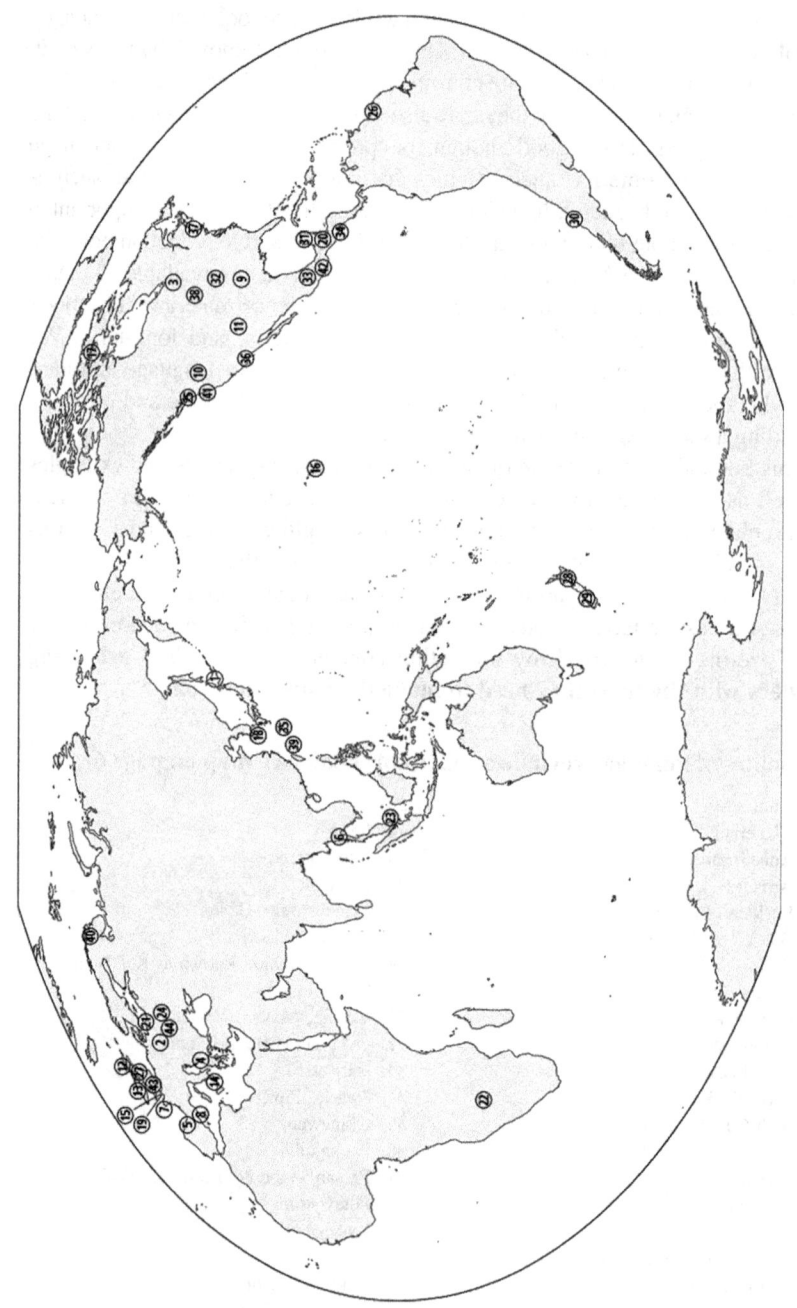

Map of examples of language revitalization in this book

Part I

Planning to Revitalize

1 Why Revitalize?

Lenore A. Grenoble

Introduction

There are a great many reasons to consider revitalization, and more than one can be a decisive factor in deciding to take this on. Language revitalization is often packaged as having the goal of creating new speakers of the target language, of building new domains for language use, and of creating a future generation of speakers. This view is overly simplistic. Although creating new speakers is an important goal (and potential benefit) of revitalization, the notion of a speaker is complicated, and achieving fluency in a language requires a lot of work. It can be very liberating to reconceive the benefits and goals of language work to focus less on creating new speakers and more on the broader advantages that revitalization can bring.

Different people have different ideas about why they want to revitalize, and there is no single right reason. It is also important to keep in mind that the motivations for revitalizing can change as one goes along. Revitalization is a dynamic, fluid process. Moreover, it is important to keep in mind that revitalization is not just about language: it is a social movement and brings benefits to society as well as to individuals.

The decision to revitalize is often a personal one; it requires time, commitment, and tenacity. But at the same time many people may decide to revitalize to benefit not only themselves, but their family, or their larger community or network of friends and acquaintances. And there may be pressure from friends and family to revitalize, or not to. This chapter provides an overview of common motivations to revitalize, and a discussion of the potential benefits of language vitality. One over-arching impetus for revitalization has to do with *identity*: defining and claiming identity for an individual or a collective group is one of the most compelling reasons for language work. And for many, it also involves reclaiming rights to self-determination and control over one's life.

The motivations listed here can be unified under the larger umbrella of identity, but it is important to consider each individually, to understand them better, and to think of how they can both be used to encourage revitalization work, and manipulated to serve its end goals. They are divided into six broad groups that encompass a range of social, psychological, and physical categories/stimuli:

(1) connecting with ancestors, the past, and cultural heritage;
(2) healing;
(3) building community;
(4) knowledge and culture;
(5) well-being; and
(6) cognitive benefits.

As these labels suggest, the categories overlap and, even if the motivation for revitalization comes from one specific area, the resulting benefits are considerably broader.

For clarity, I list these reasons to revitalize as separate points, but it is useful to keep in mind that the benefits are interconnected and a benefit in one area can spill over to another area. This is one reason motivations may change as people revitalize, because they recognize (and need) different benefits at different times. Moreover there are benefits to being bilingual, and these benefits also intersect with the benefits of revitalization. If revitalization moves people from being monolingual to bilingual, they will enjoy the advantages of being bilingual. Being bi- (or multi-) lingual has benefits that are independent of language revitalization: being bilingual in two majority languages brings not only the obvious social benefits of being able to communicate with more people, to interact with them more directly, but also cognitive benefits in improved performance in school, along with physical and mental health benefits. This is important to keep in mind at the outset, as many people mistakenly fear that learning one language interferes with speaking another, and see this as a reason not to revitalize, or not to speak an Indigenous language with their children. This is not true. There is ample evidence that bilingualism is an advantage.

Overall language vitality is related to a combination of factors –social, political, demographic, and practical – and all are usually at play at once. Of greatest relevance are the social and political factors: the use of the language in a wide variety of domains, including the home, schools, places of worship, government offices, on the streets, in stores, in the workplace (broadly defined). The availability of the target language in these various domains is not always the decision of individual speakers, but is often determined by the language and education policies. This is linked to the social prestige of a language, which is in turn related to speakers' motivations to use the language, and also connected to the economic power of a language: does knowing the language bring job possibilities or hinder them?

Finally practical considerations can also determine whether a language is used. These include such factors as whether the language has a written form, an orthography that makes it keyboard-friendly (for text messages, emails, and social media), a standardized form that is taught in the schools, is used on signage, and so on. This is not to say that any of these are requirements for a language, but rather, if a standardized form has already been sorted out, it may be functionally easier to get it into textbooks and on public signs than if it hasn't, for example.

As this list makes clear, language use is a social act, and revitalization – by its very nature – involves social transformation. The transformation may be as basic as bringing use of the language into some domain where it was not previously found, or had not been used for many years. But it may involve massive social change if it involves the (re)introduction of language use (and thus language rights) in education and administration, and increased presence and voice in matters of governance. And this is one reason that revitalization efforts are sometimes (often?) met with resistance by authorities (local or national) as they are viewed as a kind of empowerment that may be threatening. Some governments see revitalization, as well as Indigenous language use more broadly, as steps towards self-governance, autonomy from existing powers. One argument against revitalization that is often invoked is the idea that it costs too much. But in fact research shows quite the opposite. A relatively small investment in the use of local or Indigenous languages has big financial payoffs: it improves educational outcomes and improves health and well-being. It thus is more cost-effective to invest in people at an early age, to produce adults who contribute to society.

From this perspective, revitalization is not a sociolinguistic process but a sociological one, and the changes it brings may not be just locally significant, but regionally or nationally. This is a strong view, but it underscores that language revitalization is both social and political, and brings a host of potential benefits and hazards that are not, at first glance, directly related to language itself.

Revitalization is an active process, and the kinds of benefits you gain from it will depend on the investment, at an individual level, at a community level, and at a larger societal level. Because it is an active process, the goals, motivations, and benefits can and often do change over time. One of the core motivations for revitalization is to claim, or reclaim, identity. This is a consideration that drives many revitalization efforts, and in some sense is an overarching motivation that encompasses the separate points given here.

Stories and oral histories have been, and continue to be, important vehicles for teaching about one's self, for learning what it means to be a member of society, how to deal with adversity, to face challenges, and to celebrate accomplishments. These are important aspects of identity and resilience, which are acquired and accessed through language. For example, in their report on the Mi'kmaq and Maliseet/Wolastoqi immersion programs, Tompkins and Murray Orr[1] discuss community activities and benefits in revitalizing language in two First Nations groups in Canada. They note that the benefits are often framed in terms of academic impact, but they find in interviews with participants, language and identity are closely linked. They find that participants in the program evaluate knowing the language as the single route to learning to be a member of the culture. By the same token, the more children are exposed to the culture, the more they learn the language. The two cannot be separated.

1. Connecting with your Ancestors, the Past, and Cultural Heritage

Language revitalization is often a first step in cultural revitalization and reinvigorating cultural traditions. Speaking the language of one's ancestors is one obvious way to make a connection with the past, with linguistic and cultural heritage. In some cases this can mean being able to speak directly with living relatives, elders, or other people. Speaking to them in their native tongue, your ancestral tongue, is rewarding for both sides, and opens windows to closer understanding of your heritage.

In other cases there may be no speakers of the language, but the cultural heritage lives on in prayers, stories, and songs, and in many cases in written historical documents, not only from ancestors but also from outsiders, such as explorers, missionaries, and colonizers. In order to understand these texts, knowledge of the language is critical. Language revitalization often goes hand-in-hand with cultural revitalization, and connections with the past provide a stepping stone for creating a new cultural future.

As this implies, motivations for revitalizing a language can be spiritual. Language is used for spiritual purposes, to communicate with the gods, spirits, or supernatural beings. Sacred language is an important part of many cultures. While in some cultures, only certain people have access to sacred language, in others, all people do. In many societies language is the primary means for communicating with the spirits or gods, and even in places where a new religion has come to replace the old beliefs, it may not have done so entirely. In Siberia, Indigenous peoples are often Christian, but many communities still have shamans and practice animism alongside Christianity. Shamans communicate with the spirits in the ancestral language, and people need to communicate with the shamans in that language too.

The close connection between spirituality and culture is hard to understand without the ancestral language, as these connections are often

---

[1] J. Tompkins and A. Murray Orr, *Best Practices and Challenges in Mi'kmaq and Maliseet/Wolastoqi Language Immersion Programs* (Dartmouth, Nova Scotia: Atlantic Policy Congress of First Nations Chiefs Secretariat, 2011), www.deslibris.ca/ID/230705.

expressed, maintained, and negotiated through language. For some, spirits or gods can only be addressed in certain kinds of speech: specialized sacred language, or special words, or more simply in the ancestral language itself. For many Indigenous peoples, nature, spirituality, and language are deeply interwoven.

Breton provides an interesting counterpoint, illustrating that religion and language are intertwined in a variety of ways. Breton is a Celtic language, closely related to Cornish and Welsh. It is spoken in Brittany (Breizh in Breton) in France. The most up-to-date information of the total number of speakers puts it at 206,000, based on a poll conducted in 2007.[2] (This figure is deceptively high, as most speakers are elderly and the language is considered endangered.) There is a strong association between Catholicism and the use of 'good' traditional Breton. Although this attitude has led to stereotypes and strong ideologies about who counts as a speaker of Breton, it has also served as a protective factor, and has helped foster revitalization.[3]

Some revitalization programs are aimed at what Leanne Hinton calls the 'missing generations': people of parental and professional age who are not able to teach their children their ancestral language because they themselves do not speak it, but their parents, family members, or elders do. The Master-Apprentice Program[4] (also known as Mentor-Apprentice) is just one example of a program that specifically partners adults with elders to learn the language, thereby also building stronger, closer connections with at least one member of a generation that spoke it and used it in daily life. Some examples are discussed in Chapter 15. Such bridges are important for building connections that extend far beyond the language itself (a fact which pertains to most or even all revitalization). And this speaks to another motivation for revitalization: passing the language to your children (and their children), and to future speakers. This helps restore links between generations, heal possible ruptures, and nurture cohesion and well-being in the community. In this sense, connecting with generations is not only backward-looking, but forward-looking as well. Connecting with the past may not alone be sufficient motivation for younger (or even older) speakers to revitalize, but understanding history and heritage is an important part of (re)claiming identity.

---

[2] Published in TMO-Fañch Broudic 2009. *Fañch Broudic. Parler breton au XXIe siècle. Le nouveau sondage de TMO Régions* (Brest: Emgleo Breiz, 2009), www.fr.brezhoneg.bzh/5-chiffres-cles.htm.
[3] J. L. Davis, 'Intersections of religion and language revitalization', in S. D. Brunn (ed.), *The Changing World Religion Map* (Dordrecht: Springer, 2015), pp. 1091–101.
[4] L. Hinton, 'The Master-Apprentice language learning program', in L. Hinton and K. Hale (eds.), *The Green Book of Language Revitalization* (San Diego and New York: Academic Press, 2001), pp. 217–26.

2. Healing

Many Indigenous peoples cite healing as a primary reason for revitalization. They often feel (with good reason) that their languages were forcibly taken away from them, along with rights to self-determination and to deciding one's destiny. Revitalizing language is part of a larger process of decolonization, cultural revitalization, and reclaiming the right to determine one's fate. Colonial language practices have had a deleterious effect on local language vitality in many places. The forced imposition of a colonial (national) language and assimilation to a majority culture resulted in many people feeling a loss of self-worth and pride. These practices have left deep and painful scars. Reclaiming one's language is an important means to combating the colonial legacy.

Healing implies overcoming trauma, and sadly there are too many people around the world who have suffered traumatic experiences where use of their language is concerned.

In the late nineteenth century, and well into the twentieth century, in different parts of the world (including Australia, Canada, the Soviet Union, the USA, and Scandinavia), children were forcibly taken away from parents to live in residential or boarding schools, in the name of 'civilizing' them. In these schools they were often actively punished for speaking their language. This was not only painful for them but also became a driver behind language shift, as they actively avoided teaching their language to their children so as to protect them from these painful experiences. They suffered further damage by being separated from their families; in many cases children returned to their home communities as strangers, unable to speak the local language and having forgotten the local culture. The impact of the residential system cut to the very core of local societies. This also occurred, and continues to occur, in less extreme circumstances in normal day schools, with children punished or ridiculed for speaking their language.

Research has shown that many people in North America do not recognize the term 'historical trauma' per se, but speak about it in their own words, referring to it as 'disturbing times' or 'the events the ancestors went through'. They also speak about trauma with specific reference to language ('I don't understand my talk, my language') and talk about sorrow and loneliness of the soul.[5] Language revitalization can be a direct goal, with

---

[5] K. M. Reinschmidt, A. Attakai, C. B. Kahn, S. Whitewhater, and N. Teufel-Shone, 'Shaping a *Stories of Resilience Model* from urban American Indian elders' narratives of historical trauma and resilience', *American Indian and Alaskan Native Health Research* 23/4 (2016), 63–85. http://dx.doi.org/10.5820/aian.2304.2016.63.

reclamation of the language as healing. And it can be the means to an end, since language is a vehicle for culture. In addition, research shows concrete benefits for psychological and physical health related to reinforcing a sense of identity in close connection to the use of the heritage language (see section 5 of this chapter).

Healing through revitalization goes beyond language-specific trauma; it is an important means of building resilience. Using a language can be a means of reclaiming and regaining control of one's fate; it can be an act of political resistance, resistance against linguistic and cultural assimilation, against the very act of colonization. The United Nations Declaration of the Rights of Indigenous Peoples declares that all peoples have the right to self-determination: Language revitalization can be a deliberate reclamation of that right.[6]

3. Building Community and Social Change

People often begin revitalization with the goal of learning to speak their ancestral language, but then find that the benefits extend far beyond linguistic abilities. Often the very act of revitalization brings people together, creating closer community ties.

In Native North America, people used to say how the video rental truck was a major cause of language shift. Instead of coming out of their homes in the evenings to talk to one another, people would rent videos and stay home and watch them. The videos were eventually replaced by the Internet and widely accessible video content (on programs such as YouTube), but the effect has been the same. Community-based revitalization programs bring people together: in classes and workshops, in planning sessions, and in events celebrating the language. Even where groups of people convene to practice a few phrases, the very act of coming together builds stronger social ties and a sense of shared purpose and therefore community. These programs offset some of the isolating effects of modern society.

Active engagement in community language revitalization also helps create leaders and build research capacity in the community. Some community language activists – Daryl Baldwin of the Myaamia Tribe, and Jessie Little Doe Baird of the Wampanoag, both in North America – have received formal linguistics training to help them do the language work more effectively. They have brought these skills to their communities and put them to work in supporting youth to create future leaders.

---

[6] For some concrete examples about current work and successes, see the *Healing Through Language Project* at https://holisticnative.org/our-projects/healing-through-language/.

4. Knowledge and Culture

Language and culture are deeply intertwined, and knowledge of all kinds is packaged in language and cultural practices. Certain kinds of knowledge are packaged in the words of a language, and other kinds of knowledge are packaged in larger communicative practices. For example, a large number of studies have been done documenting knowledge and use of plants in traditional medicine; this work is of interest to scientists and health care specialists searching for cures for diseases that are still unknown in Western medicine. Oftentimes knowing the name of a plant will tell you about its uses. In many languages, the common name for *Euphrasia* gives a clue to its usage: in English it's 'eyebright'. In my own fieldwork in Greenland, I found that many people knew its name but not its use. It's called *isiginnaq* < *isi* 'eye' in Kalaallisut (Greenlandic); the name does give a clue here even though the usage was forgotten, but people would guess that it has something to do with eyes or vision just based on the word.

Reindeer herders have a rich vocabulary for referring to the reindeer and to the herding practices themselves, and these vocabularies can and do vary across different herding cultures. It is not just that the words vary, but what is named, and how it is named, can vary from language to language. The Evenki people of Siberia have a complex vocabulary for different kinds of reindeer, varying with age, sex, and their use in the herd, while in the Northern Sámi of Norway, the labels include categories for colour, body shape, and size in addition to age, sex, and use. In both cases, the complex lexicon encodes important information for identifying different animals for different purposes. Both groups often say that you need to know the language in order to know how to herd reindeer.

The words we use for food tell us what people eat, how they collect it, prepare it, and how they serve and eat it. Many cultures have food taboos, some for particular life cycles (e.g. foods that are banned during pregnancy); some items are eaten in certain communities but banned by one group; and in some communities women cannot eat certain foods, or only members of the royal family can eat certain foods. Food preparation in many cultures connects mothers to daughters, older women to younger women, in communities where it is women who prepare food. These specialized ways of speaking provide all kinds of information about cultural practices involving an important aspect of human life, and the knowledge that accompanies these practices.

Culture is often reflected in the ways people speak, not only the words people use, but also in how people talk about things, what they say when, and to whom. This can be as basic as the ways you greet people, joke with them (or not), or how you thank others or express gratitude, or praise. A more complicated area is child-rearing practices and the ways of speaking (or not) to

Figure 1.1 Traditional healing knowledge transmitted in Nahuatl. Engaged Humanities project field school, San Miguel Xaltipan, Mexico. Photo by Justyna Olko

children. This is a core part of cultural transmission that may be lost in contexts where the last native speakers are great grandparents. In addition, there are sacred ritualized uses of language that are found in religious contexts and provide information about the gods, cosmology, and greater spiritual and philosophical questions. In many places, language is used to communicate with spiritual beings, be it a shaman's special language found in many different communities in Siberia, or the use of Hebrew in Jewish religion. Cultural practices thus vary from very elevated to what may be seen as everyday and mundane (see Figure 1.1).

People often talk about languages as providing windows into ways of thinking and different worldviews. Language is powerful; using language can provide access to knowledge, and some kinds of information can only be accessed by using the language. Language revitalization is not just about language, but accessing these different ways of living and being, connecting with culture and the world.

5. Well-being

Both physical and mental well-being are known to be affected by language revitalization. Improved mental well-being is probably the more obvious outcome. People who actively participate in language revitalization report a better mindset and higher levels of self-esteem than before, even when they do not learn much of the language, maybe even just a few words or greetings. There are good reasons for this. Many groups who have lost (or are losing) their language suffer from trauma. This trauma can be the result of a host of causes, but frequently in endangered language communities the trauma involves a history of colonization that has had deep psychological effects and low levels of self-worth. Language revitalization means taking control, reclaiming something that was taken from you, something that was lost. It means taking time to invest in yourself and your family, your circle of friends, and your community.

Moreover, language revitalization often brings people together and unites people in a common goal of learning and using a language. It usually involves building stronger community ties, with a shared purpose. In North America, many Native groups report that those people who are committed to using their language meet more frequently, coming together to practice and learn the language. Even when they are not, strictly speaking, learning the language, they often acquire at least some basic phrases and words, perhaps some greetings, songs and learn the language in symbolic ways. Critically it brings people together. This shared experience of doing language work together connects people, and that helps create an overall positive sense, not only of yourself, but of your culture and heritage.

Thus it is no surprise that people who have access to their language have improved mental health, lower suicide rates, and lower rates of substance abuse than do comparison groups in similar communities who do not use their language. In addition, there is evidence that having access to your ancestral language improves physical health, in terms of reducing the rate of cardio-vascular disease, lowering blood pressure and hypertension, and lower rates of diabetes. These benefits are tied to many things, including living a traditional lifestyle (e.g. by following a traditional diet, which is generally healthier than a Western European diet that is higher in fat, sugar, and salt), more physical activity in engagement with the land and traditional life, and more access to the land. Perhaps some of the health benefits to revitalization come from the fact that it helps (re)connect people with *place* (see Figure 1.2).

But even studies in Australia and Canada that take into account lifestyle factors show that active engagement with language improves both mental and physical well-being at the individual level and the larger societal level. This is a strong motivation for language revitalization.

People in many parts of the world speak of 'taking back' their language. It is an active process that involves taking control of their lives and their own well-being. Jane Juuso, a Sámi researcher and educator in Norway, has done much to advance Sámi language learning for adults by making use of

Figure 1.2 Indigenous communities that lose their languages often face a youth suicide problem. Suicide prevention program, Shoshone Reservation, Fort Hall, Idaho. Photo by Justyna Olko

Cognitive Behavioural Therapy. Juuso identifies certain language barriers that hinder learners from actually speaking, and thus dubs them silent speakers. Originally published in Norwegian and Sámi, her informative how-to-book has been translated into Swedish and English, and the program is being implemented by First Nations Peoples in Canada.[7] It has proven to be a very effective mechanism for helping people overcome their fears of speaking and making mistakes.

Children who receive mother-tongue education show improvement in overall well-being across the board. A 2012 study by UNESCO shows that they have greater self-confidence, higher test scores, lower school dropout rates, and are less likely to repeat grades. These are advantages that extend to their broader community, with improved social well-being and a greater integration into society. More broadly, research shows similar benefits come from having access to the heritage language, in mother-tongue

---

[7] J. Juuso, *Tar språket mitt tilbake/Valddan giellan ruovttoluotta* (Varangerbotn/Vuonnabahta: Isak Saber senteret, 2009).

programs, language teaching programs, and in other venues for hearing and speaking the target language. Studies in different parts of the world – Māori in New Zealand, Mi'kmaq in Canada, Hawaiian in Oceania – show that Indigenous-language immersion programs improve acquisition of the majority language too (see Section 6).

Programs that are embedded in the local language and culture are highly successful in improving the well-being of children and parents. Consider, for example, the Martin Aboriginal Education Initiative in Canada. When it was launched in two Ojibwa (Anishanabeeg) schools in southeastern Ontario in 2009, the schools had very low success rates in reading proficiency: Only 13 per cent of the children in Grade 3 at the two schools met or exceeded standardized tests for reading in Ontario. By 2014, approximately 70 per cent of the children in Grade 3 were performing at the average for Ontario in reading, and 90 per cent met the writing standard, performing at better rates than the province as a whole.[8] Moreover, the number of students classified as having 'special needs' (a term used to describe children with physical, mental, or behavioural problems – or often who have a different mother tongue) in kindergarten through Grade 3 dropped from 45 per cent to just 19 per cent, and in Grades 4–6, the number went down to only 4 per cent (from 24 per cent). The children did not really have special needs or learning difficulties, they just needed better teaching.[9]

These are measurable successes because they involve standard tests. But there are numerous less tangible benefits: increased parent engagement, increased family and community engagement, increased pride in the local language and culture, and overall heightened value of local community practices and ways of knowing and learning.

6. Cognitive Benefits

Linguists often hear that parents opt to raise their children to be monolingual speakers of the majority language so that they will perform well in school. They are afraid that bilingualism will disadvantage their children, or afraid that knowledge of the home language will in some way interfere with learning the majority language, and will inhibit a child's

---

[8] J. Friesen, 'Aboriginal literacy pilot project dramatically improves test scores', *The Globe and Mail*, first published 24 February 2015 and updated 12 May 2018. See also Martin Family Initiative. 2019. *Model Schools Literacy Project*, www.themfi.ca/programs/model-schools-literacy-project.

[9] See J. Geddes, 'The new program that has First Nations' reading scores soaring', *Maclean's* June 2, 2015, www.macleans.ca/education/the-new-program-that-has-first-nations-reading-scores-soaring and Martin Family Initiative, *Model Schools Literacy Project*, Montreal, 2016: Copyright © 2016 Martin Family Initiative / Initiative de la Famille Martin, www.themfi.ca/programs/model-schools-literacy-project.

performance. There is ample evidence that this is not the case at all and that quite the opposite is true. Studies such as those by the psychologist Ellen Bialystok[10] repeatedly show that there are cognitive benefits to a bilingual brain. These benefits include a shorter processing time, an increased attention span, and a greater ability to multi-task than monolinguals. A number of experiments have shown that bilinguals perform better in tasks requiring focused attention. This probably comes from a kind of necessity: current research indicates that in the bilingual brain, both languages are activated and accessible at the same time. Rather than interfering, this helps bilinguals think in a more focused manner, with faster processing than monolinguals.[11]

Parents often fear that education in a native language will hinder the child's progress and acquisition of the majority language, but studies show that the opposite is true. Children who are educated in immersion and bilingual programs outperform children in monolingual educational programs in standardized tests. (Note here that these programs use the native language as the language of instruction, it is not a secondary subject or a tool to get children to perform in monolingual programs.) There is some controversy as to why this is the case: does knowledge of the home language provide some sort of cognitive ladder that enables performance in the other language? Or are children who receive initial schooling in the home language better adjusted (emotionally, socially) so that they are better prepared for formal education and thus able to perform well on tests? Although much of the research focuses on the use of a national language and a major immigrant language (such as English and Spanish Dual Language Immersion (DLI) in the USA, English and French in Canada), there is ample research with the same findings for Indigenous languages: Sámi in Northern Norway, and Cherokee and Navajo in the USA, are just a few examples.[12]

Another long-term benefit is that bilinguals show delayed effects of dementia and Alzheimer's disease compared to monolinguals of the same age, suggesting that the bilingual brain is more resistant to this kind of

---

[10] See E. Bialystok, *Bilingualism in Development: Language, Literacy and Cognition* (Cambridge: Cambridge University Press, 2001). For a review of recent studies, see E. Bialystok, Fergus I. M. Craik, and Gigi Luk, 'Bilingualism: Consequences for mind and brain', *Trends in Cognitive Sciences* 16 (2012), 240–50.

[11] See e.g. E. Bialystok, 'Cognitive complexity and attentional control in the bilingual mind', *Child Development* 70 (1999), 636–44. www.sfu.ca/~jcnesbit/EDUC220/week5/Bialystok1999.pdf.

[12] The American Council for Teaching of Foreign Languages has compiled a number of resources and a bibliography of representative research: www.actfl.org/advocacy/what-the-research-shows.

decline. More research is needed to determine whether bilingualism is preventative, i.e. that bilinguals are less likely to suffer from Alzheimer's, or (what is more likely) that the processing advantages of bilingualism offset the effects of the disease: bilinguals have improved cognitive capacity that enables them to function normally for longer even with Alzheimer's or dementia. That is, bilingualism appears to have an inhibitory effect on mental decline. Regardless it is clear that bilingualism brings an advantage of improved mental capacity and quality of life throughout the lifespan, an advantage that extends well into advanced age. It is a lifelong gift and a strong motivation for revitalization and multilingualism.

Conclusion

Language loss often occurs because of a combination of stressors on speaker populations, including displacement from one's homeland, which can involve forced migration due to colonization patterns, cultural disruption, and historical trauma. The combination of these stressors can seem overwhelming. But there are multiple potential benefits to revitalization, which is an important means to offset these stressors to improve overall well-being and to reclaim one's rights to self-determination.

FURTHER READING AND RESOURCES

Biddle, N. and Swee, H. (2012). The relationship between wellbeing and Indigenous land, language and culture in Australia. *Australian Geographer* 43(3), 215–32.

Evans, N. (2010). *Dying Words and What They Have to Tell Us*. Malden, MA: Wiley Blackwell.

McDermott, B. (2014). Language healers: Revitalizing languages, reclaiming identities. *Cultural Survival* 38-1. www.culturalsurvival.org/publications/cultural-survival-quarterly/language-healers-revitalizing-languages-reclaiming.

Meek, B. A. (2010). *We Are Our Language: An Ethnography of Language Revitalization in a Northern Athabascan Community*. Tucson, AZ: University of Arizona Press.

Oster, R. T., Grier, A., Lightning, R., Mayan, M. J., and Toth, E. L. (2014). Cultural continuity, traditional Indigenous language, and diabetes in Alberta First Nations: A mixed methods study. *International Journal for Equity in Health* 13(92). doi: 10.1186/s12939-014-0092-4.

Walsh, M. (2018). "Language is like food": Links between language revitalization and health and well-being. In L. Hinton, L. Huss, and G. Roche, eds., *The Routledge Handbook of Language Revitalization*. New York: Routledge, pp. 5–12.

Wyman, L. T., McCarty, T. L., and Nichols, S. E., eds. (2014). *Indigenous Youth and Multilingualism: Language Identity, Ideology and Practice in Dynamic Cultural Worlds*. New York: Routledge.

1.1 Endangered Languages and Well-being

Patrick Heinrich

General findings in language endangerment indicate that it is always dominated communities that undergo language shift, and that there is 'nothing to gain' in language loss. You lose more than 'language' in the strict sense of the word. Language loss is accompanied by the loss of knowledge, loss of linkages to the past and cultural achievements, loss of aesthetic possibilities, or loss of cultural autonomy. Such kind of loss does not leave communities undergoing these transformations unaffected. Every community undergoing language shift has its very own history of 'not being well' and 'not doing well'. An interesting contribution to how to study such problems has been promoted in Japan in recent years, where sociolinguists have been pondering the establishment of 'welfare linguistics'. Welfare linguistics starts from the view that language diversity *is always* related to some kind of inequality. Therefore, welfare linguistics identifies (1) the mechanism of oppression or exclusion and (2) studies strategies for how to cope with this. (3) It acknowledges alternative practices and (4) promotes them. Welfare linguistics is an emancipative endeavour. Language can promote or inhibit well-being ('welfare'). That is to say, an endangered language in itself is not the solution to the problems of a shifting community, but it can be made into a solution. This requires insights into the four points outlined above.

Studies in well-being conventionally distinguish between economic, physical, and psychological aspects. Language maintenance and revitalization can contribute to all of these three components. In Okinawa (Japan), we can witness a new wave of products, services, and media outlets that employ Okinawan and, hand in hand with this trend, there are new employment opportunities for speakers of Okinawan. For example, nurses and caregivers speaking Okinawan are much sought after because older people with dementia respond better to their first language, Okinawan, and many nurses and caregivers whose Okinawan skills are lacking volunteer for Okinawan language classes. Okinawa is also known for having the highest life expectancy in the world. Longevity is usually portrayed to be the result of a healthy diet and a relaxed lifestyle. However life expectancy in Okinawa has been sharply declining for more than three decades now, and it is dawning on many that those who 'eat and live well' are actually speakers of Okinawan. The decline in physical health is concurrent with a decline of Okinawan language, culture, and lifestyle. Finally, the connection between an endangered language and mental well-being is seen to be strong enough that a project studying this link in the case of the Barngarla community in Australia received one million Australian dollars of funding in 2017. This is unconventional, because 'the cure to the ills' of minorities was traditionally seen to lay in their closer assimilation to the majority (e.g. more and 'better' English). Now reviving the Barngarla language is seen as a means to improve Barngarla well-being.

Focussing on language and well-being is not simply a new research perspective. It's potentially a game changer. Modernity brought social mobility, and with that came a focus on 'merits', that is, acquiring the necessary skills to climb the social ladder. Smaller languages and their speakers do not fare well in such a setting. Indigenous languages became marginalized and relegated to (nonthreating) functions such as 'tradition', 'heritage', or 'local identity'. We know that language revitalization cannot succeed when endangered languages are only attributed such folkloristic functions. One way to improve the prospects of an endangered language and its speakers is to link it to 'well-being'. A number of factors affecting well-being have already been identified. They include income, work, marriage, health, education, housing, job satisfaction, community relations, leisure time, or crime rate. The fact that so many factors can affect well-being implies that the exact role of language in well-being will differ from case to case. In general, however, we can assume that Indigenous languages function as a protective layer for the well-being of community members. Losing them decreases well-being.

In 2007, I asked my Okinawan language teacher, Chie Inamine, if she sometimes regretted not having raised her children in Okinawan. She gave me the following answer: 'We live in a merit society, and all we care about is merit. Merit, merit, merit. And then language has to adapt to this fixation. With my grandchildren I will not fall into this trap. I will provide them with Okinawan language skinship.' Skinship (*sukinshippu*) is a widely known and used linguistic innovation on the basis of English in Japanese. It refers to intimate but nonsexual relations, where it is ok to have physical contact. A prototypical skinship relation is that between a mother and her baby, where physical contact reassures and comforts the baby and where we can see a very deep physical and psychological tie between both. Inamine applied this term to language when I interviewed her on education. In my understanding, she seeks a closer more intimate tie between the younger and the older generation, because by educating the former through Japanese a more distant relation was created than through Okinawan. Distance is not something abstract in this context, but something which affected the well-being of speakers like her and those who do not speak the language. There is an emotional and psychological gap between the generations. In Inamine's comment we have in a few words, the welfare perspective on an endangered language. It needs promotion and further study.

1.2 Benefits for Communities: The Case of the Black Tai Community in Thailand

Sumittra Suraratdecha

Several years ago I started a sociolinguistic project on linguistic and cultural rights in a Black Tai community in Phetchaburi province, Thailand. The community represents a typical marginalized ethnic group where suppression and stigmatization is present. Thailand is a hierarchical society where ethnic minority peoples are placed at the lower end of the social hierarchy. Belonging to the lower end of the hierarchy means that ethnic minority communities face stigma and discrimination, socially, ideologically, and linguistically. The Black Tai people in Thailand are descendants of former captives of wars from Muang Thaeng during the reign of King Thonburi, in the Rattanakosin period, circa 1779. Today, this is the location of Dien Bu Phu in northwest Vietnam. The Black Tai people refer to themselves as 'Lao Song', however they prefer other out-groups to call them 'Black Tai' as the word 'Lao' has connotations of suppression, insult, and disdain. Incidents of discrimination, abuse, and rape were also recorded in the history of the Black Tai.

My project started out with the aim of examining the Black Tai linguistic and cultural reclamation movements in terms of the rights that social groups claim to express themselves linguistically and culturally. I also wanted to investigate the psychological outcomes of these movements in terms of well-being.

As an outsider researcher, I was concerned about whether the Black Tai, both adults and youths, would be willing to share stories of their history and talk about acts of discrimination or prejudice they have faced. However, despite my initial concern over how to elicit such stories in a non-threatening way, responses to a simple question: 'Could you tell me about the Black Tai people in this community?' unexpectedly revealed so many stories describing discrimination and historical stigmatization experienced by all generations. Adults talked about how they were discriminated against by non-Black Tai and how embarrassed they were about their own identity as a Black Tai in Thai society. Younger generations talked about how they were teased at schools by their peers who belonged to different ethnic groups. All the stories about incidents in their everyday lives came out naturally in their narratives.

After years of working with different ethnic communities in Thailand, my colleagues and I shared a similar observation, namely that most of the people we worked with were elder members of the community. Our big question was: What if there is no next generation to inherit all of this invaluable linguistic and cultural heritage? Subsequently a long-term Participatory Action Research (PAR) project was initiated in ethnic communities in Thailand, including Black Tai. A number of local community members, particularly youth members, were actively engaged in all stages of the project. Through planning, conducting, observing, and evaluating the research process, local participants absorbed and learned through direct experience how to be an active learner and how to conduct local research by themselves (see Figure 1.2.1).

The overall outcome of the PAR project can be divided into two levels: community and self. At the community level, the community network is stronger than ever before. The PAR approach provided an opportunity for a range of people – including local government officers, community leaders, members, elders, and youths alike – to engage in all stages of the research. This created a sense of ownership among participants, and community ties and networks were restored and strengthened as a result. After the PAR project was complete, the wider community, including those who did not participate in the project, became more active and interested in learning local knowledge. Additionally, the community was able to write a successful proposal for a community development grant. Other local organizations and media have taken an interest in working with the

Figure 1.2.1 Revitalization workshop with young people. Photo by Sumittra Suraratdecha

community, or sharing stories of their success. The community now talks about their heritage with pride and encourages others to be proud of their own roots as well.

At a personal level, all members have a better attitude towards their language and culture and more self-esteem. They have also learned to be active thinkers and learners through the PAR process. Not only did youth members learn about their linguistic and cultural heritage through the PAR project, they also learned other life skills like decision making and team-working etc. From informal interviews and observations over five years, the overall well-being of the community has increased. For example, the elderly people are a resource with essential knowledge and skills, yet their skills were forgotten thanks to a formal education system that distances learners from their immediate learning environment. These resources are now recognized once again. The greatest benefit of all, however, lies in community human resource development, and witnessing the seeds of youth participation sprout from the young people who no longer avoid eye contact when talking, and are no longer ashamed to be who they are. They now serve as youth leaders who represent their community and continue to work on its development in school, university, or community projects, sharing their priceless linguistic and cultural knowledge with the whole of society (see Figure 1.2.2).

Figure 1.2.2 Linguistic and cultural revitalization program for all generations: Raising silkworm. Photo by Sumittra Suraratdecha

1.3 Language Revitalization Benefits in Wilamowice[13]

Justyna Majerska-Sznajder

When we started our activities connected to the revitalization of Wymysiöeryś culture, we encountered three main difficulties, based on different attitudes among the inhabitants.

- The youngest generation was of the opinion that Wymysiöeryś is not a practical language so there's no point in learning it.
- The middle generation saw Wymysiöeryś culture as grounds for ridicule – as had been repeated since the 1950s by neighbours from the surrounding villages.
- The oldest generation, the one that was most hurt by their fate, the one that still remembered repression related to Wymysiöeryś, did not want to use Wymysiöeryś for fear that the persecutions would return.

---

[13] The writing of this capsule has been supported by the Project 'Language as a cure: linguistic vitality as a tool for psychological well-being, health and economic sustainability' carried out within the Team programme of the Foundation for Polish Science and cofinanced by the European Union under the European Regional Development Fund.

Figure 1.3.1 Performance by the Wilamowianie Dance Group. Photo by Robert Jaworski, Polish Theatre in Warsaw

What did not help was the attitude of the local authorities, whose officials originated mostly from the surrounding villages, where the distinct Wymysiöeryś culture was derided. Their views were shaped by their upbringing, so discrimination from the 1950s translated into ongoing negativity on the part of the local authorities. The situation would probably have stayed the same until today if the Faculty of 'Artes Liberales' of the University of Warsaw had not engaged in revitalization activities. In 2014, the first international conference was organized in Wilamowice – and parts of it were in Wymysiöeryś. It raised the prestige and status of the language among the local inhabitants and authorities, who until then had considered our activities nothing but a flash in the pan. It also fell to us to change the attitude of the oldest generation – some of whom we invited to present on Wymysiöeryś culture and their histories during our various meetings and events. Thanks to this they became aware of the interest in their culture and realized that public use of Wymysiöeryś is not only unpunished, but even welcome. This helped them work through their trauma related to the persecutions.

Through various activities, e.g. theatre performances by the 'Ufa fisa' group, and song and dance by a local folk ensemble (see Figure 1.3.1) we have managed to make Wymysiöeryś trendy among our youth, who also started understanding our actions as their contribution to the conservation of their cultural heritage. They derive joy and happiness from continuing the traditions and the heritage of their ancestors. The oldest inhabitants are visited by young people to talk together and it makes them feel needed. They not only get practical help from the young people but also feel appreciated and heard – they can count on people who will gladly listen to them. We have managed to awaken the Wymysiöeryś identity in both the youngest and oldest inhabitants – and this is one of the most important markers of Wymysiöeryś culture. Thanks to that people have gotten a better acceptance regarding their own feeling of belonging. The biggest remaining challenge is the middle generation, the one that was brought up in compulsory Polish. They are the parents who have the greatest influence on effective learning of Wymysiöeryś among the youth, because they can either forbid or allow them to attend the classes. Thanks to several meetings and psycho-linguistic lectures they no longer consider learning Wymysiöeryś a waste of time, and are more conscious of the benefits of multilingualism (this is rare in Poland). A different approach to being Wymysiöeryś was also helpful – we reclaimed those aspects that previously subjected us to ridicule, changing them into assets.

We have also taken it upon ourselves to disseminate the knowledge about the persecutions and the dire fates of inhabitants which have until now been taboo. This subject has been broached many times in the public sphere and recently work has been done to collect documents and memories of the inhabitants regarding this time period. Thanks to this we can hope that (at least to a certain extent) the sufferings of the people who survived the persecutions will be recompensed. We can also hope that others will be more aware of the history and will understand that it is not a reason for shame.

The actions of Wymysiöeryś organizations related to revitalization also have a significant effect on the well-being of Wymysiöeryś. They are very strongly mobilized and engaged in community activities – thus maybe conforming to the archetype of Wymysiöeryś mainly sticking together in a closed circle. These organizations are the only ones that meet the cultural needs of the inhabitants because the local authorities have little to offer in that regard. Taking part in these activities helps to create social bonds, but participants also feel happy because through their actions they are creating something for Wilamowice – and this is one of the markers of local ideas of well-being for Wymysiöeryś. Such actions also result in measurable benefits – like in the case of the Song and Dance Ensemble 'Wilamowice' whose members get the chance not only to participate in its performances and travel with the group (for many members this is their only chance to travel) but also to further their own personal development through visits to museums and places of interest. Membership of such organizations also allows elderly people to remain physically fit longer and becomes a way of distancing oneself from problems as well as a means of relaxation. We also know about cases where the help that the older generation provides in the revitalization process has stopped the progression of dementia and served as a kind of rehabilitation.

The last type of benefit is economic. The local authorities have finally noticed the opportunities for the development of the region on the basis of Wymysiöeryś culture, and thus more and more local initiatives are starting. Huge support was provided by a project to promote the commercialization of findings from research on linguistic revitalization, and the related idea of the creation of a tourism cluster – all thanks to Bartłomiej Chromik, back then a doctoral student with a background in economics. Our activities have thus enabled the inhabitants to develop language-related tourism and, consequently, economic activity. Thanks to their participation in linguistic documentation, the youths who know Wymysiöeryś can be employed in tourism and so they begin to see knowledge of Wymysiöeryś as an economic asset.

1.4 Reading Ancestral Texts in the Heritage Language

Justyna Olko

The Nahuas first adopted alphabetic writing for their own purposes in the sixteenth century, so writings in Nahuatl go back many centuries. However, speakers of Nahuatl do not have easy access to the histories written by their ancestors. Knowledge of the long history of writing in Indigenous languages is not part of the Mexican educational program and although documents are kept in archives they are usually only explored by professional scholars. Therefore our team began to organize workshops in which native speakers and new speakers could read and discuss the colonial Nahuatl documents written by their ancestors (see Figure 1.4.1). In this way we have started together to awaken a historical memory

Figure 1.4.1 Participatory workshop on reading Nahuatl historical texts in modern Nahuatl, Archivo General de la Nación, Mexico. Photo by Justyna Olko

Figure 1.4.2 Participatory workshop in the community of San Miguel Xaltipan, Mexico. Reading a colonial document from the region. Photo by Justyna Olko

and raise awareness of the legacy of minority communities. It is a valuable way of strengthening their identity and raising both their self-esteem and the prestige of their heritage language, which has proved especially promising in the case of speakers of Nahuatl.

The workshops have been carried out every year since 2014 (since 2015 in the Mexican National Archive – *Archivo General de la Nación*). Each time some thirty to forty speakers of Nahuatl from diverse communities in Mexico City and the states of Mexico, Puebla, Tlaxcala, Guerrero, Oaxaca, and Veracruz take part in the activities, which are conducted entirely in Nahuatl. During these events all participants speak in their own variants of the language, which additionally contributes to language revitalization. They not only work collaboratively on the transcription, translation, and interpretation of the texts, but also personally examine the original documents, which turned out to be a deeply emotional experience. For this collaborative reading we choose colonial texts that are vivid testimonies of Indigenous capacity to act; for example, defending local autonomy and rights, demanding removal of Spanish officials, etc. (see Figure 1.4.2). Exposure to this information can be an important source of empowerment for modern activists. These ancestral writings allow Indigenous readers to experience a degree of continuity with the past by giving them the opportunity to see their ancestors' actions as examples, which might inspire them to take their own individual and collective initiatives. In other words, the texts make it possible for readers to 'empower themselves to come to grips with the conditions of their living'.[14]

When planning these activities, we intentionally attempt to select texts from the regions or places from which specific groups of participants originate. Connecting to the past through these places allows Indigenous people to personally experience the degree of continuity between older and modern heritage tongues and culture. During these encounters the Nahuas from different regions often compare their vocabulary and joyfully experiment with terms that do not exist in their own variety. Yet another aspect of language use that these sessions have stimulated is reevaluation of the purist attitudes shared by many speakers of Nahuatl today. Participants often recognize that Spanish influence goes back many centuries and that some loanwords became part of their language a long time ago.

Links with the past are of vital importance in many Indigenous communities: ancestors are conceived of as the source of knowledge and strength for the living. Severing links with the past has profound consequences for identity, self-esteem, and self-awareness. Therefore, opening a dialogue with the ancestors and the testimonies they left can provide an empowering stimulus to reclaim historical identity and inspire social change in the present, including the revival of language use.

---

[14] Y. Kalela, *Making History: The Historian and Uses of the Past* (London: Palgrave Macmillan, 2012), p. 164.

2 What Do We Revitalise?

Julia Sallabank and Jeanette King

Introduction

The question 'what do we revitalise' may seem a rather unusual one. After all, isn't the answer obvious? We want to revitalise our language. But in order to do so, we need to think about the kinds of questions that are tackled in Chapter 1, such as who wants to 'save' the language, and for what purposes?

For example, do we want to expand the scope of the language to be able to use it in schools, or to talk about new technology? That might require new terminology: in which case, who should decide on it, and how? Should we try to recover 'traditional' language, or should we try to re-invent our language for a new generation – or something in between? If there is a range of varieties of our language, should we focus on just one? Should we try to create a standard language (copying majority languages), or support linguistic diversity in its fullest sense? Such questions are more often related to political struggles and ideological debates about language ownership or authenticity (see Chapter 7) – and there may be bitter arguments about what the 'correct' form of a word or expression is. If a language is highly endangered, it may only be used infrequently and in a fragmented way, so it may need to be reconstructed.

In Chapter 6, Justyna Olko and José Antonio Flores Farfán discuss the varied range of people who may be involved in language revitalisation; we need to consider all their diverse needs and wishes when planning what to revitalise. An *endangered language community* consists not only of people who speak the language; it includes others who have an interest in what is to be revitalised, and whose views need to be taken into account. For example, people who would like to claim an association with the language by learning it or by supporting revitalisation efforts (e.g. by helping to develop an app) may have other ideas on what to revitalise than people who grew up speaking the language but have lost their fluency through many years of disuse. Members of the wider community also have a stake in policies directed at language (even if only through paying taxes that fund public policy measures).

In broad terms, there is frequently a distinction between *traditional* speakers and *new* speakers, whose views on what to focus on and how may diverge significantly. Diplomacy may be needed to reconcile all points of view; one possible way of handling conflicting agendas is to see a range of activities as complementary parts of an overall plan, rather than mutually exclusive.

We also need to remember that decisions we make now will affect how the language is used in the future – not just how it is used now. Do we want to focus on specific areas of use, or look at language revitalisation in a more holistic way? It is important not to limit future options by restricting language to particular areas of life; even if we don't use all the variations or topics now, we should ensure that there is a safe record of all the rich diversity of a language. But we also need to bear in mind that language revitalisation is not only, or always, just about language, as we discuss later and in Chapters 1 and 9.

There are many different types of languages. While we typically think of language as being oral, or spoken, other means can be employed to convey information, such as sign languages and whistling languages. Whatever type, people try to revitalise languages because they are regarded as being endangered, and because they feel an emotional link to that language. All types of endangered languages have both similarities and differences in why they are endangered and how we go about reversing this, so it is important both to look at our own contexts and to learn from what others have tried (see Chapter 12 on links with other groups).

Contexts of Use

Every language variety has a number of forms; that is, the ways language is used will change according to who is using it, when, where, and for what purpose. For example, the language used to interact with children will differ from that used in formal contexts. This is not just a matter of using alternative words; there will also be differences in the ways sentences are constructed. Languages aren't single, unchanging entities; because they are used in a wide range of forms by a wide range of people in various places for distinct purposes, they naturally change and evolve. There are often debates in language revitalisation movements about how much change is desirable; this is discussed more in 'Language Change' below.

The task of revitalisation can seem overwhelming when viewed in its entirety, so some prioritisation may be necessary (see Chapter 4 on planning). Assessing what resources are available, and to what extent your language is still spoken or not, will help you decide where and how you want to concentrate your revitalisation efforts. Settings where language is used include the home, school, the workplace, social media, religion, bureaucracy, political life, sports commentary, etc. Some of these require specific types of vocabulary or levels of formality (called *registers*); often minority languages don't have, or have lost, forms of language that are needed for particular settings or registers. Critics of language revitalisation may claim that this is proof that the language is inferior and not capable of being used in all areas of (especially modern) life. For this reason many language supporters want to expand the spaces in which their language is used. Language promoters may focus on useful or practically oriented areas such as grammar terminology for teaching; others may focus on high-status areas to increase the language's prestige.

Language revitalisation often focuses on transmitting language to children; the home and school are therefore key spaces of use. We need to be aware that there is a particular kind of language in those situations, that of adult–child interactions. In Guernsey, where most fluent speakers of Guernesiais are now aged over 80, Julia Sallabank has been involved in trying to collect examples of adult–child interaction, as well as children's rhymes and games, from older speakers. This has proved difficult, as there are now very few people alive who have experience of raising their children in Guernesiais. So this may be a way of using language that has to be reconstructed. Where there are still children learning the language (or people who remember raising children in the language), it is important to record this type of language.

One effective and widely used and respected revitalisation method is to implement preschool language immersion centres. These were pioneered in 1982 in New Zealand with the Māori language. The idea behind these centres is to transmit the language directly from an older generation of speakers to a new generation of child speakers. However, if the older speakers are few in number and quite elderly, this option needs to be thought out carefully. To begin with, not all older people have the stamina and desire to interact with preschoolers for many hours a day. In addition, older speakers need to understand that their role is to speak the target language, and only the target language, with the children. That is, it is not necessary or desirable to sit the children down and overtly 'teach' the language. The type of language used with small children is usually quite basic, often consisting of descriptions and commands. But as the children grow and get older, a more sophisticated repertoire is required. Ideally, if possible, children should also be exposed to adult interactions in the language. Everyday interactions between adults such as greetings, apologies, requests, etc. are often surprisingly lacking from linguists' records, but they are important if you want to use your language for conversation and social activities. In Wales, some parents have noticed that children from

English-speaking families who go to Welsh-medium school are quite direct in their speech: they have been taught simple commands, but not polite forms of language, which are often more complicated grammatically. However, they can be taught as 'chunks' of language whose grammar does not need to be analysed by the children at this stage.

While developing new uses and new words for a language, it is important not to forget traditional areas of life, especially home, socialising, and child language (including games, nursery rhymes, etc.). When schools take over the role of passing on the language, children might only learn school language, and not know how to make friends and be intimate in their language. As a result, they may not speak the language outside school, or with their own children in due course (as has been found in Wales after thirty years of immersion teaching). It has also been found in Brittany that children who learn a formalised Breton at school are unable to converse with older speakers who use regional varieties and more informal speech.

Most language use outside basic conversation involves reading and writing. If the language you are working with is not written, creating an agreed writing system is an essential area to tackle. This will be dealt with in Chapter 14.

Variation and Standardisation

It is not uncommon for one variety of a language to be quite vibrant but for other varieties to be under threat. Minority varieties are particularly vulnerable because they are often regarded as being of lesser value than the dominant or 'standard' variety, which has more status. Even speakers can believe that their way of speaking is not as important or valid as more prestigious variants. In Jersey, regional varieties of the island language Jèrriais are called accents. Some accents are disappearing because language teaching focuses on one accent, which has been formalised with a standard spelling that doesn't always take into account other accents. The formalised accent/variety used in schools is seen by some as the 'correct' variety.

Many people get involved in language revitalisation because they want to reconnect with their roots. They want to learn the variety that they identify with; for them learning another version would not fulfill that requirement. For example, most speakers of Māori live in the North Island of New Zealand, but the Kāi Tahu iwi (tribe) in the South Island are working to increase the numbers of speakers of their local variety.

In many cases, an endangered or minority language is perceived as 'only a dialect' – or designated as a dialect by the national government. This may have little to do with the degree of linguistic difference, but more to do with status and identity. In this book, we prefer to use the word 'varieties' when we talk about how ways of speaking differ across regions, age groups, etc. This is because the term 'dialect' has negative connotations of 'incorrect' and 'low status', and is often used to denigrate minority languages. Language activists often campaign to have the linguistic variety that they identify with recognised as a language in its own right. These issues are discussed in more depth in Chapter 11 on policy and Chapter 7 on ideologies.

There is often pressure to create, teach, and learn a standard version of an endangered language. In the process of standardisation of national languages, the standard is usually based on the variety used by an urban intelligentsia. However, urban varieties of endangered languages typically disappear at an early stage, leaving the choice of prestige variety unclear. Minority and endangered languages usually have extensive variation, and there is often no obvious prestige or standard variety, which can lead to disagreements. In many cases there is no tradition of written literature, or authors may write in a wide range of styles, varieties and spellings, or even different types of script.

It is often assumed that endangered languages have to copy the model of national languages, which have a standard 'correct' way of writing and speaking, especially if we want to teach our languages in schools. But this can lead to local ways of speaking being minoritised again. Some language supporters argue that it is better to prioritise more widely used varieties. But there are other models, such as in Corsica, where different varieties are recognised as equally important, and learners are given a choice of which they want to identify with.

What Is It For?

Often when we talk about language revitalisation, our ultimate aim is for the language to be used again by a range of community members from young to old. (This may be the long-term, ultimate aim, but there are many steps to be taken before you can reach it – see Chapter 2 on planning.) Being aware of what resources are available puts us in a better position to know what sort of language revitalisation is possible and achievable and for what purposes. Without considering this we run the risk of activities that fail due to lack of planning. The important thing to remember is that there is no right or wrong when deciding what aspects of your language you focus on. It is also important to ensure that what you focus on now does not limit future options.

But full community use is not the only form of language revitalisation. Your language may have very few, if any, remaining speakers. Such contexts are termed *post-vernacular*: that is, the language is no longer used as a *vernacular*, for everyday purposes. However, even in these situations there are productive things that can be done. In the USA, the Breath of Life programme addresses situations where the language hasn't been spoken for several generations but where there is documentary material, collected by linguists or anthropologists, which is housed in libraries and archives. Working together, language learners and scholars pair up with graduate linguistics students to locate relevant material and work on useful language resources, which can range from (re-)creating a prayer through to working on a spelling system for the language.

Because endangered languages are no longer widely spoken in everyday life, it can be difficult for learners to find people to converse with in their language. Many people in language revitalisation movements turn to activities such as songs, theatre and other performances in order to find ways to use and celebrate their language, as well as to create a sense of community endeavour (see Chapter 16 on arts and music). Or they may wear a T-shirt or jewelry with words in the language on, to demonstrate identity and solidarity. Performances and festivals are often very enjoyable occasions that bring together the community and raise awareness of the language and culture. A recent press release described how a school play was being performed entirely in Māori, a language which was banned in schools for over hundred years. The article mentions that not all of the performers are fluent in Māori, which could be interpreted negatively (they don't know the language properly), or positively (they are engaging with the language and trying to learn).

Another common focus of language activists is the 'linguistic landscape' – supporters campaign to have signage, public announcements, etc. in their language to raise its status, increase its presence in public life, and make non-speakers or tourists aware of it. If politicians or businesses support such measures, it is often in order to highlight local distinctiveness. These types of activities may not require fluency, but instead use parts of language symbolically or emblematically, to express identity. For many people this is a valid and adequate way of engaging with language, but it is only one way of looking at language revitalisation; for others, the aim may be to re-create a fluent speaker community, or to reclaim culture.

We are not suggesting that prioritising certain areas of language means that revitalisation should be one-dimensional; different registers and spaces of use can be complementary and mutually reinforcing, and individuals or groups may want to focus on different areas. It is important not to see these as mutually exclusive. There is a threat that if only a narrow spectrum of a given language is 'revitalised', the result may be perceived as artificial and not be sustainable.

We argue that it is important to have conscious aims (see Chapter 4 on planning) and to be aware of the ideologies that underlie these aims, as well as different people's motivations for language-related activities (see the chapter on attitudes and ideologies). If not, we run the risk of losing a language through focusing only on symbolic activities. As Adrian Cain, Manx Language Development Officer, has commented: 'Language awareness raising isn't an end in itself, and if it doesn't encourage people to learn and speak, then it hasn't worked'.

Who Is It For?

In many situations, revitalisation efforts begin when there are still at least a few older speakers in the community, but they are initiated by younger generations. This leads to a paradox of language revitalisation: the momentum for revitalisation typically emerges from those who did not grow up as speakers of the language. The younger language activists, because they did not grow up with the language, are keenly aware of what they have not had access to in respect of their culture and identity (some learners of Guernesiais have said they felt 'robbed'). In the words of the Joni Mitchell song, 'you don't know what you've got 'til it's gone'. But to be able to revitalise the language, these 'new' speakers will want and need to involve older speakers. However, the needs and desires of these two groups of people may differ, and interactions can lead to some tricky social and political issues. One effective way of getting older and younger speakers together for mutual benefit is the Mentor-Apprentice model (also known as Master-Apprentice model), where an older or fluent speaker is paired with a person committed to learning and passing on the language (see Chapter 15 on teaching and learning for details).

As discussed in Chapter 8 on types of communities, in many endangered language communities there are a significant number of people who can understand the language but not speak it fluently. In Guernsey, an informal group who call themselves 'The Rememberers' (in Guernesiais, *Les Rallumeurs* or 're-kindlers') meet weekly to chat in Guernesiais and reactivate their passive language knowledge into active use, improving both fluency and accuracy – topics often include obscure words or grammatical points. The Rememberers are mainly aged 55–70 and some have not used Guernesiais for fifty years. In some cases, parents used Guernesiais with each other but not with the children, or in other cases Rememberers stopped speaking Guernesiais after discouragement at schools. The Rememberers is a rare example of effective bottom-up language planning which focuses on rebuilding social networks and increasing participants' frequency and fluency in everyday conversation and language use (rather than formal teaching). However, their conversations often focus on 'how the old people would have talked' rather than 'how we might talk in the future'. If this goes unnoticed, it might impact the ideas and possible choices about the kind of language that should be brought to the future, taught and revitalised. So even in an informal conversation group, it is important to think about our ideologies and goals of interaction, as well as which elements of language, such as topics, registers, and vocabulary, to focus on: for example, in one session a member of The Rememberers asked others to help recall or reconstruct words for movements such as leaning forward. (This is not to say that informal sessions should become formal grammar lessons, as seems to be happening in some Mentor-Apprentice programmes.)

Language Change

All living languages change over time, especially across generations. Languages also change due to the influence of other languages. Languages don't become endangered without another language that people are shifting to, and bilingual people always mix languages. We need to be aware of and accept the dynamic nature of language: the language we revitalise will not be the same as it was in the past, and that is completely normal. Some older speakers in Guernsey have expressed concern that if Guernesiais is taught in schools, 'it won't be the language we know'. They feel a strong connection to the language of their youth, and worry that it might become 'corrupted'. But if it is not taught to a new generation, it won't be a language that anyone knows. And that new generation needs to be able to pick it up and run with it, make it their own, and develop the language for whatever they want to use it for.

Change and growth are signs of life and health, not of decline. English, for example, has been enriched by many words from other languages: Well-known examples include *pyjamas* from Hindi, *robot* from Polish or Czech, and *chocolate* from Nahuatl. Indeed, the only languages that don't change are truly dead languages, which may only exist in archives. Linguists have found that ironically, endangered languages change faster than larger or more vital languages. This is often due to influence from other languages, especially the dominant one(s), which can be difficult for some language supporters to accept, although it is impossible to prevent.

In the case of Māori and Guernesiais, practically all speakers have English as their dominant language, and most speakers under the age of around sixty are likely to have learnt Māori or Guernesiais as a second language (there are young neo-speakers of Māori, who have been brought up to speak it as a first language, but their parents are probably second language or 'new' speakers). As with all languages, we have observed differences in grammar and pronunciation between the speech of younger and older speakers (you can see this in English too, e.g. 'I'm like ...' instead of 'I said ...'.)

Linguists have observed that endangered languages undergoing change may seem to be simplified or to become more regular (e.g. in verb forms). But there can also be additions and new borrowed words or structures from a dominant language, especially given that people who are bilingual inevitably mix their languages (which is also frequently lamented, but can't be prevented). Sometimes direct translations can bring new and useful ways of saying things, such as *bailler a hao* in Guernesiais, a direct translation of English 'give up'. The pronunciation or accent of younger or new speakers may differ from that of older speakers, which again older speakers may find difficult to accept.

When the spaces where a language is used become restricted, its vocabulary and forms can also reduce, as some ways of using it become forgotten. When community members assimilate to a dominant culture and language, some of their cultural expressions may change or be lost, including traditional greetings, politeness and kinship terms, and counting systems. In the Isle of Man, a decision was taken to use the English number system rather than the traditional Manx one in the Manx-medium school, to enable the children to follow the mainstream curriculum.

We also find that highly endangered languages can fragment into many small varieties, which may be only used within one family or by one individual – all of whom may consider that they speak the correct way! These changes are often not new – for example, some can be seen in nineteenth century Guernesiais literature; in the Americas, such changes go back to the sixteenth century and are often well documented. But by the time they are noticed, it is not possible to stop them (if it were ever possible). It is important to stress that language change does not imply that our languages are inferior or unsuitable for use or for reinforcing. Neither should language change be seen as an obstacle to revitalisation.

Purism

An important part of language and cultural reclamation involves collecting and documenting the knowledge of elders and devising ways of expanding that knowledge. However, it is common to focus on the heritage aspects of the language, which link the language with the past. Even linguists are not immune to this, with one linguist recently confessing to not including borrowings from other languages when he documented a language in the 1970s in a desire to represent only the 'purest' version of the language.

The idea that there is an 'authentic' way of producing your language can lead to ideas that there is only one right way of speaking or writing. While it can be helpful to remember that all living languages change, it must be remembered that the sort of change a language undergoing revitalisation may experience can be extreme and challenging to older speakers.

One thing that hampers many revitalisation initiatives is language purism. 'Purism' is the idea that there is a 'pure' or 'real' or 'authentic' way of using your language. Typically, language purists are older speakers of a language who don't like the new pronunciations or simplified grammar used by 'new' speakers of a language (see Chapter 7 for more about language attitudes and ideologies). Along with this type of thinking comes the idea of ownership: There may be strong feelings about who owns the language and who gets to say what is right and what is wrong. There can also be new 'language owners' who stigmatise older speakers for using too many loanwords. In a revitalisation situation there are usually limited resources, so you need to include everybody who has an interest (see Chapter 10 for discussion of power dynamics).

It is worthwhile thinking about what 'authentic' really means: genuine, valid, real. If someone uses the language for a real purpose, whatever that use is, it is a valid, authentic reason for using language. For example, in Guernesiais there is a word, *warro*, which is used as informal greeting (like 'hello' or 'hi'). Although it has been documented as used by some of the oldest speakers and appears in a highly respected dictionary, the authenticity of this word has been called into question by some community members who say that it was not used in their families.[1] But whether or not it was used in the past, people nowadays feel an authentic need for an informal greeting in Guernesiais. Using this word will encourage them to use Guernesiais more and facilitate real communication.

If your aim is to have the language spoken by younger generations, you need to be aware that the language will often need to change to be relevant to their interests and needs. All too often older speakers criticise younger ones, which can put them off speaking their languages entirely. It is more productive to encourage them to use the minority language, in whatever form it takes. It is known from research into language learning that there are intermediate stages before a learner acquires the whole of a new language. The processes of language contact and revitalisation can resemble some of the stages of language learning. In any kind of learning, we have to learn to walk before we can run; once new speakers become confident with what might be seen as 'simplified' language, they

---

[1] Fragmentation into small varieties, even between neighbouring families, is another common feature of highly endangered languages.

can start to tackle more complicated traditional forms if they want to. It has to be remembered that young speakers are the future of any language. If it survives, it will belong to them.

New Words for New Uses

If your language hasn't been used as a community language for a while, it will need a big input of new vocabulary. Just think of all the technological words which have entered the major languages in just the last ten years: words for *smartphone*, *app*, to *tweet*, to *unfriend*. Not only might you need vocabulary for these concepts; if your language is to be used as a medium of instruction in schools, you will also need words for concepts such as *graph*, *molecule*, *colonisation*, and *curriculum* (see Chapter 15 on teaching and learning).

Simply borrowing words is often the easiest default option for new terms such as *refrigerator*. Some older speakers find it difficult to conceive of their language being used in new ways, and simply use the new language to describe new things. So their speech may be peppered with borrowed or *loanwords*, which some zealous new speakers may dislike. Some language planners (e.g. Irish) have been criticised for using mainly loanwords in non-traditional contexts, while others (e.g. Quechua) have been criticised for being too purist.

Languages have always had ways of creating new words, which can be studied and reproduced. If there are historical language records, traditional literature, accounts, poems, or documentary archives, one option is to rediscover, reintroduce, or repurpose some terms and structures that have fallen out of use. An example of this in English is the word *broadcast*, which originally meant to throw seed outwards in a field. It fell out of use with the mechanisation of farming, but was reintroduced as a metaphor when radio was invented. There are many additional ways of creating new terms in a language. In the late 1980s when revitalisation of the Māori language was well underway, the Māori Language Commission (Te Taura Whiri i te Reo Māori), in response to many community requests, coined a large number of new words using a variety of approaches. Their main aim was to avoid loanwords, so strategies included circumlocutions, for example, *hekerangi* to mean 'parachute' (literally *heke* 'to descend' and *rangi* 'sky'). Another frequent strategy was *calquing*, where the literal meaning of an English word was translated, for example, 'bisect' is *weherua* (*wehe* meaning 'to split' and *rua* meaning 'two'). Sometimes existing words were combined, for example *pūhiko* for 'battery', where *pū* means 'origin' and *hiko* means 'electricity'. In fact *hiko* originally meant 'lightning' and its meaning has been extended to include electricity.

Another strategy was to repurpose archaic words (for example, *ngota* for 'atom' where the original meaning was 'fragment, particle').

In several languages, such as Manx and Māori, there are committees of people seen as language experts who are tasked with creating new words; but sometimes they take too long to decide on and disseminate new words. For example, teachers of Māori needed a word for 'number' to use in lessons and did not want to borrow a word. By the time the language committee had decided on a term, each teacher had their own different word.

Another way of developing new terminology is an inclusive 'crowdsourcing' approach, which encourages groups of people to talk about the topic – both face to face and online – and collect the most popular terms. This can even be done together with the oldest speakers to reduce possible tensions in the community about 'what to revitalise'.

Not Just About Language

Jeanette King's research has found that many people are not only (or principally) interested in revitalising a language for its own sake, but they often have a personal reason such as getting in touch with their family roots, joining a language community, or gaining a sense of achievement or well-being.

Language, Culture, and Identity

Language is deeply linked with culture. Most of those involved in language revitalisation talk about how culture is intrinsically linked to language. When you learn and speak a language you are learning and speaking culture. Some of this cultural expression may be in the form of cultural values, such as terms of address, etc. In addition, language can be closely related to cultural practices. For Māori in New Zealand, for example, the rituals of encounter in a *pōwhiri* (formal welcome) have to be delivered in Māori, with opening calls being performed by women, followed by speeches which necessarily contain much ritualistic language and expectations, such as paying respects to the dead. There is also the requirement for each speech to conclude with an appropriate song.

Most of those involved in language revitalisation are involved in reclaiming aspects of identity as well as cultural practices. This means that revitalisation is just as much about revitalising people as language. In other words, it's not just about what you are revitalising but who you are revitalising.

Language revitalisation often involves campaigning for someone else to do something, e.g. for a local government authority to erect signage, or for schools to teach the language. Such campaigns are valuable and can be a way for people who don't speak the language to get involved and to contribute to revitalisation. However, we need to be aware that it can be easier to focus on what others ought to do, rather than alter one's own behaviour, especially if one is not very confident in one's language competence. So, for example, some language promoters have reported that they find it easier to perform a poem or help in a classroom, which involves less impromptu language use than speaking it with their own children. So, increasing the self-confidence of language supporters is a vital part of language revitalisation.

Conclusion

Different people in language revitalisation movements have different aims and motivations. Some have a nostalgic, purist ideal of the kind of language they want to preserve. Others want to extend the areas where their language is used and have it recognised as a fully developed, modern language which can be used for all purposes. Others want to enjoy using their language with friends and family, while others want to affirm their identity through using a few words and phrases in greetings, rituals, songs, etc. Others may find that re-connecting with their language can enhance personal and community well-being.

All of these (and more) are valid elements of an overall language plan, but different priorities are too often a source of disagreement. It is therefore important to discuss openly what we want to achieve, why, and also what is achievable – in the short term, medium term, and long term. Plans should be regularly evaluated and revised, so that different functions, uses, and spaces can grow and be added to over time, as part of a longer sustainable plan. This involves recognising the strong feelings, attitudes, and ideologies that people have about language. Above all, it will involve compromise. These are all considerations when you are thinking about what sort of language you will be revitalising.

FURTHER READING

Aitchison, J. (2012). *Language Change: Progress or Decay?* 4th ed. Cambridge: Cambridge University Press.

Bentahila, A. and Davies, E. E. (1993). Language revival: Restoration or transformation? *Journal of Multilingual and Multicultural Development* 14, 355–74.

King, J. (2014). Revitalizing the Māori Language? In P. K. Austin and J. Sallabank, eds., *Endangered Languages: Beliefs and Ideologies in Language Documentation and Revitalization*. Oxford: Oxford University Press/British Academy, pp. 213–28.

Romaine, S. (2006). Planning for the survival of linguistic diversity. *Language Policy* 5, 441–73.

Shandler, J. (2006). *Adventures in Yiddishland: Postvernacular Language and Culture.* Oakland, CA: University of California Press.

2.1 Wymysiöeryś

Tymoteusz Król

When I first started working on the revitalisation of Wymysiöeryś, I was focused on the language. The other elements of Wymysiöeryś culture seemed safer. I thought, for example, that you could collect traditional costumes and lock them in a wardrobe in a museum in order to preserve them. When we were children or teenagers, our task was to document everything that we understood as 'Wymysiöeryś': language, folk dress, recipes, old buildings, folk tales, etc. We were successful in doing this (we got a broad documentation), but mistaken in our approach (keeping it alive).

I realised our naivety as I started to write a dictionary of Wymysiöeryś. I had read all the dictionaries and grammars of Wymysiöeryś that I could find, but not a single one of these books described my language well enough to satisfy me. Later, I started to read poetry and saw that it only represented part of our language – the style is more literary and archaic than spoken usage. It was then that I realised that it is only by speaking a language can you keep it alive. It is the same in the case of Wymysiöeryś dress – when documented and closed behind glass in a museum these garments become dead artifacts of the past.

Documentation is essential: it is the basis of revitalisation but it is not the final goal. Also we have to take care of what we document. I often used to think about how I could create teaching materials using a 'pure' form of the language that was not Polonised or Germanised. But after a couple of years I stopped being so concerned with this – I gave up looking for 'the pure Wymysiöeryś language' and I started to listen to what people were actually saying (see Figure 2.1.1).

I noticed the same problem in the case of Wymysiöeryś costume. Elements of Wymysiöeryś folk dress used to be inspired by styles noticed or imported by Vilamovians living in Vienna, Paris, London, Graz, Lviv, and many other cities in Europe, and incorporated into local dress styles. Now many people bring folk costumes to Wymysoü from other cities as well, although these modern textiles and their patterns are very different from traditional local ones. Some anthropologists (and some Vilamovians as well) believe that this change is negative and that we cannot say that these new garments are truly 'Wymysiöeryś attire'. I agreed with them at first, but then I thought, 'who am I to judge'? Is the pattern on these new textiles more important than the fact that they were imported from the same cities as hundreds of years ago? Maybe the fact that they were imported from abroad is the most important tradition? In this way, I brought back textile designs and ideas from the ENGHUM field school in Mexico.

Judging these things as a scholar is, for me, a form of neocolonialism. An example of this is when Germanists argue about whether or not Slavic words, for

Figure 2.1.1 Speaking Wymysiöeryś: Tymoteusz Król, the revitaliser of the language. Photo by Justyna Olko

example, from Polish or the Silesian language, should be used in Wymysiöeryś, which is a Germanic language, or when linguists determine what is a language and what is a dialect.

I think that, as language activists and revitalisers, we can ask those linguists who decide that a language is in fact not a language, but 'only' a dialect: 'Who are you to judge a language in this way? Why are you able to reach this conclusion? What about the views of the people who speak it? Who are you to judge?'

2.2 Language Purism in Nahua Communities

Justyna Olko

Back in the 1970s, when Jane Hill and Kenneth Hill did extensive research in Nahua communities around the Volcano Malintzin in Tlaxcala, they discovered interesting facts about how Nahuatl was classified with regard to Spanish.[2] Some speakers believed that what they called *mexicano* was an *idioma* ('language', always used in reference to Spanish), but most people identified Nahuatl as a 'dialect'. The reason given was it is mixed with Spanish, which results in *tlahco mexicano, tlahco castellano*, 'half Nahuatl, half Spanish', no longer having the legitimate status of a language in its own right. Today more people in Tlaxcala seem to identify Nahuatl as a 'language', which is probably a result of a more positive ideology arriving from the outside. However, in more secluded

---

[2] J. Hill and K. Hill, *Speaking Mexicano: The Dynamics of Syncretic Language in Central Mexico*, 1st ed. (Tucson, AZ: University of Arizona Press, 1986).

mountainous communities most of the speakers believe their tongue is a 'dialect', even if they cannot explain what a dialect is. And a clear majority is deeply convinced that mixing with Spanish is negative because 'Nahuatl is disappearing if it has Spanish words' and 'if people mix languages they no longer speak Nahuatl'. But at the same time, for this very reason, many speakers think their way of speaking is bad and very different than 'the legitimate Nahuatl' spoken once by their grandparents and great grandparents. In other words, they are often convinced that the jumbled (*cuatrapeado*) nature of the results of Nahuatl-Spanish contact is reflected in how they speak.

Accelerating language shift is accompanied by purist attitudes, which are often displayed most strongly by specific individuals or a particular group within a community. Such persons present themselves as 'owners' or 'guardians' of the heritage language, advising others which terms should be used and which must be avoided. They sometimes criticise both older speakers for their loanwords from Spanish, and the youngest speakers for their limited language skills and vocabulary. Purists would focus on eliminating all loanwords from Spanish (while inadvertently accepting direct translations!), including some words, which were incorporated into Nahuatl several hundred years ago. They also 'test' speakers on their knowledge of 'good' Nahuatl, for example asking them to say complex numbers (the traditional base-20 system has only partly survived and Spanish numerals are generally used). Degrees of purism are found not only among intellectuals and professional teachers, but also among community members.

Purist attitudes often have quite counterproductive effects on language survival. A good example is that of the community of Santa Ana Tlacotenco, where 'legitimate' Nahuatl has become a tool of internal politics. In the second half of the twentieth century this community suffered strong criticism of the locally spoken variant by members of academic circles who promoted the use of 'Classical' Nahuatl as the only legitimate version of the language. Today Nahuatl is spoken by very few people, most of them from the oldest generation. This decline in language use is accompanied by purist attitudes on the part of members of the middle-aged generation, but their approach hasn't been particularly helpful in keeping the language alive. Some activists, however, take a less restrictive approach, encouraging young people to explore the traditional vocabulary of the oldest generation rather than resort to substituting 'missing' words by borrowing from Spanish. They also engage in the creation of neologisms. Creating new words from within the language for new things has always been an important response of Nahuas to contact with Spanish, especially in the colonial period when the vitality of Nahuatl was high. This kind of purism can in fact stimulate the development of language skills and encourage speakers to explore and learn vocabulary and registers of the heritage language that have almost been forgotten or fallen out of use.

3 Ethical Aspects and Cultural Sensitivity in Language Revitalization

Joanna Maryniak, Justyna Majerska-Sznajder, and Tymoteusz Król

Ethics is often broadly understood as answering the questions of 'what is good?' and 'what is bad?'. Of course, this assumes that there are simple answers to these (and similar) queries. We define ethics in language revitalization as reflection upon the problems of correct, desirable, and sensitive actions around revitalization itself. Its importance stems from the fact that decisions taken without considering such ethical questions might end up being problematic or even harmful to communities. Thus tackling this issue can contribute to the success of language revitalization. While engaging in language revitalization, we[1] often find ourselves in situations that are anything but obvious – for example, in situations where two (or more) possible good courses of action clash. For this reason, we will outline a series of discussion points for those engaged in revitalization. We have presented suggestions only where we felt we could offer potentially useful solutions or 'best practices'. Still we know that there is no valid and universal code of ethics or rules of conduct, even within a single community. For this reason, all of our points are, first and foremost, suggestions and points of departure for reflection.

Basic Questions

The first logical step to language revitalization is recognizing that a language is endangered. However this might not sit well with the community that speaks it (or that has historically spoken it). As the awareness that their language and culture is disappearing can be a depressing thought, some speakers may deny that it is happening. Therefore some people might ask whether to start a revitalization project at all? Other chapters in this book discuss reasons and benefits of language diversity and language revitalization (see Chapters 1, 8, 9), so they might provide a starting point for such a discussion within a community.

---

[1] This chapter is cowritten by two Indigenous Vilamovian activists and researchers and an external researcher collaborating with them.

This however leads us to the second question: who should start (and continue) the revitalization process? Our experience shows two main kinds of people who are normally involved: internal (often called 'activists') and external, mostly researchers, who usually become interested in the language for purely academic reasons (like documenting interesting topics) and only later become involved in the revitalization process. These two groups differ in many ways. Their knowledge about the community is different and the time and money available to them, likewise, vary. Broadly speaking, activists are more likely to have more time and flexibility (since they often live in the community and so, even with full-time work, are still at hand) but less likely to have money at their disposal than researchers. On the other hand, researchers might have impressive financial means (thanks to funded projects) but strict time constraints (due to project deadlines). This can be a cause of misunderstandings and problems. Yet the process of revitalization doesn't end with those two groups: local authorities, politicians, and governments are often important as well. There might also be some overlap in that activists can become researchers (like two of the authors of this chapter, who are currently writing their PhD theses on various topics related to their home community of Wilamowice). Furthermore a researcher might become so engaged with the community that their actions cross over into activism. However no matter how respectable the authorities helping you, no matter how much money they can offer, no matter how good the methods they employ are, revitalization won't work without local engagement and local conviction about the goal, purposes, and benefits. Likewise, it will not succeed without respecting a local sense of ethics and good practices.

A Decision-Making Process and Dealing with Dilemmas

An Indigenous community itself is never homogenous and there might be people who disagree with the need for revitalization at all. An even bigger issue arises when only a part of the community wants to revitalize their language and the other part is against it. So, if someone wishes to start a revitalization project, would it make sense to try to convince them not to do so, or is it better to just ignore them and work on one's (self)-appointed tasks? As languages are usually lost because people decide not to speak them or cannot speak them anymore, an important challenge for activists is to question majority attitudes and practices within the community.

On the other hand, other community members might see revitalization as needed and useful but might not want to collaborate with others who are involved. Being an activist means being more visible than other members of the community. More often than not activists aren't democratically elected and this might put them in conflict with others – especially those who like being in the limelight or have been in a position of power for a long time. Opinions on the language itself can also vary as some activists are more concerned about taking the language forward and some might want to preserve older forms of it and keep it as it was previously. Of course, there may also be conflicts about how to go about revitalization.

Coming from Outside and Dealing with Internal Parties

What if a community at large doesn't want revitalization at all and the only interest is from outsiders, often (but not exclusively) researchers? Outsiders cannot revitalize a language without community involvement. All they can do is raise awareness and change attitudes, but this doesn't mean they can't try their best to promote the idea of revitalization in the community. Researchers face their own set of questions. How much and in what way should outsiders learn about the community beforehand? One thing we can emphasize is that coming to a community without any knowledge of local culture, traditions, and language will likely discourage its members from collaborating in the proposed project. Thus putting in time and effort during the preparation stage is essential when establishing collaborations. We will describe this in more detail in the sub-section entitled 'Establishing Collaboration'.

An unsolvable dilemma is whether a researcher should consult the community when planning a project before asking the funding agency for money. To make sure that the planned activities do not clash with the community's ideologies, needs, and behaviors, it is best to discuss the project with members of the community beforehand – even if with just a few. However, then their hopes might be raised and they might not understand the complicated procedures and long times needed for the projects to be reviewed and chosen for funding. This could lead them to think you let them down when you are only waiting for the results of various calls for proposals. One way not to run into this problem is not to discuss it at all, but then it might turn out that the planned actions don't sit well with the community. The best course of action may be to under-promise initially (i.e. promise the bare minimum needed so as not to raise the hopes and expectations either of the community or the funding agency) and then over-deliver once the project has started (don't stop at what you promised, give back as much as possible).

Time constraints posed by academic programs are something that should also be considered carefully. While the length of the project does not have to translate into the length of engagement with a community, it might determine it – especially if the community is far removed from the researcher's residence. In general, we have seen that Indigenous communities tend to warm up to outsiders gradually and at different paces. Usually they become more open and welcoming once they get to know them better. Therefore planning a longer project (or longer engagement) might help to address better the situation and goals of the community. What counts most in our opinion is that personal engagement outlasts the funding process.

Yet the best-case scenario is not always possible and there might be situations in which it is known from the start that the engagement will end after a certain period of time. In such a situation the best thing to do is to inform the members of the local community about that from the start and keep information clear and up to date during the communication process; sometimes saying something just once might prove not enough due to cultural differences. After receiving funding to work on one language and with a specific community, some researchers might be tempted to publish the results and move on to a new one. This is often referred to as a 'data extraction' approach and its ethical aspects can be problematic, especially considering community involvement and how it might benefit them. It is also important for outsiders to care about what will happen to their local collaborators once they leave. If a researcher left a good impression, all is well. But if not everything went right, members of the community who collaborated on the project might be associated with the researcher and thus reflected negatively on. It is a good idea to stay in constant contact with them and to do one's best to leave the best impression. In such a case, it is also advisable to plan to train local activists/volunteers to continue the revitalization activities once the researcher has left. These matters relate to the broader question of establishing collaboration, which we will discuss now.

Establishing Collaboration

How to establish initial collaboration with a community? How does one choose local collaborators? Is there a way to make sure that language revitalization goes on without discriminating any group in the community and making sure that all members have equal chances to be involved rather than marginalized? These questions guide decisions about establishing collaborations. First of all, it is advisable for external researchers coming to the community to include its members and make them part of the decision-making process at all stages of the project, including planning, realization, and evaluation. Local revitalizers are often in the best position when it comes to including and consulting other community members during all the planning and decision-making stages of the revitalization process. On the other hand, a naive external researcher may unwittingly ally with one local faction and alienate others.

Creating a hierarchy as an outsider working with coworkers from the local community can cause controversies. This means, for example, avoiding favoritism, e.g. when commissioning handicrafts from specific people in the community. The eldest are not necessarily speaking the 'only correct' variant of the language or even a 'correct' one at all, as their language might have experienced attrition due to disuse. Those who do not know the language well might nevertheless have traditional knowledge, which is an important part of the culture. Local activists are not the only ones who can collaborate with researchers. Striving to understand relations among different groups of interest in the community, and remembering that sometimes the interested parties may try to hide these relations for various reasons, can prevent certain problems from arising. In some contexts, being an obvious outsider can help to avoid being associated with any faction.

Local revitalizers often act as 'radars', paying attention to the emotions, opinions, and attitudes of community members. But at the same time they might act against the 'common opinion' shared by many community members. During their activities they might tread 'uncomfortable' ground for other members of their community. This discomfort might be related to historical traumas or specific situations that the group or individuals have gone through. Local revitalizers might therefore be tempted to avoid certain subjects; caring for the well-being of community members can help the revitalization process gain more allies. However, confronting such topics – with as much tact and caution as possible so as not to hurt anybody further – might also prove a valuable experience. Local revitalizers are also in the most comfortable starting position when it comes to including the community during all the planning and decision-making stages of the revitalization process. However, they also should pay attention not to exclude any sections of the community – this means inviting everyone to get involved (and especially those who are interested). Worsening local conflicts or driving divisions deeper as a result of revitalization activities is precisely something that should be avoided. Local revitalizers have yet another advantage in that they have known the members of the community for a long time and so can choose their collaborators more thoughtfully and on the basis of longer experience.

In the case of many disappearing languages, the main language carriers are the elderly. When working in language revitalization, one must be careful not to exploit them – for example, through taking up too much of their time or reminding them too much of traumas they might have experienced. As they grow older, their health can worsen and they can eventually die, thus leaving younger people as possible collaborators. This can be emotionally difficult for researchers and activists who have got to know them. However, younger generations can't always help in the way that elders have done. If language revitalization is supported by a project with strict deadlines, taking care not to plan too much work for the elderly is even more salient, as their illness or death could result in unnecessary pressures on all the surviving parts of the community.

There may also be members of the community who do not speak the language in question and do not show any particular concern about it. Still some forms that appear in their use of the dominant language might be influenced by the minority one. Similarly, a seemingly 'worse' knowledge of the dominant language might not be a sign of an uneducated and 'worthless' interlocutor, but a new and hitherto unexplored field of research – one of language contact in that community.

It is also good to remember class and gender issues in the community, which are best analyzed on a case-by-case basis. Sometimes publishing a book or creating a movie in which the members of one class or people of one gender will be more prevalent can result in controversies. Of course, it can also be done on purpose to help to create visibility of minorities within minorities, but then it needs to be done consciously, not haphazardly without considering the implications for the group.

The position of an outsider can also be exploited by the community collaborators. A feeling of prestige or the possibility of receiving some benefits from collaborating with the academy can result in conflicts and internal discrimination. The opposite is also possible. Members of some communities do not want to get engaged in collaboration regarding the language because they fear being seen as deriving private profit from a common good, i.e. the language. There are no clear answers and solutions to such problems and they are best approached on a case-by-case basis and with the most careful use of intuition, respect, and sensitivity.

As an outsider, preparing for language revitalization in a community is less about choosing the correct kind of technical equipment or having the proper monetary means as it is about learning. Making an effort before meeting to learn as much as possible about some of the most important subjects such as local internal dependencies, cultural codes, and history of the field and community, can make a huge difference. We recommend that outsiders learn about the community's culture and history, including its rules of respect and conduct. Developing sensitivity toward the community's needs, its perspectives, and its knowledge systems might prove more different than assumed. Cultural differences are not only in play when dealing with far-away countries. There are some places that have such a vast amount of literature on them that it is not possible to read it through in a reasonable amount of time, so it is understandable that one has to limit oneself. However, there are also places that have next to nothing written about them, or that have their last description dating from a long time ago, thus making it horribly outdated. Whatever the case, effort is of paramount importance as it shows respect to the community through not coming totally unprepared. However, in no case should one treat the written word as having absolute precedence over what you are told by the members of the community – things might have changed since the writing of the books, they might reflect an external point of view or they might reflect perspectives of only one specific group within the community (and, as already remarked, most communities are not homogenous).

Even when working with communities near the researcher's home area and doing one's best to develop sensitivity and awareness of local norms and rules of respect, one can still be perceived negatively. Being conscious of that is a good step toward approaching possible issues. These might be the result of internalized negative stereotypes or judgments from both the sides: Researchers might be seen as people from huge cities, or as representatives of the dominant culture (both characteristics that can be perceived negatively). However, their actions might also prove offensive to the community without the researcher being aware. In such a case neither side is at fault and understanding that helps in approaching issues with an open mind.

Facing the Past and Dealing with Political Tensions

Many communities come with a burden of past or present oppression, persecution, experiences of ethnic discrimination, marginalization, and related traumas. In such cases, the group may ask itself difficult questions about how much visibility they want; in the context of their history, including possible traumas, minoritization, and related persecutions, it is possible that the group may not want to draw attention to itself. Would bringing up a specific subject result in the community's discomfort, fear, or insecurity? Would reminding the public of some difficult issues reignite old troubles? Sometimes it might seem that the problem does not exist or has been solved long ago, only for it to come back in the least expected moment. It might be reasonable to discuss these issues with community members – if and how they wish difficult topics to be brought up or dealt with – as sometimes time is needed for a community to realize what would be best for its members and the future of the language. In such a situation helping to create safe spaces for discussing it in the community would significantly facilitate such deliberations.

For example, in 2018 the Vilamovian youth, who were engaged in language revitalization, wrote and staged a theater play dealing with the violent ethnic persecutions suffered by the eldest generations during and after the World War II. This was not well received by local authorities and was very stressful for the youths themselves, in part because of Poland's descent into conservative authoritarianism, which sees minorities as a threat to the territorial integrity and ethnic cohesion of the state. However, the decision to stage this play was a bottom-up one, taken by the young members of the community. Instead of intimidating them, the experience became a source of pride and empowerment for them. Were it done as an external initiative (e.g. by a researcher or an institution), the negative reactions might have been seen as lacking of sensitivity toward the community and putting its young members in risky and disturbing circumstances. Thus, we believe that certain, especially difficult, decisions should be made only by members of the community. Even if they represent just one of its groups, this does not deprive them of the legitimacy to act.

Collaborating as an academic with a minority may position an outsider politically, whether they want it or not. Linguistic minorities often overlap with ethnic minorities and this raises questions about their nationality and possible separatism. Basque and Catalan in Spain are two famous cases, but similar examples abound (in Poland a very similar situation surrounds Silesia). Journalists will undoubtedly ask you for your opinions about those subjects and more. Academics may be asked to testify about such difficult topics in person, or to pen scientific opinions that will carry more weight than any research paper because on their basis some parliaments might vote yes or no to a law giving a community the right to learn in its language, or to use it in their signage etc. Writing this sort of text carries a huge responsibility so it is best to be careful not to hurt the most vulnerable party, i.e. the minoritized community. When asked whether what they are speaking is a language, the best answer is the one respecting the perspective of the community. The absolute worst course of action is to use a term that will be understood as diminishing the importance of the language. 'Dialect', 'patois', even 'ethnolect' all can be seen as dismissive and imposing such external categories on the speech of community language can be seen as unethical or as a form of violence.

Ownership, Consent, and Other Legal Issues

Legal issues also fall under the subject of ethics. Laws change so much and so often that any set of precise recommendations we might include here would quickly become outdated. Therefore we will name topics, which do not depend on a particular wording of the law but touch upon legal issues in general. While doing language revitalization, one needs not only to familiarize oneself with the laws of the land and obtain all the necessary permissions from local authorities, but also – especially in the case of academics – to comply with the legal requirements in one's own institution, with regard to national and international laws (if applicable), or the requirements of one's funding agency. If the revitalization is supported by sponsors, agreeing on these rules is also an ethical question.

There are also situations where what is legal may clash with what is ethical. This refers, for example, to intellectual property and authorship rights. These are often violated when local collaborators are treated as 'informants' and not as partners and coauthors of research and related language revitalization programmes, including scientific and educational products. It is ethical to consult people before publishing their data or transcribed utterances and, if possible, offer them the position of coauthors or named contributors. What would seem ethical and culturally sensitive may, however, clash with national or international legal regulations. For example, research participants usually do not legally own their words once recorded. The recordings legally belong to the organization that employs the person creating them. However, this does not have to be a guiding practice for sensitive researchers. Whatever the ownership rights might be in the country where one is working, including the collaborators and interlocutors as coauthors or of a publication, or at least naming them as contributors (if they agree for their identities to be revealed in a specific publication), is a commendable practice.

No matter what the laws might be in the country, there might be parts of culture that do not incur any legal protection but that the community does not want to be copied or published. For example, the Vilamovians (both generally as members of an ethnic minority who are inhabitants of the town of Wilamowice, but also more specifically as members of a tightly knit dance ensemble) have a very distinct song and dance repertoire and see any other folk group performing parts of it as a cause for outrage. Similarly the Maasai had their handicrafts copied – not only by huge Western corporations but also by other nearby tribes. So, sometimes it would be more sensitive for researchers not to engage in disseminating content which could be copied without the community's consent. Even local activists may be wary of engaging in external language revitalization because they do not want to be accused of 'betraying the group's secrets' or selling the rights to the language or culture. Of course, a full application of this principle would prevent anything from being published, so consultations are a reasonable course of action.

Another legal issue arises when the commercial benefits of revitalization go to outside parties. This is often intertwined with cultural appropriation as in the case of various big name fashion designers 'copying' or 'being closely inspired by' various Mexican traditional costumes, but it can also occur on a smaller scale as in the case of Wilamowice. Some enterprising Poles living in the region have started selling materials based on Vilamovian cultural heritage. Yet the economic profits do not reach the community who feels that they own the moral rights to those materials.

It is unacceptable to publish anything without prior consent. Of course, it does not have to be given in writing. There are groups that are historically illiterate and calling them out on it is a very bad idea. Yet there are also groups, which have been in a problematic situation vis-à-vis various bureaucratic forms, which they were forced or coerced to sign. In these cases, asking them to declare their consent in writing might recall these traumatic memories and so it is much better to include the expression of consent at the beginning of a recording. This might sometimes be problematic for academics if a funding agency or their institution asks for a written consent. Even so, it would be advisable for a researcher to prioritize the comfort and well-being of local collaborators over formal requirements, and, if necessary, negotiate oral consent with the institutions they depend on. After all, this may contribute to a greater decolonization and sensibilization of those institutions.

Moreover consent, according to the United Nations Declaration on the Rights of Indigenous Peoples, should always be understood as **FPIC**: '**F**ree, **p**rior, and **i**nformed **c**onsent'. In other words, it is valid only when it is given freely (sometimes also termed 'enthusiastically' i.e. without pressure), when it is given prior to an action deriving from it (so, for example, requesting permission to record someone after the recording has already taken place is unethical), and when the person who is asked for consent understands what they are agreeing to. It follows that both written consent forms and oral questions relating to consent should employ language that is easy to understand. This suggestion can also be helpful for other forms of communication with the community. However, precautions are not always enough, and we can find ourselves in a situation when a person who was recorded or provided some other kind of information asks for it not to be disseminated. It is easy enough to deal with this before the fact, but what to do when material created already (book, movie, etc.) prompts this person to withdraw their consent? Of course, there are perfectly legal answers here, but they might not be satisfactory to the member of the community and what to do in such a situation is an example of a serious ethical challenge.

One might sometimes be confronted with a moral dilemma connected to gathered data. Let's say one finds some older, good-quality recordings and wants to share them with the community. However, the first collaborator to hear the recording informs you that the person featured in the recording was implicated in many problematic actions in the community and being reminded of them in a language-learning material could turn people away from the language even faster. There are various points of view and various relationships and reputations here at stake, and it is by no means easy to balance them. Such a recording could be anonymized or, if it stays recognizable even after such a process, one possibility is to use such a recording for very short excerpts, like the pronunciation of single words in a digital dictionary.

Sharing the documentation (as it is also part of the language revitalization process – see Chapter 13) is also an ethical question. Recorded materials might not belong to the community according to the letter of the law, but it does not change the fact that their content originates with them. Therefore the community may wish to receive it back. Recordings can easily be transferred to a hard drive and left in the community as a sort of incipient local archive. Vocabulary gathered can be typeset as a dictionary – even using a simple word processor, printing it in a print shop, and binding it at home. What counts above all are the content and the gestures. Communities may appreciate these ways of giving back much more than seeing a fancy hardcover book published after a few years by a big-name publisher. The same applies to older sources (such as archival documents or old recordings) as they might be useful in language revitalization. Community members often do not have access to those materials, either because they do not know where to find them or because the archives demand exorbitant prices for access to the copies. In these cases, giving someone, for example, a copy of an old record or a photo of their grandmother can do wonders for the collaboration. In all cases, however, when making such materials available, it is commendable to publish them in a language that the community will understand – not necessarily in the dominant one.

Ethics is also concerned with the problem of respect toward outsiders by community members and activists. Academics and other outsiders also have their rights, dreams, and sensitivities and they may be engaged and committed individuals with the best of motivations toward the community. They may also be vulnerable human beings. An ethical collaboration should be developed in both directions, especially when the future of an endangered language and community's well-being are at stake.

The last, but by no means least important part of ethics in revitalization, is ethics toward oneself. The revitalization of Wymysiöeryś was something that the two Indigenous authors have for years treated as a 'higher thing,' having priority over all else. We often put revitalization before our private lives, sometimes working on it 24/7, even losing sleep. If this is your position, we don't want to argue that you should step down and treat it just like a hobby (though if you already do so, it is also a viable position) but remember the ethics of working with yourself: respect yourself and do not burn yourself out as it won't help the revitalization in any way. A healthy, well-rested, and positively minded person can do more for revitalization than one who is struggling to maintain a healthy work–life balance.

FURTHER READING

Austin, P. K. (2010). Communities, ethics and rights in language documentation. Language Documentation and Description, 7, 34–54. London: SOAS, University of London. www.elpublishing.org/docs/1/07/ldd07_03.pdf.

Dwyer, A. M. (2006). Ethics and practicalities of cooperative fieldwork and analysis. In J. Gippert, N. Himmelmann, and U. Mosel, eds., *Fundamentals of Language Documentation: A Handbook*. Berlin: Mouton de Gruyter, pp. 31–66. (Spanish version: Ética y aspectos prácticos del trabajo de campo cooperativo. In J. Haviland and J. A. Flores Farfan, eds. (2007). *Bases de la documentación lingüística*. Mexico City: Instituto Nacional de Lenguas Indígenas, pp. 49–89.)

Grinevald, C. (2003). Speakers and documentation of endangered languages. In P. K. Austin, ed., *Language Documentation and Description* 1, pp. 52–72. www.elpublishing.org/itempage/7

3.1 Being a Helper: A Few Ethical Considerations for Conducting Research with Indigenous Communities

Aleksandra Bergier

In this capsule, I'd like to share a few ethical lessons I learned while collaborating with the Indigenous researchers and the Friendship Centres (urban Indigenous community organizations) in Ontario, Canada, on various Indigenous knowledge and language-related projects.

I'm particularly grateful for an opportunity to enhance my understanding of what it means to be a helper. I don't use this word in a sense of being a white do-gooder within a Western charity model. Rather, I draw on the culturally grounded meanings this term holds for the urban Indigenous communities I had the privilege of working with. Being a helper means contributing to the well-being of the community with one's unique skills and knowledge. It is about being part of a community circle where individuals with a wide range of identities and ways of being in the world feel that they belong while sharing their gifts and working for the benefit of all. Navigating the role of a helper within the research context is never limited to using skills typically associated with the work of a scholar – gathering information, making sense of data, and writing down the findings. It involves many other skills and responsibilities. One of them is the willingness to listen deeply and carefully before rushing to speak your truth. Another is sensitivity to the needs of the community members and the ability to respectfully follow cultural protocols. An act as simple as helping to clean a venue before a community gathering or ensuring a knowledge keeper's appropriate transportation to and from event can go a long way.

I had one of my most enlightening research experiences as I was sitting at the kitchen table at one of the Friendship Centres. I was simply listening to women who shared incredibly complex stories about their work while helping to chop vegetables, greeting guests and serving food at the community feast. This, of course, was part of a research plan previously approved by the community. I gained more insights that day than during dozens of formal interviews.

In my experience, research done in a good way is grounded in long-term, reciprocal relationships with the knowledge keepers. It generates useful knowledge in a way that's accountable and addresses the needs of specific communities. Often this means planning the research outcomes in a way that's immediately beneficial to people, for example, designing data collection activities around community initiatives and including expenses for these initiatives in a research budget. Examples include funding a language immersion camp, a land-based experiential workshop, a video, a toolkit, a Pow Wow, or a community feast.

Finally, I learned that an integral part of a researcher's work is an ongoing examination of their positionality. To me personally, it means exploring my own cultural foundations as a Polish researcher – connecting to my country's past, looking into the history of my family, and understanding how my identity and social position impact my work.

4 Planning a Language Revitalization Project

Susan D. Penfield

In the world of language revitalization, the importance of planning should never be underestimated; the need for good language planning is critical on many levels. Ideally communities who are engaged in reclaiming their languages should put a large-scale 'strategic language plan' in place. Such a plan specifies short- and long-term goals over several years and provides a structure within which to plan and implement a wide range of projects that support those goals. Within each project is a set of activities that help reach the goals for that project. However, as the well-known language revitalization expert, Leanne Hinton, has pointed out, this does not mean that a community needs to wait for such a large strategic plan to be in place before attempting any project. Every project aimed at language sustainability counts as a learning experience for all involved and will ideally serve to better inform and advance the efforts of the community.

Having an overarching strategic plan for a revitalization program contributes to the larger vision of language sustainability for the long term in important ways. But the careful planning of individual projects is equally important. Individual projects can be positioned and implemented to help best meet the long-term goals. The best language planning entails P-I-E (Planning, Implementation, Evaluation). Leanne Hinton credits Lucile Watahomogie, Hualapai educator and pioneer in language revitalization, with this approach, and it is certainly tried and true. Every individual project is best served if these three pieces are carefully put into place.

To focus on project planning, let's begin by thinking about what a 'project' really is. At CoLang 2016 (Institute on Collaborative Language Research), Margaret Florey taught a course on project planning. Students were asked to generate ideas for projects. Here are a few of the ideas they shared:

- Start a Master-Apprentice Program.
- Record songs in my language.
- Create more language resources for my community.
- Develop a writing system for my language.

Planning a Language Revitalization Project

- Change the names of geographic landmarks in my community to their Indigenous names.
- Create an app for my language.
- Raise literacy efforts for my language.
- Start a language nest.
- Write a grammar.
- Make an online dictionary.
- Get young people involved in language work.
- Make signs and public materials in my language and more.
- Raise public awareness about Indigenous languages.
- Teach my language.

These are all good ideas for activities! But there are many more. Activities are initiated and sustained in accordance with the current needs of the specific community. Any given project may involve many activities. Remember that a project needs to be an achievable effort and planned to meet the language needs of the community.

Some of the ideas listed above may seem more like 'projects' to you than others. Strictly speaking, projects are a carefully planned set of activities within a specific time frame and with well-defined outcomes. Australian language activist Margaret Florey explains that a project must, ideally, have the following characteristics:

- definable and realistic goals,
- clear objectives,
- outcomes that can be measured,
- response to a specific need,
- fit into a larger strategic plan,
- an identifiable target audience, and
- a work plan with stages and a timeline and with an end date.

Planning a successful language revitalization project must entail, at least, the following steps:

Step 1: *The beginning of any good project begins with a good idea.* This is an idea that can be molded and shaped to fit the resources of the community and the capabilities of those involved. It is an idea that can be understood and shared with others and leads to something that will have understandable and useful outcomes when completed. A good idea, which motivates participants and guides the activities, can go a long way toward developing really important projects for communities. Such ideas are sometimes the work of a very motivated individual, or they may result from group meetings, committees, and the like. Regardless of its origin, a good idea is usually recognized by the excitement it generates. Community settings where 'brainstorming' is encouraged are good places to generate valuable ideas for language revitalization projects.

Designing such meetings to generate ideas is a process that can occur often in revitalization contexts and can breathe new life into existing projects as well as launch new and exciting ones. Start by asking broad, general questions like 'What can we do that would help with our immediate goals?' or 'What activities do you want to see continued?' – which may or may not be language-specific – and see where these lead. Perhaps it will become clear what is most important to community members, how they want to see language efforts proceed, and then more focused activities can be built around those interests.

Let's further this discussion by generating a possible project. Let's say that the community is very concerned about losing traditional agricultural practices. A language project might be initiated which would try to identify how much information about agriculture is in the existing documentation for the language. Maybe it would also be possible to document how agricultural activities are or were talked about. This would entail plant names and uses, terminology for tools, seasons, understanding how the labor was divided, planting methods and activities such as harvesting and related ceremonies. It might be good to ask who taught these traditional practices, and how. These kinds of information can be gathered through interviews with speakers, and added to what information is already documented. This could lead to the building of a large database of language related to agricultural practices that could then form the basis for generating materials for language teaching.

As well, any one of the above questions could lead to a specific project that would require all the same planning steps, on a smaller scale. For example, maybe, beginning language students could learn a short dialogue about planting seeds and learn to incorporate new vocabulary related to tools or agricultural practices. Perhaps students or teachers could create a children's book about harvesting activities, or organize a field trip to agricultural areas and have a hands-on demonstration, augmented or immersed in relevant language about traditional food sources, etc. All of this, and more, could be generated from just one good idea!

Step 2: *Decide what is already in place and what is needed.* A project can be started by an individual or a group (such as a language committee), but in any case it should respond to what is already in place within a speaking community and propose what else might be needed. If possible, begin by writing up a 'background' statement, a 'needs' statement, and a 'purpose' statement. These can be as simple as saying 'Our language has (x) remaining first language speakers. We need to start offering classes to adults to reclaim our language'. This last statement establishes both language status and existing work (and gives some background, need, and purpose). Then, look at what is *specifically* needed and propose how to accomplish it. For example, 'To continue revitalizing our language, we need to create a language nest' (or an online dictionary, or classes in schools, and so forth). These basic statements are important for several reasons: (1) they position the project you choose within any existing work that might be going on, (2) they form the base line information that will be needed for any proposals (grants or other funding requests), (3) they make clear the basic goal of the project and explain why it is needed to others in the community.

Step 3: *Putting the idea into action.* An idea is an abstract entity until it becomes a reality in the form of a serious project, which has expected tangible outcomes. This transformation usually happens when the interested parties begin to set specific goals. Goal setting is perhaps the most critical step in all language planning endeavors. It requires careful thinking and realistic considerations. If you are creating an overarching strategic plan, then you should think in terms of short-term goals such as: what can we accomplish in 6 months? 1 year? Or 2 years? And long-term goals like, what should have been accomplished by 3 years? 5 years? 10 years? Within each of those time frames would be a series of individual projects, also with goals. Within each project, there should be specific activities that will lead to the goal. This is a nested way of creating a framework to accomplish goals: the bottom tier are activities, which support a specific project, which forms a critical piece of the larger strategic plan.

Step 4: *Outline your project.* To help get started, write down the following things:

a. In a short paragraph, describe your project and give it a title. Write this as if you were trying to explain it to someone who knows nothing about it. This short paragraph is very important. It might become part of a grant proposal, part of a letter of request for help with your project, or the basic statement you use to tell everyone and anyone who needs to know what you are planning to do (maybe a tribal council? School officials? Funding agencies?). It should be concise and clear and begin with a sentence that states what the project is about, such as 'The purpose of this project is _____'.

b. List the needs your project addresses. The needs that your project responds to can be one or many. Your project should, however, clearly respond to needs stated in the larger strategic language plan (if there is one) or at least needs that the community has already identified. There is always one very broad need: 'We need to revitalize our language'. But individual projects respond to more specific needs. For example, a more specific need might be stated as, 'We need to develop better teaching materials for the existing language revitalization classes'. Whatever the case, make it very clear which needs your project is addressing and as you write them down, explain why it is important to address these needs at this particular time.

c. Consider the target audience for your project. Having a clear idea of who the project is intended to serve will help shape the project and the activities needed to complete it. For example, if you are hoping to provide language classes to adults, your project resources, locations, and leaders will be different than if you are planning language classes for school children.

d. List at least three clear outcomes your project will achieve. Any journey is made easier if there is some clear idea of where it is leading you. Stating outcomes accomplishes several things:

- It helps you plan for success.
- It helps keep the project manageable (there should not be too many outcomes).
- It informs people about the value of this project in terms of community goals for revitalization.
- It sets up the structure needed to evaluate the project.

Well-established outcomes set the stage for more work – they create building blocks toward the larger, long-term goals.

e. List the steps needed to achieve these outcomes. When you are beginning to plan a project, it is helpful just to make lists of what you need or plan to do. These can be expanded, revised, and changed in a number of ways, but they give you an initial overall picture that is really important to have. That may seem like an obvious thing to say but really, at this point, what you are creating is an outlined plan of the project you have in mind. You need a complete plan, in outline form, to start with. It helps set a picture in the minds of you and your team of the project from beginning to end in its entirety.

Sometimes it is useful to create a project template, which can guide the outline/planning for any project and which includes at least the following items (as discussed above);

Title of your project:
Description of the project: (That short paragraph mentioned above).
Purpose: (Why are you doing it?)
Objectives: (What you hope to accomplish. These also appear as expected outcomes.)
Activities: (How many? When? By whom?)

Target Audience: (Who is the project intended for?)
Dates: (When will it take place – beginning and end)
Location: (Where? What community or facility?)
Format: (Is it a class? A meeting? A workshop? A field trip?)
Budget: (Plan for all of the costs)
Partners: (Other organizations or groups to work with or who could be a resource)
Funding: (Decide if you need a grant or can get donations in time or money)
Marketing/Publicity: (How will you advertise this project? How will you recruit participants?)
Evaluation/Assessment: (Both summative and formative)

f. Consider what resources will you need. It is one thing to have a good idea, and another thing to make your project happen smoothly. Any community-based project is dependent on the locally available resources. Is there someone or some group you might want to partner with? Resources can include people, equipment, food, teaching materials, travel vehicles, local institutions (schools, libraries, museums), and more. Anything that will help you develop and carry out your project is a 'resource'. There may be additional resources available outside the community – maybe there is a nearby university, or museum, or help from other similar communities. Maybe, there are financial resources available in your state, province, district, county, or other government agencies at the federal or national level. Whatever funding you need to carry out your project will have to be secured. There may be funds available through your community-level government.

In the planning process, it is at this point that you need to consider how you will fund your project and how much it will all cost. You might consider a grant (unlike a loan, grants don't have to be paid back). There are a number of online resources that can help you find grants that support specific types of work (see also Chapter 5). There are other options too – often local government and nonprofit organizations will help support community-based projects. Crowdfunding is also an option in some contexts. Remember that first paragraph you wrote describing your project? You can put it to use as a way to introduce what you want to do to people who might want to financially support it! It is also possible that people will be willing to donate – this is especially true when it comes to food. Most community events are more successful if there are, at the very least, refreshments involved. As you plan, the need for food, the amount, source, and type must also be taken into account. Plan carefully for anything that might incur costs: food, salaries, honoraria, meeting space, travel, materials, equipment, etc.

g. Create a potential timeline with a clear beginning and end dates – be realistic because an individual project is usually part of a bigger strategic plan. Creating a realistic timeline is critical. There may be several projects launched at the same time which need to be articulated together. Even if that's not the case, planning a project around a timeline is very useful. It allows for a clear beginning and a clear ending. This helps all those involved understand what is expected of them over the course of the project. The timeline should allow for a planning stage, an implementation phase, and an evaluation phase. Again, these three things – P-I-E – compose the foundation of any project.

Step 5: *Implement your project*: On the surface, implementing you project should be as simple as following the plan. However, we all know that things don't always go as planned. As you begin to implement your project, remember to be flexible, ready to make changes as you go, and keep track of the challenges you face. The first time through any endeavor may be a bit rough – there is always a lot to learn. Be sure you have some alternative choices such as other possible locations to hold activities, a longer list of resource people than you actually need, be ready to change activities, if needed, but not to the extent that you lose sight of your original goals. You have carefully outlined and developed Plan 'A' – make sure to also have a Plan 'B' – a set of possible alternative activities if others fail. If carefully outlined, the implementation of a project should go smoothly.

Step 6: *Plan how you will evaluate or assess your project.* Ask what assessment strategies will you use? There are both formal and informal approaches to assessment. Both can be *formative* (used to provide feedback as the project moves forward and they help shape the project – this is information that contributes to the *formation* of the project) or *summative* (done near the end of a project to provide feedback on the entire results of the project). Generally, a formal assessment means that you choose to involve someone unrelated to the project, an objective observer, to do an 'external' evaluation. This might be someone who does similar projects in other communities, or a professional who is familiar with language projects. Formal evaluations are sometimes costly and therefore may occur just once near the end of a project. It's good to do a formal evaluation if you need to prove the worth of your project for large grants or other major sources of funding. For the purposes of the community, informal evaluations are always important. These are done by the project organizers or even by the project participants and take the form of a casual questionnaire or verbal feedback. Informal evaluations can occur at any stage during a project and should occur whether or not a formal evaluation is planned.

Finally, the project director or coordinator and the project team need to do their own evaluation. Take time to look back on various aspects of the project. Consider what worked well, what didn't and why. Write it all down so that if you decide to repeat the project it will probably go smoother than it did the first time. It is crucial to take the time to review the strengths and weaknesses of the project, as a project team, and to discuss what the next steps should be. Remember that revitalizing a language is just a step toward sustaining it for a very long time. Consider how your project has contributed to this effort and how will it lead to other projects aimed at this same long-range goal.

Language revitalization or reclamation takes a lot of commitment, vision, and just plain hard work. It really never ends so it is important to keep generating fresh ideas and implementing new projects. Projects should connect with each other or build on each other as they are all, ultimately, supporting the same long-range goal of keeping the language alive.

FURTHER READING

Brandt, E. A. and Ayoungman, V. (1989). A practical guide to language renewal. *Canadian Journal of Native Education* 16(2), 442–77.

First People's Cultural Council. (2013). Guide to language policy and planning. This resource specifically targets British Columbia, Canada; however, it offers a wealth of ideas for communities who are engaged in planning projects aimed at revitalization. It is available at www.fpcc.ca/files/PDF/Language_Policy_Guide/FPCC_Policy_Guide_2013.pdf.

Hinton, L. and Hale, K., eds. (2001). *The Green Book of Language Revitalization in Practice*. Leiden, the Netherlands: Brill.

Hornberger, N. (1997). *Indigenous Literacies in the Americas: Language Planning from the Bottom Up*. Berlin: Mouton de Gruyter.

4.1 Doing Things with Little Money

Werner Hernández González

Linguistic activism without funds is possible. It may happen that when you want to start revitalization efforts, you will be confronted with the specter of lack of economic resources; however, you just need to recognize that solutions are closer than you think. Below are a series of tips that have as a common point the maximum use of emotional resources and the minimum use of money. The purpose of these tips is to open possibilities to anyone interested in the revitalization of languages:

1. **Look for people who think like you.** People with the same interests with whom you can practice and study the language. You coincide in direction, actions, and results, regardless of the type of skills they have. It is also important that they all solve problems in the same way you do or perhaps can provide better solutions. Organize. Focus on talking about strengths and about what can be done together and begin to believe in that goal.
2. **Emotional resources of the group.** Share commitment, enthusiasm, identification, affection, respect, admiration, care, time, perseverance (credibility comes very close to it). Use all your ingenuity too. Build closeness and confidence. Always remember that working with minority languages involves the feelings of their speakers.
3. **Instruct yourself in the best possible way on the subject.** There is enough information on the Internet for you to develop a good understanding of the history and the specific context of your language. The damage a language could suffer occurs through multiple actions so the solutions must go in many directions too. Partial understanding only gives us partial answers. And there is also considerable information available on how speakers of other languages have gone about language revitalization.
4. **Get a compass.** Consult criteria such as those in UNESCO document 'Language vitality and Endangerment,' Paris 2003 (free material on the web) or other assessment tools. Make a table and diagnose your language's vitality: This will help you to have an overall vision. It is important to know where you are starting from to know where to go. Knowing the general score will give you an idea of the state of your language and the effort you will need to apply. Then choose which efforts must be undertaken first (see Susan Penfield's advice in the main part of this chapter). Aim for real and achievable results, both short- and long-term. Update your diagnosis/plan and compare the steps from time to time. Assess your achievements and reassess future plans.
5. **Visit the community often** – if you cannot live in it, keep in touch. Think with the people in the community to give the answers that the group needs. Avoid preaching to them.
6. **Generate speaker networks.** Open spaces to practice the language and make it visible: conversation clubs, hours in a local cafe, chats, and public forums in social networks. It is important that both activists and speakers share a sense of community. Being close to the speakers and being aware of activities, dates, or situations that are most attractive to them is highly recommended.
7. **Work on self-esteem and self-concept.** Keep sharing news of the appreciation that other people have for their language and toward the revitalization efforts.
8. **Always think of the youngest.** Propose many games that involve language for children; build an endearing link between games and language. Help teenagers to ensure effective intercultural contact, without trauma and without self-denial.

9. **Government attitudes and policies.** Echo the community work. The efforts must awake positive enthusiasm in the language community so that it attracts the favorable attention of decision-makers. Look for spaces to communicate with politicians.
10. **Make links** with language activists in other communities to get ideas and emotional support (see Chapter 12).
11. **Look back at the previous points** and check how many require money and how many require a positive attitude/commitment.

5   Getting Funding and Support

Nicholas Q. Emlen

In the course of developing an endangered language revitalization project, one must eventually face the most basic of logistical problems: how to pay for it? The costs associated with language revitalization projects vary greatly depending on their size, duration, goals, and products. Some involve the creation and publication of dictionaries, educational materials, or websites, while others require expensive technical equipment. Salaries for community language experts, travel budgets, and space rentals (or even the construction of a language center) can also be important investments.

As the field of language revitalization has become increasingly visible over the last couple of decades, new avenues of funding have emerged to meet these costs. However, the demand for funding has grown just as quickly as the supply, and the competition remains stiff. Long-term funding remains difficult to secure. Furthermore, while the process of applying for academic research grants regarding endangered languages is, by now, relatively formalized and streamlined, funding for community-based work often comes from a wide variety of places and can be difficult to identify.

This chapter offers some practical guidance for funding language revitalization projects. Consistent with the handbook's orientation, this chapter focuses on support for the work of language activists and community members. However, since language revitalization efforts are often closely related to language documentation, these two fields are considered together where appropriate. This chapter is divided into two parts: (1) identifying sources of funding and (2) how to write an effective proposal.

Identifying Sources of Funding

Many language revitalization programs are sustained by a mix of funding sources. This is because the available funds tend to be small, and because they are usually limited in duration. For language revitalization, which is a long-term process that takes place over generations, the short-term nature of most grants and fellowships presents a particular problem. Some funding sources are limited to citizens of particular countries or members of particular tribes or ethnic groups, others are open to students or members of academic institutions, and a few have no eligibility restrictions at all. In cases where language documentation and revitalization efforts are linked, it can be helpful to consider how to make academic research funding work in the service of language revitalization. For instance, some major research funders in Europe and the USA inquire about a project's 'broader impacts', defined by the National Science Foundation (US) as 'the potential to benefit society and contribute to the achievement of specific, desired societal outcomes'.[1] Language revitalization certainly qualifies as one such broader impact in many academic projects (though, despite these stated goals, some funders limit the amount of money that can actually be used to support revitalization efforts). Alliances with universities, nongovernmental organizations (NGOs), and businesses can also be fruitful, while in other cases, informal fundraising through games and contests (e.g. raffles and bingo) and online crowd funding has proven effective. A good place to start in the search for potential funding sources is to research or contact other successful language revitalization programs, and to learn about how they acquired their funding.

To begin with, a handful of funding organizations specifically devoted to endangered languages have been established in recent decades. While some of these organizations only support language documentation, the Endangered Language Fund (ELF) and the Foundation for Endangered Languages (FEL) also accept proposals for language revitalization projects. The first organization is particularly committed to funding collaborations between communities and university researchers. However, these organizations make small grants (~$2,000–$4,000 for ELF, ~$1,000 for FEL), and even these can be quite competitive. ELF also offers larger scholarships for members of some US tribes seeking academic training in linguistics, which is another important mode of community–university partnership.

Some government bodies offer larger grants for language revitalization, though these are more common in the USA and Canada than in other countries. For instance, the Administration for Native Americans, part of the US federal government, supports 'the planning, designing, restoration, and implementing of native language curriculum and education projects to support a community's language preservation goals'.[2] Similarly Canada's Aboriginal People's Program offers one funding program for 'the preservation and revitalization of Indigenous languages through community-based projects and activities', and another for 'the

---

[1] www.nsf.gov/pubs/2016/nsf16617/nsf16617.htm
[2] https://ami.grantsolutions.gov/index.cfm?switch=foa&fon=HHS-2018-ACF-ANA-NL-1342

production and distribution of Indigenous audio and video content'.[3] One benefit of these funding sources is that they offer larger quantities of money than the small NGOs mentioned above. More specific opportunities are offered by other institutions, such as the Smithsonian's Recovering Voices Community Research Program, which funds visits by community members to 'examine cultural objects, biological specimens, and archival documents related to their heritage language and knowledge systems, and engage in a dialogue with each other and with Smithsonian staff, as part of a process to revitalize their language and knowledge'.

Moving beyond funding sources that are explicitly designated for language revitalization, communities and activists need to be creative. Local, national, and international NGOs that might be receptive to the issue, but had not considered it before, are a good possibility. Communities can create their own NGOs, which can be an important step in applying for funding. Tribal funds often support language revitalization programs in the USA. Collaborations with educational institutions can be helpful as well. For instance, an innovative partnership between the Miami Tribe of Oklahoma and Miami University operates a successful program to 'assist tribal educational initiatives aimed at the preservation of language and culture' while 'expos[ing] undergraduate and graduate students at Miami University to tribal efforts in language and cultural revitalization'.[4] In some cases, speakers and language activists have gotten grants and fellowships to study and support their languages within academic institutions. Other communities might benefit from local trust funds, or companies with funds for local initiatives.

Some language revitalization projects do not require large budgets for their operations. In these cases, communities might be able to cover their costs through crowd funding. For instance, a group of students at SOAS raised more than £2,000 for a storybook in the Sylheti language (spoken in Bangladesh and India, as well as in European cities), an illustrated version of a children's story told by Sylheti speakers in London. In another case, at the time of writing, members of the Okanagan Salish language revitalization program had raised a few thousand dollars for the construction of a small, new modular building on the website www.gofundme.com. Some efforts, such as community conversation clubs or master-apprentice programs, may require no more than a bit of funding for administrative time to match lists of potential participants. Fundraising efforts need not be digital – some revitalization programs are supported by the kinds of games

---

[3] www.canada.ca/en/canadian-heritage/services/funding/aboriginal-peoples.html
[4] https://miamioh.edu/myaamia-center

and contests mentioned above. These modes of fundraising have the additional benefits of raising awareness of the language revitalization program and involving the wider community. Some communities have also generated revenue by offering language courses and extended visits to non-community members.

Writing a Good Proposal

The procedures for acquiring language revitalization funding are as diverse as the sources themselves. Some of the funding sources described above require detailed proposals, while others just involve informal coordination among a few community members. This section considers the requirements of funding institutions that review formal proposals. These tend to be organized around a few common elements. First, reviewers must determine whether the project is likely to have a significant impact, whether it is more important and urgent than the many other proposals they're considering, and whether it is well designed and ethical. Second, they need to know about the applicant(s) and their relationship to the community, and whether they have the experience, personal and institutional contacts, permissions, approvals, and other bureaucratic prerequisites that are necessary to complete the project as it is described. Third, they will examine the budget and determine whether it is appropriate, and if so, whether it is a 'good deal' in light of the anticipated outcomes of the project. Finally, they will consider whether your project furthers the specific goals of the funding institution, which vary greatly from one to the next.

Given the demanding and highly competitive nature of this process, applying for funding can feel like entering a hopeless bureaucratic labyrinth. However, one point of consolation is that there is not, in fact, much difference between preparing an effective project and preparing an effective funding application. If your project is worthwhile, carefully planned, and consistent with the goals of the funding institution, and if it enjoys the support of the community, all that remains is to convey these facts through clear writing. Conversely, a funding application can be a helpful tool for thinking through the practical aspects of your project. Just as importantly, some funders provide reviewers' feedback to the applicants, whether or not the application is approved. Receiving the thorough and candid assessment of a panel of experts is a rare and precious opportunity (even if it can sting a bit). If you receive feedback, you should use it to help improve your project.

Funding applications vary greatly in their details, particularly in a field like language revitalization that draws in money from a range of sources. However, applications tend to ask for a few general types of information, along the lines of what is mentioned above. I now take a closer look at three of these: the value and design of the project, the applicant's connection to the work, and the adequacy of the budget.

Is This a Good Project?

If a funding institution accepts formal proposals and consults reviewers, the first question that a reviewer will need to consider is whether the project itself is worth funding: is it important, feasible, ethical, and likely to generate valuable outcomes and impacts?

To begin with, how important or urgent are the outcomes that the proposal promises? For example, a language revitalization project might have an impact on a critical situation of language endangerment, or its value might lie more in developing new methods or technologies, or in moving the broader field forward in some other way (such as an attitude study). Institutions that fund language documentation efforts sometimes try to prioritize work on the most critically endangered languages, particularly in cases where little high-quality documentation already exists. Your proposal should have some substantive and clearly defined practical outcome, and you should explain it in as few words as possible at the beginning of the project description. Identifying the planned outcomes requires a good sense of the situation on the ground, and it is also helpful to demonstrate knowledge of how language revitalization projects have worked in other places and how these might be relevant to your project. In the case of a project with an academic dimension, it is important to demonstrate a strong command of the relevant scholarly literature.

Once you have identified a clear and substantive goal, reviewers will want to see that you have thought through what is required to achieve it: your methodology. What kind of work will need to be done, and who will do it? For a language revitalization project, what kind of activities will you engage in (e.g. training workshops, the development of educational materials or a website), and what kinds of technical considerations will they require? If the project involves documentation, what kinds of data will you collect, and how do these data relate to your aims? Will you make audio or video recordings? Of what, and how many? How will you select the participants? How will you obtain their informed consent? How will you process the material, and with what kinds of software? What other practical considerations might be relevant? Do the planned activities fulfill your desired outcomes? Is your timeline feasible? In all cases, the methodologies that you propose must be tightly connected to the goals.

One of the most common problems with funding applications is that they often promise too much. Reviewers want to know that you are motivated

Getting Funding and Support 77

and ambitious, but that you are realistic about the logistical constraints of the work. For instance, don't assume that you will be able to implement a large and well-functioning revitalization program right away (see Chapter 4 on planning a revitalization project). Nor, in a documentation project, are you likely to arrive somewhere you've never been before, encounter a language for the first time, and return home after a few months with a large corpus (body) of data and a sophisticated grasp of the language. The best way to develop a feasible agenda is to approach it step by step, with an exploratory or pilot first phase, and elaborating or expanding the work over longer periods. This will reassure reviewers that you know what you are getting yourself into.

Projects that involve scholarly research with living humans, and that are conducted under the auspices of an educational institution, usually require the approval of an ethical review board before you can begin the work (see Chapter 3 on ethical considerations). Projects through NGOs or communities generally do not require such approval, but it is still important to think through how you will conduct your project ethically. If your project is subject to an ethical review board, you will need to explain how you will go about getting informed consent from anyone you record or video, protecting their anonymity, and storing the data. These must be developed in close coordination with community members, and must be responsive to local expectations about privacy and research ethics. These procedures can take some time, so be sure to get started early.

Finally, reviewers will want to know what the products and outcomes of the project will be. Will you publish educational materials, or will a training program for community language workers be established? Will you organize a radio program, or add to the community's digital presence in the language? If you conduct academic research, some funding institutions require that you deposit the products of your research with them, including recordings and field notes. It is also good practice to make those products available to the community, for instance at a local library, school, or community center. Some funders may ask you to adhere to Open Access archiving standards, by which data must be publicly available on the Internet (a requirement that must be made clear to the participants before the project begins). Demonstrate that you are aware of such policies, and that you are prepared to abide by them in a way that is consistent with your plan for ethical research.

What Is the Applicant's Relationship to the Project and the Community?

Once a reviewer has considered the value of the proposed project, they must next consider the applicant. Applicants who are community members themselves have a clear connection to the work, as well as a personal investment, base of knowledge, and network of contacts that will help the project succeed. Meanwhile scholars who are not part of the community will have to demonstrate that they have the support and approval of the community, the relevant academic training, official government permissions, and ethical approval, and that all manner of other practical aspects of the work are in place.

Many applicants for language revitalization and documentation grants are affiliated with local NGOs, tribal governments, or language support groups; some are simply individual community members. Others are affiliated with universities, particularly as MA or PhD students. In all of these cases, it is important to demonstrate one's preparation for the project at hand, whatever that might be. If the application requires letters of recommendation, these will attest to this sort of preparation. It may also be helpful to demonstrate your personal experience with the cultural, scholarly, and methodological issues at stake. Have you worked with the revitalization program already, and in what capacity? What kinds of work have already been carried out in the community, and how does this project build on them?

For noncommunity members, a crucial part of preparing for some fieldwork projects is attaining the kinds of local permissions necessary for the research. For instance, nontribal members who work on a Native North American language usually need an official invitation from a tribal government, and failing to follow the proper procedures on such matters can derail the project. In some places in the world, e.g. Vanuatu, you might also need a visa or other sort of permission from an embassy or a local government. Some grants also require affiliation with a local university or other institutions. To avoid complications down the road, some funding agencies require that you submit copies of some types of permissions with your application.

Does the Budget Look Right?

Every proposal requires a budget, in which you give a detailed itemization and justification of your expenses. Some funding institutions give small grants to cover a plane ticket or the printing of education materials; others give huge grants that pay the costs of graduate school or the salaries of several people for years. The parts of the budget relating to the work itself are a concrete expression of your methodology, so you should make sure that the expenditures you list (equipment, personnel, etc.) are closely connected to the activities you describe in the proposal. Most funders provide information about what they expect to see in their budget categories. It can also be helpful to use a colleague's successful grant application as a guide as you draw up your budget.

Funding institutions categorize expenses in different ways, but there tend to be some general similarities. In the box below are some of the most common categories, with brief explanations of each.

Common Budget Categories

TRAVEL AND SUBSISTENCE: How will the project participants get around? For people who live locally, this might include bus fare, gas, or buying a bicycle. For people who do not live locally, it might involve plane or bus fare, as well as expenses for meals and lodging. For some grants, this category also includes day-to-day living expenses throughout the period of the grant.

PERSONNEL: Who will be paid a wage, stipend, or salary during the project? This category will likely include compensation for community language experts, research assistants, and, if there is an academic researcher involved, perhaps stipends or money for teaching replacement. Technology consultants like app developers might be compensated as well. You will need to find out an appropriate rate for each such recipient and calculate how much time they will be paid for.

EQUIPMENT: Revitalization and documentation projects often require new equipment, including recording devices, microphones, computers, software, hard drives, solar panels, and the like. Refer to the funder's guidelines about what kinds of expenses are allowed and consult with colleagues about what kinds of equipment they recommend.

CONSUMABLES: These are disposable supplies and day-to-day expenses such as batteries, fuel, data cards, Internet and phone usage, notebooks, etc.

Part of preparing a feasible project is requesting enough money to cover all of the relevant costs. For this reason, you shouldn't cut corners or compromise on important expenses. However, keep in mind that funding is tight, so unnecessary costs might take away from someone else's project, and will likely be noticed during the review process.

FURTHER READING

Endangered Language Fund General Resources, www.endangeredlanguagefund.org/general-resources.html.
First Peoples' Cultural Council (no date) *Grant Writing Toolkit*, www.fpcc.ca/language/toolkit/GrantWritingToolkit.aspx.
Foundation for Endangered Languages (FEL) (small grants), www.ogmios.org/home.htm.
Zepeda, O. and Penfield, S. (2008). *Grant Writing for Indigenous Languages*. Tucson, AZ: University of Arizona. http://jan.ucc.nau.edu/jar/GrantWriting.pdf.

5.1 Attitudes of NGOs in Guatemala toward the Inclusion of Indigenous Languages in the Workplace

Ebany Dohle

In 2012, I conducted a survey to investigate the role of NGOs and international organizations in the preservation of Indigenous, minority, and endangered languages. Individual representatives of the organizations that participated in the study were, at the time, key figures involved in the language revitalization movement in Guatemala, as they pushed for the inclusion of Indigenous languages in the workplace.

The Republic of Guatemala has a population of approximately 12,710,000, of whom 55 percent are Indian [Indigenous], and 45 percent *Mestizo*.[5] Linguists such as Charles Hoffling and Valentin Tavico agree that the total number of languages spoken in Guatemala is twenty-five, including Spanish. These languages belong to four language families: Indo-European, Mayan, Lenca, and Arawakan. Spanish is the national language and the one, which carries the most prestige, being the language of wider communication. It is closely followed by the four *mayoritarios*, or 'major ones': K'iche, Kaqchikel, Q'eqchi', and Mam. These four languages have the largest number of speakers and are the languages, which are regarded as having the most vitality in Guatemala, with over 100,000 speakers each.

Not unsurprisingly, the survey found that both NGOs and international organizations whose targeted communities did not include Indigenous people, were not interested in discussing language issues and did not respond to the open call for participation. Those who did respond were organizations with an interest in working and collaborating with Indigenous people. These organizations can be divided into two groups: local and international.

---

[5] The term *mestizo* refers to non-Indigenous communities, although in recent years the term has been adopted by Indigenous people who have rejected their language, culture, and heritage, choosing to become part of the mainstream Latin culture who speak Spanish instead. It is worth noting that although the term 'Indian' does not have negative connotations in English, the Spanish translation *indio* is often used in a derogatory manner. Indigenous communities therefore prefer the Spanish term *indígena*, one which I will be using throughout this work. Similarly the term *mestizo* is not commonly used. Instead it is often replaced by the term *ladino(s)*, which generally refers to mixed race or 'Westernized' communities.

The survey found that although international organizations whose headquarters were based in a different country were sympathetic to the promotion of Indigenous languages and were willing to promote their use via national policy change or education, they were not enthused by the idea of incorporating their use in the day-to-day workplace. Some of the reasons given for this were that too many languages would lead to confusion, a lack of transparency, and difficulties in communicating with headquarters back in their home countries. In contrast, it was found that despite the more limited reach and influence on a national level of local NGOs with headquarters within the country, these were more open and willing to consider and encourage the use of Indigenous languages in the workplace. This was especially the case with those organizations that sought to establish and strengthen strong and stable relationships with an established community. The NGO Wuqu' Kawoq, for example, saw a need to provide better quality healthcare in the town of Santiago Sacatepequez in Guatemala, where the predominant language is Kaqchikel Maya. To improve access to rural healthcare amongst Maya communities, the healthcare NGO was founded with the provision of services in local languages at its core.

I have since observed a similar tendency in neighboring El Salvador. Local organizations and institutions with a vested interest in local people were more likely and willing to interact with, participate in, and support language revitalization movements. Despite limited funds, local institutions like universities, museums, language schools, and even banks were willing to provide some sort of support. Universities and their students can be key allies in the creation of a public voice. A museum might provide an exhibition hall and printing services in which to hold a public event to raise awareness. Banks and other companies with a local interest often have a corporate policy to have a 'social impact' and have specific funds allocated for projects that may help achieve this. While it is unlikely that a bank may support an entire language revitalization initiative, such a funding opportunity might be useful for the printing of a book or the creation of a podcast series that can result in better outreach and new funding possibilities. In an environment where support is likely to be limited, thinking creatively and developing a varied network of interested individuals and institutions is key to making progress with the revitalization initiative. Finally, understanding what motivates individuals, organizations, or institutions to engage with local languages and cultures is beneficial to understanding how to approach and engage with a wider network.

Part II

Practical Issues

6 Types of Communities and Speakers in Language Revitalization

José Antonio Flores Farfán and Justyna Olko

In this chapter, we look at diverse communities who struggle to preserve their heritage languages or who might be interested in launching revitalization programs. We reflect on what it can mean to be a minority or endangered language community and how we can characterize different types of communities. We also look at the implications and challenges for language revitalization that should be considered when taking into account distinct types of communities. The concept of 'community' requires some clarification. As a starting point for this discussion, the community, for the purposes of language revitalization, can be considered any original or newly formed group or network of individuals. These individuals may live in a specific place or may be geographically dispersed, but they are linked by various kinds of interactions and relationships (including those based on both face-to-face and virtual social networks), and share some aspects of their identities and goals. Each community is inherently heterogeneous, variable, highly dynamic, subject to change, and sensitive to all kinds of different factors and circumstances. Communities are usually comprised of distinct groups of speakers, and are maintained or reproduced by different interaction networks.

We have to point out that the 'concept' of revitalization is also blurry and by no means well defined in the literature. Let us just stress that revitalization, as well as several other similar metaphors derived from the biological sciences, have been loosely applied to a wide range of situations, which often differ significantly. They vary from scenarios where only a few speakers prevail with a very limited use of the language (e.g. the Peninsula of Baja California, Mexico, where, for example, Kiliwa has some five speakers left), to communities with about a million speakers and a still pretty robust use of their language and future viability (e.g. Yucatec Maya in the Yucatec Peninsula, Mexico). Some languages are spoken in large communities, some in very small or dispersed ones. Some are still used in relatively isolated areas, while some are used in urban zones where they are exposed to intense contact with other languages. Some languages are valued and recognized, others are associated with trauma, shame, or poverty. In dealing with different communities we must be sensitive, flexible, and open to discussion and deep reevaluation of related attitudes in order to start any revitalization project. A strict definition of revitalization is less important than finding effective ways to recover the use of an endangered language in a specific community.

'Revitalizing' a whole community is a fiction or a utopia. Linguistic and cultural revitalization is usually developed by specific groups or individuals from a community, who take the lead in 'reviving' the language. Such activists are motivated by a range of diverse language ideologies, which may, at times, be contradictory and conflicting. For example, plans for revitalization may be met with opposition, indifference, skepticism, or, on the contrary, overenthusiasm, depending on distinct stakeholders.

In order to provide a general typology of such highly heterogeneous language revitalization communities, we will first attempt to provide an overview of their complexity. The field of language revitalization is directly linked to the process of language endangerment and language communities, each with distinct types of 'speakers'. Endangerment refers to a continuum of language use in a specific tongue; the threat of extinction is always a matter of degree. Endangerment is, in fact, faced by most of the languages of the world, which is extremely telling of modern social and political conditions of multilingualism and globalization. Current estimations of the number of tongues spoken vary between roughly six and eight thousand, the majority of which survive in different states of at least some sort of precariousness. They range from 'dormant' languages with very few, if any, speakers, to those with some levels of vitality, most of which comprise communities with a couple of thousand or hundred speakers or even fewer. 'Stable' languages are usually national languages, protected by law, institutions, and other forms of infrastructure as provided by a specific state or political organization. It is estimated that they constitute only some 30 percent of the world's linguistic diversity. Estimates regarding the number of languages still spoken in the world are based on a number of criteria, many of them being imprecise, ideological, and/or political; deciding on where a language or a 'dialect' begins often stems from political and ideological notions. For instance, within the Maya family, Yucatec Maya, Mopan, and Itzá are considered separate languages, mainly because the speakers of the first group dwell in Mexico, whereas the other two reside in Guatemala. In Scandinavia, Norwegian, Swedish, and Danish are recognized as distinct languages, spoken in three different countries, yet linguistically they form a 'dialect continuum' of regional variants that are mutually intelligible to differing degrees. Another interesting and less known example is the Wymysiöeryś language in Poland, which faces obstacles to achieving official recognition, since the basic criterion in the law is that a regional language cannot be a 'dialect' of any other national language. The argument employed against the recognition of Wymysiöeryś is its alleged status as a 'dialect' of German, despite a unique historical trajectory, linguistic features, and a low degree (or even lack) of intelligibility with German.

The causes of endangerment encompass a broad range of factors, including the historical consequences of colonialism, genocide, the slave trade, and exploitation, accompanied by discrimination, racism, political domination, economic disadvantages, etc. Postcolonial heritage and the effects of globalization have resulted in a global crisis for languages, the worst that the world has ever experienced. Its effects can be compared to 'the great dying' of species in the remote past as well as to modern processes of accelerated reduction in global biodiversity. Nonetheless these global trends also provoke grassroot responses from local communities. Such responses provide an especially important starting point for any revitalization project.

However, revitalization efforts should consider the specific conditions and situation of the group or 'community' in question. These conditions include not only the degree of language endangerment, but also the motivations, ideologies, goals, aims, desired benefits, and internal politics of its members. Thus awareness of the diversity of communities and linguistic situations needs to be considered while planning and undertaking any (re)vitalization strategy. We must emphasize that there is considerable overlap between distinct types of communities and their speakers: any typology should be considered a continuum or even a kaleidoscope of continua. In the following sections, we describe certain general features and characteristics that many communities share. However we should not forget that the complexity and combination of factors that affect each group, in fact, make each community unique.

'Original' or Ancestral Communities with Different Forms of Language Transmission

Groups that continue to live in traditional lands and territories and were established in a more or less remote past can be considered 'ancestral communities'. In the present time of linguistic unification, most communities that use their own heritage tongue or language variant that is different from a national or dominant language face the threat of language loss. They may have different degrees of language transmission as well as different forms of language socialization. Many of them suffer displacement and linguistic conflicts, that is, an ideological, functional, and political struggle between the use of the local tongue and the imposed, dominant language. In some of these communities the ancestral language is still spoken, but younger generations have lost interest and proficiency; the natural transmission of the language is weakened or broken. Skills in the heritage tongue vary considerably; there are groups of speakers who have become monolingual in a hegemonic national language after passing through a stage of substitutive or replacive bilingualism. This may, for example, be the result of school trauma, especially in residential schools where students were forced to leave their communities and home territories, and abandon the tongue that they learnt at home, as in Australia, Canada, or the USA. Imagine literally having your mouth washed out with soap or standing in the burning sun as a punishment for speaking your language. Unbelievably these practices still occur in some countries. Latin and North America are particularly good examples of the impact that school policies have on language. Across these continents boarding schools and, more recently, 'bilingual schools', have become efficient tools for eradicating Indigenous languages. Similar practices have occurred in other parts of the world, especially in postcolonial contexts or countries that adopted strong nationalistic policies aimed at cultural and linguistic unification of their citizens (Russia, postwar Poland, China, Japan, etc.). In addition, pressures on shifting communities are often linked to economic motivations, including the linguistic requirements of the job market and individuals' desire for social advancement. Typically parents will also be pressured not to pass the heritage language to new generations.

Yet there are interesting cases of resistance to language displacement, including the vital use of an endangered language in settings such as religious rituals, the market place, and other public domains. These kinds of situations are fertile ground for the particular types of (re)vitalization projects that we describe here as 'communities of learning or practice' (see later). Moreover there are also emblematic cases of language recovery and resilience, as in Euskara ('Basque') and Catalan, which were forbidden in Spain in the era of the Franco dictatorship (from the late 1930s until the mid-1970s). Both are now coofficial languages in their respective autonomous regions, yet they still face serious threats and challenges.

Māori, spoken in New Zealand, is another interesting case, with its famous 'language nests' – a methodology consisting of speaking the ancestral language almost from the womb. Even though Māori's vitality is now a fact, with official recognition, support, and institutional use, this does not mean that it is no longer endangered. This is telling of the difficulties in stabilizing a threatened language; despite its relatively successful revitalization, the Māori language is not free from constant challenges and conflicts, even from within the community. For instance, the vitality of Northern Māori varieties is much higher than that of the Southern ones, known as *Kāi Tahu,* which are in an advanced state of shift. The Māori community has been trying to recover *Kāi Tahu* for over two decades, dreaming to replenish the South with Māori and reversing language shift.

Yet one of the main problems is the conflict between the so-called obsolescent Southern Māori varieties and the vital Northern ones.[1] This can be seen in the fact that some Northern speakers even mock Southern varieties. This intolerance can happen within language communities, but also in mainstream society. In our work with Indigenous communities we have come across lay people, and even anthropologists, who value certain varieties more than others. These are often varieties that exhibit influence from the dominant language and are viewed as 'impoverished' or 'inauthentic', etc.

Thus, in 'ancestral communities' we often find complex situations when it comes to language maintenance and shift, a continuum with clear internal differences within the same language. Many subvarieties can be associated, for instance, with different generations, as is the case of several Indo-American languages. These range from 'monolingual' or traditional varieties, to highly innovative varieties that may borrow heavily from the dominant language. Such differentiation within the larger language group, as it occurs in specific communities, depends on various factors, including the status of the heritage language, the territory where it is spoken, contact with other languages, the role of migration and the nation states' language policies, etc. Other key factors include the specific ideologies, motivations, attitudes, and goals of speakers. It is important to emphasize that in the same region there may be distinct types of situations of language retention and shift, ranging from conservative groups of speakers of monolingual varieties (e.g. the elders), passing through high levels of bilingualism (e.g. younger generations), to groups within the same community who now use the hegemonic or national language as their first tongue (e.g. children). In the same geographic area, we can also find ancestral communities that have already lost their heritage language entirely or in part.

Often strong traces of the 'lost' language are left in the so-called interlanguage. In this scenario, speakers have not completely acquired the colonial or national tongue, but rather developed a version of the dominant language. Examples include Indo-American Spanish or First Nation peoples' English, which exhibit strong (lexical, phonetic, and structural) influences from the Indigenous languages that were previously or are still spoken in the area. Such scenarios are abundant in almost all parts of the world. In the case of ancestral communities whose traditional tongue has been reduced to an emblem, for symbolic use only, or who have lost the

---

[1] See H. O'Regan, 'A language to call my own', in A. M. Goodfellow (ed.), *Speaking of Endangered Languages* (Cambridge: Cambridge Scholars, 2009), pp. 184–98.

tongue entirely, revitalization efforts must be oriented toward awakening a 'sleeping' language, which had not been spoken for a while and is thus 'dormant'. In these cases, the few last speakers often belong to the eldest generation. One example of awakening a sleeping language is the revitalization of Manx on the Isle of Man, which was brought back to use only after the death of the last speaker, Ned Maddrell – a poet who lived in the isolated village of Cregneash on the island – in 1974. This case shows that the commitment of a group of activists can change the fate of a language, at least in the short- or mid-term.

Even today ancestral communities are typically under intense pressure from dominant languages as well as discriminatory or racist language ideologies (see also Chapter 7). The latter usually come from mainstream society and can also be adopted by speakers themselves. Such ideologies are usually linked to the presumed lack of economic value of the language, which leads speakers to question its utility and even its status as a self-standing language. These kinds of ideologies are evident in self-destroying stereotypes such as 'it is only a dialect, it cannot be written', etc. This is often the case for variants that are heavily influenced by the dominant language, which are therefore considered 'corrupt' and 'mixed', lacking 'purity', 'authenticity', and/or 'legitimacy'. Communities may also experience internal political struggles regarding language ownership, local language policy, and language choices; for example, what the future language of the community should be, and if there is any value in keeping or restoring the heritage tongue.

A frequent phenomenon in communities experiencing language shift is purism, an ideology focused on eliminating any features coming from the colonial language. Purism can become an extremely negative force in language maintenance, since purists, who are often people with a powerful status in the community (for example teachers), propose to eliminate any feature coming from the national language. This often hinders the use and development of the local tongue in the way that it is commonly spoken, increasing linguistic insecurity and favoring language shift. For example, both younger and older speakers can be reproached or stigmatized for their way of speaking, depending on the situation and the policy that local purists try to enforce. Yet purism can be turned into a positive force in revitalization programs, depending on specific local conditions. This seems to be the case with the Maya rappers in Yucatan, who have recovered the *hach*, or 'real Maya', due to its presumed wider repertoire and 'authenticity'. The best recommendation is to avoid favoring any variety or register of a language and to promote community members' acceptance of different contact varieties so that they can contribute to the richness and ecology of the language.

Exiled, Dispersed, or Resettled Communities

Some ancestral communities were forcibly exiled or dispersed for historical reasons; some have been completely exterminated due to invasion and aggressive colonization. This happened to the Taino during the Spanish invasion of Cuba in the sixteenth century, and in Tasmania, where the last person solely of Tasmanian descent died in 1905. In cases of almost total genocide, the few survivors that speak the ancestral tongue are the so-called last speakers of a language. Examples are found in many parts of the world, including the native groups of Australia, the USA, Salvador, Chile, Argentina, and Uruguay. Some of those groups are survivors of genocide, as in the case of Nawat/Pipil speakers in Salvador. After the genocide of 1932 they were relocated to other areas of the country, and the traumatizing experience resulted in language loss and forced change of identity. However, even in such dramatic historical circumstances, speakers of Pipil have been identified among the oldest generation, which permitted the launch of revitalization activities. In such cases, however, awakening a language must be closely linked to dealing with historical and personal trauma as well as social healing. For example, in the case of the Pipil it was common to deny speaking the heritage tongue to avoid being killed.

Yet bringing back the ancestral language is often a powerful source of healing and empowerment. One such example is the Diné/Navajo in the USA, for whom language cultivation in schools has become crucial to the recovery of the language. Another case is that of Lemko communities in Poland. Lemko speakers were exiled from their ancestral territories in the Carpathian Mountains almost overnight during the Operation Vistula of 1947. Some were sent to Ukraine, but most of them were resettled to the western region of Poland and the post-German territories, whereas others were confined to postwar concentration camps where the death toll was dramatically high. They were purposefully settled among Polish speakers to foster their linguistic and cultural assimilation. Only a few managed to return to the ancestral region: their houses and lands were occupied and they had to purchase land in their own home territory. They now are a minority in an increasingly Polish-speaking area, which, along with political pressures, has made language maintenance very difficult. Those who stayed in the new lands in the western part of the country experienced even more challenges due to dispersion and severing bonds with their homeland, which was a fundamental part of Lemko identity.

Similar situations have been experienced by many groups of Native American nations, allocated to reservations that were often away from ancestral land and divided among several locations assigned by the US government. Such resettled or dispersed communities are particularly exposed to language loss due to the severing of links between an ancestral tongue and ancestral land, which has a number of devastating consequences. Such groups and communities present continua of language maintenance, with different types of speakers who range from monolinguals in the heritage tongue, to bilinguals and monolingual speakers of the imposed language. In such communities there is also a common type of survivor who does not speak the heritage language; in these cases revitalization efforts would have to be based on reviving the language (the most famous case is Hebrew).

Diaspora and Migrant Communities

Forcibly resettled and dispersed communities are in many ways similar to diasporas of immigrant communities living in urban or other areas (e.g. Veneto in Chipilo, Mexico, or Mennonites in Latin America). These also include the Rom (also called Gypsies), who speak Romani and live in several parts of the world. They are often openly discriminated against by both mainstream society as well as the state, and not officially recognized (France, Colombia, Mexico, Poland, etc.). A common scenario in diasporic groups is language loss within one or two generations, due to the lack of opportunities to use the ancestral language outside of the home. However, at least some of these communities keep their languages as secret codes, which is also a form of 'spontaneous revitalization', meaning an unplanned form of revitalization, that does not have an 'external' agent instigating or accompanying it. In these cases, groups maintain their language as a form of 'in group' communication, as in Romani. These types of communities are remarkably diverse. Some keep strong ties with their homeland (e.g. Mexican Indigenous communities in the USA or Polish communities in the USA and the United Kingdom). Some retain their languages, as is often the case of the Chinese diaspora, and some keep the language partially or create new varieties. The latter includes the para-Romani varieties within the Rom diaspora in Europe, such as the so called Caló in Spain. Linguistic rights of such communities are not recognized by states and therefore they usually do not appear in any censuses.

Different patterns of mobility are associated with diverse types of exodus. These range from permanent migrants (e.g. several Mexican Indigenous groups in the USA or the Turkish population in Germany or the Netherlands) to temporary migrants. An ethnic group can also exhibit mixed patterns and strategies of migration that change over time and in response to political or economic circumstances. Examples include several groups in the USA or the Central American population who relocate to Mexico but then return to their homeland periodically or at least occasionally. In this case, due to the sociolinguistic environment and the languages to which they are exposed, the diaspora situation often leads to reduced repertoires in the heritage language. It also results in the creation of neo-speakers of neo-urban varieties, and 'receptive' speakers, who can understand but do not speak the language, e.g. children.

Another term that has been proposed with regard to persons who grew up listening to the heritage language but did not become active speakers is 'latent' speaker.[2] There are also 'rememberers' of dormant languages, and several types of bilinguals (e.g. incipient to almost coordinate bilinguals, that is, speakers who master the two languages almost perfectly and are able to separate them). They continuously face the colonial heritage as it manifests in many forms of discrimination, economic and social disadvantage, as well as covert, and often open, racism. Within the great diversity of migrants, we can also identify 'voluntarily assimilating' speakers who want to abandon their heritage languages as soon as possible to integrate into mainstream society. However we also find groups of speakers who, on the contrary, reaffirm and even empower themselves as immigrants in countries like the USA. This is the case of the Maya of Yucatan, who form a vigorous enclave in the San Francisco bay area, with around fifteen thousand speakers.

Communities of Practice and Learning

'Communities of practice'[3] and 'communities of learning' comprise a further category of community. They are a newly described type of group, which deliberately develops social revitalization networks. In the area of language maintenance and revitalization the focus of these groups is on collective efforts to enhance mutual learning and communication, and mobilize available resources. A central goal of such initiatives is to design and carry out specific activities that can positively influence existing practices and situations. Such communities include individuals from different fields who are united in their goal to stop and reverse language shift. Most notably, but not exclusively, these include language activists, linguists, and anthropologists. They may create partnerships with members of the ancestral community who are interested in language revival, or form multidisciplinary and multiethnic teams who are interested in achieving the same goal: language revitalization. Challenges they face involve finding novel ways to empower

---

[2] See C. Basham and A. Fathman, 'The latent speaker: Attaining adult fluency in an endangered language', *International Journal of Bilingual Education and Bilingualism* 11/5 (2008), 577–97.
[3] See https://web.stanford.edu/~eckert/csofp.html

speakers, creating revitalization methodologies through diverse types of collaborations between several stakeholders and generating external support for revitalization programs. Such groups can also include activists from one or more of the ancestral communities, who are united by the goal of keeping their language alive, despite adverse ideologies, attitudes, and educational policies.

An example of the creation of this type of community is the Language Revitalization, Maintenance and Development Project in Mexico, led by Flores Farfán. This project attempts to improve and develop participants' communicative performances and mastership of different language genres, going beyond language abilities per se, to generate highly proficient professionals, such as actors. By engaging in the production of videos or creative writing, the project aims at reactivating speakers' language competences so that they can become proficient speakers and professionals. For instance, after participating in the project, one of the female participants on this program went on to work in the Indigenous education sector in the Balsas region of Guerrero as a bilingual teacher, where she developed community workshops for relearning Nahuatl.

The project actively engaged activists and language leaders from around Mexico in practical training on a range of subjects, including: coaching revitalizers, creating language activists' self-documentation with revitalization in mind, script writing, planning and producing their own books, managing illustration programs, and producing local, culturally sensitive educational materials. This resulted in the creation of language games, animation videos, and books, which are disseminated to children during community workshops led by language leaders (for more details see Capsule 16.6). Also in Mexico, John Sullivan and Justyna Olko carried out a series of interdialectal encounters for the speakers of Nahuatl as well as participatory workshops for reading historical texts created by the ancestors of modern Nahuas and discussing them in the modern variants of this language (See Capsule 12.1). These initiatives have resulted in the creation of networks of engaged language activists (see Chapter 12). Another similar initiative has been the Engaged Humanities project aimed at extensive capacity building and connecting engaged scholars and language revitalization activities all over the world (see Capsule 12.2).

This discussion of course does not cover all possible scenarios. There might also be communities who are only interested in a very reduced use of their languages, often described as symbolic or postvernacular use. In such cases, the active presence of the heritage tongue can be limited to greeting formulas, selected culturally relevant terms, or songs. There are also such communities that do not want to use or revitalize their traditional language at all and it is only linguists who are interested in doing so.

Speakers of Heritage Languages

It is very important to emphasize that language communities are not abstract entities. They are composed of many different kinds of speakers of endangered/minority/heritage tongues and, very often, include individuals who no longer speak them. In much the same way as an awareness of diverse community types is important in processes of language shift and language revitalization, the role of distinct kinds of language users is also key. Even in communities where the language is still spoken by the majority, it is not uncommon to find families in which the grandparent and parent generations are fully proficient in the heritage language, whereas the children have different levels of proficiency.

For example, teenagers may speak the language with varying levels of proficiency, their younger siblings may understand the language but not speak it themselves, whereas the youngest siblings may neither speak nor understand the heritage language, having shifted to the dominant or national one. In contexts where language transmission has been broken in this way, scholars have identified 'semi-speakers', 'rusty speakers', 'receptive', or 'passive' speakers 'terminal speakers', 'latent speakers', or 'rememberers', 'pseudo-/quasi-speakers', etc. In revitalization efforts, however, 'labeling' individual speakers can be counterproductive and even discouraging or harmful for people struggling to speak or learn their heritage language. Speakers who struggle to develop their language skills do not want to be categorized by scholars implying their 'incomplete' knowledge and use of a heritage language. In addition, such 'labeling' does not reflect the potential they have for developing their language competence and use. Therefore, any such classifications should be treated with extreme caution; their utility is limited to an assessment of the challenges facing a given revitalization project and they should not stigmatize speakers.

The exact profile of speakers will vary from community to community, despite some common characteristics. Similar to the profile of communities, these categories should be viewed as having blurred and dynamic boundaries, existing within broad continua of language proficiency. Here we give an example of a general typology of speakers that is based on the different communities we have worked with in Mexico, especially Nahuas. However the typology can be applied, to a certain extent, to other communities, depending on their unique situation.

1. *Selected speakers with a very high Nahuatl proficiency* are often the 'top owners' of the language. They are specialized in specific types of discourses, such as bride or rain petitions or ritual activities conducted through chants by healers or enchanters. Members of conservative,

traditional communities pay high respect to this type of speakers and hire them on special occasions. Recovering such genres of speech in communities that have lost them might be one of the ways of revitalizing the language, giving it prestige and expanding its linguistic repertoires. In these cases specific revitalizing methodologies can be developed.

2. *Fully proficient speakers* – often scholars, students, writers, or activists – who are conscious users of the language and who reveal a huge capacity in the language in any domain; some of them hold purist attitudes toward the language and avoid loanwords and code mixing. They are usually bilingual with different degrees of influence from their mother tongue in their Spanish. Some use an almost 'standard' Spanish, whereas others clearly exhibit at least some influence from Nahuatl.

3. *Quasi/almost monolingual speakers* whose proficiency in Nahuatl is very high and who have limited contact with the Spanish-speaking mainstream society. These speakers are usually elders and often females, although they also include adults, young speakers, and even children who only start learning Spanish when they begin attending school. Empowering these speakers is an important strategy for revitalization. This can be achieved, for example, by legitimizing them at the school level and reestablishing intergenerational language bonds that might be weak.

4. *Fluent bilingual speakers from traditional communities* with unbroken transmission who either still use the language in their home community or who have migrated but continue speaking whenever they visit the community and sometimes even when they are abroad. The use of language and adaptation skills in different domains varies, but generally their proficiency is very high. There is even a trend to acquire a third language, such as English as in the case of Maya Yucatec speakers in the San Francisco area in the USA. This type of migrant shows that migration is not always a displacing feature, but can in fact be a revitalizing force due to the strong identity ties speakers develop while living far away from their homeland.

Depending on the region and community of origin, some of these speakers resort to heavy code mixing in certain situations. For example, this is sometimes seen in teenagers or young adults who learned the language when growing up and use it at home and among their peers but who received no school instruction in it. Sometimes it is impossible to differentiate this category of speakers from less fluent speakers. Furthermore, their proficiency may vary depending on the domain or the topic of conversation.

5. *Bilingual speakers* who are socialized in the heritage language in increasingly bilingual homes, sometimes learning it from their grandparents or other family members. Their use of the language is limited to basic domains and their vocabulary and use of grammatical structures is reduced; some of them purposefully omit loanwords and code mixing, especially in the presence of teachers or researchers. Spontaneous speaking on a wide variety of topics requires considerable efforts on their part. As with other categories, the distinction between this type of speakers and other kinds of asymmetrical bilingual speakers is fluid. Such individuals' proficiency exists on a continuum. Some of them learned the language at a later age, when they were teenagers or young adults. This may have been due to pressures from the community and their expected participation in domains such as commercial or ritual activities. Alternatively, they may have been motivated to learn the language for personal reasons. Speakers who are self-motivated to learn the ancestral tongue later in life often become committed teachers and can be important agents in revitalization efforts.
6. *Insecure or 'dormant' speakers* who learned the language as children but have not been using it regularly or for an extended period of time; some use it in very limited domains and on specific occasions. These language users are typically members of communities with broken language transmission and/or migrants with a recessive use of the heritage tongue. This broad category includes speakers who only use the language under pressure or for specific purposes (for example in commercial exchanges). We can also find second language learners who try to recover their mother tongue or, on the contrary, individuals who decided to stop using it. In general, their speech is characterized by heavy borrowing, code mixing, and code switching. They often exhibit difficulty and insecurity in expressing themselves. Such speakers are frequently ashamed of their reduced language skills, a possible prelude to language loss if revitalization actions are not taken.
7. *'Receptive' or 'latent' speakers* whose competence is restricted to understanding the language to differing degrees. In specific communicative situations they may function adequately with no difficulty in understanding. These situations may include farming or other work places, family reunions, (often religious) festivities, and the market place. Depending on the degree of contact with other more fluent speakers, this type of speaker has different degrees of comprehension of the endangered language. Activating such speakers can become an important part of revitalization efforts, helping them move from 'listeners' to 'speakers', who then may develop a high level of fluency in the language.

8. *New speakers* who are already fluent in the colonial/dominant/national language but attempt to recover their mother tongue and use it as a second or even third language. In the case of Nahuatl, this type of speaker has varying degrees of Spanish proficiency. In turn, this can have varying degrees of impact on their Nahuatl use, affecting all levels of the language (for example pronunciation, morpho-syntax). New speakers are very important, often essential, for language revitalization projects. As with other continua, this group of speakers also includes a diversity of individuals, encompassing people who are 'symbolic' speakers, that is, Spanish monolinguals with no real intention of recovering the language, who use only a few formulaic words and phrases for political reasons (for example being identified as an in-group member). Such symbolic speakers are in contrast to new speakers who are really committed to recovering their mother tongue.

Conclusions

As we have shown, language revitalization efforts take place across very broad and diverse situations and communities, and involve many types of speakers. All endangered languages and their speakers are in a permanent state of flux, existing in complex language ecologies where heterogeneity is the norm. This should be taken into account and respected; all revitalization projects must understand and deal with such complexity in order to design and develop well-informed and efficient strategies to reverse language shift. In addition to pointing out the diversity of situations, linguistic variants, speakers, proficiencies, attitudes, motivations, and goals that exist, we also want to warn against applying biological metaphors to the context of language endangerment and revitalization.

Such metaphors can be harmful when we consider, for example, that in the biological sciences, revitalizing a species can be done through intervention and even genetic reconstruction. However, when working with people and their languages, we should focus on the agency of human beings as a fundamental aspect of recovering endangered languages. For this reason, when considering any revitalization project it is important to account for the cultural strategies and practices of communities and speakers, as well as the different goals and outcomes they aspire to. By comparing distinct kinds of communities and speakers, we can conceive (re)vitalization as a continuum ranging from dormant languages to highly vital and viable languages that are, nevertheless, still threatened.

Therefore, the range of possible, and often complementary, efforts made by different actors, including academics, can be envisioned as attempts aimed at (re)vitalizing, (re)covering, (re)claiming, (re)evaluating, (re)versing, (re)creating, and (re)activating endangered languages. The many scenarios and kinds of 'communities' and 'speakers' we have outlined in this chapter can hopefully serve as useful starting points for developing additional recommendations and points of reflection for future revitalization projects, which are focused on good practices and sensitivity toward local diversity. One of several possible practical goals could be, for example, to engage with many different kinds of speakers in joint and collaborative revitalization efforts, creating a sense of 'community' by reestablishing and strengthening language bonds and identities between different generations and diverse types of speakers.

FURTHER READING

Fishman, J. (1991). *Reversing Language Shift*. Clevedon: Multilingual Matters.
McCarty, T. L. (2018). Community-based language planning. Perspectives from indigenous language revitalization. In L. Hinton, L. Huss, and G. Roche, eds., *The Routledge Handbook of Language Revitalization*. New York and London: Routledge, pp. 22–35.
Mithun, M. (1998). The significance of diversity in language endangerment and preservation. In L. Grenoble and L. Whaley, eds., *Endangered Languages. Language Loss and Community Response*. Cambridge: Cambridge University Press, pp. 163–91
O'Regan, H. (2009). A language to call my own. In A. M. Goodfellow, ed., *Speaking of Endangered Languages*. Cambridge: Cambridge Scholars, pp. 184–98.

6.1 The Community of Wymysoü

Tymoteusz Król

Wymysoü (Wilamowice) was founded in the thirteenth century by colonists of Germanic origin. It started as a small village, then in 1818 it became a town with around 2,000 inhabitants. The number of people in Wilamowice did not increase as rapidly as in the surrounding villages because a relatively large proportion of the population were students, who left to study in other cities and then remained there. Many of them were Catholic priests, who were sent to parishes far from their hometown. Moreover, Vilamovian merchants used to travel all over Europe and stay in big cities, where they had commercial interests. The biggest colony of Vilamovians was in Vienna, where there were a couple of hundred, and in Cracow, where there were also about a hundred. The Wymysiöeryś language has never been spoken outside Wilamowice and the two colonies of Vienna and Cracow. Today in Vienna there are some people who speak Wymysiöeryś, but those in Cracow became assimilated into Polish culture.

The community structure of Wymysoü before World War II was complex. There were five social strata: intelligentsia, big farmers, merchants, small farmers, and servants. In the nineteenth century there were also weavers, who used to have their own way of using the language. Marrying people outside of Wilamowice or even outside of one's own social stratum was not favored, but merchants used to marry Jews and people from Vienna. Servants in the town were often Poles and Germans from surrounding villages, and they married Vilamovian servants. There were also strong Jewish and Rom communities in the area.

The occupation of Poland by the Nazis and the following period under communism destroyed this multiculturalism. Those Jews and Rom who could not emigrate to escape the Holocaust were murdered in concentration camps. After World War II, the Vilamovians were sent to postwar concentration camps in Russia and Poland. The Polish communist authorities issued a decree forbidding people from speaking Wymysiöeryś and wearing Vilamovian folk dress. They also expelled the Vilamovians from their houses for thirteen years. At that time their Polish neighbors developed highly negative attitudes toward Vilamovians. The oldest generation remained Wymysiöeryś, but the younger one used to inform their children that they should be Poles, and not reveal their Wymysiöeryś identity. Many people married Poles because this provided protection against persecution. This was also a response to negative ideologies, which said that Vilamovians should mix their blood because, due to their previous endogamy, they were mentally handicapped. Even Vilamovians said that it would be better if their language and identity died.

But at the beginning of the twenty-first century the young generation 'woke up' and started discovering the past of their parents and grandparents and developing their own identity. As a result, the language and other elements of Vilamovian culture started to become present in public life again. Now there are plenty of Wymysiöeryś/Vilamovian identities: people feel Vilamovian and Polish, Vilamovian and Austrian, or just Vilamovian. Some people say that the young people are doing a great job in revitalizing the language and local identity. But many local activists and politicians say it is dangerous to bring the old Vilamovian identity back – an identity that is not Polish. They do not understand that times have changed and that the young generation is not bound by the old negative attitudes. The young Vilamovians are creating their own identity by selecting parts of the old Vilamovian culture and taking inspiration from other cultures – thanks to visits to such places as Nahua communities in Tlaxcala and the Isle of Man. They are building a new Wymysiöeryś identity and a new speaker community, which are not the same as the one at the beginning of twentieth century. And they have a right to do it, even if they work against the Polish nationalist mainstream, or even against some of the norms and expectations represented and expressed by the older generations.

6.2   What Is Community? Perspectives from the Mixtec Diaspora in California

Griselda Reyes Basurto, Carmen Hernández Martínez, and Eric W. Campbell

If we define 'community' broadly as a group of people who share certain linguistic, cultural, and/or social practices, then the notion of community is fluid and dynamic, and the relationship between people and communities may be many to many rather than one to one. In language documentation and revitalization, *community* has traditionally referred to a village or set of villages that share a common language or set of language varieties. However, especially in the digital age, even this narrower notion of community is not bound to physical topography, and in the postcolonial age, communities may find themselves distributed over large and discontinuous spaces and media. Here we briefly consider the notion of community in the context of the Mixtec *Indígena* diaspora in California, which may serve as an example or point of comparison for other diasporic communities around the world. We use the term *Indígena* to refer to Indigenous peoples of California whose traditional communities are located in Mexico or Central America, instead of the broader term *Indigenous*, which could also include Indigenous peoples with longer histories in present-day California.

Traditional Mixtec communities in Mexico are numerous and situated in western Oaxaca, eastern Guerrero, and southern Puebla states. The political, social, economic, and environmental effects of colonialism have led to large-scale emigration of Mixtec and other Indígena peoples to other parts of Mexico in the 1930s and to the United States in the 1940s–1960s with the Bracero Program, increasing in the 1980s. In California, diverse Indígena populations have settled in and around San Diego, Los Angeles, Ventura County, Santa Maria, Salinas, Fresno-Madera, and other locales. The settlement of large numbers of people from Mesoamerica has led to the emergence of a new, diffuse, and multiethnic community that Michael Kearney termed *Oaxacalifornia*.

Indígena workers are now an integral part of California's enormous agricultural economy. However inequality and discrimination often migrate along with the people who suffer these forms of injustice; Indígena workers may be marginalized as relatively recent arrivals in the USA on the one hand, and then further marginalized and discriminated against within the larger migrant labor force for being Indígena. They are often lumped into 'Mexican' or 'Latino' groups with whom they do not identify, and they are not provided adequate medical, educational, legal, and labor services.

Families are shifting to Spanish in many origin communities in Mexico, and especially in the diaspora. Many youth and children who do speak their native languages feel compelled to abandon them, both because of bullying and discrimination by their peers and due to the dominant society's lack of recognition of their language and culture. The result is that youth have been uprooted and disconnected from communicating in their languages, which threatens the linguistic and cultural continuity of their communities. In response to their economic and social challenges, and the discrimination that they face, Indígena peoples have created binational and local community organizations, such as the Mixteco/Indígena Community Organizing Project of Ventura County, California, to enhance collective efforts and share resources and information.

Ventura County is now home to as many as 20,000 Indígena people, most of whom are Mixtec, and they speak at least fifteen Mixtec varieties, not all of which are mutually intelligible. Each individual has a unique set of language practices that may include their Indigenous language, English, and Spanish, depending on how much time they have lived in the USA, the work that they do, and their personal interests. Most people identify with a 'hometown' community in Mexico, but for many, the community they know and experience the most is the diverse Indígena community of Ventura County. As this example illustrates, we should not essentialize or stereotype Indigenous languages and people, for example, by assuming that they only live in far-away traditional homelands. In order to meet everyone's linguistic and social needs, we should recognize that there are diverse and diaspora communities outside of traditional areas and people may belong to multiple communities.

6.3 An Introspective Analysis of One Year of Revitalization Activities: The Greko Community of Practice

Maria Olimpia Squillaci

In this capsule, I shall briefly describe a series of actions recently taken toward the revitalization of Greko, a critically endangered Greek language, spoken in southern Calabria (Italy), which favored the constitution of a community of practice.

The first attempts to revitalize Greko began in the 1960s, when a group of mostly young people started to actively campaign for the safeguarding of this language and its culture. Since then, many associations have been founded, and very many cultural activities and local/regional programs have been implemented with great opportunities for local development. All this has brought about a very significant change in the attitude of the community toward its own language, which moved from being hidden and despised to being a source of pride. However associations have not been able to secure the intergenerational transmission of Greko at home, resulting in a continuous decrease in the number of speakers. Furthermore, in the last ten to fifteen years, there has also been a progressive reduction of activities in support of the language.

For this reason, five years ago I launched a new summer school 'To Ddomadi Greko – the Greko week', thanks to the support of the old but still-active association Jalò tu Vua. In my mind the Ddomadi Greko had to be a one-week injection of language, enthusiasm, and stimuli to shake up once again the community's interest for Greko and to draw attention to its critically endangered status. My ambition was to (re-)create a strong connection between local people, especially the young generation, and their heritage language, allowing them to discover the richness of their own native place. The school included four hours of language teaching every day, a one-hour cultural seminar, and one afternoon excursion. The result was extremely positive, to the extent that two years ago, we gathered together a group of young participants, potentially interested in engaging with language revitalization.

The first step was the creation of a WhatsApp chat to practice Greko every day, favoring in particular the use of voice messages. Whoever joined the group had to use the Greko words that they knew, even inserting them in an Italian phrase, and if there was a mistake, someone had to correct it and give a grammatical explanation for it. A very useful tool that really facilitated texting in Greko was Grekopedia, the smartphone application with an Italian–Greko Greko–Italian dictionary that my father and I had launched a year before. However, to avoid the creation of a dead chat, we all decided to undertaking several tasks, the first of which was the setting up of the Facebook page 'To Ddomadi Greko' (following success using social media to promote other languages – see Chapter 17), which would cover grammatical topics, traditional songs, stories, memes, and gifs in Greko (on the model of the Colectivo Tzunhejekat facebook page for Nawat).

As trivial as it might seem, this process immediately got great results since it gave visibility to the group, encouraging other people to join in, including Calabrian emigrants and foreigners. Most importantly, however, the management of the page required the group members to practice Greko every day, to find or to create Greko material to post and, crucially, to communicate with the rest of the group. This continuous exchange enormously accelerated their learning process and fostered great collaboration within the group. Tandem activities too, even carried out on Skype for those living outside of Calabria, facilitated team building, a crucial and sensitive part of the revitalization program. To this end, we also used theater as a key tool to quickly improve language skills and a great space for teamwork. The most important results were not the activities per se, but the fact that the management and supervision of them was fully carried out in Greko among people living in different parts of Italy and Europe. In less than a year we managed to build up a community of practice whose main goal was the revitalization of Greko.[4] Crucially all this was actively supported by many older Greko speakers who constantly joined us in our events and we would regulalrly visit them at their place as part of our core activities. The collaboration between the group of new young speakers and the older ones was our strength as it fostered the creation of strong affective bonds among the young members of the group and across generations. This became the driving force of our work and also had a huge impact in terms of language learning, since younger people have progressively stopped learning new words and grammatical rules from books and began learning them by transmission, by living the language in this new kind of community.

---

[4] I soon realized that we also had to give Greko an economic value, to make all our efforts sustainable over time. For this reason, we launched the crowdfunding campaign 'If you speak me, I live – adopt Greko', in order to secure funds for revitalizers to teach and work for the language and to do so by remaining in Calabria, which is per se a big challenge, Calabria being one of the poorest regions in Italy. At present, establishing a link between people's knowledge of Greko and job opportunities in Calabria is our top priority as it might bring to substantial changes in the long run.

7 Attitudes and Ideologies in Language Revitalisation

Nicole Dołowy-Rybińska and Michael Hornsby

Introduction

While there are many reasons that we might initially have for wanting to preserve a language, as detailed in the earlier chapters of this volume, people may also have underlying assumptions about the processes of language revitalisation that go unexpressed. These are generally known as language ideologies, which we discuss in this chapter. These ideologies are often expressed and materialise in the form of language attitudes. Below, we show how language attitudes can affect attempts to save an endangered language; it is difficult to plan any positive language revitalisation without ensuring positive attitudes towards the minority languages (people must actually *want* to use the language if revitalisation is to be successful).

One of the most important tasks, then, for any language revitaliser is to listen to the various attitudes expressed within the community towards their endangered language and to try to work out what ideologies lie behind these attitudes. Such attitudes will be varied, possibly contradictory and nuanced, of course, so we need to be extremely sensitive in dealing with them. Without doing so, it is unlikely that language revitalisation will be successful. It is also very important that attitudes held by the majority language community are taken into account. Majority views affect minority language speakers, as they can influence the community and discourage actual and potential speakers from using the language. Challenging negative impressions held by majority language speakers is therefore an equally important task for language planners. In this chapter, we explore some of the more prevalent ideologies and attitudes found in minority language communities. In doing so, we aim to raise awareness of these issues amongst language planners and minority language activists, helping them to revitalise their local endangered language.

Language Ideologies

Pick up any textbook concerned with minority language sociolinguistics, or start reading an article which discusses the situation of any given minority language and, in all likelihood, it will not be long before the concept of 'language ideology' is encountered. Therefore, we start this chapter with a consideration of the term 'ideology' as it relates to languages and, in particular, to minority languages. There have been many attempts to define what a language ideology is, and some of them are quite complex. This complexity can be confusing for activists engaged in revitalisation. At the opposite end of the scale, however, some writers have used the term without any careful consideration of what they actually mean when they write 'ideology', sometimes using it as an alternative for 'attitude'. We consider that there is a significant distinction between the two terms and that, for minority language activists working on preserving their languages for the future, an understanding of the difference is very important in helping them plan their revitalisation strategies.

For our purposes here, we understand language ideologies as those beliefs, feelings, and assumptions about language that are socially shared and which attempt to make sense of different forms of the language (dialects in relation to a standard language, minority languages in relation to majority languages, youth speak in relation to older generations' way of talking, etc.) and their place in society. Most importantly, ideologies of language represent assumptions about particular linguistic forms and what they say about the people who use them. For example, we often attribute certain social values to a speaker who prefers to use one language over another, one who uses slang or swear words regularly, or who speaks with a particular accent. In this sense, language ideologies are closely connected to language stereotypes, where languages (and their speakers) can be attributed as having certain characteristics, even when these characteristics cannot be objectively demonstrated. For example, claiming that language A sounds more beautiful than language B, or that someone 'hates' the sound of a particular language, are both claims rooted in language ideology, which can then emerge through explicit statements which we call 'language attitudes'. (See below for the difference between language ideologies and attitudes.)

This idea is best demonstrated by considering a common language ideology that can be found in many societies: the so-called **standard language ideology**. The standard language ideology refers to the belief that a particular form of language, usually the variety that is used by the most powerful group in society, is superior in some way to other varieties of the language. The standard variety of a language is often based on written forms, which have been unified in some manner and are typically acquired after many years of formal education. Even though this variety may actually be spoken by only a minority of the population, the vast majority of speakers of the language recognise it as somehow 'superior' and 'prestigious'. Even in the case of many European national languages, which have only been standardised recently (e.g. the Finnish or Czech languages), they gain the status of the language that should be used and protected by the state. Ability in this standard language justifies the privileged societal positions of its speakers, whereas a lack of ability in it often results in exclusion from such positions. Thus, a standard language ideology can make this situation seem fair and equitable – both to those who benefit from it and to those who are disadvantaged by it.

Differences between Ideologies and Attitudes

It can thus be seen that ideologies operate at a subconscious level and that people may not be aware of their existence. However, ideologies can become apparent through people's attitudes towards a given language or language variety. Language attitudes are the explicit evaluations of particular languages and language varieties, expressed by people as opinions and beliefs and, more negatively, as prejudices. They influence people's thought processes and their specific language choices. We refer to the Irish example here. In the Republic of Ireland, the Irish language is viewed favourably by over 60 per cent of the population, who agreed with the statement: 'Without Irish, Ireland would lose its identity as a separate culture'.[1] However, according to the Irish Times, quoting the 2016 census figures, the percentage of people using Irish as a daily language in the Gaeltacht (the officially designated Irish-speaking areas) has fallen by 11 per cent. Outside of the Gaeltacht, where just over 90,000 people live (2.1 per cent of the total Irish population), some 53,000 people in the rest of the Republic use Irish as a daily language (1 per cent of the total population).[2] Given that there is a generally positive view of the language by most adults in the Republic, we might expect more people to be using the language for identity and cultural reasons. However, it would appear that being favourably disposed to a language does not translate into actual use. In thinking about these results, it is worth questioning the nature of the survey itself – if the questions had embraced a more complete spectrum of attitudes (including, for example, the perceived usefulness of the language, and its economic worth) then the results might have looked very different.

Common Language Ideologies in Minority Settings

Researchers have noted a number of ideologies that are regularly found in minority speech communities. The linguistic anthropologist Kathryn Woolard[3] has identified two of the most important ones as being:

---

[1] Economic and Social Research Institute (2015).   [2] *Irish Times* (2017).
[3] See K. A. Woolard, 'Language and identity choice in Catalonia: The interplay of contrasting ideologies of linguistic authority', Workshop on Language Ideology and Change in Multilingual

The ideology of authenticity, which 'links the value of a language to its relationship with a particular community'. To be considered authentic, speakers must recognise the speech variety as being 'from somewhere', and with a particular local quality. Thus, in many minority language situations, one of the markers of a good speaker is the ability to use a particular dialect, or to speak using a recognisably local accent. If such markers are absent, a linguistic variety may be seen by the community to lack value. In revitalisation contexts, authenticity can prove to be a problem when new speakers acquire the language. These learners may not see themselves as sounding sufficiently natural compared with native speakers. In turn, native speakers may 'close ranks', and exert a sort of ownership over speaker identity, privileging their position as 'authentic' speakers. This state of affairs can lead to frustration from learners, sometimes deterring them from using the language altogether.

The ideology of anonymity, which holds that a language is a neutral means of communication equally available to all users. This view is universalist in nature and seeks to include all members of a speech community, however they may have acquired the language. Anonymity is the opposite of authenticity, in that membership is not evaluated by how 'local' a speaker sounds, but more on how well or how often they use the language. This ideology is closely related to the ideology of standard language, in that some users of a particular language actively avoid using dialectal or local forms and instead use the standard variety. In this way, the ideology of anonymity promotes a shift away from an 'authentic' or 'native speaker' identity and towards a 'civic' identity that regards the minority language as a resource for constructing a cosmopolitan, modernised identity.

These two ideologies can lead to tension in minority language situations. For example, the spread of Irish outside of the traditional Irish-speaking strongholds and into areas previously dominated by English has complicated traditional ideologies of authenticity. Most commonly, native speakers of Irish were from very rural areas and their language reflected this, with highly localised dialects and a very developed vocabulary in the traditional occupations of the west of Ireland, such as fishing and farming. As a result, this group was put forward as 'ideal' (or idealised) speakers; when Irish was being revitalised in the early years of the state, language planners gave traditional native speech communities a high prestige status based on their perceived authenticity. This view has remained a deeply rooted language ideology. Yet the rise of a more educated and urban group

Communities, UC Diego, 2005, https://escholarship.org/uc/item/47n938cp; and K. A. Woolard, *Singular and Plural: Ideologies of Linguistic Authority in 21st Century Catalonia* (Oxford: Oxford University Press, 2016).

of speakers in places such as Dublin, Galway, and Cork has resulted in a series of tensions. While the ideology of authenticity positions traditional native speakers as the 'owners' of the language, this view has been rejected by language users outside of the traditional Irish-speaking areas, who perceive the language as a symbol of a newly constructed national identity.

Very often connected to the concept of authenticity are ideas about language **ownership.** In some people's view, a language is 'owned' by its native speakers. This means that their beliefs regarding the 'correct' forms of language are seen as authoritative and they have the final say on what constitutes 'good' language and a 'good' accent, etc. Accordingly, areas where the language is traditionally spoken are often perceived as repositories for the language where people can experience it in its 'natural' environment and access an authentic language-learning experience to become 'real' speakers. However this commodification (or the objectification) of the language can create tensions between those who were seen to produce the commodity (i.e. native speakers) and those who wished to consume it (i.e. learners); while the ideology of authenticity positions traditional native speakers as language 'owners', learners of the language often contest this on the grounds that they too have a right to the language.

Language ideologies based on authenticity can also relate to the perceived usefulness of a language. For a language to be perceived as authentically useful, it very often needs to have a pervasive presence in society – it needs to be seen and heard everywhere – and in that sense, normalised. A normalised (majority) language is seen as the common sense, default option in day-to-day life and official interactions. In a sense, it is the common property of all community members, including those members who also speak another language. The normalised language thus comes to be seen as the most appropriate and most useful means of communication in society. In this situation, transgressing community norms by using a minority language in public may be challenged by non-speakers, who see such behaviour as 'rude' or inappropriate. These ideologies can filter through to the minority community where they are adopted, often subconsciously, by speakers who then choose to use their minority language privately, out of the public domain. In Brittany, for example, it has been noted that when older Breton speakers are out shopping in the supermarket they tend to talk in Breton quietly to each other and will switch to French when a stranger walks past them, switching back to Breton only once they are out of earshot.

The challenge facing many minority language activists is to deal with these issues and work with speakers to help them overcome ideological barriers in using the language. If this does not happen, then it may add to the pressure on minority language speakers to switch to the majority language in all situations, including intergenerational transmission to the younger generations. In such cases a sense of shame can develop, which is often accompanied by a feeling of uselessness as far as the minority language is concerned. The majority language comes to be seen as the language of advancement and betterment, and as the way to secure a more prestigious job and the language to raise children in. Linking minority language use with a sense of purpose, a sense of pride, and above all an essential part of the group's identity, are key to securing a future for the endangered language. Furthermore, and perhaps just as importantly, activists must raise awareness amongst the majority population and attempt to involve them as allies in the preservation and revitalisation of the minority language. There is no magic formula which can be applied universally in all minority language situations and one of the main tasks of activists and concerned speakers in the minority language community is to work out just exactly how to do this, given local conditions and local language ideologies.

The anthropologist Kathryn Woolard has dissected the term 'ideology' into four strands: (1) ideology as a mental phenomenon – the domain of the ideational and conceptual; (2) ideology as the foundation of metapragmatics (the discourse of the effects and conditions of language use); (3) ideology as linked to positions of power through discursive practices – the struggle to acquire or maintain power; and (4) ideology as distortion, maintaining the relations of power by disguising or legitimating those relations. We offer some practical ways for language revitalisers to explore these four strands in the concluding section of this chapter.

Language Attitudes

Everybody has beliefs and feelings about languages based on the way that society perceives them and the stereotypes associated with them. They are socialised through various agents, including teachers, peers, family, and the media. Furthermore they tend to relate to two aspects of the community: status and solidarity. Status refers to both the personal characteristics of those who use the language (e.g. if language speakers are perceived as educated and intelligent) and the external image the community or the language itself has (e.g. if it is not perceived as a 'real' language but as a dialect of another language). Solidarity refers to the extent that a specific language or variety is associated with group membership and belonging to the community. Evaluations made regarding status and solidarity may be positive or negative, and language attitudes can be seen in people's reactions to different language forms, practices, and varieties. A speaker's accent, the vocabulary used, the particular language chosen (especially in the situation of unequal bilingualism, i.e. when minority community members are bilingual in both the minority and majority languages while the rest of population inhabiting a given territory speak only the dominant language and do not consider knowledge of the minority language as important) all give clues about who the speaker is, what their personality is like, their social status, and even their appearance. This evaluation is based on the stereotypes and language ideologies that operate in society and are learned from early childhood. This image of minority language speakers and their language influence how people react to them and how they act towards them. In this way, language attitudes may be seen as a bridge between ideologies and behaviours. Furthermore, because they directly influence language choices, they are key elements of any revitalisation program.

As we have shown, language attitudes are the opinions, ideas, and prejudices that people have towards a language or language variety. For example, some people may think that a language that does not have a written form is not a real language. Others may associate a specific accent with being uneducated, while some people feel shame when using their language in a public place, or feel attacked when other people speak a minority language in their presence. In contrast, some people may feel proud of their language and perceive it as more beautiful than other languages. They may, as in the case of Basque, claim that their language is the oldest in the world, highlighting the uniqueness of their language to create more positive attitudes towards it and secure its future. As we can see, language attitudes are based on language ideologies that are often covert and have been internalised by individuals within a community so that they are perceived as natural.

Language attitudes should be identified and addressed as a core element of language revitalisation. When a community has strong negative language prejudices regarding their way of speaking, their feelings about using the language in different domains are also negative. In this situation, reversing language shift may be very difficult or impossible. In contrast, positive attitudes towards a minority language may inspire activists and community members to act against language shift. Just like language ideologies, language attitudes can also be changed. However, this is a long and difficult process that should be planned at many different levels, including changing negative attitudes that may exist in the minority speech community, and those possessed by the dominant community. The work should target both bottom-up language policy and state language recognition. Through some examples, we will explore some different types of language attitudes and consider how it might be possible to change them.

Negative Attitudes Resulting in Negative Language Practices

Negative language attitudes in the dominant society can have serious consequences for the minoritised speech community, leading to prejudice and discrimination. Negative language attitudes that have been internalised by the group are the most difficult to change. These attitudes are the result of long-term language trauma related to discrimination and the unfair and humiliating treatment of people because of the language they use. Language ideologies and their related language attitudes can be very powerful and can become an instrument of domination. For example, the belief that one way of speaking is less prestigious than another can run very deep. This is particularly true when different methods for oppressing the language have been used, such as banning the language, negative media discourse, physical punishment for using the language, and psychological abuse. In these cases, negative attitudes can be instilled in people's minds so that they start to treat them as an objective truth. People who are linguistically discriminated against often perceive their language as worthless and a source of shame, seeing it as the cause of their own suffering and misfortune. Wanting a better life for themselves that is free from humiliation and deprivation, they often feel compelled to abandon the language and do not transmit it to their children.

Linguistic discrimination is often the reason why intergenerational transmission of a language breaks down. An example of this is the Breton language in France. The language trauma there was so strong after the Second World War that the number of speakers decreased from 1,100,000 to 200,000 over the course of the twentieth century. This was the result of a combination of several factors, including strong language ideologies associating Breton with the language of uneducated people and poverty, which led people to feel shame when using it in public; linguistic discrimination of Breton speakers at the political and social levels (e.g. social exclusion and hindered access to the labour market); direct persecution of Breton speakers at schools (e.g. corporal punishment of children, or the symbolical punishment of children caught while speaking Breton marked by an object hung around their neck until a stigmatised child caught another one speaking Breton) and the persecution of speakers in other spheres (e.g. Breton soldiers' traumatic experiences during the First World War when – because they did not understand orders issued in French and were not able to contest them – they became 'cannon fodder', with the number of Breton deaths being significantly above the French average).

The effects of this type of internalised language trauma can be seen in the following statement: 'I spoke the language X and it caused only problems. I want to forget this language and I do not want my children to use it'. When language trauma results in language shift, revitalisation projects must occur alongside efforts to end discrimination and create positive language attitudes, both within the speech community and outside of it. It is often the case that the generation who suffered because of direct language discrimination and did not transmit the language (thus making them the last 'native' speakers of a language) are not willing to participate in language revitalisation efforts. However, they should not be left behind. This situation can often cause a sense of guilt for not having transmitted the language. Sometimes this generation can downplay or even deny that linguistic discrimination against them took place. It should be stressed that language trauma can be inherited by the next generation, making any community work sensitive. Efforts to create language prestige should be linked to top-down language policy, recognition of the language, as well as bottom-up activities aimed at showing people that their language is in no way worse than the official one. Language ideologies and related language attitudes should be deconstructed in order to make people aware that they are only social constructs created to deprive them.

Positive Language Practices in the Face of Negative Attitudes

Negative language attitudes and language discrimination may lead to different behaviours in different speech communities. These can be understood as the adaptation strategies of a community and its individuals. These strategies include decisions about what language to use and what group to identify with. In many cases, to avoid discrimination, people abandon their language and choose the dominant one instead so that they are not disadvantaged socially, culturally, or politically. However, social and linguistic inequality and discrimination may also lead people to assert their right to use their language. This is illustrated by the attitude: 'My language is oppressed so I have to do my best to protect it'.

Many endangered language activists are motivated to protect their language, community, and freedom, by grievances and the rejection of discrimination and persecution. Language activists take on responsibility for the language and the future of the speech community, undertaking different activities aimed at maintaining the language. An important part of these activities is to change the negative language attitudes already internalised by many community members. This can happen at different levels, including: discursive, where the language is described as equal to the dominant one; behavioural, where the endangered language is introduced to public spheres where it was previously forbidden or perceived as inappropriate; militant, where the language is promoted through direct and indirect acts of social rebellion; and political, where official recognition of the language is campaigned for. These activities may be undertaken at both the public and the private level and act as personal 'testimonies' for those people fighting to save the language. Through all these activities, and by reversing the negative image of a language, it is possible to gradually change language attitudes.

Negative Language Practices despite the Existence of Positive Attitudes

Changing the language attitudes of a speech community is a multilayered process and does not necessarily lead directly to reversing language shift. In other words, negative language ideologies are sometimes so deeply internalised that even when erased on the conscious level, they still resonate in the actual language practices of people. This attitude may be represented by the statement: 'I support language revitalisation but I will not learn this language/I will not send my child to the bilingual school'. This situation has negative consequences for revitalisation efforts.

To illustrate this, let us take the example of the Kashubian language in Poland. This language belongs to the same language family as the Polish language and, for political reasons, was treated as a 'dialect' of the Polish language (a language ideology). Its prestige was low: it was not recognised by the state and its speakers were associated with rural life, and a lack of education and job opportunities. Moreover, after the Second World War, in the Polish People's Republic, based on the concept of building a unified – monocultural and monolingual – society, Kashubian speakers suffered language discrimination and many of them had traumatic experiences at schools with regard to their language. Although efforts to maintain the Kashubian language began two decades ago and it is now recognised as a regional language of Poland, negative attitudes and ideologies still influence people's language practices. For many years, there has been no social acceptance for establishing schools with Kashubian as the language of instruction, the argument being that those children would experience language problems in the future. These attitudes persist today. Gradually, with numerous efforts undertaken at different levels and thanks to language activists who have gradually broken down these mental barriers, the effects of language trauma and language ideologies are being eliminated.

Positive Language Attitudes and Positive Language Practices

The speech community may also have positive attitudes towards their language and assert that it should be protected and used by people in all domains. In the context of minoritised languages, these positive attitudes may result from: speakers' resistance to discrimination ('I am prevented from speaking my language but I do it anyway because I want it to survive'); strong positive ideologies related to the language ('I speak my language and I am proud of doing so'); or successful revitalisation efforts ('I have learned the language of my community and I speak it to my partner and children'). When there are numerous people with such language attitudes, there is hope for the future of a language. In the last example given, we see a person who did not acquire the language through conventional family transmission but who learnt it at schools, on a special course, or through contacts with the speech community. Moreover, this person has enough motivation to make it the language of everyday life. Finally they have decided to use the language with her or his family despite the fact that it probably has relatively low prestige.

We can say that for a minoritised language to be revitalised, three conditions must be met: people must be capable of using it, having learnt it in the home or through minority language education, they must have the opportunity to speak it, in both private and public lives, and they must have the desire to use it. All of these three conditions are interrelated with the positive attitudes towards the language. To be able to achieve these conditions, there must be a strong language policy with top-down language support. For example, there must be: opportunities to learn the language; the existence of a language infrastructure with support for families who want to bring up their children in the minority language; and job opportunities in the minority language and possibly other economic profits to increase people's motivation to learn it and use it. Furthermore, the role of media must not be underestimated. Both the language and the speech community must have a positive image in wider society. It is also important, especially for the younger generation, that the use of a language is not uniquely linked with the past and tradition, but also with what is perceived as 'modern' and 'cool'. Therefore, for people to have positive attitudes towards a language, it should be used in all domains of their daily life, from the family domain, to school, work, and social media.

Positive Attitudes towards Multilingualism

Once intergenerational transmission of the language has been interrupted or broken it is important to take into consideration not only the language attitudes of active speakers, but also the attitudes of those who do not speak it. A contemporary minority language community may include native speakers (who may or may not choose to use the language), people who have learned the language of the minority and use it, and those who are indifferent or have negative attitudes towards it. Moreover, there are individuals who are considered members of the speech community and are surrounded by and/or mix with those who do not identify themselves with any particular group, but may be interested in learning and using the language. The 'speech community' may therefore also include 'potential speakers', who should also be targeted by revitalisation activities.

Therefore, promoting positive attitudes towards multilingualism becomes one of the main aims of revitalisation efforts, allowing new speakers of an endangered language to become part of the community. In this regard, an education system, which is open to both native and non-native speakers, can play an important role. There should be a place where children can learn the language and, preferably, also learn through the medium of this language. The latter is important for changing language ideologies that claim that it is not possible to express everything in the minority language, or that learning in this language causes harm to children. Moreover these educational settings should be of the best quality in order to encourage parents to send their children there. One possible solution is to provide teaching in three languages: the minority language, the dominant/state language, and English (as a global lingua franca). Another possibility is to work with institutions and social media to raise awareness of the benefits of multilingualism. For example, multilingualism raises cognitive abilities and creativity. Moreover, children who speak at least two languages have higher language skills; find it easier to solve problems; to distinguish meaning from form; to listen and remember; and to learn any additional language faster.[4] These benefits can increase the child's chances of obtaining a good job in the future and can help them to cooperate effectively with other people. These arguments are based on the intellectual advantages of learning a minority language rather than the emotional, identity-based, benefits. This reasoning may help to create more new speakers and to convince parents from the speech community that it is good for their children to learn and use their heritage language.

Conclusion

Language ideologies which operate at a sub-conscious level express themselves in peoples' attitudes, opinions, and beliefs towards a given language or language variety. Both language ideologies and language attitudes are very important to the revitalisation process. Therefore the first step when planning new revitalisation strategies should be an examination of the

---

[4] For a summary of research on such benefits, see E. Bialystok, F. I. M. Craik, and G. Luk, 'Bilingualism: Consequences for mind and brain', *Trends in Cognitive Sciences* 16(2012), 240–50.

existing language ideologies and language attitudes in a given society or community. Without this knowledge, revitalisation efforts could fail. Recognising language ideologies, such as the ideology of the standard language, of authenticity and ownership, is the first step in overcoming them. The same concerns language attitudes. There is a need to understand attitudes towards the minority language in both the minority speech community members and wider society.

Changing language ideologies, whose power lies in the fact that they are innocuously and deeply imprinted in people's brains, is a long-term process. The best method to do so is to make people aware of their existence and how they function.

Formal and informal education can be helpful here. One of the primary goals of any revitalisation program is to activate speakerhood and to produce more speakers of an endangered language. Part of this process should consist of familiarising people with the fact that language ideologies are socially constructed and that they can be changed. Informal education also plays a vital role in producing positive attitudes towards the language and motivating people to use it. For example, creating different events and activities for speakers and people who are learning a language to meet can actively encourage them to use the endangered language, even if it is difficult for them. This can also contribute to building a common language identity amongst speakers and creating positive attitudes towards the language.

Media has the power to create a positive image of both the endangered language and the speech community (including native and new speakers). When a language that is otherwise considered 'not useful' or 'backwards' is presented in the media, online, or in computer games, it can appear modern and attractive, particularly to young people. Another role of the media is to create a positive image of the speech community, minimising their reluctance to use their language in public life. When a speech community is presented as being full of life, new ideas, and resistance, this may also contribute to changing language ideologies and attitudes and, as a result, language practices.

To change language ideologies and attitudes, it is also helpful to strengthen the presence of the endangered language in the linguistic landscape. Bilingual inscriptions signal a collective identity, as well as equality between the endangered language and the dominant language. The presence of an endangered language in the written form augments its prestige and social significance, thus breaking the symbolic domination of the majority group. Numerous studies on 'linguistic landscaping' have demonstrated how minority language spaces are symbolically defined through the medium of writing, particularly on street signs, billboards, and signs in public buildings, etc. However we should also bear in mind that some languages have more of an oral presence, and that they are more likely to be heard rather than seen in written form. In these cases, the media can also be used to create a 'soundscape', for example, through public announcements in train stations and airports and the availability of radio and TV shows in the minority language, etc. These are important considerations when engaging in language revitalisation planning.

To conclude, when speakers' and community members' language ideologies and attitudes are negative, this could jeopardise revitalisation efforts. In order to prevent this, a community should identify existing ideologies and their roots. This will help in understanding language attitudes within the community. We should establish programs aimed at diminishing the impact of negative language ideologies (for example, through community campaigns and activities) and reinforcing positive language attitudes with the use of social movements, cultural activities, supportive language policy, the linguistic landscape, and last but not the least, formal and informal education.

FURTHER READING

Baker, C. (1992). *Attitudes and Language*. Clevedon: Multilingual Matters.
Blommaert, J., ed. (1999). *Language Ideological Debates: Language, Power, and Social Process 2*. Berlin: Mouton de Gruyter.
Gal, S. and Woolard, K. A., eds. (2001). *Languages and Publics: The Making of Authority*. Manchester: St. Jerome.
Garrett, P. (2010). *Attitudes to Language*. Cambridge: Cambridge University Press.
Garrett, P., Coupland, N., and Williams, A. (2003). *Investigating Language Attitudes: Social Meanings of Dialect, Ethnicity, and Performance*. Cardiff: University of Wales Press.
Schieffelin, B. B., Woolard, K. A., and Kroskrity, P. V., eds. (1998). *Language Ideologies: Practice and Theory*. Oxford studies in anthropological linguistics 16. New York: Oxford University Press.
Woolard, K. A. (1998). Introduction: Language ideology as a field of inquiry. In B. B. Schieffelin, K. A. Woolard, and P. V. Kroskrity, eds., *Language Ideologies: Practice and Theory*. Oxford: Oxford University Press, pp. 3–47.

7.1 Language Ideologies in an Endangered Language Context: A Case Study from Zadar Arbanasi in Croatia

Klara Bilić Meštrić and Lucija Šimičić

Language ideologies can be defined as socially, historically, and politically shaped ideas about language, which often have far-reaching and irreversible effects on language attitudes and linguistic practices. This is the case in the context of Arbanasi, a language spoken by approximately three hundred, mostly elderly, people in the city of Zadar, Croatia. The language has been classified as highly endangered by UNESCO. Based on the Gheg dialect of Albanian spoken by Catholics fleeing the Ottoman wars in the early 1700s, Arbanasi underwent significant linguistic influence from Venetian, Italian, and Croatian, especially in its vocabulary. Today it is not institutionally protected as, among other reasons, its speakers do not claim a separate national minority status. Furthermore, having been classified as intangible cultural heritage in Croatia along with around twenty other minority languages and language variants grants its speakers only symbolic recognition.

The ideologies behind the loss of Arbanasi reflect several highly interrelated features, which are all related to the devalued role that many minority languages have in society. The pervasive attitude among Arbanasi speakers and the wider community that Arbanasi is not a proper language is due to: (a) a high level of 'mixing' with other languages, (b) a high degree of variability in both grammar and vocabulary, (c) a lack of written tradition accompanied by the absence of standardisation. Such attitudes are based on the ideology that languages are abstract, stable, pure, countable entities with clearly defined borders; at the same time, this belief sees all other language varieties as less valuable. However, this view often ignores the fact that languages are always a form of social reality and that the selection of a language norm is usually historically and politically motivated. Proponents of this ideology question the idea that languages marked by a high level of 'mixing' and/or variability can be perceived as fully legitimate. Consequently many Arbanasi speakers are reluctant to call Arbanasi 'a language', and prefer to refer to it as 'a dialect' or 'a speech'. For others, however, it is precisely this linguistic hybridity, that is the fact that it is so highly interspersed with Croatian and Italian (Venetian) influence, which functions as a source of pride and leads them to refer to it as a language in its own right; one that is different from modern standard Albanian (based on the Tosc variety).

Since languages proper are often equated with standardised and written varieties, many believe that Arbanasi, not having been written down, cannot be accorded the same rights as developed national languages. However the desire to prescribe written norms for Arbanasi is only marginally present in the community since not everyone considers it necessary for language learning, and much less so for (occasional) informal texting and similar. A recent attempt to write down Arbanasi using the Croatian writing system also caused heated discussions since many believe that the traditional Albanian-based writing system is more 'correct' and more likely to grant Arbanasi a legitimate 'language' status.

At a more personal level, linguistic insecurity is visible in Arbanasi as speakers become increasingly aware of language decline manifested mostly in numerous lexical gaps, with words missing even for everyday concepts. Moreover, due to reduced language productivity to create new words in Arbanasi, it is the lexical level that serves as an ideological battlefield; by endorsing either the modern Albanian standard variety (Tosc) or Croatian, (groups of) community members promote their view of a 'correct' language. Moreover occasional instances of insisting that there is an original, genuine version of Arbanasi that some, mostly senior speakers, use, only increase the reluctance of many Arbanasi to speak their language. Such a feeling is especially pronounced among those who tend to code-switch a lot and/or insert Croatian and (to a lesser extent) Italian lexical borrowings into their speech. At the same time, the myth that speaking Arbanasi at home will cause its young speakers to make mistakes in Croatian has contributed to the interruption of intergenerational language transmission in many families. This reflects an ideology of monolingualism, which is usually based on the fear that an official, national, or a language of a majority cannot be properly mastered if the traditional language is still in use.

Today, the youngest known speaker is in his early thirties and, to our knowledge, the language is not being transmitted in families (there are no children who are growing up with Arbanasi). There are a few places where the language can be heard in public and one of them is a language course in the city library. This course is a community-based initiative, where mostly traditional and latent speakers gather because it is the only chance for them to use the language. It is also an arena where the different aforementioned ideologies often come into play. Bearing in mind the decisive role that language ideologies and attitudes play in language shift in the Arbanasi context, it is clear that addressing language ideologies at the grassroots level should therefore be the starting point in any revitalisation effort.

7.2 Attitudes towards Guernesiais

Julia Sallabank

Guernesiais is the Indigenous language of Guernsey, Channel Islands (between Britain and France). Traditionally Guernesiais was seen as a 'poor relation' of French. French was used in the government, the judiciary, religion, and education, while Guernesiais was used between family and friends. Although the Channel Islands have been associated with Britain since the eleventh century, it is only since the nineteenth century that English has become widespread. English spread quickly (especially once radio brought it into homes) and it is now the dominant language, while Guernesiais has only a couple of hundred speakers: most fluent speakers are aged eighty or over, and there are very few speakers below the age of sixty.

One commonly expressed attitude towards Guernesiais is that it is 'not a proper language' but either a dialect of French or a mixture of English and French. In response, language supporters point out that Guernesiais is a variety of Norman, which has a prestigious history – reclaiming prestige is an important principle.

Until the late twentieth century, even in areas where the language was spoken most widely, people assumed that if children learnt Guernesiais they 'would never know English'. One woman remembered how in the 1950s neighbours told her mother that 'when she goes to school she won't be able to learn' if they spoke Guernesiais (she is now an accomplished musician).

By the early twenty-first century, however, it became clear from media reports and anecdotes that attitudes towards Guernesiais were becoming more and more positive. Speakers started to express pride: 'In certain company you didn't speak it – because it made you feel a bit inferior but now it's the other way round – you don't feel at all inferior if you know it, it's completely the opposite you know?'

I conducted a representative survey in 2004[5] and found overall strength of support for Guernesiais even higher than anticipated: for example, 50.5 per cent disagreed strongly and 25.3 per cent mildly with the statements, 'It doesn't matter if Guernesiais dies out' and 'Guernesiais is irrelevant to the modern world'. Attitudes towards bi/multilingualism were also much more positive. Although these results were the same across gender, job sector, and geographical origin, as well as proficiency in Guernesiais, people with higher levels of education had marginally more positive attitudes. When the results were analysed by age group, under-18s were found to be slightly more likely to have negative attitudes. Although the difference was minimal, the attitudes of young people are of course key to a language's future. However several interviewees commented that it is common to reject traditional values in your teens and twenties, but some become enthusiastic about Guernesiais in middle age or later.

This survey included not only Guernesiais speakers but reflected the general population in that only 2 per cent speak the language, and 36 per cent were born outside the island. A crucial factor in this apparent majority-population support for a minority language may be that many of the majority population see Guernesiais as part of their heritage too, not only that of the dwindling number of native speakers; this is even true of respondents who are not of local origin.

On the face of it, such majority support would appear to bode well for the future of the language. Yet not all older speakers have fully accepted a higher status for Guernesiais – some still unconsciously perceive Guernesiais as lacking in prestige. In addition, there is an influential minority who cherish Guernesiais as the language of their youth, and who seem unwilling to hand over control to a new generation or to new speakers. It is often assumed that young people and immigrants will not be interested in Guernesiais, and language maintenance activities can perpetuate this stereotype by focusing on traditional culture. Language activities need to be inclusive to attract people of all ages and backgrounds. It should be remembered, however, that attitudes are not actions: positive attitudes cannot save a language without concrete measures. However, they can lead to public support and funding for such measures.

7.3 What's the Point of Manx?

Adrian Cain

Manx is a Celtic language spoken in the Isle of Man/ Ellan Vannin, an island in the Irish Sea mid-way between Wales, Scotland, and Ireland. The last traditional native speakers died in the 1970s; at that point one might have asked 'What's the point of Manx?' Indeed Manx was categorised as 'extinct' in 2009 in the UNESCO *Atlas of*

---

[5] See J. Sallabank, 'Can majority support save an endangered language? A case study of language attitudes in Guernsey'. *Journal of Multilingual and Multicultural Development* 34/4 (2013): 332–47.

Figure 7.3.1 Language materials in Manx. Photo by Justyna Olko

Languages in Danger. But Manx is actively used through revitalisation efforts such as adult lessons, Manx music sessions, preschools, a Manx walking club, bilingual signage, radio broadcasts, conversation groups, and optional lessons in mainstream schools. There is a Manx-medium primary school which teaches all subjects through Manx, with seventy pupils (see Figures 7.3.1 and 7.3.2). According to the 2011 Census there are over 1,800 speakers.

I don't get asked the question 'what's the point of Manx Gaelic' too often these days and that probably reflects a change in attitudes towards the language; however, if I do, my usual response is, 'What's the point of the Isle of Man?'

Having lived in London for a number of years I'm aware that most people outside of the Island have a very poor understanding of the Isle of Man, which at best consist of a series of clichés such as 'tax haven', 'TT races', and 'cats without tails'. Unfortunately many such clichés are peddled by the supposedly liberal press in London too.

In this sense, the revitalisation of the language here is as much about changing perceptions towards the Island as it is about getting people speaking the language. Moreover, if the Island is to rid itself of these misconceptions and lazy journalism, it needs to be telling a different narrative about itself, its history, and its culture: the revitalisation of the language in this sense is a positive news story about the Island that tells a different narrative. We are more than just a well-regulated 'off-shore' tax jurisdiction, but an Island entitled to our independence which has a positive story to tell the rest of the world about language revitalisation and identity.

Figure 7.3.2 Manx for children. Photo by Justyna Olko

A follow-up question might indeed be 'who are the Manx?' these days. The Island has changed fundamentally from that of the last native speakers. Much of the change, but not all, has been good and the reality is that less than half of our community now were born here. 'What is the language to them?' Ironically, the language is one of the few things that the last native speakers would recognise about the Island, but if the language is to mean anything these days it needs to be seen as a language of modernity – associated more with the Internet than thatched houses and fishermen. This Island is open to anyone who wants to make it their home (it doesn't matter if you were born in Portsmouth, Port Moresby, or Port Elizabeth). What's more, the language and the culture that accompany it can belong to you as much as they belong to someone from a long line of Manx descendants who was born and brought up on the Island.

The Island has changed and will continue to do so; however, the language and culture are stronger than they have been for over 100 years. Although the future will be challenging, there is a growing acceptance from politicians and business people on the Island that the language and culture tell a different narrative for our Island; that is, that the language is forward looking and welcoming to new learners and speakers of different backgrounds.

What languages need, therefore, is a vision: a sense of what has gone and what is possible. But this vision needs to avoid arguments about how authentic modern Manx is, and offer instead a sense of what our languages can be in a rapidly changing world.

'What is the point of the Isle of Man?' Therein lies the future of our language.

FURTHER READING

Clague, M. (2009). Manx language revitalization and immersion education. *e-Keltoi: Journal of Interdisciplinary Celtic Studies*, 2, Article 5. https://dc.uwm.edu/ekeltoi/vol2/iss1/5.

Manx: Bringing a language back from the dead, www.bbc.com/news/magazine-21242667.

Manx Language Network – Your one-stop shop for all things Manx Gaelic: Learn, use and support Manx, www.learnmanx.com.

How the Manx language came back from the dead, www.theguardian.com/education/2015/apr/02/how-manx-language-came-back-from-dead-isle-of-man.

7.4 Emotions and Relationships in Language Revitalisation and Maintenance[6]

Soung-U Kim

While working on Jeju Island, South Korea, I had the opportunity to speak to people about what their local language variety 제주돗말, *Jejudommal* (pronounced ['tɕedʑudomːaɭ], aka *Jejuan*, *Jejueo*, or *Jejubangeon* among others) means to them, as opposed to the national language, Standard (South) Korean. Transmission of the speech of the oldest generation has ceased, yet a number of traces remain in the way the youngest generation speaks. Younger people may consider themselves speakers of Jejuan nonetheless, and as much as 'Jejudommal' and 'Standard Korean' do exist in speaker's minds as entities, so are emotional meanings constructed and assigned to these different ways of speaking. That is, ideological connections with the emotional meanings of language use may even persist in cases when there is no intergenerational transmission.

Jejudommal is regarded as having much richer words to express sounds, feelings, moods, and attitudes, whereas Standard Korean is seen as sounding more 'sober', with more clearly definable words. Still, people's impressions go well beyond language: Speaking Jejudommal is often considered more appropriate in a relaxed, trusting, and intimate atmosphere where emotions may be expressed freely, and where people feel much more connected to their emotional lives themselves (e.g. when talking to close relatives or friends). Contrastingly people associate speaking Standard Korean with having to keep themselves in check, and with leading rational conversations, which purely serve the purpose of communicating 'cold' information between people who have to maintain a particular distance. Naturally people often say that they feel more disconnected from their own feelings and expressing them in such situations – a classic example is that of a work meeting.

---

[6] This work was supported by the Laboratory Program for Korean Studies through the Ministry of Education of the Republic of Korea and Korean Studies Promotion Service of the Academy of Korean Studies (AKS-2016-LAB-2250003).

Isn't this interesting? When we talk about language revitalisation and maintenance, our attention is often directed towards more 'objective', 'tangible' things, for example, domains of usage, language materials, education, speaker numbers, and such. Rarely, however, do we talk about the emotional meanings and values that we attribute to the languages that we speak, and also the emotions that our very language choices evoke. Maybe it's because emotionality is stereotypically considered vague and difficult to measure, or maybe thinking and talking about our emotions may not be considered the most 'professional' approach in our revitalisation 'work'.

What we are trying to achieve here goes way beyond a task where we merely repair a dysfunctional machine; rather we are working towards a profound transformation of deeply ingrained habits – our everyday language choices – which are connected to a much wider web of being human. If that is the case, in language revitalisation we should take into account something that is crucial to us as human beings: our emotional lives, and how they relate to the language choices we make.

Thus it may be worthwhile reflecting on what feelings, thoughts, values, and images you associate with speaking your minority language(s), compared to the dominant language(s) of the majority. How does it make you feel when you speak or hear 'your language'? Which language variety do you choose in particular situations (certain people in your family, at work, at school, with friends, in a shop, etc.), and why? How would it make you and others feel if you chose to speak a different language from what people are used to in those situations? Feel free to ask your family and friends and many others – the goal is to see what emotional values and meanings are shared between members of your community to use that knowledge productively for language revitalisation work.

Taking on such a perspective may in fact inspire your language revitalisation practice and planning: what if you tried to go about strengthening language use not only by tackling certain domains, but also, with respect to strengthening particular spaces and relationships that appeal to people's emotions? Similarly how about reflecting on the emotional relationships you forge on a daily basis through your language? Can you help to foster positive emotions connected to the use of your language? Of course, one should not dismiss the insights of language revitalisation studies so far, but I do think that we must acknowledge that we are more than just 'brains with limbs and organs' exchanging facts through speech, and that language revitalisation, therefore, must be about more than language. Essentially it's about being human, together – or in the worst case, alone.

7.5 Nahuatl Language Ideologies and Attitudes

Justyna Olko

Today Nahuatl is still spoken in several Mexican states, in both rural and urbanised settings (although much less frequently in urban centres). The Mexican National Institute of Statistics and Geography (INEGI) reported in 2010 an official population of as many as 1,544,968 native speakers of the language. Nonetheless, in most Nahua communities intergenerational language transmission has drastically been weakened or has broken down entirely over the last few decades. This was accelerated, and in many cases directly provoked, by a pervasive ideology of racism, as well as by school policies. Indigenous children were subject to many forms of violence and discrimination at school, and negative ideologies were internalised by community members. Today such community-driven racist attitudes are remembered by children raised in the 1980s, such as a community member from Tlaxcalancingo in Puebla raised monolingually in Nahuatl by his mother, with whom I spoke in 2014. It took him a long time to learn the dominant tongue well and he was an object of prolonged mockery and humiliation by his peers: 'Everybody was saying that it sounded funny or that I made them laugh. [I only knew how to say] "Good bye" and "give me permission to go to the toilet." All my friends with whom we studied were laughing [at me]. I was taking a long time to learn well [Spanish]. They were insulting me, mocking me, [saying] I was an *indio*, stinker, that [I] bathe myself in a steam bath, that I carry a spittle of cactus and saying other things'.

The heritage language is seen as the most visible sign of the previous, 'uncivilised' state of existence, associated with backwardness, positioning *indios*, a derogatory term for Indigenous people that goes back to the early colonial period, as the lowest, most disadvantaged, and backward social group. As remarked by one of the few remaining elderly speakers in the community of San Pedro Tlalcuapan in Tlaxcala in 2017, 'Because they [community members] are ashamed, they do not want [to speak], they tell as we are *indios*, one who speaks Nahuatl is an *indio*'.

When Nahua people from more isolated (especially mountainous) communities come to nearby urban centres to sell their goods to earn a basic living, or when Indigenous children commute to regional schools, they often experience abuse and discrimination. Language and ways of dressing are perhaps the most obvious identification markers, so they take efforts to hide their ethnic characteristics in order to avoid mistreatment. This discrimination is experienced by members of marginalised Nahua-speaking communities, and is carried out by residents of more 'modernised' Nahua towns. A woman from a little village in the Sierra Norte de Puebla, who married into a central Tlaxcalan community and has been living there for twenty years, testified that she was mocked and discriminated against because of her origin, even by members of her new family who are themselves speakers of Nahuatl.

As pointed out by a community member from the Contla region in Tlaxcala, people feel 'denigrated' and 'ashamed' to speak Nahuatl, while the few conversations in this language are limited to the themes of agriculture and communication with workers who often come from more mountainous communities: 'We barely communicate in Nahuatl. We speak Nahuatl very rarely with my wife and kids. Sometimes we speak Nahuatl when we talk about farming and the field, when we talk with the workers. We can have a conversation with the people we meet [on the street] if they do not feel ashamed, but there are people who feel very ashamed. One denigrates himself for speaking Nahuatl. Sometimes we speak Nahuatl with the people from the *sierra* (mountainous regions) who speak Nahuatl, but when it is just us here, well, we don't'.[7]

---

[7] Interview recorded by Aleksandra Bergier in San Miguel Xaltipan, Contla, Tlaxcala.

Thus, members of native communities situate Nahuatl at the very bottom of the language hierarchy. Spanish is in the middle as a national language and that of the dominant 'modern' society. Most recently, English has taken the place at the very top as a symbol of upward social mobility and opportunities. It is associated with technology, business, youth, and popular culture. For members of a community with high rates of migration to the USA, it is also the language of remote opportunities and a symbol of a better life. Spanish, in turn, is linked to all basic aspects of social life, as the sole language of education, politics, work, legal, and public services. When compared with these two languages, Nahuatl's domains are limited to the household, family, and agriculture, as a lower-status tongue of *campesinos* (peasants). These attitudes are closely linked to a deep denial of the reasons for language shift, especially in the generation of speakers who decided not to speak Nahuatl to their children. Community members remain largely silent about the reasons and circumstances of what occurred. Some spoke some Nahuatl to their children or speak it occasionally to the grandchildren, but they say the failure is on the part of children and grandchildren who refuse to speak the heritage language. Some elder speakers deny anything really happened: they declare there was no pressure or discrimination, just everybody in the neighbourhood started to speak Spanish. This erasure of recent and painful experiences fits well into a widely shared image of modernisation and peaceful transition for a 'better status'.

Children who acquire their heritage tongue at home usually learn at school and/or in the community that it has no value. They often choose to pursue a path to a higher social position than their parents by learning English. Most of them will never go back to speaking the mother tongue. But exceptions and new role models are possible. These are the words of a young and successful engineer from a Nahuatl-speaking family in San Miguel Tenango, Puebla, who decided to invest in his skills in Nahuatl and started to promote it in his home community among the younger generation:

'And at school they say that if you want to find a good job, teach yourself to speak English. So I started studying English. When I started, I said to myself one day, "This English is indeed difficult." Then I said to myself, "So I am learning to speak English, and what about Nahuatl? I also know how to say [something], and I only do not know how to write it. I do not know how to write it, but I know how it sounds." And I said, "So, if I have studied to speak English, I should also teach myself to write and to speak my language well".' (San Miguel Tenango, Zacatlan, Puebla, 2015)

8 Some Considerations about Empowerment and Attitudes in Language Revitalization

Werner Hernández González

Talking about minority languages means talking about efforts, strategies, brave people, and perseverance through the years. The success of these processes is closely related to the way that each group understands their very own situation and assumes the required commitment.

This chapter is about the importance of attitudes and the difference that it can make to language revitalization efforts if they are included as a fundamental element. This is based on experience of more than fifteen years of supporting the process of revitalization of the Nawat language in El Salvador. I also include some reflections that have emerged from the perspectives of the two fields that I know best: as a language activist and as a mental health professional. Both approaches are, in my opinion, strongly related in the understanding that language is the reflection of thought.

On the clinical side, I have had the satisfaction of seeing how people can resolve their once problematic situations when, alongside other elements, they take a positive attitude. If human beings are able to change the course of their destiny with this change at the mental level, it is possible to apply this question to a bigger context, such as the group level. What if the speakers of a minority language took a positive attitude toward their language? Could it perhaps change their destiny? Would it be possible to prevent a tragedy?

A Little about the Case of El Salvador

Salvadoran Nawat is currently the southernmost of the Nahua languages and the only one spoken outside of Mexican territory (excluding migrant/ diaspora communities). It is spoken by a dwindling, scattered population in the central and western areas of this small Central American country. With the loss of Nawat, El Salvador would become the first monolingual country in its region, as the shift to Spanish would be complete.

Ever since the first Spanish colonization in 1524 the Nawat language has not enjoyed high status, even after the establishment of the national state in

1821. The Salvadoran Nahuas became dominated and minoritized, and their language has been weakening ever since. The already undermined language was dealt a severe blow by a major event in 1932: a peasant uprising by and in the area of Nahua villages resulted in an excessive response from the state, with the genocide of some 25,000 people (approximately 2 percent of the country's population at that time). The political dispute soon turned into an ethnic issue. The nucleus of speakers disintegrated and speaking the language could signify mortal danger for a person, whether or not they had any political involvement. The event, therefore, had serious repercussions for the health of the language.

Nawat speakers fell into a kind of hopelessness where they identified themselves as the least desirable component of Salvadoran society, along with all their traditional knowledge, including the heritage language. In order to survive many of them changed their native surnames, they moved away from their traditional areas, they changed their clothes, and finally they abandoned the use of their language (most of them completely). With the loss of positive attitudes toward themselves, intergenerational transmission of the language was also lost. It was not until eighty years later that the Nawat language would be able to experience more promising times.

Auschwitz, Nawat, and a Solution

It would be possible to consider situations of this type just from a social, historical, or political point of view. However, these events and their consequences also have psychological significance. Their impact can make a person vulnerable, provoking depression or anxiety. As a clinical condition, this problem deserves treatment, which are discussed below.

Although it was developed for individual experiences, the logotherapy approach to psychotherapy, pioneered by Viktor Frankl, lends itself to both individual and/ or group contexts, such as the case of Nawat. Frankl's approach was developed from his experiences in the face of the most extreme hardship in the genocide in Auschwitz in World War II. Threats, death, and despair were common experiences shared by both groups, despite them being quite different in both time and location.

The Logotherapy approach proposes that even when we face extreme adversity, we still have a degree of freedom in decision-making that can determine the course of individual responsibility that each person has for their own well-being. The core of Frankl's philosophy is that people can find meaning in their lives by identifying the unique roles that only they can fulfil. Logotherapy believes that lack of meaning causes mental health issues, so it attempts to help people find meaning in order to help solve their problems. Thus, in a particular scenario people could resolve either to abandon themselves, or to find their own meaning in the situation and obtain a more satisfactory outcome, at the same time as understanding their own actions as well as the benefits in the short and long terms. This point can usefully be shared among people participating in language revitalization.

As is usual during times of adversity, people can feel forced to focus on threats and stress suffered instead of using that same time, passion, and energy to find other possibilities. We are less likely to achieve a success story if we only look at complaints and not at solutions. This does not mean we should ignore problems, of course not. The causes of a problem must be known if we want to make the best decisions, but we may be surprised at all the resources that we lose when focusing on a problem, when we could instead begin to believe in joint efforts and in our very own organizational capacities to create a magnificent story.

The inspirational option to focus on solutions and on aspects that we can influence/modify, is the key to building answers. Problems are only our starting point and nothing more than that. This was what Viktor Frankl promoted among the survivors of Oświęcim (Auschwitz), but it is a lesson that traveled to El Salvador and to the world.

Attitude as a Basic Resource

Even if our language only has a small number of speakers, whatever the situation has been, we must look for strengths to make a difference. In this circumstance attitudes are highly relevant because of a very practical fact: talking about attitudes means talking about more possibilities. It is possible that in project planning, the attitude factor has not been taken into account as one of our resources. Nevertheless, it deserves attention beyond a superficial look. Positive attitudes provide resources, but if there are negative attitudes, resources could get lost.

Circumstances can be explained as the interaction of two types of events: external ones, outside our control; and internal ones, which we can control. The way in which we focus on the internal variables has emotional and behavioral consequences. This is one of the approaches proposed by emotive rational therapy. If we do not address circumstances successfully, we can become pessimistic, but on the other hand, we can start from the same experience with the positive option of going forward with optimism and enthusiasm if we focus in the right way.

Why is it important to notice this? Because minority languages are not in that condition by mere chance, but due to political, social, or economic adversity. Those of us who are interested in them must be aware of the need for an approach that gives us the greatest possibility of resolving the situation in a positive way. Understanding this and teaching it to other participants and stakeholders in the process will be beneficial.

A simple way to achieve this is using the easy initials ABCDE:

- A means 'action' (our current situation).
- B comes from 'behavior' (we must provide at least two behaviors after the action).
- C means 'consequences' (one for each behavior).
- D is for 'discussion' of each consequence.
- E means 'efficacy', where we decide on the best answer after the discussion.

How can this be applied to a specific case of linguistic revitalization? To get an idea we can look at these two simple examples:

Case 1

- Action: My local language is in a critical situation.
- Behavior: I will not do anything for my local language because languages are being lost on the planet every fifteen days. It would be better if we promote more successful languages.
- Consequences: Defeatism and loss of cultural knowledge.

Case 2

- Action: My local language is in a critical situation.
- Behavior: My language expresses very beautiful forms, caring for my language is good for my culture and for humankind. Achievements are more appreciated when we face adversity.
- Consequences: Appreciation and enthusiasm.
- Discussion: A positive approach leads to more productive ways of facing reality and opens the door to more possibilities to solve this particular situation.
- Efficacy: If we want to revitalize a language, we choose the route presented in case 2.

In the case of Nawat, taking control of their situation has enabled community members to elaborate thoughts such as:

'Firm hearts cannot be defeated. From our hearts we will continue speaking Nawat'

'They gave us death but we will give flowers and new life to words,' or the very popular

Ne nawat shuchikisa ('The Nawat language is in bloom').

Why is it important to consider attitudes in this way? Because it can make a big difference and really does not cost a penny. It does not cost anything to meet and get organized with people who are interested in the language, create joint efforts, and solve conflicts together. This reasoning allows us to see attitude as an immaterial resource that helps us manage or optimize material ones.

Help from the Outside to Help Inside

Although it might sound a bit paradoxical, this approach is effective and offers one of the fundamental ways to change attitudes of native speakers. Strategies are needed to counteract and compensate for discrimination, for reasons such as ethics, responsibility, dignity, or mental health of persons who have been discriminated against for a long time because of their language, ethnicity, and/or culture. It is important that people in the language revitalization team care about this point, not to play the role of a messiah, but as human beings sharing their experiences and feelings with the human being that is next to them.

In a recent educational project in El Salvador that involved the state, an educational institution, language activists, and some native population members, it was a Nawat speaker, Andrea López, who in personal communication said, 'Your team is looking after everything in school, you also take us and bring us safely and the classes are funny so we want to participate too because is evident the interest and good treatment you give to the Nawat language and its speakers'. She pointed out in this way that the effects of the position explained above have an emotional resonance that is translated into attitudes. If we add joy and enthusiasm, the combination becomes unbeatable as soon as we want to revitalize a language.

Some Ways of Changing Attitudes

For the past five years El Salvador has witnessed a growth in linguistic activism by citizen groups, which have recently been joined by various interested universities to create spaces and offer Nawat language classes. Despite the historical damage to the Nahua population, the involvement of native speakers stands out. Despite the advanced age of several of them, they are involved in the process of fostering language visibility, which has facilitated the presence and appreciation of these speakers inside and outside their towns. With the improvement in attitudes they have become figures in the changes they wanted to see.

It is also worth mentioning the celebrations around the language that are held today, such as the annual Day of the Mother Tongue, which is celebrated simultaneously in several places. These events require open spaces and the use of sound equipment because participants are numerous, whereas previously Nawat was only spoken sporadically in just a few homes.

Nawat is experiencing an initial process of revitalization which, the experts will agree, has not yet achieved much, but it gives enough encouragement to continue. In the words of Alan R. King, in the *Oxford Handbook of Endangered Languages*: 'An awakening has begun, as intellectually capable and socially aware young adults start asking questions and discovering their capacity for effective action and exercising choices'. Collaboration between new speakers and native speakers is an outstanding achievement that has had mutual benefits for the attitude of both groups.

Conclusions

The issue of people's attitudes toward a language is closely related to emotional factors. This makes it worthy of attention from a psychological point of view, particularly in those situations where the environment has been a determining factor in mental health, because substantial changes can have a powerful healing effect. Humans have the great ability to influence their destiny, even in the face of adversity, and to develop positive attitudes in different ways such as when taking on a commitment in a language revitalization process where attitudes are an authentic resource that must be adopted by the revitalizing community, even if they do not have material resources to start the task of preventing the tragedy of the loss of a language. The valorization of the language and ethical treatment of the speaker community by external figures can contribute to mobilizing the appreciation of speakers for their own language, and thus change their attitude to it. By doing so they can make more widespread use of their language.

The number of Nawat language speakers is still small today, but it is precisely this that gives it an interesting position. If this process runs successfully, it can become a regional model in Central America about how to go forward with the resource of attitudes, enabling us to win when history once said we should lose.

FURTHER READING

Frankl, V. (1946/2004). *Man's Search For Meaning*. London: Rider Books.
King, A. R. (2018). Language recovery paradigms. In K. L. Rehg and L. Campbell, eds., *The Oxford Handbook of Endangered Languages*. New York: Oxford University Press, pp. 531–52.
Reguera Baños, J. (2007). *Pensar bien, vivir mejor. Mediante la terapia racional emotivo-conductual*. León.

8.1 Empowerment and Motivation in the Revitalization of Wymysiöeryś

Tymoteusz Król

When I started my activities in revitalizing Wymysiöeryś, many Vilamovians in their fifties, who were too young to have learned Wymysiöeryś but old enough to remember people speaking it, told me a number of stories. They were about people who could not speak good Polish or had a Wymysiöeryś accent in Polish; about the last woman who used Vilamovian folk dress as everyday wear to her death in 2002 – Baranła-Anielka; about a man whose surname was changed from Schneider to Sznajder (to make it more Polish) and then how after many years he changed it back to Schneider. Another story was about a woman, Küba-Håla, who was expelled from her own house in connection with postwar persecutions of Vilamovians. After having spent a couple of years in a labor camp where she was sent because she had been reported by a Pole who had taken over her house, she never took up Polish citizenship and died in penury as a stateless person. All those people (who were fluent only in Wymysiöeryś) were portrayed as stupid, backward, underprivileged, or stubborn. The people who told me these stories thought that I would make fun of the people described in those stories. But for me those people were a symbol of commitment to Wymysoü, similar to my own, despite living in other times and under other conditions. And unlike the Polish national heroes who I was taught about at school, they were not committed to killing a person or to organizing an uprising, it was a commitment of their own life by continuing the Wymysiöeryś language and culture.

The older Vilamovians told me stories about Vilamovian professors, bishops, and merchants, who used to live in Cracow, Lviv, or Vienna, but spoke Wymysiöeryś when they came to visit Wymysoü. These stories revealed that Wymysiöeryś was a language of educated people as well. This made me realize how important changing local ideologies was so that others could also know Wymysiöeryś as the language of prestige, spoke by people of certain status. Several factors contributed to this change. In 2012, I received the European Union Contest for Young Scientists (EUCYS) prize in Poland for a text about Wymysoü. Later more and more activities were supported by Tomasz Wicherkiewicz from Adam Mickiewicz University in Poznań and by Justyna Olko from the Faculty 'Artes Liberales' of University of Warsaw, as both of these external institutions became involved in the revitalization of Wymysiöeryś. Because of these developments the attitudes of the municipal government changed. Also theater plays (see Figure 8.1.1) and the fact that Wymysiöeryś was being taught at the University of Warsaw started to positively influence language ideologies in the society: not only in Wymysoü, but in the whole of Poland. The same holds true for the acknowledgment of our language by SIL in 2007 and UNESCO in 2009.

For me a big motivating factor for continuing to work on revitalization is when I can show other people how we conduct our revitalization activities as well as

134   *Tymoteusz Król*

Figure 8.1.1 Performance in Wymysiöeryś, *Der Hobbit*, Polish Theatre in Warsaw. Photo by Robert Jaworski, Polish Theatre in Warsaw

experience what they do in their communities. I had an opportunity to do it for example in Mexico during a summer school of the EngHum project. Another important factor is the texts about Wymysiöeryś. Tomasz Wicherkiewicz wrote in 2001 that Wymysiöeryś will be extinct by 2010. Then, in 2011, I wrote an email to him saying that our language was still alive. After that, he came to Wymysoü and engaged himself in the revitalization process.

But the most motivating three moments of my life happened when I heard the following three statements by three Vilamovian women: first: 'I want to invite you to my 90th birthday party, because I want to have somebody there to speak Wymysiöeryś to'; second: 'If they expel you from your house as I was expelled for speaking Wymysiöeryś in 1945, come to me, I have chickens, they lay eggs, you will not starve in my house'; third: 'When I see these children wearing Vilamovian folk dress and speaking Wymysiöeryś, I think that they are my parents and my grandparents, and aunts, and uncles. They have been dead for such a long time, and here I can see their clothes waving and hear their voices speaking'.

8.2 Language Activism

Nicole Dołowy-Rybińska

Engagement on behalf of languages, frequently called language activism, can be understood as intentional, often vigorous or energetic actions that individuals and groups undertake to bring about a desired goal, such as political, social, or cultural change. Activists are highly committed people who engage in activities on behalf of their communities, develop different kinds of strategies for the future of their communities and languages, and focus a collective spotlight onto particular issues. Sometimes they are able to motivate other people into action and change indifferent or hostile people's language attitudes. Language activism embraces a range of endeavors, approaches, protest slogans, demonstrations, advocacy, and information dissemination, which aim to change a current state of affairs, and which may also raise people's consciousness. The scope and levels of actions undertaken on behalf of a specific language depend on the situation of the language, the degree of recognition or protection offered by the state, and the attitudes of minority community members toward it, as well as the attitudes of the dominant society.

Language activists attempt to encourage native and potential speakers of a language to use it. They try to persuade governments and policy makers to support their goals. They do not possess authority or decisive power; therefore, they need to rely on people with whom they cooperate. When the minority community and its language lack recognition, their only promoters and policy makers are language activists.

There are different forms of language activism depending on the time and context as well as the aim of activities: to change one's own language practices or influence the behavior of others. Actions in favor of a minority language do not have to be spectacular. There are situations where progressive assimilation poses the most significant threat to minority languages, when language ideologies encourage an opinion that minority languages are regarded as an inferior form of communication, and when current and potential users of the language remain indifferent. If this is the case, activism may start with individual language choices such as learning an endangered language, using it even when it seems not to be accepted by the dominant society (or even the minority one), speaking it with children, and showing pride in using it and in being identified as a member of the language community. Such an attitude may positively influence other people's language attitudes and practices. This type of activism may be aimed at protecting the traditional life of the community, or more concerned with global issues such as social justice, the environment, fair trade, and human rights.

Minority language activism may take the form of organizing and participating in cultural, social, and public events related to the minority language and culture. Not only does this help to strengthen the community, creating new possibilities to use the language and identify strongly with other community members; it also empowers people to move to a more public level of activism in the struggle for language rights. Examples might include actions to show the movement's strength, such as demonstrations, which gather many individuals as well as groups, communities, and associations supporting language and culture. They could also include language festivals to raise awareness in a less confrontational way.

An alternative form of language activism can be expressed through actions with political background. This often involves only a small, strongly engaged subgroup of the minority language community, because it demands considerable commitment and a higher awareness of the importance of fighting for language rights and the need to take responsibility for others. It might involve civil disobedience, for example, defacing public property such as signposts to draw people's attention to the absence of the minority language in public space; or refusing to answer tax bills or court officials in the majority language. *Cymdeithas Yr Iaith Gymraeg* (the Welsh Language Society) provides an already classic example of such activities dating from the beginning of the 1960s. By their direct, often illegal activities and campaigns, this pressure group contributed to establishing the Welsh language as the coofficial language of Wales. These actions are more focused on securing language rights than increasing the use of the minority language.

The role of language activism is significant on many levels. It encourages other people to use a language and gives them the opportunity to engage in the cultural and language life of a community. On a more public level, language activism counteracts the lack of minority language recognition and can influence state language policy to be more favorable toward endangered languages.

8.3 'I'm Revitalizing Myself!'
Jeanette King

I am not Māori, but for forty years I have been participating in and observing the revitalization of the Māori language, which started in earnest in 1982 with the formation of *kōhanga reo* (preschool language immersion centers). I learnt Māori and raised my children bilingually; they went to Māori immersion preschool and schooling options until they were high school age, and I have been teaching Māori in schools and tertiary institutions since the 1980s. With this wealth of experience I can remember feeling encouraged in what I was doing because I felt I was part of a larger movement of people who were revitalizing the Māori language.

However, in the late 1990s, when I mentioned how I felt to a colleague and noted Māori academic, Dr. Te Rita Papesch, she told me that she didn't feel like she was part of any 'movement'! This stopped me in my tracks and made me think. So when I was interviewing Māori adults for various research projects I started asking them about why they wanted to be able to speak Māori. Te Rita was right – hardly any of them mentioned that it was because they wanted to revitalize the language.

Instead these 'new speakers' of Māori talked about how the Māori language was important for their identity as Māori – 'I am Māori, so I want to speak Māori'. Often they talked about wanting to be able to participate in and understand Māori rituals at *hui* (meetings, gatherings). Those I talked to also described how the Māori language was important for their spiritual well-being. In other words, personal identity needs were their main motivator. And boy, were they motivated! Many of those I spoke to have gone on to become noted speakers and change agents. Such people are catalysts, inspiring Māori by challenging the dominant discourse. This makes sense, since one of the earliest language revitalization academics, Joshua Fishman, says that language revitalization will often involve identity (re)formation.

Apart from a focus on personal identity needs, most of those I spoke to were parents, and they mentioned the importance of ensuring that their children were speakers of Māori. In other words, they recognized their key role in establishing and maintaining intergenerational transmission of the language. I remember how one person, when asked to write down their three main motivating factors, wrote the names of their three children. Others also mentioned how they felt that the revitalization of Māori was important to the survival of their *hapū* (subtribe) and *iwi* (tribe).

The people I talked to did sometimes mention that they were motivated by the need to revitalize the Māori language, but this was in third place after their identity needs and desire to support others – in particular, their children.

In the 2000s, I noticed that national and tribal language planners in New Zealand were using promotional material to encourage people to both learn the language and also speak it as much as possible. These materials used phrases such as 'every generation has a role to play in saving our language'. In other words, they were making the same mistake I did, by assuming my motivations for being involved in the revitalization of Māori were the same as those of others. I thought that the promotional material might have resonated more with potential speakers if it emphasized the positive associations of the language with personal identity and well-being.

The message here is that you should never assume that your motivations in language revitalization are the same as others' – in fact, if you're reading this book you are quite likely focused on revitalizing a language. So don't forget that identity needs and a sense of belonging are highly motivational and that for many they aren't revitalizing a language as much as they are revitalizing themselves.

8.4 'It's Good for Your Heart': Three Motivational Steps for Language Revitalization

Maria Olimpia Squillaci

To be honest, in all these years I realized that there are very few reasons why people should keep an extremely endangered language alive. It is certainly fascinating as it brings a different worldview and allows you to reason differently. But concretely, when you live in a very poor region that does not offer any opportunities to young people, a region whose only mantra is 'learn a (dominant!) language and leave', what should your motivations be to actually pass a minority language on to your children or – for young people – to spend much time learning a *useless* endangered language (which is not easy to learn)?

The only words that come to my mind when I think about sharing my motivation are those of my dad: to *platezzi greka kanni kalà stin kardìa* 'speaking Greko is good for the heart.' Starting from this quote, I shall share here three main steps that I consider crucial when undertaking a very *frustrating* revitalization process (as phrased by Lenore Grenoble) in extremely endangered contexts with a handful of older speakers left, which can turn into *a lot of fun* (as claimed by John Sullivan) but only with very good motivations as foundations.

People start learning or revitalizing minority languages for several reasons: cultural heritage, curiosity/interest, research, and many others. I noticed, however, that the big difference comes when they feel connected to the language, when they realize that speaking this language makes them feel better to the extent that they decide not just to study or occasionally speak the language but to *live the language*, that is to embrace the world this language describes and at the same time allow it to move forward into new ones by constantly speaking it and fighting for it. This change usually occurs when people start spending much time with older speakers (even without understating a word initially). When this happens, they deeply connect with the language and crucially with the speakers. In that moment new potential revitalizers realize the treasure of the words stored in people's mouths and feel that the responsibility of transmission has moved from the old speaker down to them, to their *kardìa* – heart. This relation between the speakers and the potential revitalizers (who might be speakers themselves) adds a strong emotional value to language, which is no longer *a* language, but *the* language that people use to speak with or to listen to the people they love. This strong emotional value is the first step toward language revitalization.

The second crucial step is to build a team. It is difficult for revitalizers (either native or new speakers) to go against the flow and keep speaking the language when the rest of the community has stopped using it on a daily basis. In particular, once the initial enthusiasm fades away, revitalizers too can begin to forget the reasons for their work. By contrast, having a team of at least two or more people is a big motivation to move forward; it allows you to always be more creative and it incentivizes new actions when frustration takes over.

The third step is very much linked to the potential outcomes that speaking a minority language can bring with it. In most cases, when we tackle critically endangered languages, the economy – for instance – is a major factor to take into consideration, as its lack of economic value and the fact that 'it does not give you a job' is usually among the root causes for its abandonment. Therefore, it is important to foresee social and economic outcomes that can result from speaking the language and that can lead to concrete improvements for the community.

These three steps are a summary of what I (un)consciously promoted in Calabria, with my community. Regardless of any 'more objective' motivation, I must however go back to the title of this text and admit that the driving force for each of my actions has always been a profound love for my language and for the people who speak it.

8.5 Monolingual Space

John Sullivan

We founded the Instituto de docencia e investigación etnológica de Zacatecas (IDIEZ) in 2002 to provide scholarships to native speakers of Nahuatl who were studying careers in Spanish at the Universidad Autónoma de Zacatecas, and to furnish them with a place to continue practicing their language and culture. At first we held most of our collective discussions in Spanish. But as my command of spoken Nahuatl grew, I realized that my students were more than capable of discussing, in their own language, any of the academic topics that came up in our sessions. At that point I understood that every minute I spent working with them in Spanish was time contributing to the destruction of their native language. We decided that IDIEZ, from then on, would be a monolingual academic space. I played the role of 'language police' for a while, reminding them, when they would switch to Spanish, to look for the appropriate Nahuatl word or to paraphrase.

It's important to clarify here that we are not purists: our aim has never been to return to the time before the conquest, when Nahuatl was free of European loanwords and before the changes to pronunciation, meaning, and how words are formed and ordered that have come about as a result of contact with Spanish – as if that were even possible. The purpose of our monolingual space is akin to that of a jump start for a depleted battery. Our students have, in their brains, all of the cognitive and linguistic tools for thinking critically and creatively from the unique perspective of their language and culture, a perspective that benefits not only their community but all of humanity. They have fallen out of practice and they need to discover for themselves the richness, complexity, and power of their language: The monolingual space is the instrument for achieving this.

Students arrive at IDIEZ as native speakers who have gone through twelve years of formal education in Spanish, and have heard time after time from school, the government, and the media that their language and culture is worthless. So they no longer use Nahuatl except when they return to their villages for short family visits. When they begin to participate in the monolingual space, many ask themselves if they will be punished for speaking Spanish, as some of their former teachers punished them (with beatings, verbal abuse and humiliation, fines, extra chores, etc.) for speaking Nahuatl.

The transition is not easy: as they begin to work monolingually, many students report experiencing headaches. But at some point, each one of them realizes that their language is a powerful, complex instrument for reasoning. At that moment, a light comes on in their eyes – a light of curiosity, self-esteem, and empowerment. And then, through direct participation in monolingual teaching, research, and revitalization activities at IDIEZ, they learn that their opinions matter and their ideas are valuable; they learn that they can develop curriculum and conduct research on their own, without relying on the formulas and recipes they have been taught during their formal education. In other words, they think for themselves and express what they think, in their own language.

9 Economic Benefits
Marketing and Commercializing Language Revitalization

Justyna Olko

One of the most frequent statements one can hear in communities experiencing shift to a dominant language is that the local language does not have any value in the modern world. One of the speakers of Nahuatl whom I met during our language revitalization activities[1] recounted that he could not learn the heritage language from his parents because they would tell him that it is not useful anymore:

Neh oniczaloh nin tlahtol ihcuac nicpiyaya mahtlac huan ce xihuitl huan oniczaloh inahuac nocihtzin. Notahtzin huan nonantzin amo nechittitihqueh tlica yehhuan oquihtoayah 'yocmo, yocmo sirve, nin tlahtol yocmo sirve.'

I learned this language when I was 11 years old. And I learned it from my grandmother. My father and my mother did not teach me because they were saying it is not useful anymore. This language is not useful anymore. (2014, Contla, Tlaxcala, male speaker in his fifties)

A somewhat similar statement comes from the writings of Florian Biesik, the famous poet from Wilamowice and the author of *Uf jer wełt*, the Wymysiöeryś version of the *Divine comedy*:

I know different world languages, I have lived for half the century in exile, but the dearest to me remain the Polish and Wilamowicean tongues, although with neither of them did I earn even a piece of bread. (1924)[2]

The lack of economic usefulness of his native language did not stop Biesik from writing in Wymysiöeryś and creating a literary masterpiece. Moreover, he did it while living far away from his community with a profitable occupation as a railway official in Trieste, Italy. Clearly, for Biesik the importance and utility of the language was not affected by its perceived low

---

[1] Research reported in this chapter has been supported by the Project 'Language as a cure: linguistic vitality as a tool for psychological well-being, health and economic sustainability' carried out within the Team programme of the Foundation for Polish Science and cofinanced by the European Union under the European Regional Development Fund. I express my gratitude to Bartłomiej Chromik for his insightful comments on this paper.

[2] After T. Wicherkiewicz, *The Making of a Language. The Case of the Idiom of Wilamowice, Southern Poland* (The Gruyter Mouton, 2003), p. 48.

economic value abroad. However, the vitality of Wymysiöeryś in the community at that time was high, and it was spoken and transmitted to children. The situation changed after World War II not because of a lack of usefulness, but because of a language ban and the persecution of its speakers. Today things are different: the lack of economic value is one of the most salient arguments that the revitalizers of Wymysiöeryś have to face, even though there are other essential benefits and assets that the local language can offer the community. And numerous groups, in different geographic and cultural contexts, share this situation.

Therefore, when you engage in language revitalization you have to be prepared to face many strong counterarguments, coming both from communities themselves and from potential founders or sponsors. Unlike linguists and other academics, who usually have a stable economic situation, members of minority communities often lack job opportunities, and face highly insecure and harsh material conditions as well as a lack of prospects. For some communities at least, an important goal is not to maintain their language, which has been the source of stigmatization, shame, discrimination, and disadvantage, but to secure better living conditions. How to respond to such arguments and encourage local communities to engage in language revitalization? Furthermore, funding institutions, politicians, and state agendas – despite superficial declarations recognizing the value of linguistic-cultural diversity and minority rights – are rather unlikely to offer serious commitment to language revitalization based on arguments of the beauty of diversity, human rights, social justice, or even cognitive benefits.

The market value of learning major, dominant, and/or international languages is widely appreciated and promoted in educational and language policies. The economic value of languages is usually linked to their role as assets on the job market or as a source of added value to products or services, for instance, where languages can provide links to specific places, experiences, or a feeling of authenticity. However, the perceived and recognized economic value almost never, or rarely, extends to minority or immigrant languages and nonstandard language varieties. Economic benefits and commercialization are an often neglected dimension of language revitalization programs, despite being of key importance: many languages cease to be spoken precisely because of their perceived lack of utility and economic value.

It does not have to be this way, as the use of minority or local languages in business can lead to brand differentiation and more personalized, localized, and thus competitive offers, which increase the customer experience. The recognition of these benefits, in the eyes of both speakers and local entrepreneurs, is crucial for successful revitalization efforts. Responding to this need, minority language advocacy in a number of European countries has promoted the use of local languages in businesses, enterprises, and public services. Relatively recent efforts to embrace both grassroots and governmental initiatives have been used to promote Welsh, Scottish Gaelic, Irish, and Basque/Euskara. This can start on a microscale within selected local businesses and services. Similar policies may even be adopted by larger companies. For example, the Irish railway companies Iarnród Éireann and Luas and the national airline carrier, Aer Lingus, have incorporated some announcements in Irish. However, the airline employees use just a few words in Irish and this has a decorative function rather than a communicative role, because the safety demonstration is never given in Irish.[3] Passengers also complain about the mistakes made in the greetings and the lack of language skills of the crew. While such steps increase language visibility, they do not necessarily have a real impact on using the language and showing its utility. In this respect, local and grassroots initiatives are of key importance. Among possible strategies is the creation of local spaces, activities, and products that are closely linked to the heritage tongue, but have some economic potential. A quite different, but equally important, option is to promote multilingual workspaces. These have the potential to generate new solutions and ideas because of the creative capacity of their multiethnic members. Opportunities will of course differ from place to place. In this chapter, I discuss some possible general paths, as well as specific (but by no means exhaustive) examples, of generating economic benefits for communities based on their local linguistic and cultural heritage. A closely related challenge is that of marketing and promoting language revitalization, with regard to both community members and external actors or institutions.

Use of Traditional Knowledge for Subsistence and Environmental Strategies

An important path for generating economic benefits involves promoting the role of traditional knowledge and local languages in shaping sustainable relationships with the natural environment. It seems that biological and linguistic diversities are sometimes threatened by the same factors, such as urbanization and industrialization. Likewise, the high numbers of endangered species in these areas correlate with high levels of linguistic diversity. Some of the most evident examples of such zones are New Guinea, the Amazon rainforest, the Congo basin forests, and the North American deserts. As shrinkage of the natural landscape leads to the endangerment of certain plants and animals, it also makes it difficult for Indigenous minorities to

---

[3] See, for example, H. Kelly-Holmes, *Advertising as Multilingual Communication* (Basingstoke: Palgrave Macmillan, 2005). On a similar case of the Corsica Airlines see: A. Jaffe and C. Oliva, 'Linguistic Creativity in Corsican Tourist Context', in S. Pietikäinen and H. Kelly-Holmes (eds.), *Multilingualism and the Periphery* (Oxford/New York: Oxford University Press, 2013), pp. 102–103.

practice their traditional ways of life and, consequently, their languages. And traditional Indigenous models of managing natural resources are known to indirectly support biological diversity and balanced economic activities. However, because of policies of cultural and linguistic assimilation, Indigenous communities sometimes lose their knowledge of the environment and thus their ability to interact with it.

Such losses can be disastrous for whole ways of life, like abandoning agriculture as the subsistence base of existence or losing access to certain kinds of animals and plants (because of their extinction or due to forced resettlements, as was the case of Indigenous people in the USA, who were moved to reservations). Often, as in the case of the Nahuas in Tlaxcala, Mexico, losing the language and accepting national culture is accompanied by a switch to wage labor, usually outside the home community. At the same time, members of Nahua communities explain that increased levels of diabetes and obesity are caused by the introduction of artificial fertilizers and nontraditional foods. And the access to modern medical services does not seem to recompense the diminishing role of traditional healing. As the oldest speakers say, many of the beneficial plants that had been accessible before ceased to grow in the community, while knowledge about them that had been conveyed in the heritage language waned too. Such changes – and many others – have severe consequences, not only for local communities, but also for entire regions and so should be of interest for policy makers at regional and state levels. Therefore, language revitalization can be seen as an efficient strategy for maintaining, promoting, and exploiting local knowledge and managing the environment. Local language may become an essential 'brick' in a wider development strategy. A part of this should include its recognition as an important asset for both local sustainability and its attractiveness for visitors and entrepreneurs. All of these assets and arguments can be used by revitalizers to deal with institutions, politicians, entrepreneurs, and the communities where they work.

But what can be done in practice? It is widely documented that local languages are valuable reservoirs of environmental and practical knowledge. They are often keys to ethnobotany and ethnozoology, as well as very practical applications of local knowledge. It may refer, for example, to the use of herbs and medicinal plants, balanced management of crops and edible plants, or wise usage of animal resources with regard to their reproductive cycles. This kind of knowledge, ordered, classified, and expressed in local languages and combined with traditional practices, is often essential for maintaining sustainable relations with flora and fauna. On the other hand, cultural practices related to the environment include the ways in which natural resources are extracted and used. The study of this can be an essential part of language documentation and language revitalization projects, be they driven by the community or in partnership with external actors. This knowledge, in turn, can be recovered and reintroduced into the community, taking into account new contexts and dynamic environmental, social and economic conditions. Its potential in fact reaches beyond one particular place and should become an important element of marketing language revitalization outside the community. Specific strategies can embrace a very broad range of activities, approaches, and economic goals, depending on the environmental and cultural context. This may include balanced approaches to agriculture and ecological crop production, fishing, herding, pasturing, harvesting, gathering, raising livestock, and combining traditional subsistence modes with small-scale production (textiles, ceramics, wood products, etc.).

A good example of such an approach is provided by the linguistic-cultural revitalization programs run by the Sámi people in Norway and Finland, for example in Kautokeino. Language instruction and academic research there are closely linked to local food production and conservation, reindeer herding, fishing, and traditional medicine. In 2005 the Norwegian Government established the International Centre for Reindeer Husbandry in Kautokeino. It aims to maintain and develop sustainable reindeer husbandry in the north, to foster cooperation between the reindeer herding peoples, and to document and apply their traditional knowledge. In 2016 a calendar called 'Boazojahki', written entirely in the Sámi language, was created and launched by Karen Marie Eira Buljo. Aimed primarily at children and youth, it detailed the calendar year in terms of what it means for reindeer, reindeer herders, and the activities prescribed for each specific time of the year. Each month unveiled rich insights into the cyclical world of reindeer husbandry based on the natural environment. Importantly, theoretical and practical aspects of food production, reindeer herding, and traditional environmental strategies are an important focus of classes and seminars in Sámi Allaskuvla, or the Sámi University of Applied Sciences. Students learn the heritage language through active participation in traditional activities, such as fishing or preparing food. They also learn about subsistence strategies and the food production modes of traditional cultures in other parts of the world. This example may serve as inspiration for developing educational programs aimed at a deeper understanding of the role of the local environment (see Capsule 15.6). Ideally, as in the Sámi case, programmes should combine learning of the ancestral language with environmental studies and practical knowledge.

A useful framework for this kind of approach toward language, environment, and economic strategies is that of social economy, which addresses consumer behaviors and needs in the context of social justice, ethics, and other humanitarian values. Initiatives in social economy are run by cooperatives, NGOs (associations, foundations), social enterprises, and institutions. These groups often focus their efforts on the ideas of solidarity and responsibility, fostering socially inclusive wealth and well-being, or developing new solutions for social or environmental challenges. An important principle is that of not-for-profit aims; gains and resources are reinvested for the benefit of disadvantaged groups or communities. Such an approach contributes to a more sustainable and inclusive society. It also perfectly fits the situation of marginalized communities struggling to preserve their languages. Thus, a possible strategy to link the improvement of environmental and/or subsistence issues with language maintenance or revitalization is through community-based cooperatives and/or associations, as well as external NGOs or institutions interested in developing partnership with local community members and activists.

Linguistic, Cultural, and Educational Tourism

The economic potential of linguistic-cultural heritage can be specifically oriented toward tourism. Recent processes of globalization and homogenization have created a demand for unique and original products and services. Many people are no longer interested in highly commoditized and standardized forms of experience and mass tourism. Rather, they seek uniqueness and authenticity, experiencing the history, culture, and natural environment of less explored places and their inhabitants. Research on tourism in Europe reveals that 'cultural visitors' usually have a higher level of education and professional status. Many of them look for 'authentic' cultural traditions and ways of life, which they wish to experience themselves. Such preferences are, for example, addressed through the creation of 'cultural villages' in South Africa.[4] Located in different environments and in the territories of ethnic groups, such 'villages' offer unique opportunities for experiencing their lifestyles, including cultural and religious activities, crafts, and food – and also for hearing different local languages. For example, DumaZulu Lodge & Traditional Village (Hluhluwe) is advertised as 'A unique cross-cultural experience in the authentic Zulu Village and Hotel. Traditional Zulu customs, tribal dancing, tales of ancient lore.' Lesedi cultural village lures visitors with an 'amazing multicultural dance show. As the sun sets over the African bush, you're escorted to the Boma for a very interactive affair of traditional singing and dancing, which depict stories dating back to the days of their ancestors'. Of course, visitors are offered comfortable lodging and exquisite restaurants that only remotely resemble traditional life, if at all. And local languages are usually presented as an exotic extra on 'polished' tourist products and services. However, this basic idea can be adapted for a community-driven or community-managed (and more economically accessible!) touristic experience, where local ways and languages are not reduced to merely decorative functions. And if the communities can be in charge of this 'offer' and play a decisive role in

---

[4] www.places.co.za/html/cultural_villages.html

developing services, then the income generated can support language revitalization activities and the general well-being of inhabitants.[5]

The concept behind this type of tourism has been called the experience economy. It focuses not on offering commodities and commoditized services, but on different forms of experience, often based on 'memorable' events. When thinking about language revitalization and the commercialization of linguistic heritage, the experience economy can be seen as a particularly useful concept for tourism, cultural and artistic activities, or even the linguistic-cultural landscape. Products offered in the market can range from being entirely standardized and undifferentiated to being highly differentiated 'special' goods or services. Those related to a unique endangered heritage will definitely be at the latter end of this continuum. And because there is high interest among consumers in having 'unique' experiences, more and more businesses take this demand into account. Emotional responses, experiences of authenticity and uniqueness, exposure to local stories and local knowledge – all this can be brought into play when thinking about commercializing endangered linguistic and cultural heritage. Being exposed to and, ultimately, learning an endangered language is an important aspect of the experience economy. No wonder, heritage marketing has become a growing branch of the tourism industry where local and lesser-known languages are employed. However, this is often done rather superficially at the level of limited (and usually bilingual) 'labeling', which is an easy way of providing nostalgic or authenticity-seeking tourists with experiences of 'traditional culture'.

The real challenge – and opportunity – is to link those experiences to genuine language revitalization and promotion efforts, without reducing them to purely symbolic or folkloric dimensions. Folklorization or 'self-folklorization', the marketing of one's culture to outsiders, is characterized by some as 'identity for sale', the result of prolonged symbolic violence and colonization that reduces cultural differences to the level of esthetics, but replicates social inequalities and divisions.[6] However, it can also be understood as a strategy against social degradation and cultural annihilation. Hylton White, who did extensive anthropological research in the Republic of South Africa, relates the case of one of the groups of Bushmen, who lived in urban slums but earned their living performing the traditional skills and cultural activities of nomads in a setting arranged for tourists. Of course, this can be interpreted as gain-motivated performance designed to meet the expectations of visitors and detached from the way of life of its actors. However, the words of the leader

---

[5] See, for example, H. Kelly-Holmes and S. Pietikäinen, 'Commodifying Sámi Culture in an Indigenous Tourism Site', *Journal of Sociolinguistics*, 18/4 (2014), 518–538.

[6] E. Klekot, 'Samofolkloryzacja. Współczesna sztuka ludowa z perspektywy postkolonialnej', *Kultura Współczesna*, 81 (2014), 86–99.

of this group, shared with the anthropologist, challenge this perspective: 'I am an animal of nature. I want people to see me and know who I am. The only way our tradition and way of life can survive is to live in the memory of the people who see us'.[7]

Keeping in mind tangible risks associated with the folklorization and commodification of local heritage, possible initiatives could focus on developing tourist enclaves distinguished by a unique language spoken in the area. Preserving a local tongue may be combined with creating both physical 'living' museums in the community, as well as virtual digital museums. What would distinguish such places over other local or regional museums would be the focus on an endangered language that could actually be heard in those spaces, with its speakers and their unique histories, local knowledge, and traditions expressed in the heritage tongue. Local knowledge – for example, environmental knowledge and sustainable management of natural resources – can also be useful for the present and future of visitors. Digital tools, such as interactive displays or games, will certainly be an important component of this kind of initiative, greatly enhancing the attractiveness of the language and its association with modern technology. Such places are also excellent venues for organizing regular workshops and artistic or educational activities linked to local heritage, both for the local community and for outsiders. The participation of visitors in these activities would generate an economic gain for local activists. Thus, such spaces could be used both to foster language learning and use, increase community engagement, generate funding by attracting tourists, stimulate positive language attitudes, and, finally, become an important venue for marketing language revitalization.

Of course, both the physical space and digital tools needed for these activities require substantial funding. When a community or municipality is unable to secure funds locally, they can look for them outside. Creating cultural infrastructures and digital tools is often supported by programs that are offered by regional, federal, or state agencies and institutions, or even private foundations. In the countries of the European Union it is possible to compete for funding within special programs available at both state and pan-European level. In some of them it is useful to have an academic partner to apply with: others, however, are only available for municipalities, cultural institutions, and NGOs (see Chapter 5). Initiatives linked to the creation of local language spaces are also likely to increase the sense of community and vitality of a given group, to promote local activism and language specialists, as well as to deepen the awareness of linguistic-cultural heritage in the region and beyond. Examples of linking local languages to tourism include Gaelic in

---

[7] H. White, *In the Tradition of the Forefathers: Bushman Traditionality at Kagga Kamma: The Politics and History of a Performative Identity* (Cape Town: University of Cape Town Press, 1995), p. 1.

Figure 9.1 The performance and agency of Indigenous communities. The group of Zohuameh Citlalimeh, San Francisco Tetlanohcan, Mexico. Photo by Justyna Olko

Scotland and Ireland, Manx on the Isle of Man, Māori in New Zealand, or Welsh in the United Kingdom. However, it is difficult to estimate to what degree touristic interest in these languages has in fact increased their vitality and use. Nevertheless, they have received more visibility and at least some of the local communities have benefitted from tourism.

No doubt, showing the usefulness and value of an endangered language is an important outcome of these initiatives and can foster actual language use. One can also hope to mobilize the community and attract new speakers. An example of one such ongoing initiative comes from Wilamowice, a small town in southern Poland preserving a unique language, Wymysiöeryś, which has developed and been spoken since the thirteenth century (see Capsule 6.1). Persecution and the language ban of 1945 meant that Wymysiöeryś almost became extinct toward the end of the past century. However, it is now the focus of vigorous revitalization efforts. Alongside other components of the revitalization program, some of its most engaged participants and researchers, Bartłomiej Chromik, along with local activists Justyna Majerska-Sznajder and Tymoteusz Król, launched the project *Creation of a tourist cluster in the Wilamowice Commune on the basis of Wymysiöeryś* in 2015 (with the support of the Foundation for Polish Science).

This project was undertaken due to concerns that positive language attitudes and practices in Wilamowice may reverse when new users of Wymysiöeryś move out of the town after completing their education. With the aim of preventing or limiting this situation, project members designed a strategy for creating workplaces that would stimulate the usage of Wymysiöeryś through the development of tourism. The basic assumption was that the creation of a tourism cluster embracing the whole municipality (both Wilamowice and surrounding villages) would not only bring economic impact to language revitalization activities, but also help to create a more sustainable, long-term strategy for the community. Young Polish designers, ethnographers, and an IT specialist were invited to collaborate on this initiative. Together with local activists, they designed and created prototype souvenirs inspired by the culture of Wilamowice, as well as board and computer games and a system of plaques with tourist information.[8] These products are being sold at all events focusing on Wymysiöeryś and organized by the local NGO. They will also be available for sale in the future museum of local linguistic-cultural heritage. The concept of this museum was in fact developed during a collaborative international field school of the Engaged Humanities project of the University of Warsaw, SOAS, University of London, and Leiden University in 2016 held in Wilamowice. After the field school had finished local authorities decided to support the idea of a 'living museum' that would serve both as the focus of the tourist cluster and as an artistic and educational space linked to the revitalization of Wymysiöeryś. The selected architectural design of the museum envisions a large space for the local amateur theater group performing in Wymysiöeryś and for educational workshops that will be offered for local and external participants.

Developing linguistic tourism can be enhanced by commercializing handicrafts and ethno-design products, especially when they can be explicitly linked to the local language. In Wilamowice these products embrace T-shirts, mugs, badges, and bags with word plays in Wymysiöeryś, a wide range of woven products (a traditional industry in the town) including items of clothing and accessories, and a language game (see Figure 9.2). On the Isle of Man, widely distributed products include T-shirts, home textiles, and coasters for cups and glasses with texts in Manx. All traditional communities have their own craftwork, be it ceramics, basketry, wood carvings, or textiles, and these can be linked to the heritage language in numerous ways, as can their distribution, marketing, and sale.

The activities in Wilamowice also involved marking out tourist paths and preparing plaques in Wymysiöeryś, Polish, and English about spots of historical and present-day importance. These plaques provide rich information about the town and its heritage. In addition, they form important components of the local linguistic landscape and this has a strong positive impact, improving previously negative attitudes toward Wymysiöeryś, and giving more visibility

---

[8] http://etnoprojekt.pl/2.0

Figure 9.2 Local products sold during the Mother Tongue Day in Wilamowice. Photo by Piotr Strojnowski, © Engaged Humanities Project, University of Warsaw

Figure 9.3 A local store with some names and announcements in Nahuatl, San Miguel Tenango, Mexico. Photo by Justyna Olko

to ongoing revitalization activities. The project also created a tourist guide that is available in Polish and English. It is downloadable from a special webpage focusing on tourism in Willamowice.[9] This website serves as a virtual substitute for the traditional tourist information point and it can encourage visitors to come to the town. To make city tours even more attractive, the team created and tested a quest game based on the topography of Wilamowice. It was developed together with local teenagers who learn the language and wanted to be involved in the development of tourism. The description of questing is available on the website, which also provides information about activities and workshops that can be of interest for both community members and visitors. In fact, scenarios of workshops focusing on the local language, traditions, and handicrafts (costume, weaving, dances, etc.) were also developed during the same project. Additionally, young new speakers of the language were trained to serve as guides in the town for tours based on linguistic-cultural heritage.

Taken together, these initiatives and activities are expected to create permanent jobs associated with language revitalization, as well as stable forms of social and community engagement. This includes language classes in the local school (initiated in 2013 as a result of collaborative efforts of local activists and engaged researchers from the University of Warsaw and Adam Mickiewicz University in Poznań), the production of local souvenirs and ethno-design merchandize, a soon-to-be-opened living museum, the creation of a new infrastructure for touristic groups, as well as workshops and artistic activities with a strong potential for commercialization. Artistic activities include a local theater group operating under the patronage of the Polish Theatre in Warsaw, which also hosts special plays in Wymysiöeryś performed by Wilamovian youths. Such events (along with media campaigns launched in all our collaborative projects) are essential for the positive marketing of minority languages in Poland. They increase awareness of linguistic diversity in the country (despite postwar homogenization and dominant national ideology) and create more supportive attitudes within broader society.

The example of Wilamowice shows that such strategies have made a difference in one relatively small community. However, they can also be applied on a larger scale for languages with more speakers. For example, in Wales, and especially in its northern part, proficiency in Welsh is seen as a valuable asset in the labor market, especially in the domains of local and national governments, administration, education, tourism, and media. Creating work opportunities for Welsh speakers in their communities has shown the economic potential of the language and has contributed to its growth. The language is also seen as an

---

[9] www.turystyka.wilamowice.pl

opportunity for manufacturers and retailers, and is one of the driving forces for the economic growth in Wales. Also in the case of Irish, local organizations promote the value of incorporating the language visually into businesses, with product labels, signage, menus, or stationery. Here the Irish language is used as a resource for business, a domain that has, until now, been reserved for English. They also encourage nonfluent new speakers of Irish to engage in such initiatives. More fluent entrepreneurs and shopkeepers go beyond bilingual signage, as they create an Irish-language experience for their customers, encouraging them to develop their language skills and use.[10] An important impact of such initiatives is to link the minority language to practical day-to-day life, including economic and social activities.

Marketing and Promoting Language Revitalization

Both linguistic tourism and management of environment should become essential elements of marketing and promoting language revitalization. This, in turn, is essential for improving language attitudes, language use, and levels of activism or support both inside and outside a specific community. Marketing a minority language is needed to increase its social status and to encourage a higher level of commitment from native speakers, language learners, potential new speakers, as well as broader society. The awareness of this necessity is growing. Over two decades ago it was pointed out that although the New Zealand government had started to spend large sums of money on preschool language nests, immersion primary schools as well as other initiatives, its language policies were not accompanied by marketing a sufficiently positive image of the language. This lack of marketing hindered some of the investments in language revitalization, even though promoting the Māori language has been one of the major tasks of the Māori Language Commission, established in 1987. The target audience of Māori campaigns has become the wider population of New Zealand. Also marketing intergenerational transmission among Māori families and learners of the language has been seen as another key necessity.[11]

Marketing language revitalization is also crucial for generating funding for revitalization activities. What kind of solid arguments can you give to skeptical community members, parents, or grandparents, who remember

---

[10] S. Brennan and B. O'Rourke, 'Commercialising the cúpla focal: New speakers, language ownership, and the promotion of Irish as a business resource', *Language in Society* 48 (2018), 125–45. doi: 10.1017/S0047404518001148.

[11] R. Nicholson, 'Marketing the Māori Language', in J. Reyhner (ed.), *Teaching Indigenous Languages* (Flagstaff, AZ: Northern Arizona University, 1997), pp. 206–13.

language discrimination and violence, or to policy makers, academics, and sponsors? Connecting language revitalization to local tourism and to sound environmental knowledge is not the only possible advantage: there are also other benefits with significant economic impact. As we learned in Chapter 1, multilingual individuals have increased intellectual potential, reflected in greater flexibility and capacity for task solving as well as higher social skills. This applies to children, adults, and the elderly – for the latter the usage of more than one language can hinder cognitive decline and possibly delay the onset of symptoms of dementia. Research also shows that language revitalization and the use of the mother tongue throughout the stages of an individual's development are not only closely linked to improvements in self-esteem, but also to better health. Moreover, we know that a strong correlation exists between language loss and deterioration in Indigenous health (e.g. the presence of diabetes), with symptoms associated with posttraumatic stress, elevated suicide rates, and alcoholism.[12]

Preserving the heritage language simply helps to prevent these problems and to deal with them if they are present. As numerous studies and testimonies have shown, speaking a heritage or ancestral language or going back to it in the process of 'individual revitalization' in connection to ancestral roots and ethnic identity, greatly improves psychological well-being. As psychological and medical studies have revealed it also allows us to deal better with stress, illness, and experienced trauma or discrimination.[13] Thus, if the negative forces of language loss are reversed, we can expect beneficial results: not only better health, but also better functioning in society and in the job market. And this, in turn, has impact for the cost of medical healthcare and the general economy. Indeed, language revitalizers could argue that a relatively modest investment in an endangered language (in the scale of a state's expenditures!) can substantially lower the costs of healthcare and social services. And, as argued before, it can generate economic assets for marginalized, often poor communities, reducing the need for the state's help. Put in economic jargon, language revitalization has the

---

[12] E.g. J. Ball and K. Moselle, *Contributions of Culture and Language in Aboriginal Head Start in Urban and Northern Communities to Children's Health Outcomes: A Review of Theory and Research* (Division of Children, Seniors & Healthy Development, Health Promotion and Chronic Disease Prevention Branch, Public Health Agency of Canada, 2013); O. McIvor, A. Napoleon, and K. Dickie, 'Language and culture as protective factors for at-risk communities', *Journal of Aboriginal Health* 5/1 (2009), 6–25.

[13] E.g. C. Haslam, J. Jetten, and S. A. Haslam, 'Advancing the social cure. Implications for theory, practice and policy', in J. Jetten, C. Haslam, and S. A. Haslam (eds.), *The Social Cure: Identity, Health and Well-Being* (London: Psychology Press, 2011), pp. 319–44; M. Skrodzka, K. Hansen, J. Olko, M. Bilewicz, 'The twofold role of a minority language in historical trauma: The case of Lemko minority in Poland', *Journal of Language and Social Psychology*, 39/4 (2020), 551–566.

potential to contribute to a reduction in the direct and indirect costs of many diseases, improving the human capital (the knowledge, skills, and habits crucial for the ability to work and create economic value) of a given region.

Speakers of minority languages can also positively influence the labor market. We already know that multilingual individuals, including users of nondominant languages, are important assets for employers because they represent an investment in the diversity of the creative potential of a company. Individuals with high esteem who are proud of their ethnic origin will perform much better than those who are ashamed of their identity and no longer communicate in their heritage languages. The promotion of multilingualism may also help to reduce poor labor choices driven by racism and dominant linguistic ideologies. Persons with lower self-esteem are often underemployed in positions below their actual potential. This may also happen if employers are driven by prejudice based on the origin or ethnic affiliation of potential workers, so it is essential to raise their awareness about the benefits of multi-ethnic labor force. Thus, the efficient marketing of minority languages can bring economic benefits not only to their speakers, but also to other sectors or groups in wider society.

The positive image and recognition of a minority language can sometimes do more good for language use than concrete revitalization or teaching activities. And, conversely, the absence of positive marketing in prestigious spaces may effectively hinder the use of the language. To give an example of such a situation I will quote the words of one of the young speakers of Nahuatl in the Mexican state of Puebla:

Quemman, quemman polihuiz nahuatlahtolli naltepeuh, tleca tlacameh ihuan cihuameh amo quimatih ihuipan sirve para qué, para qué sirve, tleca, tlen ipatiuh. Nochtin tlacameh ihuan cihuameh amo tlahtoah ipan iyolloco centro, ipan Ayuntamiento [...] Porque tleca personas amo tlahtoah nahuatlahtolli, entonces amo patiyoh. Amo patiyoh quimatih nahuatlahtolli.

Yes, yes Nahuatl will perish in my town because the men and the women do not know what it can be used for, what it can be used for, why, what is its value. All the men and the women, they don't speak [Nahuatl] in the town center, in the municipality. Because those people do not speak Nahuatl, so it has no value. They know that Nahuatl has no value. (Cuetlaxcoapan, Puebla, 2015, speaker in his late twenties)

The absence of the language in municipal offices and local businesses is a powerful negative sign for speakers, signifying denial of the value and utility of the local language. However, even a small investment in visual recognition in the public sphere ('linguistic landscape') or the presence of the language in public services not only creates jobs for speakers and gives their language some prestige, but also conveys a message to the community that the language actually *is* useful. For this reason, some of the stores in Wilamowice and the local vicinity, as part of an initiative with local entrepreneurs, plan to adopt bilingual marking of their products. At the same time, our more recent step in Wilamowice, accomplished in collaboration with the local NGO and the municipal authorities, was to hang a huge banner on the municipal building located in the main square in the town. It announced to the inhabitants and visitors that *S'Wymysiöeryśy śtejt uf,* 'Wymysiöeryś rises to its feet'.

10 Local Power Relationships, Community Dynamics, and Stakeholders

Wesley Y. Leonard

Among the lessons I learned from my late grandfather, Miami Tribe of Oklahoma Chief waapimaankwa (White Loon, 1925–2008), is the importance of understanding relationships – among people, places, ideas, and institutions – and the associated community dynamics. He knew that in order for the Miami people to be successful, the efforts of our tribal government had to be aligned with the values and norms of our community, and he thus spent a lot of time talking to community members and asking about their perspectives. My grandfather's wisdom combined traditional Miami tribal knowledge with Western education, along with years of experience in leading our tribal nation toward economic sustainability and reclamation of our culture and language, myaamia. He championed the revitalization of myaamia, which was erroneously labeled 'extinct' in the categories of Western science because it went out of use almost completely in the 1960s. As such, a foundational means of fostering relationships within our community – through our language – became compromised. However, myaamia was well documented in a large body of written records prior to its dormancy, and from these records the Miami community started learning myaamia so that we could build stronger relationships with each other, with our tribal lands, and with our ancestors. I did not have access to myaamia until I was a young adult in the 1990s, when revitalization efforts began, but I am proud that I now hear Miami children speaking it.

In this chapter, I offer a synthesis of key ideas that have emerged from the application of my grandfather's wisdom to my language revitalization experiences within the Miami community and in other Indigenous communities, primarily smaller groups in the United States and Canada. I began this work in the late 1990s as a Miami tribal member and a (then nascent, now professional) linguist, and I write from this perspective. I offer this commentary with the caveat that lessons from my experiences will not apply to all communities that are engaged in language revitalization. Indeed, communities and language situations are diverse; each must be examined in its own context because revitalization is ultimately a local phenomenon, even though it occurs with global influences. Having said this, as also shown throughout the other chapters in this book, there are recurrent themes in language endangerment and the associated responses. The key theme for the current chapter is that language revitalization occurs among people who have relationships with each other and with their languages. It is important to focus on these relationships when planning, implementing, or assessing a revitalization effort.

I begin this discussion by clarifying my use of certain terms: POWER, POWER RELATIONS, and COMMUNITY DYNAMICS. Often, particularly in discussions of politics or economics, 'power' refers to the authority, and the associated ability, to *control* people and resources. For the current discussion, I adopt a more general definition of 'power', one that is more representative of my grandfather's approach to leadership: the ability of individuals or groups to produce an effect, including *guiding and empowering* the actions of others.[1] I use 'power relations' as it is commonly employed in social sciences to refer to relationships in which one person or group has higher ability, by virtue of their social positions and resources, to influence the actions of another person or group. By 'community dynamics', I refer to the totality of relationships and power relations in a given community, as well as the underlying historical, cultural, legal, and other factors that inform how people relate to each other.

Understanding Power and Community Dynamics

A general principle of language revitalization is that it both builds and disrupts community dynamics at the same time. To understand why this is so, it is useful to consider two questions that are closely related conceptually, but whose answers can be very different:

- What are the social dynamics within a given community?
- What do the members of a given community believe to be their ideal social dynamics?

While language revitalization occurs within a context of actual community dynamics, it is very often linked to broader efforts to restore traditional values and community health – that is, to move toward a different community dynamics. In other words, language revitalization is a response to a misalignment between a community's actual practices and its ideal practices, and although it ultimately restores community well-being, the mismatches that occur during the process can be a source of significant tension.

---

[1] 'Power' is meant neutrally here, but in contexts where it has come to have specific (especially negative) connotations, one might instead use different terms or clarify power relations through questions such as, 'Who is expected to guide whom, who listens to whom, and why?'

The disconnect between actual and ideal community dynamics can be particularly severe when a language has gone out of use completely, as occurred with myaamia. In these situations, the traditional norms of language transmission and socialization that many people believe to be ideal must at least temporarily be modified. For example, an ideal I have frequently heard articulated in Indigenous communities is that languages should be transmitted through everyday cultural practices from older generations to youth. In my community, this ideal of course could not be realized in our initial stage of revitalization, which entailed learning myaamia from documents. In communities where the only first-language speakers are elders, a different problem sometimes results: 'speaker' may become overly associated with 'elder', although this link exists only because of language endangerment. Such thinking can work against revitalization if it fosters a situation in which younger people are deemed to never be legitimate speakers, even when they learn a language to a high level of proficiency. The role of writing presents another noteworthy example: The ideal may be for a language to *not* be written. However, given that revitalization responds to a situation in which traditional language transmission mechanisms have been compromised, writing may become necessary. Ideas about gender provide yet another example: Community members' ideas about gendered cultural roles may clash with the values held by other community members, and might also conflict with practical needs even when there is agreement about gender roles. For instance, there may not be any speakers of the appropriate gender to perform a given traditional activity.

I have found two interventions to be useful for addressing conflicts that arise in these situations. First is open acknowledgement and discussion of the idea that language revitalization often entails engaging in social practices that are different from the 'ideal' community dynamic, but that can serve as a means of moving toward different social norms should community members want this. Second is recognition that conflicting opinions about community dynamics, while challenging to deal with in the moment, provide evidence that people are invested in their community's future, and this is a good thing.

Power also can guide beliefs about language structure (grammar and vocabulary in particular) and norms of use.[2] Describing, researching, and especially learning and speaking languages promote certain ways of understanding, and by extension of thinking about, language. A common

---

[2] Here I refer not only to the possible ways a given idea could be expressed in a given language, but also to whether an idea would be expressed at all, and if so, who would be expected to say it to whom in what context.

phenomenon is that whatever is true for the people who have social power becomes the 'correct' grammar and pronunciation for a given language, as well as the 'right' way to think about it. Key for revitalization planning, therefore, is the identification of the underlying community dynamics in a language revitalization effort and consideration of how these play out in guiding language beliefs and practices.

The same principle also applies to language resource materials. Even something that is called 'language description' and has no intent of imposing a certain way of speaking may nevertheless have this effect, especially when the person creating the description has higher social status than the person learning from it. Commonly this happens in language revitalization contexts with published language materials, such as grammar reference books whose descriptions can take on a level of truth, though they are arguably examples of possible analyses by experts trained with particular tools. A strategy for minimizing this problem is to acknowledge (and celebrate) the specific backgrounds of individual speakers and researchers who have contributed to creating language resources. For language speakers, this includes mention of where they learned the language and other factors that inform how they speak and think about language. For researchers, this includes noting how their training influences what they notice and conclude, as well as how they present their analyses.

Another important issue arises with outside researchers, such as linguists, which is that their credentials and expert status often cooccur with racial and socioeconomic privilege, both of which enhance social power. Even researchers who are themselves members of language communities, as is the case for me, often enjoy relatively high social power, though of course equally important as professional credentials are their other traits such as age, gender, membership in a given family, and previous community engagement. As a general lesson, one might say that everybody involved in a language revitalization effort benefits from being aware of these issues, and that the people with higher social power have an increased responsibility to acknowledge how what they say and do may influence others, regardless of intent.

Identifying and Respecting All Stakeholders

Recognizing that tribal community dynamics do not occur in a vacuum, a general practice of my grandfather was to look beyond our tribal community and to foster alliances with members of other communities. This practice has come to characterize myaamia language revitalization programs, which ultimately are for Miami people but nevertheless include non-Miami people in a variety of roles. That is to say, myaamia language revitalization, similar to other cases of Indigenous language revitalization, has many STAKEHOLDERS – people and institutions with a concern and interest in the process. In this section, I address types of stakeholders and the importance of identifying and considering their perspectives.

For this discussion, I call attention to two major categories of stakeholders in situations of language endangerment and revitalization: COMMUNITY-INTERNAL STAKEHOLDERS and COMMUNITY-EXTERNAL STAKEHOLDERS. Within the former group are the community members with language knowledge,[3] current and future language learners, community leaders in language programs and elsewhere, and others with various levels of community engagement. Within the latter group are researchers whose professional work engages with Indigenous languages, various governments, funding agencies, educational institutions and educators, and the wider public.[4]

Frequently omitted in discussions of stakeholders, but very important for understanding Indigenous language revitalization and related work, is that many communities also recognize stakeholders beyond living humans. Ancestors, for example, may be stakeholders; my late grandfather is among the stakeholders of myaamia language revitalization. A higher power, however conceived of or named, may have provided the gift of language to the community and thus becomes a stakeholder that must be thanked and honored. Similarly, beyond being the literal foundation on which people speak and transmit languages, land may be a key stakeholder. Indeed, specific landscapes are reflected in the grammar and vocabulary of Indigenous languages, and this reflects the relationship between communities and places. To ensure that the full set of stakeholders in a given context can emerge, it is important that 'relationship' be defined broadly.

After identifying all stakeholders in a given language context, I have found it useful to consider the following areas to understand their engagement and perspectives: NEEDS, EXPERTISE, and GOALS. For ease of presentation, I discuss each area separately, though they are interrelated (as with everything else) and thus must be evaluated together.

---

[3] In much of the literature on language endangerment and revitalization, there is strong emphasis on fluent speakers who acquired the language as children through prototypical intergenerational transmission, with much less recognition of the linguistic knowledge held by others who do not meet this 'speaker' prototype. I use the term 'language knowledge' in recognition that speakerhood exists in many forms, all of which have value.

[4] In real-life situations, there is rarely a clean split between community-internal and community-external stakeholders. Community members can take on the interests of outside institutions that they are part of, and so-called external stakeholders, despite lacking heritage in a given community, may have very strong community relationships.

NEEDS: Community needs will presumably include language resources, but I omit a discussion of this point because, in my experience, it is generally self-evident to most stakeholders (though the usefulness of the resources that get provided varies significantly). Somewhat less self-evident, in my experience, have been needs that go beyond language such as a means to earn a living, whether direct (a salary for language work, for example), or indirect (as might occur when university-based scholars are expected to publish about the revitalization work they are engaged in). Identifying and responding to these kinds of needs is crucial for revitalization program sustainability over the long term. Also tremendously important, and in my experience frequently overlooked by community-external stakeholders (though sometimes also by community-internal stakeholders), is that language revitalization requires great emotional and spiritual work, thus creating the need for appropriate support. For example, I have found learning myaamia to be very empowering, but it also serves as a reminder of the colonial violence that my ancestors experienced. I thus seek support through relationships with other Indigenous people, both within my community and beyond, who are also reclaiming their languages of heritage in the face of ongoing colonialism.

EXPERTISE: While there are sometimes expectations about what one *should* give to a revitalization effort, I argue that focusing instead on what one *can* give, and *wants to* give, is a better practice. Linguistic knowledge is often highlighted as the key resource in contexts of language endangerment, and indeed many people emphasize language speakers and their importance. However, there is a problem with reducing full persons, who have a variety of roles and relationships, to 'speakers' and evaluating them accordingly. Speakers, as with other stakeholders, have various types of knowledge and experience beyond language, and bring preexisting relationships and networks into revitalization projects. They also have diverse needs, which are easy to overlook when a person is reduced to a single trait, such as being a speaker. Putting the focus instead on full persons and all of their relationships is thus called for. More generally, 'expertise' for speakers *and* other stakeholders must be understood broadly to include cultural knowledge, professional training, personal connections, and other abilities that are important to language revitalization efforts.

GOALS: I have frequently observed a difference in the goals of community-internal stakeholders, especially those who are most actively engaged in language revitalization programs, compared to community-external stakeholders, especially those that are less directly connected to Indigenous communities. A recurrent pattern is that they all claim to support language revitalization, but have notably different understandings of what 'language' is and also of what constitutes successful language revitalization. This has significant implications for understanding goals.

Among many community-external stakeholders, there is recognition of language's social value and how it reflects and shapes culture, but often in a less direct way than is commonly expressed by members of Indigenous communities. In linguistic science, for example, there is a tendency to privilege structural definitions of 'language', where the emphasis is on grammatical patterns. While the discipline of Linguistics is increasingly recognizing cultural approaches to 'language', it is nevertheless still common for endangered languages to be analyzed and talked about without reference to the people who claim them. Also common with community-external stakeholders, particularly large groups such as governments and funding agencies, is a tendency for languages to be talked about as if they are objects that can be counted, organized into scientific categories, and preserved.

This contrasts significantly with community members who define 'language' in terms of their peoplehood (for example, saying 'language is us' or 'we would not be [community name] without our language'), in terms of spirituality, or with respect to responsibilities they have to acquire and pass on their cultures. I have also heard that 'language is power' from many people in revitalization contexts. This may refer to the idea of social power as discussed earlier, or it could refer to 'power' in a different way (and of course the definition in a specific context should be clarified) – but the general idea of language's importance is clear regardless.

It is only after the different stakeholders in a given effort have clarified their definitions of 'language' that it becomes feasible to truly understand their language revitalization goals, which tend to be framed both by definitions of 'language' and ideas about what constitutes successful revitalization. For second-language learning of major world languages, 'success' often entails proficiency in speaking and/or writing. However, while the ability to speak is a widely articulated goal of Indigenous communities – perhaps the most common – it is problematic to assume that dominant language norms map onto those of endangered language communities, or that it is appropriate to overly focus on a revitalization endpoint that may take multiple generations to achieve. Instead I argue that it is more useful to conceive of smaller, measurable goals (for example, 'I aim to be able to ____ in my language by the end of the summer' or 'I want to be able to pray in my language') that may be located within larger objectives (for example, 'I want to honor my ancestors').

In summary, when cultural marginalization has led a community to shift away from its language, revitalization goes far beyond mastering vocabulary and grammar because it includes restoring cultural practices, beliefs, and pride. In other words, it entails building better community dynamics. I conclude this discussion by returning to what I best understand to be my grandfather's general goals as a tribal leader of the Miami people, and also specifically for myaamia language revitalization. His general goals for the Miami people focused on creating a positive future, which he saw as emerging from a healthy, sustainable community based in strong relationships. His language revitalization goal was the same: a healthy, sustainable community based in strong relationships.

10.1 Power Relationships and Stakeholders: How to Orient Yourself in Complex Situations

Gregory Haimovich

For those who want to contribute to revitalization of an endangered language, it is useful to remember that there are many situations in which no acknowledged language authority exists. In addition to this, if the language still has a significant number of speakers, with even more nonspeakers who share the ethnic identity associated with the language and are interested in its revitalization, one has to deal with multiple stakeholders who are linked to each other by complex socio-political relations. In such a case, it is undoubtedly important to respect all the stakeholders and mediate between them for the sake of common cause. However, the circumstances may also require an activist to be selective and decide which party it is more advantageous to side with. Based on my experience with the Makushi community in Guyana, I will share an example of how the variety of stakeholders can present an activist with difficult choices.

The Makushi language, which is spoken in Guyana and Brazil, has been in decline in Guyana for several decades, and although there are probably about 7,000 speakers left in the country, the overwhelming majority of Guyanese Makushi children do not learn the language at home. They are shifting toward English, or more precisely, its local creolized variety.

The main organization involved in the revitalization of the Makushi language in Guyana has been the Makushi Research Unit (MRU), which is also engaged in the promotion of Makushi cultural heritage in general. Each member of the MRU is a native speaker who is a trained translator and/or teacher, and who represents a particular village of the North Rupununi district, where Makushi people are predominant. For about ten years from the end of 1990s, the MRU had the opportunity to teach the Makushi language in local schools and publish several language teaching materials, but a lack of financial support has forced the group to reduce its activities. As a result, the language is currently taught only at the Bina Hill Institute to interested students of high-school and post-high-school age.

Bina Hill Institute is an educational organization coordinated and funded by the North Rupununi District Development Board (NRDDB), which consists mainly of Makushi Indigenous leaders. NRDDB relies on village councils, led by village chiefs or *toshaos*. The Ministry of Indigenous Peoples Affairs also exerts a strong influence upon policies in North Rupununi. The ministry controls the work of NRDDB as well as the NGOs supported by it. In addition, it supervises elections of *toshaos* and issues permissions for foreign researchers to conduct fieldwork in Indigenous territories. In the case of Makushi, the MRU can be considered an active stakeholder in language policy making; however, there are also other, more passive or potential stakeholders, who may nevertheless have more power and resources. These include: the Ministry of Indigenous Peoples' Affairs, NRDDB, *toshaos* and village councils, Bina Hill Institute, elderly native speakers, and foreign researchers. In the event that there is a burst of activity around the language, any of these 'sleeping' stakeholders may insist on taking a role in decision-making. So the complexity of relations between them becomes a significant factor in language revitalization process.

It is important to remember that there is rarely an ideal situation in which all stakeholders can act together as a well-coordinated organism, where each of them understands and accepts their role, and does not try to challenge others about authority. Sometimes issues that have nothing to do with language and language revitalization can provoke conflicts between stakeholders. If it is not possible to solve a conflict rapidly, a language activist or researcher will have to decide which stakeholder deserves more respect and support in a given situation.

In revitalization activities, stakeholders will usually differ according to the following criteria:

(1) level of local expertise (knowledge about relevant language, culture, and the social context);
(2) level of general expertise (linguistic knowledge, technical knowledge, teaching skills, social skills, marketing skills, etc.);
(3) level of commitment/engagement;
(4) quantity of resources (including material and human resources).

I view the importance of these criteria in the same order as they are listed above. Most stakeholders are lacking in at least one of these criteria. In other words, an organization can be well funded and present itself as a stakeholder, but if it is not committed to the cause and lacks necessary expertise, it is justifiable for new contributors to give preference to another organization, or even a small group of people, who are already engaged in revitalization activities and represent home-grown experts. Next, even the greatest commitment to language revitalization cannot replace the knowledge and skills mentioned in the first two criteria. And finally, general expertise may be efficiently applied only when paired with local expertise, which is rarely found among external stakeholders.

11 Dealing with Institutions and Policy Makers

Tomasz Wicherkiewicz

Revitalization of a language is a combination of ideas and actions that focus on the language system itself, language users, their attitudes to the language, as well as the methods and domains of language acquisition and usage. Language communities, though, never function in isolation and rarely can fully decide on the future of their language. Most revitalization efforts are eventually confronted with authorities and official policy makers. These higher institutions usually represent the state, whose dominant language is different from the language being revitalized. Obviously the language policies of these institutions do not deal solely with endangered languages. What is more, they usually focus on maintaining and supporting the national, official, dominant languages of the state. The communities who endeavor to revive and strengthen their languages often launch their own strategies, that is they also have a language policy.

Language policies are decisions, positions, and principles regarding language, its nature, and role – any actions that affect language use and usage. This might include language education, writing and spelling, or the choice of language(s) in the public space.

When we think about language policies, we usually mean state or administrative language policies, or 'TOP-DOWN' policies as they are known. On the other hand, all parts of society have language policies, for example, schools, commercial companies, communities, language movements, families, and even individuals. These are called 'BOTTOM-UP' language policies. Both kinds of policy may be either overt or implicit and unstated, and they are often based on language ideologies (see Chapter 7). Nevertheless, the most powerful and influential parties are often INSTITUTIONS and/or other 'top-down' POLICY MAKERS.

The political concepts and practices of nation states were born and developed in Europe, and are commonly reproduced in other parts of the world. The simplistic image of a 'nation state' functioning in just one 'state-national' language has been destructive for language diversity; TOP-DOWN language policy has been widely used as a crucial part of nation building, and these 'TOP-DOWN' policies have largely been based on the imposition of one 'superior' language over lesser 'vernaculars' or 'dialects'.

Traditionally 'nation states' have been key players in the design and implementation of language policy. In fact, the role of the state has both increased and become more nuanced, as new 'agenda-setting' political actors have emerged, both in supranational institutions and agencies, and in subnational (regional, interregional, municipal) administrative bodies and organizations.

The relationship between states, societies, and the economic sector has altered profoundly; social-economic factors now play a much more prominent role in institutional negotiations and affect power relations in language revitalization, maintenance, and planning. For example, recently, there has been growing interest among large (global) retail chains, some financial companies, and local small businesses, in using nonofficial, coofficial, and semiofficial languages (languages recognized and used only in some domains) as part of their promotional strategy. Using BILINGUAL PRODUCT NAMES, or offering MENUS OR COMMERCIALS in regional languages, contributes to the promotion of these language varieties and these activities could be used as an argument in favor of further language planning negotiations that aim to promote these language varieties. Therefore, the economic sector might become a valuable ally in language revitalization, regardless of the official attitude of the authorities.

Because some aspects of language are commonly held to be symbolic, that is emblematic of identity, dealing with language policy can arouse strong feelings and highlight the politics of language(s). The politics of language is firmly based on, and also reflects, the relationship between state, nation, ethnicity, language, and identity. It also relates to other issues, such as LANGUAGE RIGHTS and language protection, but also social exclusion or restriction based on the language(s) used, enforcement of monolingualism or promotion of multilingualism, migrants' languages, suppression of dialects, etc. Language rights are often treated as a part of human rights, and can be addressed by NONGOVERNMENTAL ORGANIZATIONS or INTERNATIONAL INSTITUTIONS (see later).

For many people, language policy refers to the goals and intentions of a group or institution, expressed in statements of a political nature. Language communities, activists, and revitalizers can of course express such POLITICAL STATEMENTS, too. While such statements vary with time and according to the political constellations of individual languages and their communities, they might include:

- public petitions, including those on social media,
- media campaigns, including those supported by famous people/celebrities,

- nonviolent protest actions, rallies, and demonstrations,
- political lobbying through parties or individual MPs,
- lobbying through the MEPs (Members of European Parliament), some of whom have formed the Intergroup for Traditional Minorities, National Communities and Languages.

LANGUAGE PLANNING involves concrete actions or measures to implement policy decisions. Language planning as a concept is less political, although in practice, all aspects of language planning can become political when combined with power relations, and when requiring negotiations with institutions and policy makers. Both policy and planning need to take into account linguistic and extralinguistic factors. LINGUISTIC factors refer to features of the language itself (such as vocabulary or grammar), whereas EXTRALINGUISTIC factors refer to external influences such as politics, laws, economic factors, attitudes, ideologies, etc.

Traditionally language PLANNING is subdivided into three main types: corpus planning, status and prestige planning, as well as acquisition planning. These subcategories are distinct but interdependent, and each needs to be taken into account when planning language revitalization.

Corpus planning aims at adapting the language to meet the needs and objectives defined in policy making. Usually it seeks to increase the usage of a language by developing its linguistic resources, including vocabulary, grammar, and often writing conventions. For example, the *Académie française* was founded in 1653 to act as France's official authority on the usage, vocabulary, and grammar of the French language. Following the example of nation-state language planning activities, minority language communities often establish ACADEMIES, LANGUAGE BOARDS, or COMMITTEES of their own, with the objective of developing literary standards and eliminating 'impurities' from their language. The very existence of such language agencies is often a prerequisite for language-status recognition by authorities or amongst the general public. Authorities, for example, often require that minority language communities standardize their dialect clusters or linguistic continua to resemble 'developed' nation-state languages, whereas public opinion tends to consider nonstandardized language varieties as substandard, for example, dialects, slang, *patois*, etc. Even though it is not strictly necessary for the revitalization or maintenance of endangered languages, STANDARDIZATION might constitute a decisive argument in negotiations on official recognition of a language.

Status planning aims at changing the functions and uses of a language by influencing who uses it, in which situations and for which purposes. The status of a language can be raised or lowered in relation to other languages, and this often involves the change of its political or legal status.

Negotiating the status of a language variety usually starts as a 'bottom-up' initiative by a grassroots actor, and it is this aspect of language planning that most often involves intense power negotiations and deals with institutions and policy makers at various levels.

Grassroots movements and organizations use collective action at the community level to effect change at the local, regional, national, or international level. Grassroots movements are associated with 'bottom-up' decision-making and are considered more 'natural' or spontaneous than 'top-down' initiatives by more traditional power structures. Grassroots movements self-organize to inspire and encourage community members to engage and contribute to actions for their own community; therefore, the profile of their activities also matches language revitalization and language maintenance strategies. In the case of language revitalization programs, it is more and more frequent to have the active participation of engaged outsiders, be it nonnative new speakers of endangered languages or invited experts or researchers. Nevertheless, most studies of language revitalization programs stress that revitalization efforts must not be undertaken without the community of (potential) speakers, let alone against the community.

Grassroots movements not only represent (minority) communities in terms of language-related campaigns or negotiations, they can also advocate environmental issues of vital importance to local, Indigenous communities, such as the Ainu in Hokkaido/Japan, or communities in China and Brazil who oppose construction of dams on their life-giving rivers, or the Sorbs in Lusatia, whose land has been badly damaged by lignite mining. Good leadership is of great importance in 'bottom-up' language status planning actions vis-à-vis policy makers. Grenoble and Whaley[1] stress that successful leaders have good organizational abilities and are sensitive to both individual differences and collective needs. According to Grenoble and Whaley, the following factors must be taken into account:

- an honest assessment of its own level of autonomy and the possibilities or limitations offered to it by its national structure,
- an honest assessment of human resources, and
- a clear articulation of what community members want to do with their language, along with an honest assessment of the attitudes, beliefs, and other obstacles that may prevent them from achieving their goals.

At times, it is the authorities themselves who resolve to settle the political status of a language variety through 'top-down' measures. However it would seem much more common for 'top-down' language policy to favor

---

[1] L.A. Grenoble and J. Whaley, *Saving Languages: An Introduction to language revitalization.* Cambridge: Cambridge University Press, 2006), p. 34.

the state official language and subordinately rank nondominant languages as coofficial, auxiliary, or heritage, usually refusing any status to languages spoken by immigrants or to varieties that are labeled as dialects.

There are, though, counterexamples to this rule of thumb. A case in point might be the arrangements undertaken by the Portuguese state in reference to the Mirandese language. This geographically peripheral variety of the Astur-Leonese language continuum, which is divided by the Spain–Portugal state border, had been used alongside official Portuguese. Its community had not striven for any particular status or undertaken language-planning activities until the 1990s. At the time, (Western) Europe was intensifying institutional efforts aimed at protecting and promoting the continent's language diversity. Portugal, despite being an active member of the European community, was nevertheless reluctant to support such institutional initiatives (e.g. refusing to sign or ratify the below-discussed *European Charter for Regional or Minority Languages* or to accede the European Bureau for Lesser-Used Languages). As a sort of replacement for the European initiatives for endangered languages, in 1999 the Republic of Portugal implemented an arbitrary set of legal measures in support of Mirandese, creating an entirely 'top-down' language maintenance program as far as corpus, status, prestige, and acquisition planning were concerned.

Prestige planning is in some ways different from status planning. It aims to make a language acceptable in contexts with high(er) prestige (like science, arts and literature, media) or to create opportunities for use in these types of settings, for example, by establishing new institutions (scientific, educational, artistic, etc.) which function in the language. Prestige planning is also about trying to influence language ideologies and language attitudes (see Chapter 8). Both 'top-down' and 'bottom-up' actions may aim to influence a language's prestige. Prestige planning also requires good public relations to ensure that policy and planning measures are accepted by the public; if this is not done, they are unlikely to succeed. It is also important to pay attention to the attitudes of majority populations, especially if public money is requested to support minority languages, as their taxes will be spent on it.

Dealing with policy makers to build up and strengthen the prestige of a community language might be quite challenging in the case of varieties that are perceived as ugly, un(der)developed, poor, corroded, spoiled, transitional, uneducated, etc. Throughout modern history many, if not most, nondominant languages all over the world have been stigmatized by nation-state societies with the above labels. Therefore, it is crucial for there to be a sustained DESTIGMATIZATION of nondominant language varieties, as well as the promotion of multilingualism and language diversity. For some communities this includes destigmatization at the lowest level of linguistic variation (e.g. dialectal).

Destigmatization may sometimes lead to a CHANGE OF STATUS of language varieties. For instance, a long-term 'bottom-up' campaign in favor of the endangered Ryukyuan languages has recently resulted in a 'top-down' agreement amongst many Japanese linguists to revise and restructure the hitherto linguistic classification of Ryukyuan as dialects of Japanese. Ryukyu is a southern archipelago of Japan, where each of the islands used to form a separate speech community. Recently the term 'Japanese language' has been replaced by 'Japonic languages' (or 'Japanese–Ryukyuan language family'), to include Ryukyuan as a complex of individual languages. This change of terminology clearly resulted in a reinforcement of revitalization efforts by some of the Ryukyuan insular communities.

In Europe, there has been a significant change in the prestige of individual language varieties, which were previously considered 'dialects', 'patois', 'platt', or 'speech'. This has been a result of the introduction of the term 'regional languages' by the European Charter for Regional or Minority Languages (see later). Following the introduction of the Charter, Germany decided to recognize Low German as *Regionalsprache*, Poland declared Kashubian a *język regionalny,* the Netherlands sanctioned Low Saxon and Limburgian as *streektalen*, whereas Scots and Ulster Scots gained recognition as regional languages in the United Kingdom. Other language communities, such as Venetian, Piedmontese or Sicilian in Italy, or Latgalian in Latvia, have actively sought the same status when strengthening their language revitalization efforts.

It is common for top-down policy and planning actions officially (but very superficially) to promote minority languages among minority communities themselves. This is often done instead of adopting a more inclusive and multifaceted campaigns, which simultaneously address minority speakers, government administration, societal authorities (experts, specialists, celebrities, distinguished activists), nongovernment organizations, and other policy actors. An example of the former may be the relatively ineffective Campaign promoting the use of national/ethnic minority/regional languages, carried out by the Polish government in 2014. This action was actually required by the European Charter for Regional or Minority Languages Committee of Experts' Report, so ministry officials hastily prepared and published some web materials and printed texts regarding certain minorities. These materials were then sent out to the very same minority institutions, who had actually been involved in preparing them. As might be expected, the next report that the Polish authorities sent to the Council of Europe referred to the 'effective promotion of use of minority languages'.

Achieving an internationally recognized language status should also be an important aim for a community when negotiating other language planning issues and policies with decision makers. One possible option is to apply for an ISO CODE, also known as Codes for the Representation of Names of Languages. These codes are used to classify languages by the Library of Congress in Washington, DC (USA) and by the lists of languages published by Ethnologue[2] and Glottolog.[3] Each language is assigned two or three letters – the most common three-letter codes are allotted by an institution called SIL International,[4] which receives and reviews applications for requesting new language codes and for any changes to existing ones. Languages are eligible for a code if they are 'in use by a group of people for human communication, and [...] have been in use for a period of time'. For example, previously unrecognized language communities in Poland, including Kashubian, Silesian, and Wilamowice's Wymysiöeryś, have been successful in receiving the codes: *csb*, *szl*, and *wym* respectively. Kashubian is now a recognized regional language, while the two latter communities strive for state recognition as a part of their intense campaigns for language maintenance and revitalization. Although some applications for ISO codes are rejected, they are often given suggestions on how to modify proposals for resubmission.

Acquisition planning focuses on language transmission, language learning and teaching, (re)gaining language skills, language shift, bi- or multilingualism patterns, plus – in a wider context – foreign and second language learning. Occasionally acquisition planning is considered to be the same as language revitalization and maintenance. People assume that because schools are so good at killing languages, they can also save languages. Therefore, many minority communities perceive teaching their endangered language in school as THE objective and/or the main tool of language revitalization.

Acquisition policy is often not compatible with educational policy (of a state, region, group, denomination, etc.). However, every so often, an institutional language teaching curriculum is an important factor when negotiating language planning strategies such as revitalization, or when dealing with regulations. Granting the right to **teach** a language often means giving access to the education system, and providing teaching of a language (usually) means that it has official recognition. Therefore, communities often strive to have their language used in the school system as proof of the status of their language.

All over the world, educational authorities, as well as communities themselves, delude their societies and international institutions into believing that a couple of hours of lessons a week in a school curriculum is effective for

---

[2] www.ethnologue.com/   [3] https://glottolog.org/glottolog/language
[4] https://iso639–3.sil.org/

language acquisition. This overlooks the difference between the teaching *of* a language (usually on a much less effective base than the official or and foreign languages) and teaching *in* a native language. Many minority-language communities, not to mention the dominant society majorities or decision-making authorities, are not aware of issues relating to language acquisition in minority–majority situations, the bi-/multilingual development of a child, or effective teaching methods. Furthermore, when planning teaching provisions for minority languages, it seems quite common for both minority groups and educational authorities to ignore findings from psycholinguistics, multilingualism, and language acquisition studies. Therefore, more information and education are basic requirements when negotiating and developing a model of language teaching.

As in many revitalization efforts, community engagement is crucial when designing language acquisition strategies. One should remember that it is not the school itself that helps the young members of a community to acquire the language; when negotiating educational provisions with the policy makers, special attention should be devoted to the particular language teaching methods that will be used, such as (early) IMMERSION, LANGUAGE NESTS, BI-/MULTILINGUAL TEACHING, or CONTENT AND LANGUAGE INTEGRATED LEARNING (CLIL, which can be understood as 'culture-and-language-integrated learning'). Not infrequent are cases when schools put children off the minority language, by teaching them in a mostly ineffective and boring way.

There are some minority-language teaching programs that were started entirely on the initiative of the communities, for example, the *Diwan* Federation of Breton-medium schools in Brittany/France, or *АББА* – Association of Belarusian parents (now active as the Association for Belarusian-learning children and youth) in Podlachia/Poland. Through intense and far-sighted activity, both organizations managed to get recognition from educational authorities and introduce their community languages into mainstream school curricula.

The most effective teaching programs seem to be those that not only offer teaching *of* and *in* the community language, but also try to (re)create, (re)describe, research, and (re)interpret holistically the Indigenous worldview. Innovative curricula have been implemented at *Sámi allaskuvla* (Sámi University of Applied Sciences) in Guovdageaidnu=Kautokeino, Norway, *Ka Haka 'Ula O Keʻelikōlani* (University of Hawai'i College of Hawaiian) at Hilo, and in native Northern American institutions, who act in accordance with the Indigenous Nations' Higher Education Program as part of the World Indigenous Nations University initiative. Such institutions themselves become productive and influential policy makers, acting as language planners and community representatives at both regional and international levels.

Teaching of an (endangered) language must include many, if not all of the above aspects of language planning, and not solely a teaching network. A language should possess a developed corpus, and have an established status and a stable or growing level of prestige to function efficiently within the society.

Of course, some forms of language planning in revitalization contexts go beyond the simple three-part classification described above. One example is so-called LANGUAGE NORMALIZATION, which involves incorporating many aspects of language planning into holistic projects aimed at language empowerment in many social and public domains – for example, the *normalización lingüística* adapted for the communities of Basque, Catalan, Galician, Asturian in Spain.

Another example is the STANDARDIZATION of a language, which involves both corpus and status planning. A common opinion is that different human societies speak, or at least ought to speak, distinct languages with clear boundaries. This belief is strongly influenced by ideas of state nationalism originating in Europe. According to this belief, linguistic boundaries involve a clearly defined grammar, lexicon, phonetic inventory, and rules of usage, and, if possible, a writing system. Moreover it is commonly believed that linguistic boundaries should correspond to a particular political and geographical context. Generally many societies and authorities would gladly see the world neatly structured into distinct nation states, each with a fully fledged nation-state-language, a standardized stable communication system, with defined numbers of speakers, names of languages, norms, status, etc.

Historically the term STANDARD LANGUAGE was established over the course of the nineteenth century. It is only in the twenty-first century, however, that this otherwise technical term has become more prominent in modern discourse. The standard language ideology suggests that certain languages exist mainly, or only, in standardized forms. This belief affects the way in which speakers' communities think about their own language and about 'language' in general. One may say that speakers of these languages live in STANDARD LANGUAGE CULTURES. Given these widely held beliefs, it seems important to have regular information campaigns addressed to the authorities, policy makers, and also the dominant speech communities. These campaigns should shed light on the diversity of languages, demonstrating how linguistic variation occurs over time and territories, and according to social factors. This is especially important for minority, lesser-standardized, and endangered languages. Majorities should be systematically familiarized with terms and ideas such as language revival, maintenance, spread, modernization, normalization, etc.

Since the mid-twentieth century, language planning processes have gained a supra-national or trans-national dimension, particularly in light of a global interest in (linguistic) human rights. Minority language communities and, sometimes, individual speakers, may refer to certain international legal instruments when dealing with state-level authorities.

Worth mentioning are the following:

- United Nations *Universal Declaration of Human Rights*
- United Nations *International Covenant on Civil and Political Rights*
- United Nations *Declaration on the Rights of Indigenous Peoples*
- United Nations *Declaration on the Rights of Persons belonging to National, Ethnic, Religious and Linguistic Minorities*.[5]

These can be referred to or invoked when (re)claiming rights to native heritage and Indigenous languages. It should be mentioned, however, that the international language rights regimes has, in recent times, come under harsh criticism for their vagueness, ineffectiveness and lack of consistent legal instruments of enforcement.

Nevertheless, one useful outcome of the UNESCO programs concerning endangered languages and linguistic diversity is its 2003 framework for assessing the relationship between attitudes as articulated by government policy and language vitality. It differentiates six levels of explicit policy and/or implicit attitudes toward the dominant and subordinate languages (vis-à-vis the national language) by governments and institutions:

Equal support: All of a country's languages are valued as assets. All languages are protected by law, and the government encourages the maintenance of all languages by implementing explicit policies.

Differentiated support: Nondominant languages are explicitly protected by the government, but there are clear differences in the contexts in which the dominant/official language(s) and nondominant (protected) language(s) are used. The government encourages ethnolinguistic groups to maintain and use their languages, most often in private domains (as the home language), rather than in public domains (e.g. in schools). Some of the domains of nondominant language use enjoy high prestige (e.g. at ceremonial occasions).

Passive assimilation: The dominant group is indifferent as to whether or not minority languages are spoken, as long as the dominant group's language is the language of interaction. Though this is not an explicit language policy, the dominant group's language is the de facto official language. Most domains of nondominant language use do not enjoy high prestige.

---

[5] The 1996 *Universal Declaration of Linguistic Rights* has not gained formal approval from UNESCO.

Active assimilation: The government encourages minority groups to abandon their own languages by providing education for the minority group members in the dominant language. Speaking and/or writing in nondominant languages is not encouraged.

Forced assimilation: The government has an explicit language policy declaring the dominant group's language to be the only official national language, whereas the languages of subordinate groups are neither recognized nor supported.

Prohibition: Minority languages are prohibited from use in any domain. Languages may be tolerated in private domains.

Minority language communities in European states might also use and invoke some of the legal provisions concerning the rights of Europe's minorities and their languages. In the 1990s and 2000s, institutionalized and legally binding protection and promotion of ethnic and linguistic diversity in Europe dominated the agenda of institutions like the Council of Europe, who prepared and promoted three significant documents:

- *European Convention on Human Rights*,
- *Framework Convention for the Protection of National Minorities*, and particularly
- the *European Charter for Regional or Minority Languages*.

The latter has been proclaimed the first international instrument directed solely at the question of language, setting language rights firmly in the context of the value of cultural diversity for its own sake. The preamble to the Charter states, for example, that 'the protection of the historical regional or minority languages of Europe, some of which are in danger of eventual extinction, contributes to the maintenance and development of Europe's cultural wealth and traditions'. Another innovation has been the implementation instruments of the Charter, as the selection of provisions adopted for each individual language depended on their situation. Member states of the Council of Europe have been vigorously encouraged to sign and ratify the Charter, and countries that have implemented it have been submitted to periodical monitoring by the Committee of Experts, who were to be independent specialists.

After almost thirty years, views on the Charter's efficacy are divided. It is in force in twenty-five states, but the attitudes of individual states vary considerably – from diligent fulfillment of all the commitments (in states that already had developed systems of support for endangered language communities) to propaganda simulation (as in the above-mentioned case of Poland). This is not to mention the states that refuse to apply the Charter in the foreseeable future (as in the interesting case of Portugal, referred to earlier). Indeed, some state authorities, in accordance with their general language policies, refuse to officially recognize (or to support in any form) languages and language communities (such as Wymysiöeryś or Silesian in Poland, Rusyn in Ukraine). Hardly any appeals made by language communities in Europe regarding the legal obligations set out in the Charter have proven successful.

FURTHER READING

Grenoble, L. A. and Whaley, J. (2006). *Saving Languages: An Introduction to language revitalization*. Cambridge University Press.
Olko, J., Wicherkiewicz, T., and Borges R., eds. (2016). *Integral Strategies for Language Revitalization*. Warsaw: Faculty of 'Artes Liberales', University of Warsaw. http://revitalization.al.uw.edu.pl/Content/Uploaded/Documents/integral-strategies-a91f7f0d-ae2f-4977-8615-90e4b7678fcc.pdf.
Sallabank, J. (2013). *Attitudes to Endangered Languages Identities and Policies*. Cambridge University Press.
Tollefson, J. W. and Pérez-Milans M., eds. (2018). *The Oxford Handbook of Language Policy and Planning*. Oxford University Press.
UNESCO Ad Hoc Expert Group on Endangered Languages (2003) *Language vitality and endangerment*. Document submitted to the International Expert Meeting on UNESCO Programme Safeguarding of Endangered Languages, Paris, 10–12.03.2003. www.unesco.org/new/fileadmin/MULTIMEDIA/HQ/CLT/pdf/Language_vitality_and_endangerment_EN.pdf

11.1 Language Revitalization and Academic Institutions: Refocusing Linguistic Field Methods Courses

Eric W. Campbell, Griselda Reyes Basurto, and Carmen Hernández Martínez

Language revitalization can only be successful if it is community-driven, addressing the needs and goals of community members. There is therefore an inherent challenge for carrying out revitalization projects within academic institutions, where Indigenous community members are typically under-represented, and where the primary focus is on research – that is, research in the narrower sense of systematic investigation for the purpose of advancing (Western) scientific knowledge. Here we discuss one model for initiating or advancing language revitalization or maintenance projects in a graduate-level field methods course in a US academic institution.

Not all graduate linguistics programs value language revitalization, language documentation, or even linguistic fieldwork, and not all programs offer courses on these topics. When field methods courses are offered, they often involve a single community member, and the primary goal is to do linguistic analysis through elicitation. Such courses follow a traditional, colonial model that reinforces the divide between researchers and a research 'subject'. In field methods courses that follow such a model, community-driven language revitalization may be impossible.

The traditional mold can be broken by using a field methods course to establish a community-based language research project, or by building the course into an existing one. For example, as part of an ongoing collaboration, University of California, Santa Barbara (UCSB) linguists and the Mixteco/Indígena Community Organizing Project (MICOP) recruited community members for UCSB's 2015–16 and 2017–18 field methods courses. MICOP's mission is to aid, organize, and empower the migrant community along California's central coast (see Capsule 6.2), and the courses have advanced MICOP's mission by supporting a community-based language research and activism project (see Capsule 13.2).

In these field methods courses at UCSB, graduate students and community members work in close collaboration to gain extensive training in language documentation and linguistic analysis in a community-based research model. While traditional field methods activities such as analysis of the sound system (phonology), orthography design, documentation of lexis (vocabulary), audio-video recording, transcription and translation, grammar writing, ethics, and archival deposit preparation are part of the course, graduate students and community members learn these skills together. The activities and outcomes are shaped by the goals and interests of the community members, and a special focus is placed on developing practical materials for language maintenance and use in the community, such as trilingual illustrated text collections, games, and language activities that are shared with the wider Indígena community of Ventura County, California during MICOP's monthly meetings.

Crucially the course provides extensive training to community members who then go on to use its tools and methods as leaders in their own language maintenance or pedagogical activities in the community. While some graduate students in the course pursue or continue research in other subfields of linguistics or with communities in other parts of the world, other students continue working with and supporting the local community members in their language-related activities as they themselves progress through their graduate education. Although not every institution is located near a potential partner community, field methods courses can refocus institutional resources to train students in a community-based model in which course activities and assignments are determined by the interests and goals of the speaker in order to support their language community.

12 Making Links

Learning from the Experience of Others in Language Revitalisation

Beñat Garaio Mendizabal and Robbie Felix Penman

Introduction

Over recent decades, many individuals, communities, peoples, and nations worldwide have been trying to 'revitalise' their languages, namely to keep using them despite great pressure to switch to more widely spoken languages such as English, Spanish, Chinese and so on. Across roughly the same time period, we have seen the emergence of new kinds of cooperation, communication, networking, solidarity, or 'making links' (we generally keep to the term 'cooperation' throughout this chapter). Think, for example, of the Zapatista movement in Mexico and its international links, or the many instances of Basque-Mapuche solidarity, such as the organisation Millaray, which operate on the basis that these two peoples have similar struggles. Yet there is not much overlap between these two types of initiative. In many cases, it seems that endangered language (EL) activists carry out their work in relative isolation from other EL communities, despite the fact that thousands of other language communities worldwide are in the same situation. Similarly, most cooperation initiatives of the Zapatista kind do not directly address language endangerment and revitalisation.

In this chapter, we draw attention to those few initiatives that are working in the intersection between language revitalisation and international cooperation (using 'international' in the broadest sense, to include unrecognised nations). We explain why working in this intersection is a good idea; we then look at some of the features that define cooperation for language revitalisation, before going on to highlight some of the features that make for especially effective cooperation.

Advantages to Cooperating with Other EL Communities

We believe there are at least four ways in which EL communities can benefit from communication and cooperation with other EL communities.

First, language endangerment can be emotionally painful, and language revitalisation can be hard work with little reward. These two burdens are often made worse by being borne in isolation: EL communities are often isolated in some way, even if not always geographically. In fact, it is often thanks to this isolation that the language has survived up until now, but isolation can also mean isolation from other EL communities. However, when a member of one EL community connects with one from a different EL community, they may realise that their community is not the only one struggling with language endangerment.

Different EL communities go through different stages of activity and passivity. Connecting a community that has little 'revitalisation momentum' to another that is full of activity can inspire enthusiasm for revitalisation in the first community. For example, language activists in the Basque Country, where some people perceive revitalisation momentum to have stagnated, have felt the benefit of connecting with Indigenous language activists from Latin America, where language revitalisation is, in some ways, a more recent phenomenon.

Second, the field of language revitalisation is very young in human history. There is no 'ABC' of language revitalisation and there are few success stories. Therefore, it is vital for those involved to learn from each other.

Third, revitalisation may be easier if EL communities share resources (methodologies, staff, materials, software, etc.) or even implement initiatives together (e.g. applying for major funding together).

Fourth, linked to the third point, when EL communities join forces they can improve their prospects for lobbying large institutions and have more success in putting language revitalisation on the political agenda.

What Are Cooperation and Communication?

The following six points help to distinguish cooperation-oriented initiatives from other kinds of language revitalisation initiatives, although the boundary inevitably blurs in places: the concept of language revitalisation has emerged out of the connections between EL communities around the world (think, for example, of the Māori language nests which have inspired similar projects worldwide). We also recognise that people in different EL contexts may consider different factors relevant, and so these six points sometimes highlight ways in which initiatives can vary. Under each heading we also provide suggestions for starting, or furthering, cooperation, and communication.

Direct Contact between EL Communities

We consider cooperation to involve direct contact between representatives of different endangered language communities, for example between members of two different nations in North America (one author witnessed such a visit during a language camp). We believe it is important to hear about the experiences of other communities 'from the horse's mouth' rather than through the filter of a third party, especially since this third party is often associated with an institution of power built upon European colonialism, at least in the Americas, Australia and Aotearoa (New Zealand). In saying this, we would like to bring language revitalisation a little more in line with decolonisation and grassroots solidarity in other fields, an idea developed by Khelselim Rivers of the Sk̲wx̲wú7mesh (Squamish) Nation in Canada in his talk on 'Decolonizing Language Revitalization'.[1]

Nonetheless, a third party, often a university, can play a role in bringing about direct contact between speakers from different EL communities. The Foundation for Endangered Languages conferences, the Congreso de Lenguas Indígenas in Chile, and the International Conference on Language Documentation and Conservation are three such events we know of. In such situations it is essential to bear in mind the historical relationship between EL speakers and the institution in question. For example, at academic conferences we have heard some speakers acknowledging, at the beginning of their talk, that they represent a colonial institution.

It is worth considering whether cooperation occurs between just two EL communities, or between three, four, or even more. For example, there have been links for many years between Basque and Mapuche language activists in the Basque Country (Spain/France) and the Wallmapu (Chile/Argentina) respectively. In terms of three-way cooperation there have been links between Mi'kmaw, Gaelic, and Acadian revitalisation efforts in Nova Scotia (Canada). Other initiatives are designed to create links between members of many different EL communities, such as HIGA! 2nd Summit of Young Speakers of Minoritized Languages. This was held in July 2018 in the Basque city of Gasteiz and for four days seventy young language activists from thirty-two different language communities from around the world attended workshops, shared their experiences, and strengthened relationships that could promote future cooperation in language revitalisation.

We suggest: Take advantage of any existing opportunities to meet activists from other EL communities (often through third parties), and/or take the initiative in making links yourself. It may take several tries before you find someone with whom you can establish a good relationship: don't give up!

---

[1] www.youtube.com/watch?v=EcekBQceyN8

One-to-One Contact, NGO-to-NGO Contact, Ministry-to-Ministry Contact

As soon as a member of one EL community begins a conversation with a member of another, this could be seen as communication or cooperation. Indeed, much valuable exchange of experiences arises from such encounters: for example, Mick Mallon from Ireland helps Inuktitut teachers in language pedagogy, teaches Inuktitut himself, and is regarded as one of Canada's top scholars in the academic study of Inuktitut.[2] However, it seems to us that the majority of cooperation initiatives probably occur with the involvement of NGOs or similar organisations, such as The Language Conservancy, Mugarik Gabe, or the Endangered Language Alliance.

There are also some instances of communication and cooperation at a more institutional level, such as the First Peoples' Cultural Council (FPCC), which coordinates much language revitalisation work between First Nations in British Columbia, Canada. One rare example on an international scale is the agreement to cooperate on language policy signed between the CONADI in Chile and the representatives of the Vice Secretariat of Language Policy from the Basque Autonomous Community.[3] While some initiatives are thought of as more 'top-down', e.g. The Network for Promoting Linguistic Diversity, others are more 'bottom-up', e.g. Mapuche language camps.

We suggest: Think carefully about the pros and cons of going through a larger organisation. If it will be helpful, how exactly? Sometimes it is politically necessary, although not helpful; but accepting this (at least for the time being) is better than having political controversy jeopardise the initiative. How much time and effort will you need to invest in the organisational framework, for instance communicating with a government ministry and following all of their procedural requirements, and will it be worth it?

Each of these levels of cooperation can help in different ways, and it will depend on the EL community which level is most appropriate and most valuable. One author's experiences in both Mapuche and Yanesha territories (the former in Chile and Argentina, the latter in Peru) provide an example of this. In the Yanesha case, all interested parties considered the Yanesha Federation a crucial institution for any project involving the Yanesha language, and the Federation seemed to have widespread

---

[2] www.cbc.ca/radio/thesundayedition/the-sunday-edition-november-26-2017-1.4417692/how-a-rascally-irish-immigrant-became-one-of-canada-s-top-scholars-of-inuktitut-1.4417724
[3] www.habe.euskadi.eus/s23-edukiak/es/contenidos/informacion/20132016_legealdia_dok/es_def/index.shtml#6876

recognition as legitimately representing the Yanesha. By contrast, in the Mapuche case there is no such organisation and contacts are much more one-to-one.

This chapter is not the place to discuss all of the possible activities that can come under the umbrella of language revitalisation. Instead, in this section, we outline only those activities that EL communities have engaged in when working together, in the cases we know of. We have categorised these under the headings of training, reflection/evaluation, art, and language policy. By training we mean activities where EL communities share skills relevant to any aspects of revitalisation, from second language learning/ teaching to awareness raising. An example of training is the diploma in language revitalisation strategy run by the Basque NGO Garabide, which has been attended mostly by participants from Latin American Indigenous groups.

Training activities aim to share established best practices in revitalisation strategy, for example the principle of not spending all your energy trying to make the language an official language while ignoring the fact that parents are no longer speaking the language to their children. By contrast, other initiatives focus on identifying, reflecting upon, or evaluating best practices. Many academic initiatives have this focus. One example is Hitzargiak (Summit of Good Practices in Language Revitalization), a project designed to encourage the exchange of ideas between EL communities in Europe. Slightly less academic is Hitz Adina Mintzo, a seminar on minoritised languages organised by Oihaneder, the House of the Basque Language.

A rather different kind of approach is seen in artistic activities, where participants from different language communities reflect on their language (s) through art and draw motivation from hearing about other experiences. An excellent example of this is Wapikoni Mobile, which is a First Nations film studio in Quebec that supports Indigenous directors in producing films, often in Indigenous languages. Other examples of such initiatives, which we leave the reader to look up at their leisure, include the Last Whispers project, TOSTA, European Capitals of Culture (a more top-down initiative), Europa bat-batean (Summit of Sung Improvised Poetry genres, a more bottom-up initiative), or Celtic Neighbours/Y Fro (a culture-related regional entity).

Lastly efforts to influence language policy are a distinct kind of activity. This includes demonstrations against oppressive language policy, legal efforts to change language legislation and initiatives to monitor language policy and language rights such as the European Network for Language Equality (ELEN) or Linguoresistencia.

There can be much overlap between training, reflection/evaluation, art, and language policy. For example, an event focused on the language may raise awareness, provide opportunities for speakers to meet each other and use the language, stimulate people to reflect on revitalisation strategy, and also include artwork to inspire people.

We suggest: Different resources are needed in different EL contexts. For example, some EL activists may be enthusiastic about teaching the language but need more effective language teaching methodology; others may be the opposite. Some may be so caught up in the day-to-day activities that they have no time to reflect whether they are putting their time and energy to the most effective use; others may be the opposite. So it is important to assess community needs first, and structure cooperation so that it addresses the most urgent needs. This might even mean choosing which EL community you cooperate with according to whether it has expertise in the area needed: for example, the Catalan initiative Taller d'Espai Linguistic Personal (TELP) seems to be unique in offering workshops focussing on language choice in daily interaction. Once you have identified these needs, you can then think about what activities best address them.

Long-Lasting, Tangible Outputs from Cooperation: Language Materials, Films, Legal Documents

Sometimes communication and cooperation between EL communities results in tangible outputs such as language materials, films, and legal documents. Unlike the activities mentioned above, these may outlast the link between two particular EL communities. Some examples of films are:

- Beltzean Mintzo and ArNasa TxiKitxuak, two documentaries by Garabide on the sociolinguistic situation of Latin American Indigenous communities,
- The documentary Don de Lenguas, an attempt by Spanish state TV (RTVE) to inform Spanish citizens about language diversity within its territories and
- The documentary Yezhoù, by the Breton language activist Morgan Lincy Fercot, who travelled around Europe for almost a year visiting minoritised language communities, discovering local language revitalisation initiatives and interviewing local people.

Although media outputs may be designed to influence majority communities, we have observed that they have an important impact on other EL communities. For example, Basque documentaries on language revitalisation have received attention within revitalisation movements in Indigenous Latin America.

Other initiatives are, or result in, legal documents, such as the Protocol to Ensure Language Rights or The European Charter for Regional or Minority

Languages, developed by the Council of Europe, which has played a fundamental role in language revitalisation in Europe. We consider these a form of cooperation since they result from an exchange between EL communities on their language rights.

We suggest: If you are producing outputs of this kind with other EL communities in mind, consider which will give most 'bang for your buck', i.e. be most useful to as many other EL communities as possible. For example, in producing the documentary ArNasa TxiKitxuak, filmed in Spanish, subtitled in Basque, and covering a wide variety of Latin American Indigenous groups, Mondragon University created something accessible to EL activists throughout Spanish-speaking Latin America.

Regional, National or International Cooperation: Who to Cooperate With?

Cooperation and communication may occur entirely in the place where people speak, or spoke, the languages in question, particularly in cases where EL communities live in the same or nearby territories, e.g. Tehuelche, Mapuche, and Welsh in Chubut, Argentina, or Mi'kmaw, Gaelic, and Acadian in Nova Scotia, Canada. Some instances of cooperation and communication occur at an international or intercontinental level, such as solidarity between the Basque Country and Latin America. Others occur at a more regional level, such as the many instances of solidarity within North America, within Latin America (e.g. PROEIB in the Andes), or between peoples of the Atlantic coast (e.g. the Atlantic Meeting). Others operate at a national level, in cases where there are multiple languages spoken within the country, e.g. NETOLNEW for Indigenous languages in Canada. Still others occur between EL communities of a particular language family, e.g. the Celtic League or North American Association of Celtic Language Teachers. This may be the case even if the language family has expanded beyond its traditional geographical boundaries, e.g. Gaelic in Scotland and Nova Scotia or Welsh in Wales and Chubut. Solidarity may also happen in geographical locations alien to EL speakers/activists. For instance, the First Symposium of Minority Languages and Varieties of the Iberian Peninsula was held in Alcanena, where mainly Portuguese is spoken (Minderico is spoken just a few kilometers away).

We suggest: Consider carefully who you can keep up a long-term connection with. We have seen cases where language activists were in touch with Basque language activists on another continent but were unaware of revitalisation efforts for immigrant languages going on in their own town. Not only is a local connection more sustainable ecologically (avoiding international flights etc.), but it is likely to be more sustainable socially. A long-distance trip might be exciting, but how much will you be able to keep up long-distance contact, realistically? Activists operating in the same place also tend to better understand the context that their neighbour has to deal with. To give a simple example, Mapuche, Quechua and Haitian activists in Chile understand how the Chilean governmental grants for cultural activities work. Of course, they are also likely to share a common dominant language, e.g. English in the case of Gaelic, Mi'kmaw, and Acadian activists.

We recognise that our understanding is strongly shaped by our geographical focus on Europe and the Americas, and particularly by cooperation between the two. At the same time, this geographical bias is not coincidental. It is a result of the uneven distribution of resources between EL communities in Europe as distinct from EL communities elsewhere. We hope that in the future others will be inspired to undertake and write about similar kinds of cooperation in other regions of the world, e.g. links between the Ainu in Japan and other EL communities, about which we know little.

Cooperating and Communicating Online

The Internet is an important medium for cooperation and communication: take, for example, the many Facebook groups created with the aim of language revitalisation. Social media is a major asset for language revitalisation and networking, as it enables individuals to interact with others and share experiences, organise activities, and learn about a greater number of initiatives, events, and people.

We suggest: Think carefully about what kind of cooperation can be carried out online. This might range from everything to nothing. For example, in the case of language learning/teaching methodologies, we believe it is essential to cooperate in person, as learning/teaching is such a holistic experience. Generally we believe strongly in the value of cooperation in person, because we believe in the continuing importance of using the language in face-to-face communication even if, ultimately, you would like to be using your language in all areas of life. Other contexts for language use (e.g. written, film) are secondary in promoting revitalisation, although they can be very important supports.

What Leads to Effective Cooperation and Communication

In this section, we outline factors that have seemed to help cooperation and communication in the cases we know of, and expand these into suggestions for EL activists who are interested in working with another EL community. However we wouldn't want our readers to be discouraged from communicating with another EL community just because they do not tick all of these 'boxes'; all EL communities are different and an issue that is crucial in one context may be less important in another, and vice versa.

Finding People Who Are Interested in Language Revitalisation in the Other Community and Establishing a Productive Relationship

There is no point trying to engage in cooperation with an EL community where everyone has decided they are not interested in language revitalisation. Similarly, even if there are people interested in revitalisation, there is no point trying to engage in cooperation if nobody is interested in cooperation. Cooperation may often begin with a simple inquiry and, over time, links between the communities may strengthen.

We suggest: Look for people in another community that are already most active in language revitalisation. These are likely to be the people you will find anyway, since they are the people you will be able to track down. This could be by word of mouth, searching for relevant groups online, or by contacting a third party such as a linguist or anthropologist who knows the community. Look for people who have already shown an interest in connecting with other EL activists. There are not many such people; so don't rule out cooperation just because you can't find anyone. Meeting someone with whom you establish a productive relationship is probably more important than anything else.

The Historical Relationship between the EL Communities

Cooperation and communication seem to be most likely between EL communities that have suffered under the same colonial power, e.g. speakers of Mi'kmaw, Gaelic and Acadian French in the English-speaking British colonial system. However, cooperation between people who have suffered under the same colonial power but in different ways, especially speakers of European ELs versus other ELs, must be aware of these differences and take them into account. One must also acknowledge the fact that speakers of European ELs were themselves part of the European colonisation of the Americas and elsewhere.

If the relationship between two EL communities dates back a long time, then cooperation and communication are likely to be more effective and enduring. For example, Catalans and Basques have cooperated for decades in language revitalisation and this is partly due to a shared struggle with the same two states, Spain and France.

Nowadays, perhaps the most common situation that brings together speakers of ELs is migration to the same city, in which case they share a common experience of migration. The Endangered Language Alliance in New York and Toronto are initiatives to facilitate cooperation in this situation.

We suggest: Look for people who have an experience of language endangerment that is similar to yours. Acknowledge any important differences in the experience of language endangerment and revitalisation, but do not let these differences stand in the way of communicating and collaborating.

A Shared Language

EL communities that have been subject to the same colonial power (e.g. Spain) usually also face the same dominant language (e.g. Spanish). Clearly, having a common language makes cooperation and communication a lot easier: for example, in 2016 Inuit visitors to Wales learning about Welsh revitalisation were able to communicate through English.[4] Unfortunately, this common language is often precisely the dominant language against which you are struggling, meaning that your cooperation involves yet more time speaking that dominant language; nevertheless, this may be a price worth paying in the long term, if the cooperation is fruitful.

In a few cases people manage to cooperate without using the dominant language, e.g. Hitz Adina Mintzo, the series of talks on EL issues that is mostly held in Basque, or the Casa Amaziga de Catalunya (for Catalan-Tamazight cooperation) that seems to operate in Catalan. Although this turns cooperation into another opportunity actually to use an EL, it may not be realistic for most EL activists to learn a second EL on top of their own. On the other hand, in some cases (such as Irish and Scottish Gaelic, or the Algonquian languages in Canada), the similarity between minority languages may make this task much easier.

We suggest: Prioritise cooperation where you have a shared language, even if this shared language has to be the dominant language.

Success in Language Revitalisation

It seems that EL communities that are relatively successful in revitalising their language are those most likely to be found engaging in cooperation (e.g. Māori and Basque). Naturally, these are the communities that others want to engage with, in order to learn from their experience. There are other

---

[4] www.cbc.ca/news/canada/north/welsh-inuktitut-save-language-inuit-canada-wales-1.3904064

communities with reportedly successful experiences, such as the Mohawk community in Kahnawà:ke, Quebec, but we do not know enough about cooperation in these contexts to comment.

We suggest: We agree that there is much to learn from 'success stories', and recommend looking for these; they are not all well known, and you will likely have to visit the area yourself to decide how successful revitalisation is. At the same time, there is much to learn from less successful experiences, and this may help you avoid falling into the same traps.

Degree of Language Endangerment/Revitalisation

It seems that cooperation has happened most often between EL communities that have similar levels of language endangerment which are generally quite low levels by global standards. For example, there is a similar situation in Wales and the Basque Country, with around three million inhabitants and 700,000 speakers of the minority language in both cases, strong institutional support, well-developed bilingual education, and widespread opportunities to learn the language as a second language.

We suggest: EL communities facing similar levels of language endangerment are more likely to be able to help each other, so we would generally advise collaborating with such communities.

However, this is not always the case. A good example is Professor Ghil'ad Zuckermann's contribution to Aboriginal Australian language revitalisation, in which he draws lessons from the Hebrew experience, the revitalisation of Hebrew being perhaps the most successful case of language revitalisation in human history, while Australian languages are among the world's most endangered. There are some lessons to be learnt about language revitalisation that have little to do with the level of endangerment, for example, recognising that influence from the dominant language(s) on the 'revitalised' language is inevitable.

Other Shared Projects and Interests

Besides a shared degree of language endangerment/revitalisation, EL communities may have other shared interests. Both Corsican and some Guernesiais activists advocate using writing systems with multiple norms; both Asturians and Yucatec Mayas want their state to declare their languages official; there are issues with both Inuktitut and Cree languages in choosing between the Latin alphabet and Canadian aboriginal syllabics; and both Inuit and Welsh activists are concerned with regional autonomy in connection to language policy.

We suggest: Look for specific shared interests within your general interest in language revitalisation. Being specific about these interests and starting with specific questions may help both communities to support each other more efficiently.

Other Cultural Factors

Besides the shared experience of oppression by a particular power, and besides sharing a common language, two EL communities may have other cultural features that ease, or complicate, cooperation and communication. For example, although there is a shared history of Spanish and Spanish-language colonisation in Chile and Colombia, there are significant cultural differences between the two countries which may create challenges in communication between Indigenous groups from each country. Conversely two EL communities may find communication easy despite not sharing much history.

We suggest: These other cultural factors are rather hard to define or anticipate, so we can only suggest being aware that they may arise, perhaps unexpectedly.

Resources Available

Resources are a deciding factor in being able to engage in communication and cooperation. Travelling, accommodation, material resources, taking time off paid work, delivery costs, and so on require a certain economic position. EL communities from Europe are greatly over-represented in this chapter because of their economically privileged position relative to other EL communities.

We suggest: It is important to evaluate realistically the resources you have available to engage in communication and cooperation. Moreover, we believe that it is an ethical responsibility for EL communities with greater resources to cooperate with less well-resourced communities, especially since these well-resourced communities in Europe were also implicated in the colonisation that led to language endangerment in the Americas and elsewhere (think of the Basque role in the colonisation of Latin America, or the Scottish in Canada). These well-resourced communities, who benefit from the educational systems of European states and are close to global centres of language-related research, also tend to have access to precisely the resources that less-resourced communities want, such as expertise in second-language teaching/learning or language documentation.

Globalisation and 'Connectedness'

Some EL communities are more present than others on the Internet and at events related to language revitalisation, and it is these better-connected communities that seem to be the most likely to engage with other EL communities. The best-connected communities also tend to be the communities that are best-off economically, although the correlation isn't perfect. For example, Mapuche language activists are probably some of the best connected within South America. These well-connected EL communities may already serve as regional 'hubs' for language revitalisation activity to some extent.

We suggest: Take advantage of any such 'hubs'. For example, for a non-Mapuche language activist in Chile it may make sense to connect with Mapuche language activists first, in order them to connect with other EL communities, simply because Mapuche activists in Chile are well connected to the 'wider world' of language revitalisation.

Some international funding bodies actively encourage EL communities to engage in cooperation, as is the case with the SMiLE funding scheme. In fact, some of the projects that have previously been awarded SMiLE funding involve cooperation between communities, and this was encouraged in the call for applications.

Final Thoughts

In writing this chapter we have aimed to (1) create awareness of cooperation for language revitalisation, a phenomenon that has received little attention within the field of language revitalisation; (2) argue for the benefits it can bring to language revitalisation; and (3) suggest factors that make cooperation and communication easier and more productive.

We hope that this inspires EL speakers/learners/activists who are not yet involved in cooperation to think about the possibility. In particular, we are thinking of cases that offer good opportunities for cooperation that have not yet been taken up. For example, there is an inspiring story to tell regarding the revitalisation of French in Quebec. Quebecois language activists would have relative economic freedom resources to pursue such initiatives; and Quebecois of European descent share a common language (French) with Indigenous people in Quebec itself, as well as French Guyana, and French-speaking Africa. Yet we know of no initiatives to share that experience with other groups facing language endangerment (although we would be very happy to be corrected on this).

In our experience cooperation and communication are possible for any member of an EL community who has the opportunity and motivation to contact members of another. One author, himself a speaker of a minority language, was in contact with members of other EL communities even before working and doing research in the field.

Similarly, we hope that this chapter also provides encouragement to those few who are already engaged in such cooperation, as we believe they are doing invaluable work. We also hope to bring the world of language revitalisation a little closer to a global conversation about cooperation, or solidarity, between peoples or social groups suffering oppression and discrimination. We believe that this, too, is essential to avoid any tendency to ethnocentricity ('I want to speak my language but those immigrants should stop speaking theirs!') and for ensuring the ethical foundations of language revitalisation as a field of thought and action.

FURTHER READING

Garabide, a Basque NGO that works on language revitalization with Indigenous language activists mainly from Latin America, www.garabide.eus.

Wapikoni Mobile, a First Nations organisation in Quebec that works with Indigenous film directors across Canada, Latin America, and elsewhere, www.wapikoni.ca.

Y Fro/Celtic Neighbours, a network supporting cooperation between minority language communities across Europe, www.celtic-neighbours.eu/y-fro.html.

12.1 Networking and Collaboration between Speakers

John Sullivan

The Instituto de docencia e investigación etnológica de Zacatecas (IDIEZ, see Capsule 8.5) held its first interdialectical encounter in 2011. We invited about twenty native speakers representing ten different variants of Nahuatl, as well as a few non-native speakers who had attained fluency, to participate in a five-day workshop.

There were three goals:

(1) allow speakers from different regions to experience the monolingual space we had been developing at IDIEZ;
(2) test the commonly held belief that the many variants of Nahuatl were mutually unintelligible;
(3) open a forum for speakers from different regions to share their experiences, thus breaking down the barriers of geographical distance that had prevented this in the past.

We began our activities by issuing two rules for participation in the workshop: first, everyone must speak in their own variant of Nahuatl, with no use of Spanish; and second, no fighting over contentious topics such as orthographic standardisation (see Chapter 14). We then proceeded, in Nahuatl, to propose, discuss and set the topics that would be covered during the five days. This was especially important, because in the past, meetings of speakers of Indigenous languages in Mexico had always been held in Spanish, and organised by government institutions that determined the topics of discussion beforehand.

We got off to a rocky start. The participants were not accustomed to using their language outside of their homes and communities. And those who were, had learned that this needed to be immediately followed by a translation into Spanish. Words, expressions and structures specific to the variant of one person were met by laughter and puzzlement on the part of those who spoke different variants. But in a very short period of time everyone adapted to the monolingual but multi-variant space. Spontaneous conversations sprang up, comparing and contrasting ways of expressing different things in each variant. And most importantly, the mutual intelligibility between variants was high enough to permit five days of animated, monolingual discussion on a wide range of topics, including identity, revitalisation, rituals and local festivals, ways of greeting, education, immigration, grammatical terminology, linguistic policy, intergenerational language transmission, and gender issues.

We have continued with the encounters, always experimenting with new formats and content. In 2017, for example, the Engaged Humanities project of the University of Warsaw, SOAS and Leiden University, along with Indigenous activists, invited native speakers of Nahuatl to participate in a revitalisation field school held in San Miguel Xaltipan, Tlaxcala, working alongside revitalisers of endangered languages from all over the world. The concluding activity was a monolingual academic conference in which speakers of many variants of Nahuatl gave papers on their current projects in curriculum development, teaching methodology, scientific research, revitalisation and art. Engaged discussion followed each talk and performance (see also Capsule 1.4).

The interdialectical encounter is an important way of getting native speakers of different variants of endangered languages who are geographically isolated from each other together to share problems and experiences, exchange ideas, and plan collective projects. We will begin experimenting with videoconferencing technology in order to reduce the cost and increase the frequency and coverage of these encounters.

Finally, oral speech is not the only vehicle for communication among speakers of Nahuatl variants. Writing in all of its manifestations (artistic, academic, personal and commercial genres, social media, etc.) is an important tool for linguistic interaction. However, in order for this to work with maximum efficiency in the Nahuatl context, IDIEZ promotes orthographic standardisation based on the aspect of the language that unifies its variants, morphology rather than sounds, which differ not only from variant to variant, but often from village to village and town to town.

12.2 The Engaged Humanities Project and Networking for Language Revitalisation

Justyna Olko

Networking opportunities can emerge from large-scale projects that cross boundaries between academia and communities. An example is our *Engaged Humanities* (ENGHUM) project funded by the European Commission within Horizon 2020 in

Figure 12.2.1 Mixtec, Ayuuk, and Nahua activists at the field school of the Engaged Humanities project, Mexico. © Engaged Humanities Project, University of Warsaw

2016–2018. It was carried out by a consortium from the University of Warsaw, SOAS University of London, and Leiden University, with direct participation by speakers of many Indigenous and minority languages. We organised and carried out together a number of practically oriented activities: summer schools, field schools and field stays, workshops and cultural and dissemination events (see Figure 12.2.1). They provided networking between representatives of ethnic minorities from Poland (speakers of Wymysiöeryś, Lemko, Kashubian, Silesian and Masurian), other parts of Europe (speakers of Guernesiais, Sámi, Sylheti, Manx, Catalan, Greko, Euskara/Basque) and from Latin America (Makushi, Mixtec, Ayuuk, Pipil/Nawat), Asia (Buryat, Uruk, Tai, Zaiwa) and Africa (Ịzọn).

A good example of intense networking and mutual learning was our 2016 Field School in Wilamowice. It involved a meeting of activists, scholars, experts, and users of almost twenty minority languages and nonstandard linguistic varieties from all over the world. Its forty-five participants came from fourteen countries on four continents. All of them became very engaged not only in joint activities focusing on fieldwork, developing teaching materials for a local community or creating a project for a local museum, but they also participated in the social life of Wilamowice. They carried out a series of workshops for a local school, investigated local language attitudes, and focused on their own languages, cultures, or writing systems and visited local senior citizens' houses. The empowerment resulting from this intense cross-cultural and multilingual networking was deeply felt both by visitors and – also in the long term – by the local community struggling to revitalise its language.

Figure 12.2.2 Justyna Majerska-Sznajder and Tymoteusz Król, revitalisers of Wymysiöeryś, greeted by a speaker of Nahuatl. San Miguel Tenango, Mexico. © Engaged Humanities Project, University of Warsaw

A similar idea guided our Field School in San Miguel Xaltipan (Tlaxcala, Mexico) in 2017. This two-week event was organised in a Nahuatl-speaking zone and participants included speakers of various variants of the Nahuatl language. Nahuatl was also one of the working languages throughout the Field School alongside Spanish. Speakers of other Indigenous languages of Mexico, including Yucatec Maya, Ayuuk and Mixtec, were also among participants. Also gathered in San Miguel Xaltipan were a number of scholars working on language documentation and language revitalisation, as well as language activists from Catalonia, El Salvador, Italy, Mexico, Poland, United Kingdom and USA (see Figure 12.2.2). Our activities included workshops on language documentation techniques and tools, creation of teaching materials and practical fieldwork training in, with, and for collaborating communities. The field school was also an opportunity for the exchange of experiences and making valuable contacts with fellow language activists working in language revitalisation in other parts of the world.

Thus, INTENSE NETWORKING among speakers of endangered languages from communities all over the world was one of the most important and enduring outcomes of the project. Bringing people together and stimulating the exchange of experiences and ideas has helped create long-lasting links and '**communities of practice**' that are crucial for language revitalisation initiatives.

We have made some documentaries about our ENGHUM field schools which are available to view online:

'Amo miquiz totlahtol. Our language will not die':
https://youtu.be/xSp4AMiOIWU
Field school in Wilamowice:
www.youtube.com/watch?v=0yveONt5kuM

Part III

Tools and Materials

13 Language Documentation and Language Revitalization

Peter K. Austin

Introduction

Across the world, minority languages have been under pressure from regional, national, or global languages as these larger tongues became associated with greater social, cultural, economic, and political opportunities compared to local languages. This was particularly true during the period of European colonization and has accelerated in the last seventy years with the rise of independent nations from the colonies, and the spread of national and global languages through government, education, workplaces, service contexts, media, and the Internet. As a consequence, and because of negative attitudes towards them, minority languages have become endangered as they are no longer learned by children.

One response by linguistic researchers to these threats to minority languages has been the development of a way of researching languages and their use that has come to be called 'language documentation'. In this chapter, I explore what documentation is, whether and how the outcomes of documentation can be used for revitalization (which aims to increase the domains and numbers of speakers of threatened languages), and some of the limitations and challenges of working with language documentation materials. I end by discussing some possible opportunities for documentation to be more creatively used both for and with revitalization.[1]

What Is Language Documentation?

In about 1995, a new approach to studying languages around the world was developed that has come to be known as 'language documentation' or 'documentary linguistics'. This approach aims to create audio-visual samples of language use and performances, ranging from everyday conversations to

---

[1] I am grateful to Julia Sallabank and David Nathan for discussion over several years of many of the ideas presented in this chapter. The editors and David Nathan also provided useful feedback and comments on an earlier version of this chapter.

narratives (story telling) to more ritualized activities such as prayers, ceremonies, and recitations. The idea is to create an organized collection (called a 'corpus') of examples of the use of the language in their social and cultural contexts. The outputs from language documentation are intended to be a multipurpose record that could give an idea of how a language is actually employed in a range of contexts and situations by a range of speakers (e.g. male, female, old, young). These records could then be used by both current and future speakers and learners as resources to support the minority language, e.g. in mother-tongue education, or to increase its social status, and for learning or re-learning the language, and thereby revitalize it (I discuss the relationship between documentation and revitalization in more detail below). To this end, language documenters emphasize that a copy of the corpus should be placed in an archive, along with relevant metadata (information about the information in the corpus) such as the names and ages of speakers, where the recordings were made, who collected them etc. Later I discuss what I mean by archiving and some of the challenges it entails.

Just like researchers who create nature documentaries, language documenters frequently work as a team and emphasize the importance of making high-quality audio and video recordings in their environmental, social, and cultural contexts, ideally in the locations where the people who speak the language live. This typically involves fieldwork and participant observation, where speakers are recorded using the language in their daily life, with their informed consent and following proper ethical consultation. Such work is best carried out by a documentation team which ideally includes local researchers and/or assistants who can contribute their knowledge and skills to the documentation and its local impact. In the process, the documentary team will learn about the structures and organization of the languages used in the community and how they function, especially the different domains that different languages or ways of speaking are employed in. They can also study the attitudes and beliefs that people have towards the various languages they know, and how they are used. There may also be interviews with speakers, asking them to translate from their languages into a language of wider communication (a lingua franca) or vice versa, or checking words and sentence constructions (grammar), or the social and cultural significance of different ways of speaking. The corpus would typically contain transcriptions of the audio-visual recordings (which sometimes involves creating a script or writing system for unwritten languages), and translations into a language of wider communication so that it can be accessed by people who do not speak the languages being documented. In addition, explanatory notes or information about words, grammatical structures, and uses may be included in the corpus, along with information about the records in the corpus, called metadata (who is speaking, when, where, why, etc.). This is needed for records in the corpus to be findable, and for the audio-visual collection to be maximally useful, especially for language learners or those who partially speak the language or do not know it at all.

Language documentation can be distinguished from language description, which is the study of the structure of languages, looking at their pronunciation (phonology), word structure (morphology), sentence structure (syntax), and how meaning is expressed (semantics and pragmatics). In language description researchers aim to identify the significant parts of languages and how they work together in a structured way, typically producing grammatical descriptions (or grammars) that explain how the language is organized. Language description also often involves cross-linguistic comparisons to identify properties that are rare, unusual, or common among the languages of the world. Language descriptions can be based on a language documentation corpus, but they do not have to be. They can be produced by studying words and meanings in isolation, especially where the description is based on the author's own language and their own intuitions about how it is structured. Note that description and documentation are different but related activities: Language documentation must include a certain amount of language description in order to create the transcriptions and translations and other metadata that are an essential component of the corpus, linked to the audio-visual recordings. Without description, documentation is difficult, if not impossible, to access and use. I discuss the relationship between documentation, description, and revitalization further below.

For some languages, there may be audio or video recordings, written records, and descriptions that date from some time ago. They may have been collected by explorers, colonists, missionaries, or interested amateurs who lived in or passed through the region and learnt something of the language. We can refer to these as 'legacy materials', a term that can also be used for written or audio-visual materials that were collected by other people and passed on to another (typically later) research team, including those working on revitalization or language support. These legacy materials present particular challenges if we wish to include them in the documentary corpus and/or use them for description and revitalization – I discuss these challenges later.

The Relationship between Documentation and Revitalization

Language documenters often say that one of their goals in creating their corpus is to make it available for use in language revitalization. However language documentation corpuses may not be ideal or even useful for the purposes of language revitalization.[2] There are several reasons for this:

(1) The records in the corpus may focus on interesting or unusual linguistic features rather than how conversations are organized in the particular community (how we begin, end, or change and interrupt a conversation varies from language to language), how to use language to get people to do things, what is appropriate to say or not say in what situation, how to agree, disagree, or argue with someone, and how to be a functioning speaker of the language;

(2) Conversations, narratives, and interviews may focus on the past, looking back nostalgically to the 'good old days' before social, cultural, and linguistic shifts began to take place, often highlighting the childhood or early adulthood of the current oldest generations of speakers. This may be accompanied by negative evaluations by those speakers of the changes that have taken place, with a sense of 'loss' or 'corruption' of older ways of speaking and thinking. Such materials and attitudes can be off-putting for children and young learners, and those who wish to see a positive image for the future of the languages;

(3) The linguistic analyses created by language documenters, including transcriptions and grammatical annotations, may be produced in orthographies or languages unknown to the community and using specialized terminology which is not easily understandable to non-linguists;

(4) The language practices included in a corpus may not match the perceptions or preferences of teachers and language activists, especially when there is evidence of language shift in the form of language switching, borrowing or mixing, and variation and change. Revitalizers may prefer purism when creating learning materials, rather than using the documentary resources. There can be tensions between teaching ways of speaking or structures based on the usage of traditional native speakers (usually 'elders') documented in the corpus versus those of younger or 'new' speakers, especially for languages where there is no established standard form;

---

[2] See P. Austin and J. Sallabank, 'Language documentation and language revitalisation: Some methodological considerations' in L. Hinton, L. Huss, and G. Roche (eds.), *Handbook of Language Revitalisation* (London: Routledge), pp. 207–15; U. Mosel, 'Creating educational materials in language documentation projects – Creating innovative resources for linguistic research' in F. Seifart, F. Geoffrey Haig, N. P. Himmelmann, D. Jung, A. Margetts, and P. Trilsbeek (eds.), *Potentials of Language Documentation: Methods, Analyses, and Utilization* (Hawaii: Language Documentation and Conservation Special Publication 3), pp. 111–17. scholarspace.manoa.hawaii.edu/bitstream/10125/4524/15mosel.pdf.

(5) Because researchers often aim to capture usage by 'the best speakers', the resulting recordings may be difficult to use for revitalization because they are heavily biased towards older people who speak fast, mumble, slur, or elide their utterances, or even have speech impediments (including lack of teeth) or are hard of hearing. Fluent speakers may also rely heavily on background knowledge or history of the people and places involved that might not be clear or obvious from the conversation or story. Such material can be difficult for learners, especially at an early stage, to understand, process, or model;

(6) Documenters rarely record speech directed towards children and language learners so the corpus may tell us nothing about how to speak to them. Missing may be such things as lullabies, children's games or rhymes, jokes, or simple exchanges or routines that would be useful for an early or intermediate learner to acquire;

(7) The conversations or narratives in the corpus may include topics such as secret or sacred practices, death, or sexual relationships, swearing or impolite expressions, or gossip, which are not appropriate for language learners, especially children.

For these reasons, materials in a documentary corpus might be useful for revitalization, but they must be approached with care, and the attitudes and reactions of speakers and learners of all types need to be taken into account. It is often a difficult balancing act to use documentary and descriptive materials for revitalization purposes, and in some cases it may be that documentary corpuses or descriptive grammars and dictionaries are of very little use for language learning and revitalization. Later I suggest some ways that documenters can make their current and future work more useful for these purposes.

Working with Legacy Materials

In some situations, especially for areas that were colonized in the sixteenth to nineteenth centuries, there may be few or no contemporary speakers of the languages, and the main resources available for revitalization are written wordlists, texts, translations, or old recordings (on tapes or cassettes) collected by explorers, missionaries, or settlers. Sometimes we find notes and letters written by speakers themselves who were writing in their own languages to express their thoughts and feelings, to communicate with colonial or missionary authorities about legal, cultural, educational, and economic matters, or to preserve threatened knowledge, like stories or vocabulary. This is true in areas such as eastern Australia, the north-east coast of the USA, Mexico, or southern South Africa. Occasionally we may also find written records or audio-visual recordings made in the nineteenth and twentieth centuries by professional linguists that have been preserved (sometimes after the person has died) in private collections or libraries and archives. We can refer to all of this as 'legacy material', and for some communities, such as the Kaurna people of Adelaide, Australia,[3] it has proven to be extremely valuable and a major source for language revitalization and re-learning (see Capsule 1.4 on reading historical texts in Nahuatl). Legacy materials may present opportunities for being adapted for use in revitalization, and may be a great source of information about languages and social and cultural practices that are only dimly remembered or have gone out of use. They can be a source of idioms, metaphors, and sayings that are no longer known, as a result of the impact of the dominant languages. They can also provide valuable insights into how languages can adapt to changing circumstances to create new words or expressions (called 'neologisms'). For example, in missionary Bible translations for Diyari, spoken in South Australia, we find the verb *dakarna*, which originally meant 'to stab with a pointed instrument' (like a spear or stone knife), was extended by the missionaries to mean 'to write' (with a pen or pencil). This might be further extended to mean 'to type on a keyboard' (of a computer or mobile device) since we now use our fingers as pointed instruments to do this.

However legacy texts and recordings can also present special challenges, and must be approached carefully. It may require specialist help from librarians, technicians, historians, or linguists to make sense of the legacy materials and to make them maximally useful, for the following reasons:

(1) Ethical and political issues – often it is unclear how the legacy materials were collected and whether the collectors had permission to distribute them to others or were given instructions about how they could be used. If the collector is alive we can ask about this, but frequently this may not be possible. Sometimes there are living descendants of the collector and/or the people whose languages and cultures are recorded (including particular individuals if their names are known from the sources) and there may be complex issues about ownership of and rights to the knowledge and intellectual property contained in them. This needs to be discussed properly and openly when approaching older records, and may require legal advice in difficult situations;

---

[3] See R. Amery, 'Phoenix or relic? Documentation of languages with revitalization in mind', *Language Documentation and Conservation* 3/2 (2009), 138–48. scholarspace.manoa.hawaii.edu/bitstream/10125/4436/1/amery.pdf.

(2) Form and content issues – the legacy materials may be written in an obsolete or obscure writing system, or spelled in an inconsistent or inaccurate way that does not properly represent the pronunciation, structure, or use of the language. If there are translations, they may be unclear, incomplete, or wrong. Sometimes we may need to do detective work, cross-checking different sources to ascertain what particular forms or meanings are intended, or to compare them to information about neighbouring and/or related languages to search for clues. In some instances, it may not be possible to decide, and a given spelling, translation, or expression has to remain ambiguous or unknown. Old sound and video recordings (on tapes or cassettes) may be affected by wear-and-tear (including mould or tape degradation, or stretching) and it can be difficult nowadays to find equipment that will play them so that they can be copied and digitized. It is best to seek professional advice from librarians, archivists, or media specialists (including radio and television organizations) before taking on the task of using such recordings for revitalization. Also, old digital files (on floppy disks or other storage devices) may need to be converted if the fonts and software used to create them are now obsolete. In the worst case, some old computer files may simply be unreadable and hence unusable;

(3) Context issues – for legacy materials that include stories or songs, we may not have information about who the audience is intended to be, or on what occasions they can be told or sung (e.g. is it a story for children or a sacred myth only to be shared with older people, or perhaps only with men? Is it a ribald song not meant for young people?). A community's social, cultural, or religious beliefs may also have changed over time so that certain older materials are no longer considered appropriate for public performances, especially for younger people or those outside a given group. Sometimes collectors can make remarks or comments in the materials, or use words and expressions that were common at the time of writing or recording but would now be considered to be inappropriate, racist, or sexist (and perhaps were never intended for public consumption anyway). There may also be references to people, places, or things that are obscure, or only known to certain individuals or groups. This means we need to take care when thinking about how such materials might be employed in revitalization, and seek advice from relevant knowledge holders if possible.

In summary, legacy materials can be very valuable sources of information about languages and cultures for use in revitalization and recovery of knowledge and practices, but they need to be approached circumspectly and used appropriately. It is advisable to seek professional advice and training when necessary.

Working with Archives

An archive is a trusted repository set-up to collect and preserve historical materials of a certain type. Archives can be analogue (collecting physical objects like letters, notes, books, photographs, or video and audio tapes) or digital (collecting computer files of various types, including photographs or scans of physical objects), or a mixture of both. All archives have a collection policy that sets out the types of things they are interested in. For material on languages and cultures, there are several types, which differ in their resources, staffing, coverage, and interests:

(1) National archives like the British Library, British Museum, Library of Congress, Smithsonian Institution, National Archives of Australia etc.;
(2) Regional archives like the Alaska Native Language Centre (ANLA), Archive of the Indigenous Languages of Latin America (AILLA), California Language Archive, Australian Institute of Aboriginal and Torres Strait Islander Studies (AIATSIS) etc.;
(3) Local archives like those of the boroughs of London, the *Dialekt-, ortnamns och folkminnesarkivet i Umeå* Department of Dialectology, Onomastics and Folklore Research in Umeå, Sweden, etc.;
(4) Professional institution archives like the American Philosophical Society, Royal Anthropological Institute, or collections that are housed within university libraries.

Individuals may have personal collections of materials or objects they have amassed over many years, but we do not normally consider these to be an archive as they do not usually have an explicit collection policy, a publicly accessible catalogue, or institutional backing for long-term preservation and sustainability. There is a useful listing of digital language archives that collect documentary and descriptive materials for endangered languages on the website of the Digital Endangered Languages and Musics Archives Network (DELAMAN).[4]

Archives can be important sources of information on languages and cultures (both tangible and intangible cultural heritage) that can be valuable for language revitalization, though it often takes some work and efforts to track down and identify what materials are held where.[5] Above I have identified issues and challenges with making use of legacy materials that may be stored in an archive, but in addition to these there

---

[4] See www.delaman.org
[5] The Open Language Archives Community (www.language-archives.org) provides searching across a wide range of archives around the world and may be a useful place to start in order to identify potentially useful materials in digital archives.

can be particular matters relating to using archives themselves, especially digital language archives:

(1) Archives will have a usage and access policy that sets out who may use the materials in the archive (everyone, or certain types of people only), and how they may be used (read or listen to only, copy but not distribute to others, or freely copy and distribute). Sometimes it is necessary to pay for access (e.g. to receive a digital copy of a document or recording). In some archives, especially wholly digital ones, access may require permission from the person or group who deposited the corpus, folder, or individual file that the user is interested in;

(2) The archive may contain materials on a language you are interested in but list it under a name which is not the one used in the community (it may even be an outdated or insulting term dating back to colonial times or legacy materials). You may need to try various spellings of the language name when searching in the archive catalogue listing;

(3) The archive catalogue may be complicated or difficult to use, even if it is available online, and might be only accessible in a language that is not widely known to the speech community. For example, most DELAMAN archives mentioned above have catalogues in English only. AILLA, which focuses on Latin America, does have its catalogue in Spanish and English, but not in Portuguese (for users in Brazil), or in any minority regional language, such as Guarani or Quechua, both of which have millions of speakers and active research and revitalization communities;

(4) Deposits in archives may be incomplete, or in the case of digital archives in particular, only partial or inconsistent. It is frequently the case that researchers working on minority languages deposit their corpuses incrementally as their documentation and description project progresses, which can result in audio-visual recordings with incomplete or no transcriptions and translations, different versions of a given file, inconsistencies in representation as the researchers learn more about the language forms, meanings, and contexts over time, or change their mind about how words should be spelled or what things mean;

(5) Access to digital archive materials may require particular computer software, and training on its installation and how to use it for the purposes the user is interested in. For example, documenters frequently employ a software tool called ELAN[6] to link their audio-visual recordings to their transcriptions and translations, and occasionally to the metadata and linguistic description. It is a powerful and complex tool that is difficult to use and requires individual instruction to learn, but without it the archival materials may be unusable;

---

[6] See tla.mpi.nl/tools/tla-tools/elan/

(6) There may be some metadata about the deposit (information about the information within it); however, this is frequently limited or incomplete, especially in providing contextual background about why and how particular recordings, transcriptions, or translations were made, and how they relate to other material in the corpus (e.g. is a given song connected to a certain myth story? Are different stories about a character part of a larger story cycle or stages in a life history? Is a particular file the researcher's reanalysis of another file, perhaps from a different researcher?). Metadata can also be inaccurate, especially if the project was done in a limited time, with people or places mis-identified, personal names misspelled or wrongly assigned, and so on. Sometimes these gaps and inconsistencies can be resolved by checking with the depositor (if they are still alive), or community members, or individuals who have relevant knowledge (such as an assistant who worked on a project, or a family member who knows the history of fieldwork or the people who participated).

For these reasons, it is important to discuss your needs and plans with the staff who run the archive, and seek their professional advice or training about the collection and the materials that make it up, as well as the ways it might be used for revitalization. In the USA, there is a national series of training workshops for this purpose called *Breath of Life* that involves University of California Berkeley and the Smithsonian Institution.[7] You may also need to interact and negotiate with the depositors or the people recorded in the particular materials you are interested in, or their descendants.

Documentation for Revitalization

We have seen above that the relationships between language documentation, language description, and language revitalization are complex, and need to be approached with care and attention, seeking advice and training where required. Sometimes language activists and communities can become disappointed when they find that a given document, recording, or digital corpus is difficult to use or not particularly useful for their needs. In this section, I provide some suggestions about how current and future language documentation could be made more valuable for revitalization purposes, without necessarily detracting from the other goals that the documenters may have. I suggest that:[8]

---

[7] See miamioh.edu/myaamia-center/breath-of-life/index.html
[8] See also Amery, 'Phoenix or Relic?'; Mosel, 'Creating educational materials'; Y. Sugita, 'Language revitalization or language fossilization? Some suggestions for language documentation from the viewpoint of interactional linguistics' in P. K. Austin, O. Bond, and D. Nathan (eds.), *Language Documentation & Linguistic Theory* 1 (London: SOAS, 2007), pp. 243–50.

(1) A wide range of members of the community, including those living outside the original location, should be encouraged to participate in the documentation, description, and revitalization planning and activities, rather than focusing on a limited number of older or 'best' speakers on the one hand, while considering outsiders to be 'experts' or 'specialists' on the other hand. Community members, activists, students, and enthusiasts can get involved in various ways which may lead to an increase in their language skills and practices, create stronger links with other speakers and elders in particular, and promote local language revitalization activities and changes in language attitudes. Such engagement can also lead to the creation and development of local community-based and community-driven language and culture archives, and often contributes to improving the quality of the resulting documentation (better translations, more culturally appropriate situations, a wider range of social activities recorded, etc.). Documentation and revitalization projects that include training, e.g. through grassroots workshops, can spread knowledge and skills more broadly, improve capacity building for community members, and increase their awareness of their own knowledge, skills, and agency;

(2) The range of speakers documented should include younger generations and those who may be less fluent in the heritage language. This will result in documentation of how non-traditional speakers use the full linguistic resources at their disposal, including the neighbouring or majority languages, which may involve borrowing or mixing. For some older speakers this kind of language use may be negatively evaluated, but for revitalization it is important to document how younger speakers and learners are actually speaking, and to determine what other sorts of language and expressions can be taught to them;

(3) The range of contexts documented should include non-traditional and contemporary interactional events, activities, and locations, such as community meetings, medical centres, places of employment, Internet and social media, and interactive games. This will generate examples of language use that learners, especially children, can engage with and put to actual use in their own daily lives;

(4) The kinds of interactions that are documented in the corpus should be expanded to include everyday, but often overlooked, aspects such as greetings, farewells, fillers, and discourse markers (like the equivalents of 'umm', 'aah', 'mmm', 'well then', 'go on', etc.), how to start, stop, continue, and change a conversation, as well as how to make an apology, tell a joke, express one's disagreement, disappointment, or anger, and so on. These kinds of elements, which may be short and easy to remember, can be very useful for language learners, especially when they have more passive than active language ability (i.e. they can

understand but have less ability to speak). An appropriately placed word or phrase like these can keep an interaction in the language going, or give a language teacher an indication that the learner is following, and thereby provide further opportunities for practice and learning;

(5) Researchers should document family language such as that between parents or grandparents and children as this can be useful for re-establishing transmission of the language between generations. This could include lullabies, songs, riddles, or other culturally appropriate language use, but also affective terms like the equivalents of 'grandma', 'honey', 'sweetie' etc., as well as terms of respect used to elders;

(6) Attention should be paid to short, fixed, or formulaic expressions that learners can productively use on a range of occasions. These might be things like the culturally appropriate equivalents of 'excuse me', 'sorry', 'can I take that?' or idioms, sayings and metaphors like 'pass away', 'take the bull by the horns', 'don't cry over spilt milk' and so on. For more advanced learners, the formulaic or ritualized speech used within meetings or on ceremonial occasions can be very useful, both in terms of active proficiency in the language but also for acquiring culturally relevant knowledge (in Australia routines and short speeches like 'welcome to country' expressed in local Aboriginal languages at the beginning of a significant event are among those highly valued in language revitalization);

(7) The metadata associated with recordings could indicate that they might be particularly useful in certain ways for different kinds of language revitalization activities, such as 'this is a good example of apologizing for intermediate level'. This could also include indications of potentials for adaptation in language learning, e.g. particularly clear recordings of individual words in a certain cultural domain that could be used for a quiz or puzzle;

(8) Contextual information that is notated for audio-visual recordings and provided with archival deposits should be as wide and detailed as possible, so that users now and in the future will be more easily able to make sense of how and why particular recordings were made, processed, analysed, and used. This kind of metadocumentation (documentation of the documentation), e.g. 'this is a traditional story often told by grandmothers to children at bed time', is extremely useful for language revitalizers (as well as subsequent researchers of all types). However it is frequently omitted as scholars and students concentrate their energies on recording, transcribing, and translating the examples of language features or use that they are particularly interested in, e.g. only the sentences containing a particular kind of grammatical structure. There is a balance to be struck between the work of documentation

and metadocumentation, but more attention to the latter can have important and valuable consequences into the future for everyone.

If some or all of these ideas can be adopted and adapted in language documentation and description, then the people, contexts, and ways of speaking that are incorporated in the corpus can be made more relevant and useful for language revitalization.

Documentation of Revitalization

Individuals and communities engaged in language revitalization should be encouraged to document the processes, decision-making, events, successes, and failures of their work so that they and others can learn from them. Such documentation can also provide valuable resources for and feed back into ongoing curriculum design, materials development, testing, and evaluation. Language revitalizers can adopt the methods, practices, and tools of language documenters and make high-quality audio-visual records of learners' knowledge and use of language and cultural phenomena, and accompany them with transcriptions, translations, notes, metadata, and metadocumentation, using the documenters' software and data models where appropriate. In doing so revitalizers can contribute to the development and sustainability of efforts to increase the current and future domains of use and/or the numbers of speakers of the threatened languages they are concerned with. Some specific recommendations[9] for activities that could be documented in this way include asking learners, either individually or in groups, to speak about their experiences in intergenerational activities, in families, in schools, or in other contexts. They could report what the older generation talked about, explain the situations, or describe what they saw or heard. By documenting these kinds of intergenerational activities as well as the ways that learners use the languages available to them after engaging in such activities, revitalizers should be able to identify psychological or interactional factors involved in successful or unsuccessful transmission of the language. This new understanding can then be used in further language planning and development, and can help to foster the vitality of the threatened languages.

FURTHER READING

Amery, R. (2009). Phoenix or relic? Documentation of languages with revitalization in mind. *Language Documentation and Conservation* 3(2), 138–48. http://hdl.handle.net/10125/4436.

---

[9] See Sugita, 'Language revitalization or language fossilization?'

Austin, P. K. and Sallabank, J. (2018). Language documentation and language revitalisation: Some methodological considerations. In L. Hinton, L. Huss, and G. Roche, eds., *Handbook of Language Revitalisation*. London: Routledge, pp. 207–15.

Mosel, U. (2012). Creating educational materials in language documentation projects – Creating innovative resources for linguistic research. In F. Seifart, F. G. Haig, N. P. Himmelmann, D. Jung, A. Margetts, and P. Trilsbeek, eds., *Potentials of Language Documentation: Methods, Analyses, and Utilization*. Hawaii: Language Documentation and Conservation Special Publication 3, pp. 111–17. http://hdl.handle.net/10125/4524.

Sugita, Y. (2007). Language revitalization or language fossilization? Some suggestions for language documentation from the viewpoint of interactional linguistics. In P. K. Austin, O. Bond, and D. Nathan, eds., *Language Documentation & Linguistic Theory 1*. London: SOAS, pp. 243–50.

13.1 Technical Questions in Language Documentation
Joanna Maryniak

Most of our attestations of languages that are no longer transmitted intergenerationally or orally only exist in written form. The earliest audio recording that we can listen to nowadays is the so-called phonautogram of *Au clair de la lune* created on 9 April 1860 by Édouard-Léon Scott de Martinville. Since 1877, when Edison recorded *Mary Had a Little Lamb*, people have been able to record and play back sounds. The usefulness of recording equipment for documenting endangered languages was understood very quickly, and so the Passamaquoddy people living in Maine and Canada can now listen to the recordings of their language made in 1890 by Jesse Walter Fewkes. This documentation was done using technologies no longer used: wax cylinders.

Technological advances of the last few decades have transformed the language documentation processes. People are no longer likely to struggle with wax cylinders and less likely to have to deal with cassette tapes. A huge proportion of the human population has a cellphone. Most cellphones, and probably all smartphones, have some sort of an audio recording functionality. While most of them don't yet compare to the professional quality that can be achieved using specialized digital recording devices with good quality microphones, they are more useful because they are readily at hand.

Before starting the documentation, it is a good idea to check the cellphone and especially its recording capabilities, the placement of the internal microphone (this should be considered the last resort – to be used only if there is no way of obtaining an external one), and possibilities of upgrading it. Simple and relatively cheap upgrade possibilities include buying an external microphone with a mini-jack or another appropriate connector (as more and more smartphones are moving towards USB Type-C and Lightning ports), or installing a dedicated recording application (as opposed to the one that comes preinstalled on the phone).

No matter whether one is recording on a phone or professional equipment, one quickly encounters the issue of file formats. In general, it is better to record in lossless formats (like .wav and .flac) as in this way more data is preserved and can serve for more purposes. The alternative (lossy) format is most often .mp3, which has two main advantages:

- It consumes significantly less storage space: this might be important if there isn't likely to be more space on the recording device and no possibility to copy the files anywhere else soon.
- The second advantage of .mp3 is that one can be sure that everyone with a modern computer or cellphone is able to listen to it. The other popular format (.wav) is relatively old and can also be played back on many devices, but the files tend to become huge once the recording gets longer and might thus cause memory (RAM) problems when played.

The newer lossless format (.flac) creates smaller files, but many older devices lack the capability to play them back at all.

It is quite easy to convert a recording from a lossless format (especially .wav but also .flac) to a lossy format (.mp3) but not the other way around.

However, .mp3 also has disadvantages. One needs to keep in mind that converting .wav to .mp3 means losing sound quality and sometimes information. In the process of compressing the recording, some information gets lost and cannot be recovered. For some revitalization purposes .mp3 files are adequate because they are smaller and easier to share via the internet, but if we want high-quality, multipurpose recordings (e.g. to analyse the sounds of a language), high-definition formats are necessary. So it is recommended to record in .wav if you have the option, and convert to .mp3 if required.[10]

In the end, the decision about the format is not as impactful as the quality of the recording. There are a few things that need to be kept in mind to ensure better quality. The first is to make sure that the device is actually in good condition (fully charged, with backup batteries or external powerbanks, and a well-functioning microphone). The choice of an appropriate microphone is also very important – depending on the context it might be a stereo or mono microphone of different configurations, eg. omnidirectional, cardioid, or hypercardioid. However it is good to remember the wise words of Chase Jarvis: 'the best camera is the one that's with you' as here the same principle applies to microphones. If you cannot afford the perfect or even recommended microphone for the occasion, it is better to record with the device you have than to forgo recording altogether. The second is to try to eliminate background noises: maybe ask to close a window to a busy street or make sure the recorded person doesn't have other commitments (like pre-arranged calls). If you can do it without causing discomfort to the person being recorded, consider

---

[10] See https://www.audiobuzz.com/blog/wav-or-mp3-whats-the-difference/

bringing the microphone as close to them as is reasonable. The closer it will be, the better the recording quality.

Ideally the recording should be monitored through earbuds or headphones to make sure that you are actually recording what you think you are, and that the recording level is not too high nor too low. However, it is best to check first with the person being recorded if they are OK with this as it could create the impression of paying more attention to the technology than to themselves. You may want to do some practice recordings and let them listen back via earbuds or headphones to help understand the value of monitoring,

Similar concerns apply to video recording, but one also needs to think about image quality. This means choosing the best resolution (1080p is probably the best choice, with 4K being problematic to play back) as well as framing the subject, paying attention to lighting (avoiding over-exposure and underexposure), and making sure the video is stable for example by using a tripod (if possible) and by avoiding zooming.

Framing means creating compositions which are visually pleasing and appropriate to the subject (for example a wide angle for performances and rituals, and a closer one for personal interviews). It is always better to record video in landscape (horizontal), not portrait mode.

Avoiding over-exposure and underexposure is necessary because cameras try to balance the light and dark in what they are recording, so a poorly lit person on a bright background will be only a dark silhouette. If you have more time and space to set the stage for the recording, you can use a reflector, or a white sheet, out of shot to light a dark subject.

Making sure that the video is stable is easier in some cases and more difficult in others. When recording indoors one can often put the camera on a piece of furniture, which is a fast and simple option. However, it is not without disadvantages as things on furniture can fall off, or pick up noise from the furniture itself. It is not so easy outdoors and one might often want to use a tripod. These can sometimes be heavy, expensive, and unwieldy, however there are inexpensive lighter alternatives like GorillaPods, and many fold up to convenient sizes. A selfie stick can often double as a tripod (especially for a cellphone). If the video is recorded in motion (while walking, dancing, etc.), it might be a good idea to invest in a pocket gimbal, which can stabilize it.

When recording a movie resist the temptation to zoom in and out. Once you set the focus, leave it, and do not change it. In general, it is better to put the camera a good distance from the subject. This doesn't mean that movies will only include wide shots: high resolution video can later be cropped digitally to create closer frames, so an edited finished product can include both wide framing and close ups.

Because of the need to place the camera away from the subject you might run into the problem of reduced audio recording quality – after all the microphone should be as close as possible to the people speaking, which stands in opposition to the need to place the camera away from the subject. Moreover, inbuilt camera microphones do not measure up to the standards of external microphones. Once again, it is a good idea to use an external microphone whenever it is possible. You can also record audio separately on a recorder or cellphone using a microphone near the people speaking. This can be combined with the video later to replace any poor audio from the camera itself.

Taking all the above points into consideration, it is often better to have someone else to help with recording. This isn't so crucial in the case of audio, which often only requires starting the recording device and periodically checking if it still works. However, when a second person helps you with an audio recording, they can also monitor it using ear buds or headphones and thus ensure that not only it is working but also that the level is correct. Video requires devoting more attention to filming, so it is easy to become distracted from the topic of conversation, which might be offensive to the person who is being recorded and waste their time. Therefore, the help of another person or two with the camera, lighting, and recording might be very useful. Younger members of the community may be interested in getting involved in your project and can be trained to help with these things.

Documentary materials are in general very valuable, and safeguarding is important. This is done most effectively through multiple backups – copies of data created to protect it from accidental destruction. The golden rule is 3:2:1 – always keeping **three** backups. **Two** of those backups should use different media or ways of storing (for example having 2 hard drives and a flash drive or a CD/DVD). Each way of storing data has its problems and thus your files should be properly stored and periodically checked, e.g. by recovering sample backup files and making sure they work properly. Hard drives (HDDs) can lose data if they are demagnetized. Disks (CDs and DVDs) require an optical drive and special software, and can fail over time. Even the newest solid-state drives (SSDs) can suddenly fail unaccountably. This is precisely why we recommend storing in at least 2 different ways and checking them periodically – to reduce the likelihood of all backups failing at once, and to restore any missing ones.

At least **one** backup should be kept separately from the others – in a different place (a different room, or even better, building) or in the cloud (on a dedicated Internet server). 'Free' cloud storage (that is available without having to pay for it) is available from many providers (like Google, Microsoft – OneDrive, Dropbox, mega, and many others) but using it always means that the data is uploaded to a corporation's server, which might be an ethical problem for many people or a data privacy issue if the server is outside the user's country, e.g. there are issues with the GDPR if cloud storage is in the USA. Still, these providers offer a lot of space without having to spend any money. However, no matter what kind of backup one chooses, it is important to do so. In general, it is recommended to do a backup at least every week, but when conducting fieldwork, it is best done whenever time permits – preferably every day.

You should also consider archiving important materials (audio, video, photos, text, computer files) to ensure long-term storage and availability. Archiving requires working with a trusted repository and involves selecting and editing the materials and describing them using metadata, e.g. who is in the recording, where it was made, what languages are being used. More information about archiving for endangered languages is available from www.delaman.org.

13.2 MILPA (Mexican Indigenous Language Promotion and Advocacy): A Community-Centered Linguistic Collaboration Supporting Indigenous Mexican Languages in California

Carmen Hernández Martínez, Eric W. Campbell, and Griselda Reyes Basurto

In response to the social and linguistic challenges faced by Ventura County's diasporic Indígena community (see Capsule 6.2), the Mixteco/Indígena Community Organizing Project (MICOP) has teamed up with linguists from the University of California, Santa Barbara (UCSB) to create programs that foster language maintenance, multiliteracy, social justice, and Indígena pride. We refer to these activities collectively as the Mexican Indigenous Language Promotion and Advocacy project (MILPA).

MILPA brings together methods from sociocultural linguistics and documentary linguistics to carry out a range of community-based activities, some of which we outline in this capsule:

(i) Tu'un Savi (Mixtec) literacy classes;
(ii) Collaborative documentation of multiple Mixtec varieties;
(iii) College-level courses on language, culture, and society offered to Indígena youth;
(iv) A community language survey that explores language use and attitudes;
(v) The creation of Indigenous language materials for community use.

Community members gain technical training while collaboratively documenting their particular language varieties in UCSB's year-long graduate field methods course, and from there they go on to lead MILPA programs while advancing their own language-related goals (see Capsule 11.1).

In 2015, MICOP extended an invitation to UCSB linguists to help provide training to community members interested in becoming Indigenous language literacy instructors. The team launched the program *Tu'un Savi: Aprendo a Leer y Escribir en mi Lengua* ('I Learn to Read and Write in my Language'). Ten Indigenous students, UCSB graduate students, and university teachers participated in an online training course offered by María Gloria Santos Hernández of INEA (the Mexican National Institute for the Education of Adults). Out of the ten students, Gabriel Mendoza and Griselda Reyes Basurto were chosen to lead the first such pilot Indigenous language literacy course outside of Mexico, focusing on the Mixtec variety spoken by the greatest number of Ventura County's Indígena population: San Martín Peras Mixtec. Course outcomes included basic vocabulary documentation and analysis of the sound system, or phonology (including tone), to enable the development of a writing system (orthography) (see Chapter 14), and revision of the course materials to match the San Martín Peras variety.

In 2017, the team continued to offer the beginning literacy course and began offering biweekly workshops to document and develop writing systems for other

Mixtec varieties. The team works collectively on shared online spreadsheets to compile a multivariety Mixtec–Spanish–English dictionary, sheets for each variety that organize words by tonal melodies, a comparative verb database, and literacy primers.

MILPA offers a yearly course on language, culture, and society for MICOP's Tequio Indígena youth activist group as part of UCSB's School Kids Investigating Language in Life and Society program (SKILLS). This course is facilitated by UCSB graduate students and the Tequio Youth Coordinator, and high school and community college students earn college credit at California Lutheran University for their participation. Young people design and carry out ethnographic and linguistic research and community action projects that have resulted in the creation of a documentary film about Indígena youth identity, multilingual podcasts, poetry, online videos, and social media engagement written in Indigenous languages.

The first survey of Indigenous language use, language attitudes, and linguistic diversity among Ventura County's Indígena population is being carried out by community leaders of the MILPA project with support from UCSB linguists. The survey explores community members' and their families' multilingual practices, linguistic challenges, and language attitudes, to better understand if and how Indigenous languages are being maintained, lost, or discriminated against in the community. In this way, we can get a clearer picture of language use and linguistic diversity among Ventura County's Indígena population that can inform initiatives that foster language maintenance and justice.

The multivariety language documentation workshops, Tequio SKILLS courses, and UCSB field methods courses produce Indigenous language materials for expanding domains of language use and visibility in the community. Other examples of MILPA products include trilingual story books, coloring pages, card games, *lotería* (Bingo) games, vocabulary activities, and online language pedagogy activities that now have a Mixtec interface. Multimedia and multivariety materials foster language use and Indígena pride in the face of language shift and the challenges experienced by a diverse and marginalized community.

MILPA offers one model of community-based and multifaceted language maintenance and advocacy work. While designed to meet the various needs of this diverse and multilingual diasporic community, aspects of the project may be applicable for similar projects elsewhere.

13.3 Developing Innovative Models for Fieldwork and Linguistic Documentation: ENGHUM Experience in Hałcnów, Poland

Bartłomiej Chromik

Hałcnów, called Alzen in standard German and Alza in a local linguistic variety, was formerly a separate village. It now belongs to the city of Bielsko-Biała in southern Poland. Until the end of the World War II it was predominantly German; however, its inhabitants spoke Alznerish, a variety which is scarcely mutually intelligible with High German. Although most of the Halcnovians were not politically connected to Nazism, after the end of the war they suffered from severe persecution. The majority were either killed, banished to the Soviet Union, or resettled to Germany. The communist regime tried to erase all 'signs of Germanness' from public and private spaces. As a consequence, Alznerish also became invisible. When the political situation in Poland changed and post-war anti-German sentiment declined, most scholars supposed that it was too late to find any native speakers of the language. The fieldwork conducted in 2013 by the scholars from Adam Mickiewicz University in Poznań proved that they were wrong.

During the 2016 ENGHUM field school (see Capsule 12.2) in the nearby town of Wilamowice (where another endangered language is spoken – see Capsule 6.1), the major task of one of working groups was to document the linguistic and cultural heritage of Hałcnów. A multiethnic group consisting of seven people developed an innovative methodological approach to the problem. In the first phase of the fieldwork they focused on tracing the (hidden) elements of the linguistic landscape of Hałcnów. These actions were an attempt to discover material culture connected with Alznerish, but they also attempted to establish whether the German past of the village is now seen as an integral part of local heritage.

In the second part of the fieldwork the group was divided. While the first sub-group started to meet the native speakers and conducted unstructured conversations in Alznerish, German, and Polish, or some elicitation in Alznerish, the second group attempted to meet and talk to the most socially prominent people in Hałcnów: the priest, teachers, local historians, and activists. Except for the overt aim of this work – gaining knowledge on current ideologies and attitudes towards the language, asking about some other people who may know Alznerish, there was also another essential purpose for the fieldwork. In Poland researchers enjoy high respect in society. Moreover, as a result of the isolation of Poland in the communist period, foreigners from beyond the Iron Curtain are treated with esteem, especially outside big urban centres. Taking this into account, the interest of foreign scholars in Alznerish inevitably increased the prestige of the local linguistic variety. It was an indirect and non-intrusive way to change linguistic ideologies. The work of this group led to some unexpected discoveries. It appeared that local school students created a short glossary of the Polish variety used in Hałcnów, which is a testimony of emergence of a new linguistic community. What is of even greater importance, a previously unknown fluent speaker of Alznerish was identified. In addition, the fact that we were the first visitors ever to show interest in the villagers' experiences meant that they felt able to share with us some previously unheard personal accounts of suffering in the post-war period.

In the third stage, the group acted together again. A meeting was organized of all Alznerish speakers. Strikingly, despite being neighbours, in some cases they did not know about one another's skills in their mother tongue. Their joy from this discovery was noticeable. It has to be admitted that the scholars did not know Alznerish, but they could communicate in German or Polish. Very soon it turned out that using the latter language was more beneficial. When Halcnovians were asked questions in German, they replied in German, while the 'distance' between Polish and Alznerish was big enough to prevent constant code switching. The conversation concerned the pre-war time in the village and its 'ethnography'. Currently, it is perhaps the only domain where Alznerish can be used. It was also interesting to find that the villagers could only use the past tense to talk about their experiences.

The last phase of research activities took place in Wilamowice. Halcnovians were asked to participate in an event summarizing the field school. They were treated as special guests and received an opportunity to speak publicly in their language. It was perhaps the first time after the end of the World War II, when Alznerish was not only used publicly without fear, but also attracted positive media attention.

The described pilot study is an innovative methodological proposal for short-term studies. It was focused on documentation of the language, networking of its users and either external or internal promotion of Alznerish. The combination of these three factors may give some hope that the effects of the study will be extended in time.

14 Writing Our Language

Sheena Shah and Matthias Brenzinger

Introduction

Language communities and individual speakers of oral languages often express interest in the development of community orthographies, i.e. writing conventions for their ancestral languages. In this chapter, we review practical and ideological considerations in the writing of oral languages by asking some questions: 'Who will write / read?', 'What will be written?', 'How will oral languages be reduced to writing?' In our discussion, we focus on languages which have not been written before and where orthographies have been introduced only recently.

Purposes and Uses of Writing

Speakers of minority languages often accept discriminatory judgments from others about them and their languages, e.g. that their mother tongues are merely utterances without grammatical rules, which therefore cannot be written. The following example from the Khwe community in Namibia demonstrates the importance of writing in challenging these negative stereotypes. When community members wrote their language for the first time at a community workshop on the 15th of September 1996, Khwe became a written language. In a collaborative effort between Khwe speakers and linguists, an alphabet and other writing conventions were developed for their oral language. When writing his first Khwe words, David Soza Naudé, one of the workshop participants, who later became the key person in running community literacy workshops, stated with surprise and astonishment, 'So we actually speak a real language'.

While reading and writing do not commonly play important roles in the daily life activities among the Khwe and other marginalized rural communities, establishing a community orthography might have an immense impact for them on a symbolic level. Although equating 'real language' with 'written language' reflects the widespread discriminatory judgments mentioned above, writing their language can boost their self-esteem and enhance their confidence and respect for their own language and culture (for more on attitudes and ideologies, see Chapter 8). For example, the Sandawe in Tanzania felt that their worth as a group increased after a Sandawe orthography was developed. Elisabeth Hunziker of SIL International recalls that for many years, 'they had gotten used to being looked down upon by other ethnic groups of the country as being the ones whose language was impossible to pronounce, let alone write. Now with the alphabet, this was no longer the case'. Community members often desire written materials in their languages, which, once developed, are cherished and treasured. Books, booklets or even just small pamphlets are shared among community members and shown with pride to outsiders.

The practical use of community orthographies often begins with the production of sign boards with local place names that testify the ancestry of the land. These sign boards on the one hand may support community-based tourism, but on the other hand can also constitute arguments for claims for ancestral lands.

The publication of religious texts, such as hymns, prayers and the Bible, in as many languages as possible was for a long time at the core of Christian mission work in Africa, Latin America and Asia. With this aim in mind, missionaries wrote grammars and dictionaries of local languages. Many speakers of marginalized languages became literate by reading Christian texts, which still make up the bulk of publications in languages of many smaller-sized communities.

Another level in writing community languages is reached when they are used to take memos and to make notes at community meetings, to record decisions and detail agreements, etc. This is, for example, practised by the Ju|'hoan community in Namibia. The advantage of using their own language in these official contexts is that the non-literate speakers, who often constitute the majority in many such communities, can also participate in and contribute to discussions concerning community affairs because the notes can be read back to them.

Writing oral languages can also serve as a means to document the community's intellectual heritage, namely oral traditions relating to their history, rituals, environmental management, traditional economies, healing and spiritual well-being, etc. (see Figure 14.1). A critical take on reading and writing in hitherto oral languages emphasizes the importance of oral practices in many traditional societies. While oral traditions can be recorded in audio and video sessions and stored electronically, due to lack of basic infrastructure (access to electricity, Internet, etc.) in most rural areas, written documents are much easier to manage and access.

Writing a language is essential for mother tongue-based multilingual education, and also for immersion education for language revitalization

Figure 14.1 A Nahua boy reading an ancient creation story written in his variant. Chicontepec, Mexico. Photo by Justyna Olko

(see Chapter 15). This is particularly important, because literacy rates among speakers of threatened languages are often low and illiteracy is one of the crucial indicators to identify discrimination and marginalization. Children from such marginalized communities regularly perform poorly when their own languages are not used in the educational system.[1] Countless studies have demonstrated that children learn best in and through their mother tongues; despite this common knowledge, millions of children around the world are educated in languages other than their own. The plea for mother tongue-based multilingual education is an important argument for supporting the writing of oral languages. Government institutions, NGOs, as well as linguists may play supporting roles in communities' attempts towards developing writing conventions, producing teaching and learning materials, fostering the use of the language and establishing language rights.

Finally, writing can play a crucial role in the survival of threatened languages. Where ancestral languages are no longer spoken in the family,

---

[1] See e.g. UNESCO, *Improving the Quality of Mother Tongue-Based Literacy and Learning: Case Studies from Asia, Africa and South America* (Bangkok: UNESCO Bangkok, 2008), https://unesdoc.unesco.org/ark:/48223/pf0000177738.

children no longer acquire them naturally in their home environment. For this reason, ancestral languages are increasingly transmitted through formal and informal teaching. The design and production of teaching and learning materials for community languages are often considered central by language revival and revitalization movements. In these cases, the development and establishment of community orthographies are prerequisites, since these materials are mainly written, for example in booklets, readers, textbooks and dictionaries. When we work with last speakers of languages, learners don't speak the languages fluently and often acquire new words through reading them. For this purpose, learning can be made easier if orthographies represent the speech sounds as closely as possible.

Designing Community Orthographies

Many linguists treat orthography development as a technical issue in which they identify the phoneme inventory and then aim at representing one distinctive speech sound with one character or symbol. Hangul, the alphabetic system used in writing Korean, represents the distinctive speech sounds of that language perfectly: words can be correctly pronounced simply by reading them, even by non-speakers. Most orthographies, however, especially those with long traditions, do not follow this principle. For example, the idiosyncratic nature of spelling is an obstacle in learning and writing English. Irregular spellings and pronunciation in English are the topic of many poems, including, for example, the classic English poem 'The Chaos', written by the Dutch traveller Gerard Nolst Trenité in 1920. It contains about 800 of the worst irregularities in English spelling and pronunciation, questioning for example why 'done' rhymes with 'fun' and not with 'gone'. English is one of those languages in which the written forms of spoken words must be learned in addition to the oral pronunciation. Learning to speak English from written texts alone is therefore not possible. In Korean, on the other hand, it is possible to do so after having learnt the Korean alphabet, which in itself takes only a few hours.

Socio-political contexts and cultural traditions are often determining factors in the choice of specific orthography conventions, or even of different writing systems. Socio-political conditions affect all levels, namely the writing systems, orthographies or even the use of specific characters or symbols representing speech sounds.

Speakers of threatened languages commonly speak or even write other languages, which are more dominant than theirs. The orthographies and writing systems established for dominant languages are crucial in choosing writing conventions for a threatened language, especially when these dominant languages are used in literacy campaigns and formal education. There are often heated debates within communities between proponents of different orthographies, e.g. those who want to make it easier to switch to and from majority languages vs. those who want to use orthography to stress distinctiveness.

Religious affiliation has triggered the use of different orthographies for one and the same language, for example, when missionaries of different denominations introduced distinct writing conventions for Tumbuka in Malawi. Dialectal variation may also lead to different orthographies. For example, the Western Aranda people in central Australia want to distinguish themselves from the neighbouring Eastern Arrernte people through the spelling used in their language. For them, their own orthography is a key symbol of their distinct identity.

National governmental policies may demand the use of specific writing conventions, so cross-border languages may develop parallel writing systems in different countries. This led, for example, to different writing systems for Afar, a Cushitic language, in the three countries in which it is spoken: Afar is written in the Ethiopian script in Ethiopia, in the Roman alphabet in Eritrea, and in the Arabic script in Djibouti. Another example of state regulations on writing conventions is the enforcement of the use of Roman letters for the representation of click consonants by the government of Botswana. The orthography of Naro was developed according to this directive, whereas the orthographies of all related languages, including the well-established orthography of Khoekhoegowab, use the click symbols from the International Phonetic Alphabet, which are easily acquired and used by community members, and which are used in all community orthographies of non-Bantu click languages in southern Africa (Figure 14.2).

In the past, when starting to write an oral language, it was often the case that a 'standard' language was imposed, which ignored the regional, socio-economic, gender and generational variation that is characteristic of spoken languages. Progress in information and documentation technologies makes it possible to represent different types of variation, and to produce materials, which reflect local ways of speaking as alternatives. Modern dictionaries and grammars are based on substantial collections of oral usage and might include 'crowd sourcing', i.e. the gathering of information from large numbers of people through the Internet. With this focus on spoken natural conversation, linguistic diversity and variation are recognized and respected. In such projects, speakers are instrumental in carrying out this research as well as in the processing and analysis of the language data.

Figure 14.2 Katrina Esau and Sheena Shah introduce the newly developed N|uu alphabet charts. Photo by Matthias Brenzinger

Ownership and Management of Orthographies

Community orthographies can stimulate intense emotional reactions among communities, for example, related to who controls and has the authority over language standardization efforts, or even more fundamentally, who owns a language. Communities have different options to coordinate and manage language activities. Community language boards may manage the development and establishment of writing conventions. This, however, is often not a straightforward exercise due to intra-community disagreements about writing conventions that can arise. Communities are not monolithic and there might be disagreements about whether and how to write languages. For example, different generations may have different opinions on the use of digital technologies; while younger generations may favour the use of social media, online video, text messaging, podcasts and various other technologies, older generations may be opposed to this (but see Figure 14.3). Interventions through government policies, conflicting conventions of different religious traditions, etc., often add to the complexities of the task of establishing writing systems for oral languages. It is imperative, however, that language communities themselves head and direct these efforts to ensure that their own interests are respected.

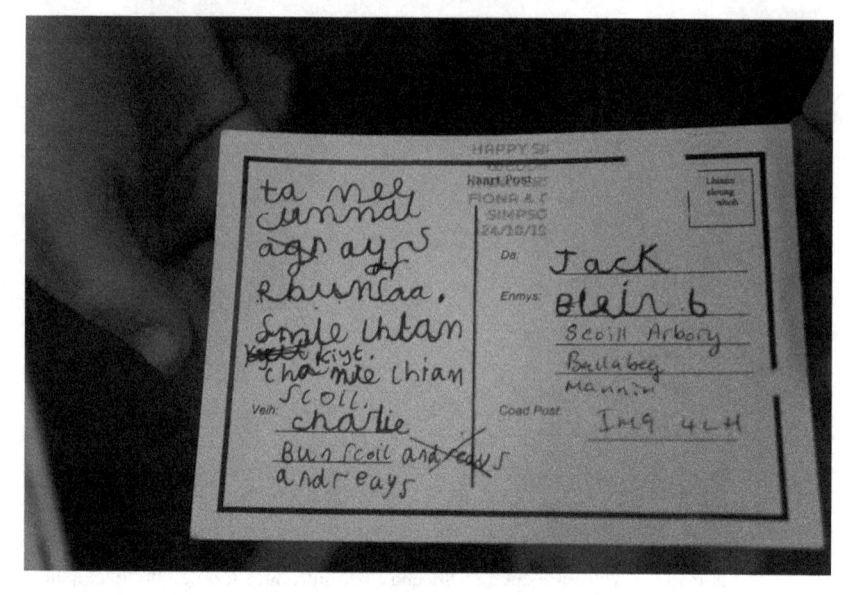

Figure 14.3 A postcard written by a young student of Manx. Photo by Justyna Olko

Summary

There is no single best way to establish literacy in previously unwritten languages of predominantly oral communities. Even though one can learn from the various previous and ongoing attempts to write languages, community settings and conditions differ substantially. The level of literacy among community members (also in languages other than their own), whether a closely related language is already written, or if national policies prescribe writing systems or alphabets, are among the core factors that need to be considered when developing community orthographies for previously unwritten languages.

The possible purposes for and the uses of written forms for oral languages are numerous. In most cases, the development and production of written teaching and learning materials are essential when intergenerational language transmission is interrupted and when languages are thus learned mainly in formal or informal teaching settings. Where archived recordings of past or living speakers exist, such as in Australia or Hawai'i, community members can also relearn and regain oral competence in dormant ancestral languages.

Introducing writing for oral languages often has a positive impact on the self-esteem of their speakers and contributes to the improvement of their well-being. Visualizing their languages in writing can be an important tool

4. До поданых примет допиш приметы ім противны.

богатий –

голосний –

веселий –

ясний –

Figure 14.4 An exercise book for (writing) the Lemko language (*Робочий зошыт до лемківского языка*), Barbara Duć/Варвара Дуць, © Engaged Humanities Project, University of Warsaw

in the empowerment of marginalized communities. Furthermore, many rural communities in various parts of the world have very little or no access to electronic language resources (e.g. no electricity, no recording devices, no smartphones, etc.), making the use of audio or video clips in teaching efforts problematic. For that reason, in the foreseeable future, writing an oral language may still prove to be essential for the production of teaching materials, and literacy will remain the main tool for accessing knowledge and information (Figure 14.4).

Most important for the development and establishment of writing for oral languages – besides communities being in control of all activities that aim at establishing community orthographies for their languages – is that community members wish to have their languages written.

FURTHER READING

Cahill, M. and Karan, E. (2008). Factors in designing effective orthographies for unwritten languages. *SIL Electronic Working Paper* 2008-001. www.sil.org/resources/archives/7830.

Jones, M. and Mooney, D., eds. (2017). *Creating Orthographies for Endangered Languages*. Cambridge: Cambridge University Press.

Seifart, F. (2006). Orthography development. In J. Gippert, N. P. Himmelmann, and U. Mosel, eds., *Essentials of Language Documentation* (Trends in Linguistics. Studies and Monographs 178). Berlin: Mouton de Gruyter, pp. 275–99.

14.1 Orthographies and Ideologies

Tomasz Wicherkiewicz

Very often, language communities and activists want to make their language visible through developing a script, writing system, orthography, individual letters or type fonts. The choices involved in deciding the graphic layout make language ideologies tangible. Developing a written form (*graphization*) of a language (variety) not only involves the selection of an appropriate orthography, but also making decisions concerning cultural, religious, political and historical matters.

Ideological factors are therefore fundamental when considering how to write minority languages. However, it is always the community who should have the decisive voice when adopting script, writing system and orthography. Of course, there are often disagreements within a community on writing and/ or orthography.

Many minorities use writing to symbolically mark their territory, using public signs to mark the names of settlements, municipalities or other places within the area of a dominant language. Sometimes the languages used in the signs are perceived as rival or competing against each other – occasionally this also applies to rival orthographies for the same 'language' (e.g. Provençal/Occitan orthographies in southern France, or 'standard' vs. 'dialectal' forms, e.g. in Italian Lombardy, Piedmont or Veneto). Place names may be written in two or more languages or writing systems, and it is quite common for a name in one language to be removed, altered or painted over as a visible sign of ethno-linguistic conflict, an example being a letter **V** in an Anglicized place-name in Wales replaced by an **F**.

> **Explanation of Terms**
>
> A *script* is a set of graphic signs (*graphemes*) for writing languages, which contains information about the basic level of language to which its signs correspond: words, syllables or phonemes.
>
> A *writing system* is the implementation of a script (or sometimes elements of more than one script) to form a complete system for writing a particular language variety; a writing system can be standardized by means of an orthography, i.e. norms for spelling, *diacritics* (e.g. accents etc.) and punctuation, which are often arranged and published as spelling rules and orthographic dictionaries. These norms may be explicit or implicit: implicit norms often allow a greater degree of variation than explicit orthographic norms.
>
> *Fonts* or *typefaces* are graphical variants, which can be distinguished within a script.

Traditionally, a script or graphic layout has been ideologically related to culture, and even more often with religion. Many people spontaneously associate the Cyrillic script with the Christian Eastern Orthodoxy, Arabic with Islamic tradition, Hebrew with Judaism, Devanagari with Hinduism and Chinese characters with the East Asian cultural sphere. For a long time, the Latin script was linked to the Western European tradition and Western Christianity. In regions of Europe where Protestant and Catholic traditions rivaled each other, the visible factor used to differentiate them was a type font: protestant writings adopted 𝔅𝔩𝔞𝔠𝔨𝔩𝔢𝔱𝔱𝔢𝔯 or 𝔊𝔬𝔱𝔥𝔦𝔠 script, while Catholic publications used Antiqua typeface.

Throughout history, scripts have been designed specifically for individual languages – examples being the Georgian scripts (ქართული დამწერლობა): *Asomtavruli*, *Nuskhuri*, and *Mkhedruli*, the Armenian Հայերենի այբուբեն / *Hayereni aybuben* for Armenian, the Korean 한글 / *Hangul*, or the syllabaries ひらがな / *Hiragana* and カタカナ / *Katakana* for Japanese. These and other 'national' scripts became carriers and symbols of various 'nation-state' ideologies in the nineteenth and twentieth centuries.

The same nation-state ideologies were also behind the adoption or imposition of dominant scripts as writing systems for minority languages (no matter whether they were linguistically related or not), e.g. in Georgia for Abkhazian, Ossetian, Svan, Megrelian, or in Japan for Ainu or Ryūkyūan.

The Hebrew alphabet (אָלֶף־בֵּית עִבְרִי / *Alefbet 'Ivri*) has served as a marker of Jewishness, and as such has been applied to most of the Jewish languages spoken all over the world (Yiddish, Ladino, Judeo-Persian, and many others). The same alphabet was originally adopted by the Karaims, a Turkic people of Judaic religious tradition. In the nineteenth/twentieth centuries, the Karaim communities in Lithuania and Poland decided to switch from Hebrew to Latin script in order to visually mark their separation from Jewish ethnicity. Later, Karaims under Soviet rule had to adopt a Russian Cyrillic-based orthography. Even some Yiddish speakers in the same period thought about switching from the Hebrew script to the Polish Latin-based writing system. From a contemporary educational perspective, it might be easier to learn using the same script as the dominant education system, although it can also encourage faster language shift. The majority of world's languages have not been recorded in writing and there are fewer scripts and writing systems than language varieties in the world. Furthermore, many language communities have made changes to their orthographies or individual graphemes (e.g. Vietnamese and Turkish switching to Latin script).

Any language or language variety can be written with any writing system or script, although e.g. arguably syllabaries are more suitable for languages with *Consonant+Vowel* syllables. However, there are many factors involved in devising or adapting a writing system or orthography, and these must be considered in order for an orthography to be effective. The process is more complex than is commonly realized.

Here are some key factors to be taken into consideration when designing effective orthographies:

(1) Governmental, administrative and legal policies, obligations and restrictions, which must be considered when working on community-driven (bottom-up or grassroots) projects. For example, in Ghana all writing systems have to use the national orthographical conventions.[2]
(2) Cultural or religious traditions, e.g. ease of access to earlier written materials such as pre-Conquest Central American manuscripts, visual appearance (i.e. symbolic meaning of individual graphemes), the values attached to a script or typeface (e.g. the close relationship between Arabic script and Islam).
(3) Linguistic factors, including sound-grapheme or meaning-grapheme correspondence (according to the script type), or how to decide where word breaks come.
(4) Educational and social factors, including literacy issues and ease of learning, access to the learning of additional language.
(5) Sociolinguistic aspects – including language ideologies, attitudes, how to choose the 'standard' variety and its applicability to other varieties of the language in question.
(6) Need and importance of written language documentation for the community.

Inventing a script is one way that a community can try to create a distinct identity. Sometimes creating and developing a uniquely new script is the most accepted way to develop and promote social literacy within a language community. One such case is the well-documented Indigenous script of N'ko in West Africa. The N'ko 'social orthography' has successfully competed against other older writing systems that have been better propagated in the colonial and national literacy education programs. N'ko's popularity results from the script's

---

[2] See M. Cahill, 'Non-linguistic factors in orthographies', in M. Cahill and K. Rice (eds.), *Developing Orthographies for Unwritten Languages* (Dallas: SIL International, 2014), pp. 9–25.

strong linguistic and cultural relevance to the Mande communities and their Indigenous knowledge.

Some minority language communities prefer to use a special font (such as the contemporary Basque *Harri / Vasca* or the historical Gaelic script for the Celtic languages), or a unique, recognizable type style (e.g. mixed-case oblique Irish vs. capital lettered English on road signs in the Republic of Ireland). In such cases, the graphic features of the script became symbolically relevant, acting as distinctive markers of the linguistic landscape. On the other hand, some members of the community might object to such 'ethnic fonts' as markers of folklorization or archaization.

If a language community uses the same script as the surrounding dominant language(s), individual graphemes (e.g. particular letters in alphabets) or even individual diacritic signs, i.e. additional graphic marks of letters, might become ideological carriers and visible indices of identity. Examples of the latter include, e.g.

- the letters **ë ė à** are, respectively, considered the most Kashubian, most Lithuanian, and most Wymysiöeryś (all three are minority/regional languages in Poland);
- the letter **q** marks plurals in Võro (or Southern Estonian – an unrecognized regional language in Estonia), while Standard Estonian uses **d** for the same function;
- the letter **ō** is used in some orthographies of Latgalian (a regional language in Latvia), but was officially outlawed by the Latvian language authorities for not corresponding to the general Latvian graphic tradition;
- the letter **r** was used traditionally in Ukrainian orthography, but forbidden by the Soviet orthographic reforms in the 1930s, as 'too much Western and too little Soviet';
- the letters **q, w** and **x** were forbidden by Turkish law since 1928, when Turkey changed its alphabet from an Arabic-based system to a Latin one. The change was intended to standardize Turkish spelling and improve literacy. However, the reform also had a political aim: assimilating Turkey's minorities, chiefly the Kurds. For many years, any Kurdish person whose name contained a Q, W or X, for example, could not have those letters included on their official documents. In the 2000s, Kurdish language activists launched a 'Q-X-W' campaign, which led to the abolishment of the ban in 2013.

FURTHER READING

Anderson, B. (1983). *Imagined Communities*. London: Verso.

Bielenberg, B. (1999). Indigenous language codification: Cultural effects. In J. Reyhner et al., eds., *Revitalizing Indigenous Languages*. Flagstaff, AZ: Northern Arizona University, pp. 103–12. http://jan.ucc.nau.edu/~jar/RIL_8.html.

Cahill, M. and Rice, K., eds. (2014). *Developing Orthographies for Unwritten Languages*. Dallas: SIL International; see especially the 'Introduction' and 'Orthography Wars' by Leanne Hinton.

Sebba, M. (2007). *Spelling and Society: The Culture and Politics of Orthography around the World*. Cambridge: Cambridge University Press.

14.2 Writing Your Language: The Case of Wymysiöeryś

Tymoteusz Król

When I was ten I became aware of a big threat to my language, Wymysiöeryś, and so I wanted to protect it. The problem was, I did not know how to do it. Somebody told me that the more recordings and texts there are of a language the better. The first thing I did was to record my grandma and her friends speaking Wymysiöeryś. But I knew that my recordings should include more literary forms of the language. As a child I had no access to Biesik's poetry. Florian Biesik (1850–1926) is a Wymysiöeryś poet who spent most of his life in Trieste. I knew the local songs and oral poetry, but there were very few texts which I could read, as all of them were written in various orthographies.

I had the good fortune to meet Józef Gara fum Toler, who was the only person publishing poems in Wymysiöeryś at that time. He taught me how to use his orthography and he checked my poems for me. Another person who helped me with my first poems was Ingeborg Matzner-Danek: she translated some poems from the Bielitz-Bialaer variant of German into Wymysiöeryś.

The goal of these first texts that I wrote was language documentation. Of course, this documentation was the work of an eleven-year-old child and it was not like the documentation carried out by professionals. The most important part of the work was the inclusion of a variety of themes and grammatical forms, but I was afraid of inventing new words. Inventing new words is always a political or ideological decision: should it be a word taken from a foreign language like Polish, German, English, or maybe a new word created by myself? Those texts from when I was child are now sometimes used as teaching materials, but they are mostly kept 'in the drawer'.

Then, there was a request for Wymysiöeryś texts from the local Dance Group 'Wilamowice': sometimes they needed a translation of a Polish song that they sung, sometimes I would tell them a poem or some greetings in rhyme for an important person and sometimes I would invent a new song for a special occasion. I often still do this.

Then I started writing some 'bigger' texts, including novels and poems. But I often heard people say: 'Your language is not really a language. We Poles have a large and varied literature with many poets, such as Mickiewicz etc.' I was angry about this, because the goal of these statements was to humiliate speakers of Wymysiöeryś. So I decided to change this and I wrote many poems and prose in different genres. When I was sixteen, one of the stories I wrote was called *S'ława fum Wilhelm* ('The life of Wilhelm'). It recounted the genesis of Wymysoü-Wilamowice and was printed by the Association 'Wilamowianie'. However, for me the most important texts are those that I wrote for the Dance Group because they are the texts that are most 'alive': they are sung by the Dance Group as 'old Wymysiöeryś songs' and nobody remembers that I am the author. The Christmas carols I translated from Polish to Wymysiöeryś are sung alongside their Polish equivalents by children going from house to house at Christmas time. For me it is beautiful that my texts, of whose quality I was so anxious, are now a part of the Vilamovian oral poetry collection. I also find it beautiful that, for Vilamovians, I am equal with tens of authors whose names are not known anymore, but whose texts have been sung for hundreds of years.

The second piece of luck I have had is that my students started writing their own texts. I must say, when I was being taught by Inga-Müm and Jüza-Feter, I never dreamt about having my own pupils in the future. As I wrote above, I was previously afraid of inventing new words which could be used for new things that I wanted to include in teaching materials that I created. Now, after the two successes that I have written about, I feel authorized to do so.

14.3 Indigenous Research, Methodology and Writing
John Sullivan

The books and articles that have been written recently on the topic of Indigenous research and methodology have two things in common. First, they are written in dominant languages, such as English and Spanish, rather than in the Indigenous languages themselves. Second, they are largely theoretical; in other words, they talk about what Indigenous research and methodology should look like and what its political function should be, but they rarely actually do it. At the *Instituto de docencia e investigación etnológica de Zacatecas* (IDIEZ, see Capsule 8.5) we have been conducting curriculum development and research in the area of Nahuatl language and culture for the past seventeen years, and we have done it monolingually, in Nahuatl. We work on the premise that for research and methodology to be considered 'Indigenous', it should be performed from within the unique worldview and cognitive structures of each specific culture. And these can best be accessed, understood, developed and expressed through each culture's language. Here are four examples of how we perform research at IDIEZ.

Example 1: During the course of writing *Tlahtolxitlauhcayotl, Chicontepec, Veracruz*, our monolingual dictionary of Modern Huastecan Nahuatl, we created a tremendous amount of neologisms for grammatical terminology. But we never simply translate terminology from European languages, as is common with the Mexican bilingual school system. We always begin with a concept, discuss it collectively in Nahuatl, and when we understand what we want to express, we use the morphological resources of Nahuatl to create a term. For example, we took the verb *tocaxtia* 'to name something' and turned it into a gerund *tlatocaxtiliztli* 'the act of providing something with a name'. This is the neologism we use to express the concept of 'noun'. Nahuatl nouns have subjects; rather than a simple label, they constitute a process for providing a subject with a name.

Example 2: At a conference in Chihuahua in 2016, a panel of native speakers of different Uto-Aztecan languages gave talks in Spanish about colour terminology in their culture. During the question and answer session, I explained that Modern Huastecan Nahuatl, also a Uto-Aztecan language, doesn't employ the concept of colour; rather it uses *ixnezcayotl* 'something's surface appearance', which includes colours, but also such things as stripes, polka dots, stains, and certain types of visible textures. The panel participants responded that their languages worked in the same ways, but they had just uncritically assumed that the Western concept of colour was universal.

Example 3: Eduardo de la Cruz Cruz wrote his master's thesis in Nahuatl on the topic of corn, at the Universidad Autónoma de Zacatecas in 2016. When we were discussing how to organize his work, I suggested a typical Western model with chapters on land, planting methods, tools and deities, etc. But Eduardo responded that as an Indigenous person this didn't make sense to him at all. He proposed chapters on each one of the ceremonies that comprised the yearly agriculture cycle, with each chapter discussing the aspects of land, planting methods and tools, deities, etc., that it employed. He chose to focus on the interrelation of his topics, rather than to compartmentalize them.

During five hundred years of contact with Europe, Nahuas have never been purists: they have adopted foreign things that are useful and ignored those that are not. At IDIEZ we do not seek to discard all foreign ways of perception and principles of organization. Rather we conduct research to discover what in today's Nahuatl culture is native and what is of foreign origin, so that native speakers can make informed decisions about how they wish to generate and organize knowledge and how they write about their culture in their own language.

15 Teaching Strategies for Language Revitalization and Maintenance

Janne Underriner, Lindsay Marean, Pigga Keskitalo, Zalmai Zahir, Pyuwa Bommelyn, and Ruby Tuttle

Introduction

Teaching in a language revitalization context is not always about acquiring an Indigenous or heritage language as a second language; sometimes it is about awakening and strengthening the first language. Teachers of Indigenous languages come to teaching either as a speaker or as a second language learner. Our intention in writing this chapter is to present teaching methods and strategies that will strengthen both types of teachers – to give the reader a solid and meaningful understanding of how language learning theories can serve teaching Indigenous languages. We will then present various teaching methodologies and strategies that have come from these theories to show what they look like in the classroom, at home and in the community. The authors are Indigenous language teachers and learners in the Pacific Northwest of the United States and in Finland, implementing various teaching strategies in our communities, schools, and homes. Each of us has years of experience learning an Indigenous language, and we bring our insights in teaching language to this chapter.[*]

We begin the chapter with a broad overview of second language acquisition research from the last fifty years. Here Lindsay Marean links theories of second language acquisition and widely used methods of language teaching to the specific context of language revitalization. We then discuss, in a practical way, language learning theories and how they can better inform Indigenous language teaching choices. We introduce second language acquisition terminology that we then define in a real-world way and support with case studies. This will help the reader to become familiar with language learning situations and behaviors. Understanding these learning behaviors will help with teaching, creating lessons and materials, and language assessment.

---

[*] This chapter represents decades of ongoing collaborations with Indigenous peoples. We offer wholehearted thanks to all community members and coresearchers who have helped with these projects over the years and who have contributed to this chapter.

We then ground this research in teaching experiences, using case studies from communities. The case studies we present are relevant to both first and second language teaching and learning situations.[1] Lindsay Marean discusses distance language study in Potawatomi, a Central Algonquian language of North America, and the use of Can-Do Statements from the National Council of State Supervisors for Languages – American Council on the Teaching of Foreign Languages (NCSSFL-ACTFL) Benchmarks – in Pahka'anil in central California. Zalmai Zahir then discusses teaching and learning in language nests and reclaiming domains in the Lushootseed language from the Puget Sound region of Washington state. Next Pyuwa Bommelyn shares his experiences of teaching Tolowa Dee-ni' from northern coastal California. He discusses two teaching methods: Accelerated Second Language Acquisition (ASLA) and reclaiming domains. Also included in this section is a sketch of learning Tolowa Dee-ni' using the Master-Apprentice method, based on the experiences of Pyuwa's father, Loren Me-lash-ne' Bommelyn. Pigga Keskitalo then discusses how Sámi language and culture can meaningfully enhance education in the classroom, citing an example of a classroom modeled after a *goahti* – a traditional Sámi dwelling. Ruby Tuttle then looks at teaching language in a classroom at home as opposed to at school, and discusses homeschooling activities and strategies for elementary age learners in Tolowa Dee-ni'. Finally, Janne Underriner ends the chapter by sharing ways that teachers who have limited speaking fluency can teach lessons using rich language.

From Second Language Acquisition Theory to Indigenous Language Revitalization Teaching Practices

Second Language Acquisition Research

During the last fifty years, the study of how language is acquired has emerged and developed among those who are curious about human language and how our discoveries can be applied to language teaching and learning. Indigenous language activists often seek out applied linguists to guide their work. In turn, applied linguists seek out language practitioners to test their ideas and to gather information about the experiences and needs of language teachers and learners. However, Western science has a history of not valuing Indigenous ways of

---

[1] We understand that in some of the case studies we use methodologies or assessment measures that are US-centric (e.g. ACTFL below, for example). If our descriptions and use of them leave the reader wondering, we have provided references to refer to, or you may contact us with questions.

knowing. Indigenous people likewise are often distrustful of recommendations coming from colonizer institutions. In recent times, we have seen calls for a 'productive symbiosis' between the two perspectives, so that Western science and Indigenous ways of knowing can inform each other in mutually beneficial ways.[2]

In the late 1960s and early 1970s, Stephen Pit Corder[3] and Larry Selinker[4] observed that second language learners are not making one-off mistakes but are in fact fairly consistent in the sorts of errors they make during the development of their second language. Consequently, researchers started investigating how learners *process* the language that they are learning, and the role of cognition.[5] Researchers looked at the importance of language *input*,[6] or the language that learners are exposed to; and language *output*,[7] the language that learners are able to produce/use and its role in helping learners to *notice* errors that hinder their communication. They also studied language *interaction*,[8] or the way that speakers and listeners convey meaning even when their communication breaks down. This demonstrates the need for teachers to understand that making mistakes is part of learning and that it is the teacher's role to create lessons that address natural learning errors.

If we look at the process of learning the past tense in English, we see that first learners want to use the rule 'add -*ed* (/d, t/) on all verbs': *walk – walked; appear – appeared; is – ised; teach – teached; give – gived.*[9] Learners need many opportunities to hear and make errors so they can learn that many of the most frequently used verbs in English do not in fact follow this rule. In teaching and designing curriculum then, we need to offer

---

[2] R. Kimmerer, R. LaPier, M. Nelson, and K. Whyte, 'Let Our Indigenous Voices Be Heard' (2017). www.esf.edu/indigenous-science-letter/Indigenous_Science_Declaration.pdf.

[3] S. P. Corder, 'The significance of learners' errors', *IRAL: International Review of Applied Linguistics in Language Teaching* 5/4 (1967), 161–70.

[4] L. Selinker, 'Interlanguage', *IRAL: International Review of Applied Linguistics in Language Teaching* 10/3 (1972), 209–31.

[5] 'Cognition is a term referring to the mental processes involved in gaining knowledge and comprehension. These processes include thinking, knowing, remembering, judging and problem-solving' (www.verywellmind.com/what-is-cognition-2794982).

[6] S. Krashen, 'Some issues relating to the monitor model', in H. Brown, C. Yorio, and R. Crymes (eds.), *On TESOL '77*. (Washington, DC: Teachers of English to Speakers of Other Languages, 1977), pp. 144–58.

[7] M. Swain, 'Communicative competence: Some roles of comprehensible input and comprehensive output in its development', in S. Gass and C. Madden (eds.), *Input in Second Language Acquisition* (Rowley, MA: Newbury House, 1985), pp. 235–53.

[8] M. H. Long, 'The role of the linguistic environment in second language acquisition', in W. C. Ritchie and T. K. Bhatia (eds.), *Handbook of Second Language Acquisition*, Vol. 2 (New York: Academic, 1996), pp. 413–68.

[9] P. M. Lightbown and N. Spada, *How Languages Are Learned*, 4th ed. (Oxford: Oxford University Press, 2013).

learners a rich language environment (and find ways to do this even if as a teacher you are not fluent in the language; examples of how follow). Teachers also need to provide sufficient time for learners to practise using language, so that they can progress their learning through interacting in the language.

> input → output → interaction → adjust error → move toward proficiency[10]

In this new millennium, second language researchers have started paying more attention to the diversity of people who are learning and teaching languages and how their life experiences affect this process. This has been called the 'social turn' in language acquisition research. Researchers are looking at issues such as the relationship between second language knowledge and community membership, and how one's sense of identity impacts one's use of a language. This is new and complicated territory for researchers. However, these are exactly the sorts of issues that some Indigenous language activists navigate in communities that are recovering from historical trauma in a world that still favors settler colonialism. A teacher who creates a thriving language learning environment considers such relationships – integrating their knowledge of how learners acquire language with teaching practices that best serve their learners. At the same time, they reflect on how their own upbringing, traditional practices, language exposure, and language learning experiences can support learner identity and well-being.

Language Teaching and Learning Methods Overview

No single theory of second language acquisition fully accounts for all aspects of language learning, yet each new perspective fills in gaps that are unaddressed in previous theories. This growth is indicative of good scientific inquiry. No single 'best practice' exists in language teaching and learning methodology. Each approach has its own strengths and weaknesses and the decision to employ an approach depends on the particular context, taking into account community history, needs, and desires. Some language activists seize on the first method that is presented to them (or the one that they found helped them to learn a language) and

---

[10] See S. M. Gass and A. Mackey, 'Input, interaction and output: An overview', *AILA Review* 19/1 (2006), 3–17.

Figure 15.1 A Manx picture dictionary. Photo by Justyna Olko

implement it without critical reflection and adaptation. However, it can be more effective to step back from a method and consider its theoretical assumptions and the context in which it was developed. From there, activists can identify which aspects of the model are well matched to their learners' needs, as well as gaps that need to be addressed. It is necessary to emphasize that regardless of the path that led them to language teaching and learning, language activists have the greatest impact when they feel equal to the researchers and practitioners that they learn with and from. There are also practical challenges to teaching and learning a language with limited learning materials and limited opportunities to speak it. These are not necessarily accounted for by researchers, who typically work with large languages such as English.

Some Methods

In this section, we describe some popular, currently used methods for teaching and learning language.

IMMERSION is often seen as an ideal model for learning Indigenous languages. The simplest form of immersion is natural intergenerational language transmission. We simply grow up speaking the language of our caregivers as a first language. This is the form of language teaching and learning that Indigenous communities used prior to the disruptions caused by settler colonialism. Native communities have responded to the disruption of intergenerational transmission in a number of innovative ways. Language nests, pioneered by the Māori, involve immersing young children in a nurturing environment of Indigenous language and culture, often involving elders and knowledge bearers in children's lives. Pyuwa Bommelyn (Case Study 4) shows ways to use language in a classroom-nest setting.

Immersion is a life-long process, extending beyond early childhood. Immersion schools continue or start the immersion process by educating children in their Indigenous languages. In some cases, children come to school already speaking their Indigenous language, and immersion schools help them to develop specialized and academic language use. In other cases, children's first exposure to their Indigenous language is in school. For adults, several approaches have had good results. The Advocates for Indigenous California Language Survival pioneered the Master–Apprentice model, in which an adult (or teenage) language learner is paired with an older or more proficient speaker over a period of several years for intensive one-on-one immersion sessions.[11] The Nishnaabemwin Pane program, offered through Bay Mills Community College in Michigan, runs large-group adult immersion in a classroom-like setting. Proficient speakers tell stories and perform skits in a low-stress, language-rich program. Another promising direction is the emergence of language houses where dedicated adults choose to live in a space entirely dedicated to Indigenous language learning and use.[12] A related approach is Zalmai Zahir's[13] method of creating language nests within the home through a process of reclaiming domains (see Case Study 3).

The GRAMMAR-TRANSLATION method of language teaching has been around for millennia. Learners study texts written or spoken by proficient language speakers, they note key vocabulary and memorize it, and they observe language patterns, especially the ways that nouns and verbs behave. They also memorize charts of word forms to help translate from one language to another with accuracy. In grammar-translation classes, the original text is of great importance. Teachers and learners end up spending a lot of time talking *about* the text and the language in it, and less time speaking *in* the language or producing their own meaningful utterances.

---

[11] L. Hinton, M. Vera, and N. Steele, *How to Keep Your Language Alive: A Common Sense Approach to One-on-One Language Learning* (Berkeley, CA: Heyday Books, 2002).

[12] M. K. S. Johnson, 'Ax toowú át wudikeen, my spirit soars: Tlingit direct acquisition and co-learning pilot project', *Language Documentation and Conservation* 10 (2016), 306–36. https://scholarspace.manoa.hawaii.edu/bitstream/handle/10125/24695/johnson.pdf.

[13] Z. Zahir, 'Language nesting in the home', in L. Hinton, L. Huss, and G. Roche (eds.), *The Routledge Handbook of Language Revitalization* (New York: Routledge, 2018), pp. 156–66.

On the other hand, DIRECT and AUDIO-LINGUAL methods prioritize use of the target language at all times. Grammar is not directly taught. Instead learners listen to and pronounce sentence after sentence after sentence. In this way, they learn grammar rules through exposure and practice. Correct pronunciation is emphasized, and students 'overlearn', practicing learned phrases until they become automatic. Most language-learning apps that are marketed today (such as Rosetta and Berlitz) make use of the direct method. Similarly, many Indigenous language-learning apps are also based on these approaches. The Ulpan method, popular for teaching Celtic languages, is an example of the audio-lingual approach. The kinetic activities described in Case Study 6 are also inspired by these methods.

In the world of 'foreign' language teaching, especially in the United States and other Western countries, professional teachers are trained to focus on language proficiency through a COMMUNICATIVE or PROFICIENCY-BASED approach. In this framework, students develop proficiency by engaging in tasks that simulate real-life use of language and by interacting with authentic materials in the target language. For example, students might study a French-language map of the subway system in Paris to figure out how to get from one place to another. They might converse with other students to find out how many pets they have and what their names are. Curriculum is often organized thematically, and it follows the principle of BACKWARDS DESIGN, in which curriculum is developed by first thinking about the proficiency goals and how to assess them, and then what sorts of activities directly prepare students to meet those goals. The 'five step' approach and pair activities mentioned in Case Study 6 are examples of a communicative approach.

Another popular trend among language teachers is RADICALLY INPUT-BASED TEACHING. Lindsay uses this term to describe a collection of approaches[14] used by a growing number of teachers, which focus on making language completely comprehensible to students. Students are only expected to *produce* language voluntarily. Extensive reading to expose learners to more language is often important in this approach. These approaches are especially well suited for teachers who are themselves still learning the Indigenous language but who nevertheless want to expose their students to extensive language input, as described in Case Study 8.

Be Informed, Be Empowered

None of the above methods is perfect. There is no proven single best practice in language teaching and learning. Rather, there are good practices,

---

[14] Examples include Total Physical Response Storytelling (TRPS) and Comprehensible Input (CI) approaches.

and a good language teacher or program leader uses those that best fit the local context. Immersion can produce second language speakers who sound very similar to first language speakers and who are strong in their Indigenous identity. However, such programs are resource-intensive and rely on having teachers who are confident and proficient in their Indigenous language. Also, if the Indigenous language is not used outside of schools, that is, in the wider community and in learners' homes, then language gains can disappear as quickly as they came once students leave school.

Grammar-Translation may give students insights into language patterns and the way that proficient users speak, and they make good use of the sort of text collections that language activists frequently find in archives. However, learners using this method are often unable to participate in basic conversations because they have not had any practice with interpersonal communication.

Direct methods can address community concerns about how one's first language, which is typically a colonizing language, affects the learner's second language use and becomes the new norm for the Indigenous language in future generations. However, their reliance on repetition and practice of provided language means that learners may not be able to express original thoughts in their own words and with their unique voices.

Proficiency-based approaches offer a broad framework that makes it easy for learners to see their progress, leading to greater retention in community language programs. However, these approaches have not been used much yet in Indigenous and endangered language contexts.

Heavily input-based approaches are especially good for adults who may have a number of emotional barriers around their Indigenous language, since they are not pressured to speak unless they want to. However, most adults' language goals include the ability to produce language, which is not emphasized in these approaches.

In other words, every method has its own strengths and weaknesses. Language activists must consider their own desires, the desires and resources of their communities, and the traditional worldview and lifeways that frame their language revitalization efforts. In conclusion, theories and methods of second language acquisition can really inform the work of language revitalization and save us all time as we learn from those who have come before us. In doing so, we must be unafraid to question and challenge researchers and practitioners that we interact with. If you have chosen to be an activist for your heritage language, you have already navigated a complex universe of identity, loss, relationships, and rich cultural knowledge. Your lived experience is irreplaceable and should guide you as you decide how you will proceed with your language activism.

Teaching Strategies 243

Figure 15.2 A Manx language class taught by Jonathan Ayres, Arbory School, Isle of Man. Photo by Justyna Olko

Figure 15.3 Nahua children reading a pictorial dictionary. Chicontepec, Mexico. Photo by Justyna Olko

Case Studies

We turn now to eight case studies to illustrate on-the-ground practices for first or second language teachers and learners of Indigenous languages.

Case Study 1 Lindsay Marean
Potawatomi Distance Learning and Workshops

Lindsay Marean is a language activist,[15] who is both a learner of her community's language, Potawatomi, and a linguist working for the Tübatulabal community in California. In addition to her experience working on documentation projects, such as a Potawatomi dictionary and corpus, she has also taught Spanish in public schools, supervised preservice language teachers, and worked to connect teachers with second language teaching and learning research projects at the Center for Applied Second Language Studies. She says that, as an Indigenous language activist, she has been lucky to meet and work with many other language activists.

Every Monday night, Lindsay meets online with some fellow Potawatomi people, and they use the grammar-translation method as they work through recordings of their elders speaking Potawatomi. They look up words in dictionaries or ask people who speak different regional varieties if they have heard certain words before. They study verb prefixes and suffixes, and puzzle over why certain discourse markers are used in different places. Lindsay explains, 'We have these wonderful recordings, we have curious adults who are interested in how Potawatomi works, and I don't have time to prepare any formal lessons. I recognize that we aren't developing our conversational skills or learning to do things like pray before a meal when we dissect these texts, but we are developing a feel for how our first language speakers use our language, and we are gaining new insights into traditional Potawatomi ways of thinking as we listen, line-by-line, to our elders sharing with us what they thought merited being recorded in our language'.

In another case, Lindsay, who usually favors communicative approaches, chose to use a radically input-based approach two years ago at an event hosted by the Pokagon Band of Potawatomis. She rephrased an incident from Potawatomi history into simple sentences and presented them one at time, followed by a prescribed set of questions that first require with yes/no answers, then progress through either/or answers, and end with more open-ended who/what/where/when type questions

---

[15] Our use of the term 'language activist' includes both Indigenous and non-Indigenous individuals from communities and academia, typically from the fields of theoretical and applied linguistics, education, and other related areas, who bring a diversity of skills, training, and interests in hands-on and theoretical practices in language revitalization, maintenance, and documentation.

Case Study 1 (*cont.*)

(this sequence is called 'circling'). By the end of the week quite a few people in the class could tell the entire anecdote in Potawatomi. Participants may not have learned how to express their own original thoughts during the lessons that week, but they reclaimed a little-known part of their history as part of an oral tradition that they now share.

Case Study 2 Lindsay Marean – Can-Do Statements in Pahka'anil

In her work as a Practical Linguist for the members of the Tübatulabal Tribe in California who are teaching their language, Pahka'anil, Lindsay uses a proficiency-based approach for tracking language growth. She and the teachers she works with are piloting the use of the NCSSFL-ACTFL Can-Do Statements,[16] a set of examples of what learners can be expected to do in their target language (for example, can introduce him/herself and others and can ask and answer questions about personal details), arranged by proficiency level (Novice, Intermediate, Advanced, Superior, and Distinguished) and mode of communication (interpretive, presentational, and interpersonal). Language teachers collect evidence of their students' language development and maintain language portfolios showcasing their growth. This is one very small piece of what these teachers do in their work to carry Pahka'anil on in future generations, and also one very small piece of what Lindsay does as their linguist. However, their experience so far is that using language portfolios aligned with the Can-Do Statements is helpful for guiding development of curriculum and for setting goals for ongoing growth as Pahka'anil users.

Case Study 3 Zalmai Zahir
Lushootseed Language Nesting in the Home

Zalmai Zahir is of Sioux ancestry on his mother's side and was raised by his mother and Puyallup step-father. It was from them that he learned the importance of language and culture. He began learning Lushootseed from his step-father at age eleven and began teaching it in 1989. He also studied and apprenticed with Lushootseed elder, scholar, and professor, Dr. Vi Hilbert. Using various teaching methods over the years with limited success, Zalmai developed a methodology that borrows from various approaches, including reclaiming domains and 'language nesting'. He has turned portions of his home into a Lushootseed language nest by focusing on using language with specific activities, such as sweeping the floor,

---

[16] www.actfl.org/publications/guidelines-and-manuals/ncssfl-actfl-can-do-statements

Case Study 3 (*cont.*)

making breakfast, and washing the dishes. Zalmai is reclaiming these activities as Lushootseed domains within his home. He teaches and assists other learners and language programs on how to use this approach.

Over the past thirty plus years we have seen that learning language in 'nests', places where language is fostered and cared for as a parent cares for a child, places where learning is nurtured and respected, has proven to produce fluent speakers.[17] And, in particular, speakers of Indigenous languages who are using this model to revitalize their languages are finding it vital to language use as it requires learners to speak and converse on a regular basis. Zalmai defines two types of nests that exist for language revitalization – a *nest for children*, and a *nest for language*. 'A "nest for children" is a physical location where the **children are nested** in the language. This is the primary accepted definition by language revitalizationists. A "nest for language" is a physical location where **the language is nested**, not the learners. It is not limited to the involvement of children, and it can occur in the home.'[18] Zalmai broadens the definition of a language nest to a 'place in the home, or the whole home itself, where adult learners and speakers with or without children will use the language. This can facilitate the growth of language use to several hours per day, and it provides a means for language transmission to friends, family and children'. It allows for activities of daily living to be 'reclaimed' in the language of the home.

As we will see in other case studies, language nesting can occur in locations in and outside of the home. Wherever it occurs, the goal is to speak the Indigenous language every time one is in that space. The dominant language is not allowed to be spoken in language nests. When a physical space is created to specifically support language use, learners have to speak the language. Teachers then create learning materials for real-life activities and teaching occurs one activity at a time.

For example, choose a room where you want to use the language. If you live in a family or with friends, decide together which space you want to begin with. For example, if you eat together, cook together, and use the kitchen to socialize, consider beginning in the kitchen. Because the kitchen functions as a gathering space, it supports the extended learning of friends and family. Many domains can be reclaimed in the kitchen (we list a few below).

Activities to support learning in the kitchen:

(1) using the sink
(2) washing your hands
(3) cleaning the counter
(4) washing dishes

---

[17] W. Wilson and K. Kamanā, 'Mai Loko Mai O Ka 'Īini: Proceeding from a dream: The Aha Pūnana Leo connection in Hawaiian language revitalization', in L. Hinton and K. Hale (eds.), *The Green Book of Language Revitalization in Practice* (San Diego, CA: Academic Press, 2008), pp. 147–78.

[18] Zahir, 'Language nesting in the home'.

Case Study 3 (*cont.*)

(5) putting away groceries
(6) making a sandwich
(7) making a cup of tea
(8) making coffee
(9) frying an egg
(10) boiling vegetables

Once you have an idea of the activities you want to reclaim, then the next step is to identify the language phrases you will need and to teach them. We suggest you begin with self-narration, saying aloud the words and phrases as you do each of the actions. This will help you decide if the phrases you chose are relevant to the activity, and it will help you to determine the ordering of the actions in the activity. Additionally, this process reinforces language learning by physically doing what you are learning. As a teacher you can see how these activities create a framework for learning and how they contribute to building your kitchen curriculum.

Here is an example script to try if you want to reclaim the domain of *washing your hands*.

(1) I turn on the water.
(2) (Now) I take the soap.
(3) I put it on my hands.
(4) I wash my hands.
(5) I rinse my hands.
(6) I turn off the water.
(7) I take the towel.
(8) I dry my hands.

Zalmai has found that if he is more prescriptive with the process, i.e. 'Take this activity and post it in your bathroom. Do it each time you wash your hands, increasing your daily language use by five minutes per day', learners have better success.

If you need help coming up with the phrases you want to teach, you can go to other speakers in your community. For communities who no longer have first speakers, you can look at documented language materials such as texts, grammars and dictionaries, or work with a linguist to gather words and phrases. These sentences will grow as your lesson plans develop.

Here is a visual learning tip:

- Make labels writing the needed vocabulary and phrases on them.
  - Write the names (nouns) of each object you want to learn
  - Write the actions (verbs) you are wanting to learn
- Post names and phrases in areas of your home (or other places) where activities will take place, so for this activity, in the kitchen.
  - Use the labels to learn nouns.
  - Use phrases to learn actions

Case Study 3 (*cont.*)

Say the vocabulary and phrases aloud as you are doing the actions and teaching them. Record them on your phone and listen to them during the day. Ask your students to do the same in their homes. The key for all activities is using the language.

Case Study 4 Loren Me-lash-ne' Bommelyn Master-Apprentice Language Learning Model

Loren Me'-lash-ne Bommelyn is Tolowa, Karuk, and Wintu and is a tradition bearer for the Tolowa tribe. He has dedicated himself to preserving traditional songs, language, and basketry. He is the foremost ceremonial leader of the tribe, and its most prolific basketweaver. Me'-lash-ne is an enrolled member of the federally recognized Tolowa Dee-ni'. His mother, Eunice Bommelyn, was a prominent first speaker of the Tolowa Dee-ni' language, an Athabaskan language spoken in coastal Northern California, at Crescent City and Smith River, and a cultural advocate. Me'-lash-ne is a fluent speaker of the Tolowa Dee-ni' language and taught for over thirty years as a Tolowa high-school language teacher in Crescent City, California.

From the time Me-lash-ne' was a child he wanted to know everything there was about plants. It was his dream to be an ethno-botanist and horticulturist. Also, he was curious about his family's language, Tolowa Dee-ni', as his mother was a speaker. He would go with her to visit elders and family and listen to them as they spoke. He would practice and put to use the language he learned. His interest in plants and language was known in the community, and he would ask many questions of his elders on these visits.

One of the learning strategies Me-lash-ne' used when walking to school, or to family and friends' homes, or to anywhere really, was that when looking at an object, he would replace the English word for the Tolowa Dee-ni' word, and over time he saw his environment through Tolowa Dee-ni' eyes.

Me-lash-ne' studied traditional dance and song with an elder and through these teachings he created his own songs in Tolowa Dee-ni' to which dancers dance today. For everything Me-lash-ne' wanted to learn and know about, he found an elder to teach him, to apprentice with. It was in this way that he learned Tolowa Dee-ni', and now as a master himself, learners apprentice with him. The essence of this teaching/learning method is to immerse oneself with the language in an environment with an elder, relying on the environment and one's curiosity to guide learning.[19]

---

[19] Hinton et al., *How to Keep Your Language Alive*.

Case Study 5 Pyuwa Bommelyn
Tolowa Dee-ni' Programs and Teaching Strategies

Pyuwa Bommelyn is a Tolowa Dee-ni' Nation tribal member and a second language speaker of Tolowa Dee-ni'. He is the son of Loren Me-lash-ne' and Lena Bommelyn, and grandson of Eunice Bommelyn. Me-lash-ne' and Lena raised their three children in the Tolowa Dee-ni' language, with Me-lash-ne' speaking to his children, and now grandchildren, primarily in Tolowa Dee-ni'. Because of this, Pyuwa and his wife Ruby Tuttle are able to raise their three children in Tolowa Dee-ni'. Ruby teaches their children at home (homeschools) providing an education rich in language, culture, and academics.

In this section we share different teaching methods of Tolowa Dee-ni' in early education, home, high school, and community language programs that serve three-year olds to seniors (60+ years).

Accelerated Second Language Acquisition

The Accelerated Second Language Acquisition (ASLA) approach, attributed to Dr. Stephen Greymorning (Neyooxet), is used in community and high-school classrooms.

ASLA teaching goals first target 'imprinting' nouns and verbs (the heart of the language), using concrete examples in the language. Once learners can use these with each other, they move onto the more abstract parts of the language, such as descriptors, adverbials, and classifiers, for example. Verbs are kept in the first and second person singular form most of the time to make learning more tangible.

Depending upon what class it is, Tolowa Dee-ni' teachers make their own teaching materials (language learning skill sets) which they call 'Indintivities'. Activities include Total Physical Response commands to support learners doing the motions they are learning, providing a kinesthetic input to learning. Once learners are familiar with the vocabulary, pair and group learning activities focus on using the vocabulary in specific domains. For example, in a lesson on *Vine tea* learners work on associated nouns, verbs of actions, and commands on plant identification: where the plant is located; when and how it is gathered and processed; why it is used; and its health benefits. This learning includes cultural knowledge about what one needs to know before picking the plant.

ASLA Learning in Domains – Reclaiming the Language of Place

As seen above with Vine tea, ASLA learning techniques can be used to reclaim domains and to bring language into daily life in specific spaces where it had not been used for some time. Here are some examples of developing language fluency within specific domains using ASLA strategies.

Classroom – In the classroom, young children learn to respond to and ask phrases like: come and sit at the circle; please set the table; would you like some milk?; time to brush teeth; I have to go to the bathroom; will you be my partner?; time to clean up.

Case Study 5 (*cont.*)

Home – learners learn vocabulary related to cooking a meal, beginning with a scripted conversation until enough language is learned to be conversational.

Community – In the community, a cultural location can act as a domain – a particular place on the reservation tied to a traditional lifeway. An example for the Tolowa Dee-ni' is the place where smelt fish are found. Fish are caught with a net and are then dried on the beach. Prior to learners fishing at the beach, teachers will teach vocabulary and phrases in the classroom. They will teach the cultural traditions of smelt fishing and drying so learners are better prepared to do the activities in the language. Once learners are at fish camp, this language will be used as they fish, prepare, and dry the fish.

High School – Teaching at the high school provides the most consistent learning environment. Students can take two years of daily Tolowa Dee-ni' classes for credit at the local high school, Del Norte High School (DNHS), taught by Guylish Bommelyn. This structure provides a framework for successful learning in contrast to the weekly community classes that have varying levels of attendance and thus pose a challenge to consistent learning. At the beginning of the year, Guylish gives students a survey, asking them to identify their learning interests. From this he plans lessons in the domains that students suggest. Initial lessons taught using ASLA include nouns, adjectives, and verbs, including commands. Additionally, he uses games, and incorporates body movement to learn Tolowa Dee-ni' verbs.

For example, 'ice cream' was identified as a domain that students wanted to learn. Guylish brings ice cream into the classroom using language to: (a) ask for ice cream, (b) explain how to get the ice cream out of the container; (c) give ice cream to classmates/each other; (d) describe the taste; and (e) discuss likes and dislikes. Language domains change throughout the year.

Pole fishing is another example. There are Tolowa Dee-ni' words for fish, pole fishing, stream, and hook, but not words for bobber, weight, spool. Thus, new vocabulary is needed for these domains. So teachers look at how nouns are formed and come up with a new word based on this same pattern so that learners can use the language longer in the domain for longer. Then learners can talk about 'catching a fish, reeling it in, and attaching a weight'; all the actions needed for pole fishing. Videos of this particular unit have been created, and lessons are posted on Instagram that are linked to the Tolowa Dee-ni' Language Program's Facebook page and the Tribe's website for tribal members to access when wanting to integrate language into their activities.

Language in the Home Program

The Tolowa Dee-Nation's Language Program implemented a *language in the home* program over three years ago. Families are required to commit to learning Tolowa Dee-ni' for at least one year. To begin with, a pre- and exit assessment on each family's general attitude toward learning the language was created and used to design the year of Tolowa Dee-ni' lessons, which provides a benchmark of what families learn in the year. The first part of the program engaged families in

Case Study 5 (cont.)

discussing their language learning attitudes. A Tolowa Dee-ni' teacher goes to a home to talk about language barriers, asking, for example, 'What are the barriers to family language learning; How does it make you feel learning language now?'

Families received a visit once a week from a Tolowa Dee-ni' language teacher. Tolowa Dee-ni' materials were made for that home by the language teacher, and families were taught how to use the materials for meaningful language learning in their home. Each family had a language quota (how much Tolowa Dee-ni' language they can/want to learn in a year). The Tolowa Dee-ni' teacher and family members then talk about what is realistic for them and language learning techniques. The Māori language program philosophy and the questions the Māori use to learn language are used as a guide for family learning. The Language in the Home program has been successful for five families. An important aspect for the families is that they need to set their own goals and be responsible for their own learning. This is emphasized throughout the year.

Some Closing Remarks
The point of learning the language of many domains, and why the Tolowa Language Program emphasizes language use and creating new words, is that they want learners to use language on a daily basis. They support learners to use 'everyday' speech. What strategies are used to support this? Extending immersion times in the classroom; learning in domains; building up language so learners can stay in the language and use it for longer periods of time; working on language attitudes in the community because any negativity impedes language learning; and sharing the language to accommodate Tolowa sister language varieties to be inclusive of how all folks learned to say things.

Case Study 6 Ruby Tuttle
Tolowa Dee-ni' as the Language of Homeschooling

Ruby Tuttle (Yurok/Yuki/Maidu/Karuk) and Pyuwa Bommelyn began schooling their children at home (homeschooling) in the language of their family, Tolowa Dee-ni', in 2013. Ruby and Pyuwa made the decision prior to the birth of their children that they would raise their children in Tolowa Dee-ni'. And as the children grew and decisions needed to be made about how they would be educated, it became apparent that if the children were to be speakers of Tolowa Dee-ni', sending them to schools where English was the medium of educating was not an option. Schooling then extended the children's Tolowa Dee-ni' language and cultural foundation and identity to embrace academic learning in their home.

Case Study 6 (*cont.*)

Homeschooling Teaching Strategies
The homeschooling space serves multiple functions. It is a language nest for early Tolowa Dee-ni' learners and for adult learner-teachers, and it is a lab to pilot and test developing elementary Tolowa Dee-ni' curriculum. Homeschooling demands that teachers are skilled in numerous language immersion methods, and in determining which strategy or activity to use in any given situation. One needs to be able to have a cache of lessons or activities that will engage students as their attention moves from one thing to the next. Ruby notes that she uses every method she knows about that promotes talking Tolowa Dee-ni'.

New vocabulary is introduced using ASLA language sets, then, to reinforce language use, Ruby uses immersion language teaching strategies. She reinforces learning with the 'five steps' where she introduces language to be learned, asks learners to listen as she says it, and then she asks learners to mimic her, putting off independent production until the end of the lesson. Ruby emphasizes that if you expect learners to speak too soon it sets up disappointment when they are unable to follow through.

Ruby and Pyuwa teach their children to be autonomous learners. One way is through using the Tolowa Dee-ni' dictionary. Another way is using a *word wall* on which the children write a word in English that they want to know in Dee-ni', and Ruby or Pyuwa add the Tolowa Dee-ni' word next to it.

Teaching Activities
Ruby stresses learning through pair activities, where the children work together to find solutions to language 'problems', and through kinetic learning.

Kinetic Activities – Children Learn through Movement
- taping a vocabulary word to a bowling pin. The children have to say the word on the pin as they roll the ball to knock the pin down;
- beachball volley. Here the children throw a beachball (or other soft ball) back and forth to each other, saying the word taped to the ball. Two balls can be thrown at the same time, one ball with a noun taped to it and the other a verb;
- an addition to volleying two balls after learning the words on each ball, is making a sentence using the two words.

Drawing – Ruby emphasizes that children need to take ownership of the language they are learning and, as a teacher, she needs to support them in that. She has had success with activities that allow children to create pictures and drawings with the language that they know.

The penny game – The Baldwin family created this game when their children were learning the Miami language. It positively reinforces language learning and use, and Ruby and Pyuwa have adapted it to learning Tolowa Dee-ni'. It goes like this: when you 'catch' someone using a Tolowa Dee-ni' word, you give them a penny for using the word. It helps children recognize that what they are doing is a good thing and good things come from what they are learning. It also gets a little

Case Study 6 (*cont.*)

competitive and the children will inquire how to say new words so they can say them and add pennies to their jars.

Some Thoughts
Ruby stresses that being consistent in how one teaches and not giving up are two of the most important elements of teaching. The grind of creating curriculum and making sure you are meeting your own cultural standards as well as school standards can be demotivating, making you feel like you are not doing enough. Ruby reminds us that the biggest thing is to just keep going. When she feels she is losing motivation for teaching, she goes back to her own motivation goals for learning and teaching Tolowa Dee-ni'. She asks, 'What is my motivation for doing this in the first place?' And she answers, 'Someone sacrificed for me to be here. Hearing the children using the language. Seeing them speaking to each other.' Those are some of the personal motivations that keep her going.

In summary, you have to think about what motivates you from within. If your reasons for doing it are your own, if they come from within you, they will remotivate you to start again and continue the language work.

Case Study 7 Pigga Keskitalo
Realizing Sámi Culturally Meaningful Education in the Classroom

Pigga Keskitalo is of Sámi origin, born in Finland in a small village in Nuorgam. She lived next to her grandmother's farm, with extended family living nearby. She learned Sámi at home as both her parents were Sámi speaking. Ville Ásllat Piggá is her Sámi name according to her father's father and means 'daughter Piggá of Aslak of Ville'.

During her studies and her work in pre- and in-service teacher education, she has been interested in developing an Indigenous schooling system. Discussions with students and classroom teachers have focused on the need to organize teaching in a culturally meaningful way, and how to teach students so that they understand and can practice cultural traditions. An example of cultural traditions taught to primary school pupils includes *smoking meat* – here traditional knowledge is used to teach Sámi language concepts, and academic content about the physics of smoking meat.

We see that in ideal circumstances, successful teaching and Sámi learning are based on the values of the surrounding community,[20] which considers the elements of Sámi cultural well-being. Culturally sensitive teaching is achieved when Sámi

---

[20] E. R. Hollins, 'Foreword', in T. H. Kohl (ed.), *Culture in School Learning: Revealing the Deep Meaning* (New York, NY: Routledge, 2008), pp. xi–xii.

Case Study 7 (*cont.*)

education is grounded on the Sámi concepts of place, time, and knowledge.[21] In the old culture, the concept of time was sun-centered and bound to observing the nature. The Sámi conception of space is not bound to square feet, rather it is circular.[22] Sámi reindeer herding, like many other traditional livelihoods, is an example of how these concepts influence life, as herders function according to time-honored environmental practices that require 'flexible' thinking, meaning one's ability to respond to one's immediate environment.

Sámi Dwelling Place – Goahti

In teaching arrangements, the Sámi conception of space would lead to a wider place of learning than the classroom. Information that pupils need also exists outside the school walls. The traditional Sámi dwelling place *goahti* is one example. The inner organization of the *goahti* can be applied to classroom organization, creating a more traditional Sámi school setting. A *goahti* has several physical areas where various tasks take place, with different people carrying out each task. When applied in a classroom, for example, a teacher could set up various teaching areas with individual tasks for student learning. The classroom would be divided into 'posts' with various work tasks that could be cultural and academic in nature, thereby transforming the usual classroom organization into one that represented a *goahti,* both physically and culturally. Widening hyper-traditional approaches may include teachers, elders, and others introducing new vocabulary. Sámi immersive teaching methods include doing traditional activities while using the language, like fishing and preparing food. In addition, suburban challenges are included, like taking into account the challenges of Indigenous peoples in suburban areas.

Case Study 8 Janne Underriner – When Full Immersion Is Not an Option in the Classroom What Can You Do to Stay in the Language?

Janne Underriner is a teacher of Chinuk Wawa, an Indigenous creole language of the Pacific Northwest.

We have seen in this chapter examples from teachers using language-learning strategies that support speaking Indigenous language in various contexts. Their common goal is to have learners using the language in daily settings outside of the

---

[21] P. Keskitalo, 'Saamelaiskoulun kulttuurisensitiivisyyttä etsimässä kasvatusantropologian keinoin' [Searching cultural sensitivity of Sámi School], *Dieđut 1* (Guovdageaidnu: Sámi allaskuvla); P. Keskitalo, K. Määttä, and S. Uusiautti, 'Toward the practical framework of Sámi education', *British Journal of Educational Research* 1/2 (2011), 84–106.

[22] P. Fjellström, *Samernas samhälle. I tradition och nutid* [Society of the Sámi people, In tradition and today] (Stockholm: Norstedt & Söners Förlag, 1985).

Case Study 8 (*cont.*)

classroom; engaged in day-to-day communication in the Indigenous language. In the Pacific Northwest, where for most communities it is not possible to provide language-rich learning environments with first language speakers, teaching language can be as much about strengthening learner's self-esteem and providing a heightened awareness of culture, place, and history as it is about teaching language. Teaching may focus more on learning vocabulary and phrases for situations of cultural relevance through stories and song; teaching words and phrases that are used in religious ceremonies or while gathering food; or learning how to count living things from nonliving things.

For many Pacific Northwest Indigenous language teachers, teaching within a traditional immersion model where learning occurs for a day or half-day in the Indigenous language is not realistic. As we saw earlier, immersion teaching requires a high degree of fluency; higher than many teachers in this area have, so teachers are working to incorporate immersion teaching into their classrooms by presenting limited topics in which they have the ability to teach in the language for short periods of time. In the Pacific Northwest, most language teachers are typically language learners, younger adults who have a strong commitment to their language. Their challenge is to keep at least a step ahead of their students, providing a language-rich classroom environment within their own level of proficiency. Hinton suggests that a teacher who is learning her own language while she is teaching it focus on learning various components of a lesson. If a teacher learns the lesson elements – not only the new and review material presented in the lesson but also greetings, classroom management vocabulary, and informal patter – she can have an immersion classroom.[23]

The benefits of using immersion techniques for a shorter time are available to less than fully fluent teachers. In these situations, immersion teaching calls for a strategy of beginning with using the Indigenous language in five, ten, fifteen-minute intervals and increasing from there. Teachers can use specific activities to stretch what they do know, for example, counting from 1 to 10 could be a ten-minute activity that maintained student's interest throughout with song, humor, and physical movements. Or teaching about spring foods (roots) can include a traditional story taught in the dominant language using the Indigenous words for roots, colors, season, and place names. Learners can then use the language that they have learned in the classroom at their community celebrations and when they are root digging in their traditional gathering places. This teaching strategy nurtures authentic language use in everyday communication and traditional practices, meaning that it has immediate application for learners in their community.

---

[23] L. Hinton, 'How to teach when the teacher isn't fluent', in J. Reyner, O. V. Trujillo, R. L. Carrasco, and L. Lockard (eds.), *Nurturing Native Languages* (Flagstaff: Northern Arizona University, 2003), pp. 79–92.

Some Concluding Words

Our goal in writing this chapter was to share teaching methods and strategies that support language use. The hands-on activities highlighted show how learning can be accessible and support language use in daily life. Our experience has shown us that these activities motivate learning, bridge classroom and home learning, and bring language use into the community. We hope you will try these activities and that they enrich your teaching, and that, ultimately, you will experience similar results. Please feel free to contact any one of us.

FURTHER READING

Hinton, L. (2003). How to teach when the teacher isn't fluent. In J. Reyner, O. V. Trujillo, R. L. Carrasco, and L. Lockard, eds., *Nurturing Native Languages*. Flagstaff: Northern Arizona University, pp. 79–92.

Hinton, L. and Hale, K., eds. (2008). *The Green Book of Language Revitalization in Practice*. San Diego, CA: Academic Press.

Hinton, L., Huss, L., and Roche, G., eds. (2018). *The Routledge Handbook of Language Revitalization*. New York: Routledge.

Hinton, L., Vera, M., and Steele, N. (2002). *How to Keep Your Language Alive: A Common Sense Approach to One-on-One Language Learning*. Berkeley, CA: Heyday Books.

Johnson, M. K. S. (2016). Ax toowú át wudikeen, my spirit soars: Tlingit direct acquisition and co-learning pilot project. *Language Documentation and Conservation*, 10, 306–36. https://scholarspace.manoa.hawaii.edu/bitstream/handle/10125/24695/johnson.pdf.

Lightbown, P. M. and Spada, N. (2013). *How Languages Are Learned*, 4th ed., Oxford: Oxford University Press.

15.1 Ka Hoʻōla ʻŌlelo Hawaiʻi I O Nā Kula: Hawaiian Language Revitalization through Schooling

Larry L. Kimura

Hawaiian revitalization efforts currently focus on Hawaiian-medium education as an effective framework to reverse the demise of the marginalized Indigenous Hawaiian language and cultural identity. Using the Native Hawaiian language as the medium of education began with the founding of the ʻAha Pūnana Leo in 1983, a nonprofit education organization that established its first preschools in 1984–1985 for children aged three to five. These schools continue until today and are conducted five days a week throughout the school year, from 7:00 AM to 4:00 PM, where Hawaiian is the only language heard while education takes place. The ʻAha Pūnana Leo preschool children served as the impetus for the first

Hawai'i[24] Department of Education's Hawaiian Language Immersion Program, started in 1987. Currently there are twenty-four Hawaiian immersion school sites in the Hawaiian Islands. In 2019 the Hawai'i public schools Hawaiian immersion program graduated its twentieth consecutive preschool (three to five years old) through twelfth grade high school (sixteen to seventeen years old), or P-12 Hawaiian immersion class since the first such Hawaiian immersion graduation cycle was achieved in 1999.

The term 'Hawaiian immersion' is now moving into 'Hawaiian-medium' education, where Hawai'i's Indigenous language is more than just a 'novel' way of 'immersing' a child in a foreign language separate from a country's mainstream language to conduct a child's education. Hawaiian medium education utilizes the endangered, unconventional Native Hawaiian language totally as the language of instruction, interweaving the Indigenous Hawaiian cultural identity and rendering the Hawaiian language as the Hawaiian foundation to engage the world. This Hawaiian medium education philosophy establishes its own conventions of education, and in the case of Hawai'i, also achieving the educational standards of a mainstream English society.[25]

Currently, the Hawaiian Language College, Ka Haka 'Ula O Ke'elikōlani, of the University of Hawai'i at the Hilo campus, serves as the major source for Hawaiian medium teacher certification and the College's Hale Kuamo'o Hawaiian Language Center develops Hawaiian medium curriculum resources for use in schools. The Hawaiian Language College offers a Bachelor's degree in Hawaiian language as well as Master's degrees in Hawaiian language and the state's first Doctorate degree for the Revitalization of Hawaiian and Indigenous Language and Culture. These graduate degrees represent the first graduate degrees to be offered in the USA for any Indigenous language. So as Hawai'i now witnesses the death of its very last native speakers and the success of its Hawaiian immersion and Hawaiian medium P-12 programs, it is imperative that the College of Hawaiian Language continues to generate highly fluent second language speakers of Hawaiian focused on Hawaiian medium tertiary education.

Since the establishment of the 'Aha Pūnana Leo in 1983 for Hawai'i's first Hawaiian language-medium Pūnana Leo preschools, thirty-six years of advancement in Hawaiian language-medium preschool to twelfth grade education into the public school system has resulted in unprecedented outcomes for Hawai'i. A standard of 100 percent high school graduation and 80 percent college entry rate for Hawaiian medium education students has been attained. These positive outcomes have uplifted the confidence and pride of a colonized minority Native population and have instilled achievable goals for the survival of the Hawaiian language and culture in its own homeland. Perhaps more significant has been the

---

[24] Hawai'i is a state of the USA. It was annexed by the USA as a territory in 1898, then officially admitted as state in 1959.

[25] Nāwahīokalani'ōpu'u is one of the College of Hawaiian Language's laboratory P-12 Hawaiian Medium schools. Please visit: www.nawahi.org.

creation of highly fluent second language speaking parents who are now raising the new generation of Hawaiian first language speakers from the home. This sets the stage for further developments in formal Hawaiian-medium education that will continue to reach into the economic, social, legal, and political structures of society to regain the Hawaiian language and cultural identity's rightful place in its own Native land while moving into the wider world.

FURTHER READING

'Aha Pūnana Leo preschool language nest movement, www.ahapunanaleo.org/.
Kaiapuni schools – Hawaiian language immersion, www.hawaiipublicschools.org/TeachingAndLearning/StudentLearning/HawaiianEducation/Pages/Hawaiian-language-immersion-schools.aspx.

15.2 Kristang Language Revitalization in Singapore under the Kodrah Kristang Initiative, 2016–Present

Kevin Martens Wong

Kristang is an endangered Portuguese creole, once spoken in various forms across Southeast Asia from the seventeenth century. Today, it is spoken mostly by older speakers in Melaka, Malaysia, where the language arose after the Portuguese conquest of the city in 1511, and Singapore, whose Kristang community (today known as Portuguese-Eurasians) developed in the early nineteenth century following the establishment of a British trading outpost in 1819. The dominance of the English language in colonial and then independent Singapore, together with the perception of Kristang as 'patois Portuguese', ensured that by the late twentieth century, knowledge of the language's very existence in Singapore was almost forgotten, even by younger Portuguese-Eurasians. Intergenerational transmission most likely ceased by the late 1960s, and the language is not taught in schools, or used in media or publications. As a result, it was estimated that, in 2015, less than 100 speakers of Kristang remained in Singapore.

Kodrah Kristang ('Awaken, Kristang') is a youth-led grassroots revitalization movement that started in March 2016 with a free pilot class for adult learners in Kristang following a year of documentation in Singapore. This first class was a collaboration between an older speaker involved in documentation who wanted the language preserved, and a younger Kristang learner who led the documentation effort. Successive rounds of this class were then developed into a full structured 160-hour curriculum based on Communicative Language Teaching and Task-Based Language Teaching principles (for more details see below). A thirty-year revitalization plan for the language, developed in 2016 at the Institute on Collaborative Language Research (CoLang) at the University of Alaska Fairbanks, also informed the development of the curriculum. This plan is divided into five phases: Prendeh ('Learning': 2016–2017), Abrasah ('Embracing': 2017–2018), Alkansah ('Achieving': 2018–2021), Kriseh

('Increasing': 2021–2035), and Subih ('Elevating': 2035–2045). Ultimately, the plan seeks to redevelop space for Kristang in the Singaporean home, whether Portuguese-Eurasian or otherwise, and invite, encourage, and sustain community ownership in the revitalization of the language.

The Kodrah Kristang initiative focuses on outreach and collaboration, building a broad base of contacts while maintaining a strong focus on attracting young people and ensuring that the effort is grassroots/community-oriented and low-cost. Kodrah's youth-led core team is multiethnic, with only two out of five of the present team being of Portuguese-Eurasian descent. Classes are open to anyone of any ethnicity, not just Portuguese-Eurasians. This is due to the initiative's urban context, the small size of the Portuguese-Eurasian community (about 0.4 percent of the population, or 16,000 individuals), and strong sensitivities in Singaporean society and the Singapore Eurasian community about language and race. The core team continues to work with remaining Kristang speakers to deliver lessons, with a (younger) core team member leading classes from the front and one or more Kristang speakers usually present among the students to provide feedback and support. Lessons are structured almost entirely around games and interactive activities to facilitate the growth of a new Kristang-speaking community founded on strong interpersonal relationships.

All classes and class-related materials are free, as the initiative has cultivated a system of reusable long-term capital and strong relationships with venue partners to reduce financial barriers to long-term sustainability. Broadly speaking, most class activities make use of common household items and games (e.g. poker cards, dice, rough paper) that cost little and can be reused as long-term capital. Slides are uploaded online so printing is left to the individual learner's discretion. The team makes use of a small amount of funds accumulated from the Kristang Language Festival in 2017 (see below) and sales of Kristang dictionaries and games fund the printing of some worksheets and purchasing of long-term capital such as dice and cards. Meanwhile the current Core Team are all registered People's Association (PA) trainers in Singapore, which allows them to run classes at any community center in Singapore for a very minimal fee.

As of May 2019, about 280 individuals, including 15 children of various ages, have completed the entry-level Kodrah 1A course and the associated ALKAS assessment, a diagnostic tool developed to determine learners' progress after two modules. Thirty students from the pioneer group in July 2016 completed the first round of highest-level 4A and 4B courses in November 2018. Meanwhile wider public outreach has been extensive, with the initiative nominated for the prestigious Singapore President's Volunteer and Philanthropy Award in 2017 and 2018, for demonstrating Kampong Spirit. Other initiatives include a pilot children's class in July 2017 and the successful launch of the first Kristang Language Festival, held in May 2017 and attended by over 1,400 individuals. A number of Kodrah students have independently initiated projects of their own featuring Kristang, including a film (*Nina Boboi*), a graphic novel (*Boka di Stori*), a children's book series, and a Massive Multiplayer Online Roleplaying Game (MMORPG). These are not part of the revitalization plan but have seen significant support from both the Eurasian community and wider Singaporean society; *Nina Boboi* featured on the online streaming service Toggle and the graphic novel *Boka di Stori* was funded by a Yale-NUS Futures of Our Pasts grant.

15.3 Teaching and Learning of Wymysiöeryś

Tymoteusz Król

As a child I was obsessed with thinking about what would happen if the native speakers of my language died out. When I was ten, the youngest of them were over seventy years old, so I realized that it would unfortunately come fast. Then I would be alone in Wilamowice as if in a *fremd* (foreign) place.

I knew that the only way to change this situation was to teach my friends. At that time, they would rather tease me than show an interest in learning Wymysiöeryś. As I was thinking about how to deal with it, I discovered that lessons in Wymysiöeryś were to be organized at the school, led by an old Vilamovian – Józef Gara fum Toler. He taught a few children, but unfortunately, because of his age (he was about eighty), he could not do it for long. Then, after two years, the lessons stopped. It was the year 2006. I thought that may be the time spent teaching children, who do not learn much, could be better spent recording the last living native speakers and undertaking language documentation.

Then, in 2011, I decided to start teaching the language. I thought about focusing on documentation, but I realized that I did not want to feel guilty that I kept the new generation of speakers from knowing the old native speakers. The first group were children from the Dance Group 'Wilamowice', then came their friends and I had to organize a couple of groups at different levels. They did their homework with the Wymysiöeryś native speakers: they helped them with housework while speaking Wymysiöeryś together. The old people are often alone, so they were very happy to have guests who were young and interested in their language and in their life stories.

There were years when I had about twelve groups and I taught about twenty-four hours per week. In 2011 I was eighteen, so my workload included preparation for the secondary school exit exams and then university, where I also had many exams. My parents did not like that I would spend more time teaching than learning and I failed my university exams twice. For them and for some friends of mine it was a big tragedy and they could not understand why I kept teaching children and teens who would sometimes stop learning or not treat me well: what if nobody wanted to continue? But I knew that it was the price and the risk that we as Indigenous people take every day. That was not the only decision that I took in 2011. I was thinking every day that while there were many children here who stopped learning, there were also many academics who abandoned their activities in Wilamowice, because they felt dissatisfied with their effectiveness. For example, some people wanted to start projects, but then they realized that their work would remain unknown, or that there are too few native speakers, or that young people do not speak in the same way as before World War II, or that this town is too small for them and they cannot spend a couple of months here because of the lack of entertainment. So why should I believe more in scholars than in my pupils?

There were many moments when I was in doubt, but now, I see my students writing poems and songs, playing in theatrical performances in Wymysiöeryś, teaching other children, speaking Wymysiöeryś with each other, using it on Facebook and creating websites about Wymysiöeryś. I can confirm for people who are thinking about taking a similar decision, that I do not regret it. I remember all the moments of doubt, but I know that this is the price that we, as locals, have to pay and nobody can do it for us. We are grateful for help from the universities in Warsaw and Poznan in preparing teaching materials and negotiating with local authorities, but organizing things on an everyday basis, teaching and as looking for new students, are all up to us.

15.4 Immersive Łemko Ethnophilology

Ołena Duć-Fajfer (translated by Joanna Maryniak)

Łemko ethnophilology was a degree course at the Pedagogical University of Kraków between 2001 and 2017. This program was needed because the Łemko training had been available only at the level of primary and high school and there was not space to prepare Łemko teachers and Łemko intelligentsia. It was closed because of standardized majority criteria for university programs: The university authorities decided there were not enough participants, whereas the recruitment rules were not adjusted to the specific situation of an ethnic minority. It was the only higher education course in Poland designed to prepare students for using the Łemko language in the public spaces and domains where minority languages are used in Poland, i.e. teaching, journalism, cultural animation, social work, research.

Students learned through common creative activities. During group and individual work they created texts in Łemko. These are published in a special section of Łemko newspapers and include book reviews as well as reports about Łemko events. The students participated not only in classes but also in journalism and music workshops. They also took part in linguistic and cultural practices in various places where Łemkos live and learn. This means that the development of their Łemko training was also shaped by the local socio-political and cultural life of this minority community. Students also had teaching practice in schools where Łemko is taught and during summer camps for Łemko youth. The most important part of these activities was the emphasis on their social meaning and social utility. The positive, family-like emotions they felt while learning creatively in Łemko-language situations reinforced their language awareness and learning.

A very important achievement of this program was the originality of the teaching method, which meets the needs of members of minority language communities and cultures. The main feature of this method was full immersion from the very start. It was possible because the lecturers were native users of Łemko who uphold Łemko customs in their private and social lives. Those students who were brought up knowing the Łemko language and culture provided important support for new

Figure 15.4.1 A presentation of Łemko books by Olena Duć-Fajfer, the founder of the Łemko philology, and Petro Murianka, a Łemko poet, writer, and teacher. Photo by Jarosław Mazur

speakers. Their innate knowledge of the domains of language and culture had positive impact on all the students – including those who had never had any contact with Łemko before. Working in such a diverse group of people is most effective as it shapes immersion dynamically and creates a special communicative and emotional sensitivity. If there are no native speakers in the group (and it happens), contact with the broadest possible range of students and Łemko youth is needed. This should happen in an environment where cultural and linguistic patterns of behavior are continued. Such emerging relationships among students bring about good results in the domains of information and emotion (and this is a priority when it comes to minority languages) as they motivate learning through approval – like in family relations. Students who aren't Łemkos are symbolically introduced into the family as they obtain their Łemko names and acquire the community language. This makes them feel special but also creates an obligation for them with regard to the language and its transmission. Students who are native speakers of Łemko are put in the position of teachers and supervisors. They also become aware of the mechanisms how the language is passed down in family environment along a number of contexts of its use and what is special about it. All this helps them have the confidence to use it in public spaces. The alumni of the Łemko ethnophilology course are among the most engaged revitalizers of the Łemko language and traditions (Figure 15.4.1).

15.5 Culture Place-Based Language Basketry Curriculum at the Confederated Tribes of the Grand Ronde Community

Janne Underriner

Place-based learning has emerged in Indigenous communities as a promising approach for language learning, revitalization, and maintenance. Place-based education has links to communicative and culturally based approaches. With community at the center, students learn about core values, culture, their homelands, their people's history, and current tribal affairs as they learn their language. Students become connected to what is essential to their tribal community *and* to the ways of their ancestors. It also links students with members of their larger, not just tribal, community who contribute to its diverseness, and in so doing it opens students' awareness to elders, leaders, mentors, and peers they might not have encountered in a more teacher-centered classroom learning experience. 'Diverseness' means that students learn about people in their community; they learn about jobs and what people do; they learn about their government and the departments in their government. Students drive learning as much as teachers.

Place-based education supports recommendations of Indigenous educators for Indigenous students. Place-based education meets the call for the integration of the local and the inclusion of cultural knowledge in teaching, as well as increased involvement by the community. Incorporating culture into learning affords the opportunity for students to participate in traditional practices of the community today, linking the past to the present. In addition, culture place-based language learning builds identity and connection to surroundings. By design, it is collaborative and cultivates relationship building. It is experiential and so nurtures learners' curiosity, builds cooperation among students, and strengthens problem-solving abilities.

A culture place-based learning approach positions curriculum and lessons in local events and places, and acknowledges that learning happens not only in formal educational settings but also outside of school in families and communities. This reinforces connections to one's home, family, community, and world. Included components can be the cultural, historical, social, religious, and/or economic relevance of specific locations or regions.[26]

Culture place-based learning supports communicative language use as students work together on projects to investigate and understand the world at large. Here, for example, they use learned skills to make observations, collect data, and interview community members to carry out a group learning task. At the end of a project they disseminate the result in presentations at school and to community groups. Cooperation and communication are essential throughout the process, and team members learn to respect each other's views and contributions.

---

[26] G. Smith, 'Place-based education: Learning to be where we are', *Phi Delta Kappan* 83 (2002), 584–94; D. Gruenewald, 'Foundations of place: A Multidisciplinary framework for place-conscious education', *American Educational Research Journal* 40 (2003), 619–54.

Since 2000, I have been a member of the curriculum team at the Confederated Tribes of the Grand Ronde Community (CTGR) in Grand Ronde, Oregon in the United States. We have been writing culture place-based curriculum for their preschool, elementary, and high-school Chinuk Wawa immersion classroom where students three to ten and thirteen to seventeen years of age receive instruction. Our goal has been to create lessons that will promote learning, foster curiosity, and develop the connection to community. And they must be written and taught in ways that inspire learners to want to learn more.

Initially, a curriculum team (teachers, elders, curriculum writers, linguists, science, language arts teachers, community cultural specialists, parents) brainstorms ideas, and develops a topical curriculum web that provides interrelated themes, language needed, the sequence of what will be taught, and accompanying materials and resources (people as well as objects). Throughout, culture place-based objectives are incorporated into academic standards that meet school district requirements.

In developing culture place-based curriculum, we begin with:

(1) Curricular TOPIC idea that comes from teachers, students, a member of the community, and parents, for example, 'basketry'. From a topic,
(2) THEMATIC UNITS are determined and created; one could be material resources for basket-making: cedar basketry, hazel basketry, juncus basketry (plant resources). Or a unit could center on basket types (function) – for root digging, storage, holding water, for cooking. Another unit can center on basketry patterns. After units are determined we develop
(3) Lessons and materials

Here are some other topic examples:

- traditional lifeways (basketry, canoe making, digging roots) – each of these can be its own topic as seen above with basketry
- animals (beaver, elk, deer, condor)
- elders past and present
- storytellers
- roots (celery, camas)
- fish (salmon)
- berries (huckleberry, salal)
- acorns
- canoes
- land
- water and forest management
- health

An example of a place-based curriculum is the project *Basketry: Place, Community, and Voices*, a multidisciplinary, year-long unit. The project emerged from parent–community Chinuk Wawa language curriculum meetings. For decades, adult basketry-making classes/workshops have occurred year-round in Grand Ronde. Now parents wanted their children to learn about basket-making and initiated that classes be taught in the schools. Specifically parents and teachers wanted students to:

- understand that baskets are an important part of Grand Ronde culture
- know that juncus and hazel are used in creating traditional baskets
- identify different weaving materials in situ and in class
- be able to talk about weaving processes in both Chinuk Wawa and English
- weave different types of baskets with these materials.

Curricula meet Oregon State standards in math, science, social studies, history, art, and literary arts. Some examples of preschool – fifth-grade lessons include:

(1) *Math* – counting weavers; Geometric basket designs; Estimation; Even and odd numbers.
(2) *Social Studies and History* – Use of baskets and basket weavers past and present; Influence of outside communities.
(3) *Stories and Literature* – *Hattie Hudson* – a story of a past elder basket weaver.
(4) *We Go Gather* – a story about giving back to nature when taking from it.
(5) *Science* – Where, when, and how to harvest; Charring sticks for bark removal; Best management practices for guaranteeing future harvests; Processing materials; Qualities of good basketry materials; Experimenting with materials.

In workshops, specific basketry skills are targeted, so a year's curriculum can be taught in four or five intensive workshops. In schools, the curriculum is year-long and follows the seasons and time of year when gathering, processing, and weaving are carried out traditionally. For example, hazel is collected in the spring when sap is running throughout the plant. This is climate dependent, so one year it could occur in March, another year could be earlier or later. Learners travel to areas in their community on the Reservation to gather it. They begin weaving in the late spring and summer (also in the fall and winter) after hazel sticks have been prepared. In the summer and early fall, they use hazel baskets to gather berries, and in the early spring in digging roots. Winter lessons include learning basketry stories as traditional stories are told after the first freeze, learning gathering and digging songs and prayers, and learning basketry patterns. Each season learners are taught how to identify hazel in its environment, and how to care for it.

In developing curricular products, we considered those that would benefit the school and the community in general. Thus materials that resulted from the project serve various learner groups. Materials were made by students, parent and family members, basket weavers in the community, teachers, and the curriculum team and include: a multidisciplinary, twenty lesson year-long unit on hazel and juncus basketry of the Grand Ronde people; story, material processing, and pictorial books; and workshop videos.

Summing up, we find that culture place-based curriculum engages youth and children in learning their language in culturally appropriate ways. It builds relationships among mentors and youth, and supports older children to be role models for younger children. We experienced first-hand that a strength of culture place-based curriculum is that it is collaborative and local. It supports the understanding of plant materials, and traditional uses and practices of basketry. This aids in developing better natural resource management practices on tribal, private, and national forest lands. The curriculum informs learners about the health of the environment and land.

We see that learners, young and older, from traditional and nontraditional homes, are more willing to participate in community events at their tribal gym, longhouse/plankhouse (places where ceremony is practiced), and on reservation land (gathering natural resources for weaving, for example) because the curriculum familiarizes learners with traditional and community practices – learning holds at its center the values and traditions (past and present) of its elders, families, learners, and community members. In this way culture place-based learning offers an opportunity for community centered learning that promotes learners' well-being.

15.6 Sámi School Education and Cultural Environmentally Based Curriculum

Pigga Keskitalo

In 1997, a separate Sámi School was established in Norway. It follows the principles of the Sámi curriculum in the district area of the Sámi language, emphasizing the importance of bilingualism and the improvement of the status of this Indigenous language after it became officially recognized in the Sámi administrative district in 1990.

Ideally, teaching should be sensitive to the cultural values of the surrounding community. The Sámi curriculum has been developed by working groups including Sámi representatives. This model is based on cultural sensitivity and multilingualism.

Culturally sensitive teaching goals are fulfilled when Sámi education is grounded in Sámi conceptions of place, time, and knowledge (as discussed in Case Study 7 in this chapter). In Sámi culture, the concept of space is circular. Time is sun-centered and bound to observing nature. As a result, teaching takes into account the Sámi understanding of time by organizing classes in a more flexible way and giving up the forty-five-minute scheduling typical for school culture. In addition, the eight Sámi seasons are respected by considering the livelihoods and seasonal work of the Sámi. Traditional local knowledge and linguistic concepts are also included in the learning process.

Learning centered around Sámi values guides students and helps them to understand the social connections of community, their surroundings and nature. Teaching also has to include learning about flora and fauna and should reveal the strong connections between people and nature. Sámi traditional knowledge is derived directly from the environment where people live: concrete working situations and cottages, lean-to shelters, and campfires function as venues for a type of scientific seminar, as discussions are held there and traditional knowledge spreads. Culture-based learning is achieved through storytelling, conversations, and direct participation in these activities, as well as recalled memories and experiences. When applied in the school context, it means that knowledge is a shared

Figure 15.6.1 A girl in a *gákti* (traditional Sámi dress). Photo by Ibbá Lauhamaa

experience, which has at its foundation an ecological approach. Thus, education connects to every area of Sámi life, and promotes pupils' well-being and their links to the environment and land. Building on the school educational context, community members, parents, and elders also help children to recognize and incorporate traditional upbringing practices and working methods (Figure 15.6.1).

Parents and pupils need to be at the center of learning. The starting point in developing a curriculum involves organizing practical 'idea circles' for parents and pupils to discuss what they expect, what they dream of, and what their values are. To make sure that interaction and cooperation between pupils and parents works well, teachers need to set aside their role as an authority of school knowledge. It is also important to incorporate meaningful rituals into the curriculum. For example, you can reflect on how you start your teaching in the morning, maybe including morning circles and storytelling, and other kinds of culturally meaningful rituals to engage students each day. Employing traditional storytelling will support content learning and increase students' engagement in the learning process. You can also start your day by singing traditional music and songs, *luohti,* reading stories from books, and also presenting stories orally. Then the day can continue with tasks that pupils themselves plan, based on the week's goals. According to the Sámi values, learning should include working outside as well as inside, with physical activities that are connected to the day's learning goals.

Phenomenon-based curricular units can be organized around stories, for example, a chapter dealing with reindeer herding can include a story on drying

Figure 15.6.2 Reindeer meat will be smoked in a *lávvu* (lean-to-shelter). Photo by Pigga Keskitalo

meat in a *lávvu* (see Figure 15.6.2). We can also talk about drying fish or elk meat or smoking fish or meat. Students will learn traditional knowledge and Sámi values both through stories and more academic learning. For example, units can include:

- *Stories and language arts* – students learn traditional stories and create their own storybooks. Digital education materials can be included.
- *Science* – simple chemistry that is connected to traditional knowledge
  - What happens to meat when it is dried?
  - Does it weigh more or less when it dries?
  - Does the color change?
  - How is it dried?
  - How and why is it stored?
  - When is it eaten?
- *Ecology and natural resources*
  - Taking care of the environment
  - Taking care of reindeer
  - Sustainable development
- *Art and Music*
  - Sámi traditional handicrafts
  - Traditional music
  - Documenting the drying of reindeer meat through pictures, photos, and digitally (blogs, social media)

- *Social Studies and History*
  – History and present-day practices of reindeer herding
- *Food and cooking*
  – Traditional knowledge about drying reindeer meat
  – Interviewing traditional knowledge holders
  – Cooking traditional food and serving it to the community.

Where an endangered language is no longer being passed on in the family, activities focused on language learning should take the cultural contexts into account. Language learning should take an approach that integrates both content and language. Integrating content into language learning will support children without high levels of proficiency in the target language, providing them with concrete stimuli and practical situations that help them understand both the concepts and language.

15.7 'Use It, Don't Lose It'

ᏎᎶᏈᎣᎠ ᏙᎣᎠ, ᏣᎻᎦ꓄Ꭿ

Micah Swimmer

In 2001–2003, I was an Intern at the Cherokee Immersion program inside a daycare on the Qualla Boundary in Cherokee North Carolina. It was there that I first learned the importance of immersion. I was placed in a classroom with three fluent speakers and seven babies around one to two years of age. My most fond recollection was running out ahead of the class on their group walks to let everyone in our path know that 'we've got immersion babies coming, please speak only Cherokee to them, don't use English'. To us, English was like a sickness that we didn't want to expose our babies to. It was our effort to give them an environment of Cherokee Language and Culture only, and it was working.

Somewhere along the way of adding more classrooms, we began to stretch our speakers out too thin in order to accommodate the vast amount of interest the community had for wanting their children to be able to speak Cherokee. As years went on, the Immersion Academy administration, as well as the parents of the students, became concerned for their children's inability to read English on the child's grade level. This was the beginning of when English took over.

I can recall a pivotal moment that happened in 2014 as I was the Early Childhood Supervisor. When supervising the three-year-old room, I overheard the children saying things like, 'Come down here and fight me', 'Oh no I fell off the cliff', and 'Hurry up or the dinosaur is going to eat you'. Simple sentences but in English. I started writing down what they were saying, and they were things that I didn't know how to say in Cherokee. After a page and a half, I asked the second language learner teacher, who has been there for ten years if she could translate all these into Cherokee. After she read through it, she handed the paper back to me and said a few. It was then that I realized we needed to teach our teachers. We can't teach what we don't know.

I started an adult program like the one our brothers and sisters from Cherokee Nation of Oklahoma had. It was geared toward my early childhood staff, but failed because of the teachers not having enough time to work in their classrooms and spend enough time to learn the language.

In July 2018, I took on our first cohort of adult-language learners. We started out with something I call 'Interview, Lexicon and Pre-test (ILP)'. The first day we gave the learners an interview or 'hot-seat' if you will. The learners would come in one at a time and sit in front of myself and the (7) speakers, where we would ask them random questions such as 'What is your name', 'Where do you live', 'Where did you grow up,' 'How old are you', 'Do you have any kids', 'Who are your parents,' 'What is your clan', etc. This was done to give us a baseline of where each learner was at with their language skills. Some learners were able to answer a few of the questions, and some were unable to answer even one. Every four to six months we would reinterview them, and they would show tremendous improvement. By the end of the first year they were all able to answer every single one of those same questions without hesitation.

Once the interviews were complete, I had each learner create a lexicon. They were asked to write down every word and phrase that they knew how to say in the Cherokee language. I believe that we as second language learners know how much we know and that we could effectively display what we know in the lexicon. Just like the interviews, after around four to six months the learners would add new words and phrases that they had learned to their lexicons. The new words and phrases were entered under a separate color so that we could see the growth that they had made.

Finally, a pretest was given. The test content was randomly selected lessons that we would eventually cover in the future. I would also administer the same test after the first year of learning in the program, and again at the end of the second year of the program.

Our classes would focus on our speakers, and our elders, and the great knowledge they have about the way our ancestors might have done things many years ago. For example, this past year we planted a garden. We got to harvest our flour corn, our beans, and our squash that we had grown all while still focusing on and using the language. I believe that hands-on learning is the best way to learn a language. We were able to take our classroom outside of the traditional classroom setting, but still making sure we would be able to stay in the language while taking trips outside. Our trips consisted of learning traditional medicines, wild foods, and stories from long ago. We would practice in the classroom before going out and doing it. We practiced on our pronunciations, the words we could use, and the techniques for proper planting or harvesting.

My experience with teaching adults has been amazing and rewarding. To see people come in and know nothing of the language, go to being able to have basic conversations in the language, and some even going back out into the community to teach some classes has made it all worthwhile. Creating more teachers and creating more speakers is what keeps our fire burning. Each year we will have a new cohort and each year from here on out we will be graduating students who can teach what they've learned and most importantly, we're adding another language speaker into our community. They're not fluent by any means, but they are not afraid to use what they know and learn as they grow. I am extremely proud of our group and their drive to learn our language. I will leave you with this. Language and culture doesn't care about color or creed. Language and culture cares about who loves it and will take the time to learn it.

15.8 We Stand Strong in Our Knowledge: Learning Anishinaabemowin One Word Bundle at a Time

Aleksandra Bergier, Kim Anderson, and Rene Meshake

During the time when residential schools operated in Canada, the ancestral languages were beaten out of Indigenous children and speakers were shamed for using their mother tongues. Today, many Indigenous people feel embarrassed and dispossessed because they did not learn their language or because they don't speak it perfectly. In spring 2018, our group of scholars and community practitioners set out to jumpstart Anishinaabemowin language revitalization at the University of Guelph – an institution, which at the time had practically no Indigenous language activity. We called our project 'We stand strong in our knowledge' because we wanted to offer the campus community members (both Indigenous and non-Indigenous) opportunities to develop personal 'language bundles' – a collection of Anishinaabemowin words built around their own knowledge, identities, and stories. We also wanted to create spaces where the language learners could feel a sense of safety and belonging.

Our university is situated on the treaty lands and the territory of the Mississaugas of the Credit whose language is Anishinaabemowin. It is also located on a Dish with One Spoon territory that honors the agreement between the Anishinaabe, the Mississaugas, and the Haudenosaunee to share and protect this land. Yet, the buildings on our campus are named after educational philanthropists, university deans, and presidents with no reference to the Indigenous people who have been the stewards of this place for countless generations. And so, we decide to start our revitalization activities with a symbolic act of renaming several university buildings. In a unique walk around campus our group of students, faculty and staff members explored the names of familiar spaces with the help of an Anishinaabe language keeper Rene Meshake. Rene, who likes to call himself a funky Elder, has been working with Anishinaabemowin concepts most of his life, unpacking their meaning morpheme by morpheme through storytelling and art.

We start our walk at the University Centre – the main hub on campus with access to the food court, study spaces, and administration offices. The participants tell stories about vibrant community events, the feeling of excitement, and constant movement they associate with this place. Rene names it *Odena* (the heart lodge). He compares the youth arriving at the University Centre to new blood coming into the heart.

We then visit the science complex where students have their biology, physics, and chemistry labs. They talk about a sense of accomplishment and the joy that comes from learning about the diversity of life forms. Rene gifts us with another word – *Mino bimaadiziwin* (good life). He explains that *Bimaadiz* means 'full of life, spirit, and soul' and that's exactly how we feel standing in the middle of a beautiful atrium filled with warm spring light.

We repeat the same activity in other places on campus and each time a new word bundle emerges, followed by stories and life lessons generously shared by Rene. *Kino'amadiwigamig* (a place of giving directions) describes the helpers' room at the library where students support their peers in becoming better writers and communicators. As we enter the next building, often used for exams, the participants share stories of anxiety, but also of relief and newly built courage. Rene reciprocates with stories about times of great struggle in his personal life. We then decide on a name – *Godjiewisiwin* (a place of trial/testing).

The concept of *Nanda wendjige* (seeking sustenance from the earth) comes up when we visit a building with small classrooms where students typically use hallways to brainstorm and work on collective projects. This place makes us reflect on the ability to be creative and make use of the limited space and resources one has available. Rene connects this contemporary learning context with traditional land use, trapping, and hunting skills he learned back in his home territory. These activities honored the earth as people took only what was needed for their communities.

In a similar way, we only take away from this activity that which resonates with us. We finish our walk amazed at the abundance of stories captured by the word bundles and we feel enriched by the opportunity to look at our everyday experiences through the lens of Indigenous knowledge. We might not be speakers of Anishinaabemowin (yet), but we can weave the new words into the fabrics of our lives with gratitude for the meaningful relationships we created with each other and with the place where we work and learn.

16 Art, Music and Cultural Activities

Genner Llanes Ortiz

Introduction

As has been discussed in the previous chapters, a great number of languages in the world have experienced a significant displacement in their national and regional contexts, particularly in the last two centuries. Displacement comes from a process that forces certain languages into a 'minority' status – which rather than being a mere reflection of their demographic stature or grammatical integrity is the result of political and economic marginalisation. For these reasons, minoritised or minorised languages in the world are associated with marginal populations and spaces. Speakers are also discouraged by the lack of education in minoritised languages, as well as the lack of recognition of their art forms, like literature, music, or performance, among others. This, in turn, dissuades people from using these languages in new intellectual or artistic productions.

Language activists in different parts of the world are confronting this situation by reclaiming forsaken linguistic art forms, like traditional storytelling, song and oratory performances, among others. They are also experimenting with new forms of literature, performance and poetry, song composition and music, and other cultural activities like radio production, TV series dubbing, news and social media publications, multimedia installations and advertising. These art forms are used as strategic ways to revitalise their minoritised languages. In this chapter, we will introduce a handful of examples from the Americas, Oceania and parts of Europe, which could provide some general principles and guidelines.

When discussing arts in minoritised languages, we must keep in mind that while most art forms are meant to be enjoyed without linguistic interference – think of dance, painting, sculpture, architecture, photography and graphic design – virtually all artistic endeavours rely, to a certain degree, on language to be made sense of. In what follows, we will focus on arts that rely more significantly on words, speech or discourse, for example, literature (written and oral) and song. We will also look at mixed arts which combine image and speech in creative ways. I will divide the chapter into literary arts, musical arts and mixed arts (cinema, video and TV) to examine the potential of these social and cultural strategies to resist and prevent language displacement.

Literature in Minoritised Languages

Literacy in minoritised or endangered languages is significantly low at present, due to historical marginalisation, political hostility, and a lack of trained educators and teaching resources. In some cases, this is the after-effect of the destruction and prohibition of previous traditions and forms of writing. One clear example of this was the systematic eradication of Mexica and Mixtec pictographic codices and Maya hieroglyphic books during the colonisation of Mexico and Guatemala. Many other minoritised languages do not have an agreed writing system (see Chapter 14). Consequently, reclaiming minoritised literatures and developing new literary traditions are necessarily tied to questions of literacy, standardisation, normalisation and publishing.

For writers and publishers of minoritised languages, the main challenge is to create a readership, particularly in contexts where speakers are not even literate in the dominant language. Global concerns about the loss of linguistic diversity have moved a few national governments (especially in parts of Western Europe and Latin America) to provide funds and infrastructure in order to address these disadvantages. However, money and publications are not the only resources that an endangered language needs.

Language activists are trying to redress the interruption of local, unwritten literary traditions by compiling examples of spoken art, like storytelling, recitation, ritual dialogue, chanting and other surviving oral traditions. A growing number of states now offer support to revitalisers. For example, the Mexican government has sponsored the publication of literature in Indigenous languages since the 1980s. These publications, although always in bilingual form (Spanish and Indigenous languages), represent an important shift in relation to the previous monolingual policies of the Mexican state. The Contemporary Indigenous Literature series initially consisted of cultural monographs, collections of folktales, songs and prayers, and community theatre scripts. Later series have included new narrative forms such as fiction stories and novels, poetry and playwriting. Although these series purportedly aim to revitalise Indigenous languages, several critics point out that these bilingual books end up being used more by literary scholars and linguists than by Indigenous speakers. Distribution is crucial since these books tend to circulate predominantly within government and higher education institutions and community libraries, but rarely in commercial bookshops. An even more pressing challenge is that Mexican Indigenous speakers are still rarely taught and even less encouraged to read in their own languages.

Mexico's case shows that increasing publication of books in endangered languages is not enough; guaranteeing their circulation and access, and encouraging their consumption by speakers is also necessary. Promotion of literacy in minoritised languages is an enterprise that requires both institutional and grassroots support. Growing access to the Internet in minoritised language contexts might provide new opportunities to promote literacy, but this is yet to be determined.

Compilation of traditional oral literature has been deemed an important way to identify aesthetic principles which could support the development of new literary styles. A good example of this is the investigative and creative work of Ana Patricia Martínez Huchim in Yucatan, Mexico. She was one of the first Maya women to research Maya oral literature, working first with children and later with adults. In spite of not being a fluent speaker, Huchim became a prolific writer, drawing inspiration from community stories and turning them into new tales that followed the Maya storytelling canon. Her collections of stories feature acute social commentary, shedding light on forgotten historical events, as well as denouncing gender injustice in community life, in true literary form.

Play-writing and theatrical performance also offer significant opportunities to dynamise minoritised languages. This literary and performative hybrid art form integrates different skills and taps from different sources which makes it an even more effective way to reinsert endangered languages in the public sphere. Among its sources we could have story compilations, historical re-enactment, or creative writing. Preparation of theatrical performances involves speech training, rhythm awareness, dialogue practice, memorisation, recitation, and improvisation. Plays are social events that prompt conversation, analysis and, on occasion, even debate, all of which could invigorate threatened and minoritised languages. These secondary, meta-performative events are key to infusing endangered languages with new life. Because these art forms require group work and cooperation, they could also strengthen collective identity and help to associate the language with play and socialisation. This is not only the case with theatre but could also potentially be a part of dance.

This is how the Kaqchikel-speaking members of the Sotz'il Art Group in the Guatemalan highlands understand their artistic and political work, which mixes theatre and dance to recount mythic stories in a contemporary fashion. The Sotz'il Group has developed an investigative and experimental practice that reclaims ancient Maya literary and performance aesthetics. The group formed in 2002 on the initiative of Lisandro Guarcax and a group of

Kaqchikel-speaking high-school students. Their work echoed traditional community performances. Indeed, traditional performers from the community supported them with learning about customs, instruments, props and cultural knowledge. Confronted by stereotypical and offensive portrayals of their ancient art and historical heroes in schools and other public institutions, Sotz'il members have sought inspiration from representations of Maya musicians and dancers found in ancient books and paintings. They have used these images as a template to create new performances, copying postures, improvising movements, reinventing costumes, and writing dialogues for plays that deal with both the historical and the political challenges of today. Without strictly relying on text, Sotz'il's recreations of theatre and dance creatively assemble myth, memory, and movement to reconnect young people with Kaqchikel culture and language. A more conventional literary outlet for Sotz'il's experimentation has been the publication of artistic theory in their bilingual (Spanish–Kaqchikel) anthology *Ka'i' oxi' tzij pa ruwi' rupatän Samaj Ri Ajch'owen* [Some words about the work of the Maya Artist], 2014.

A broad definition of literature in the context of minoritised languages should not only include playwriting, but also other forms of spoken art like singing and praying. The Royal Academy of the Spanish Language, for example, defines literature as 'the art of *verbal* expression' (my emphasis). Following this, 'literature' would have to include public storytelling (including 'call' and 'response'), civic rhetoric, ceremonial discourse, ritual song, religious or historical dances, carnival speech or jokes, political chants or slogans, everyday sayings and proverbs, all of which encapsulate specific aesthetic principles. One form of performative literature that has become a favoured strategy for language activists will be the focus of our next section.

Minoritised Sounds in Emerging New Languages

The strong connection between music and language is not a new discovery. It was during the twentieth century, however, that language activists started to use song composition and performance in a more conscious and political way. One example of this was the *Nova Cançó* (New Catalan Song) movement during the late 1950s under Francisco Franco's dictatorship in Spain. The Francoist regime had banned the use of regional Iberian languages, like Basque, Galician and Catalan, in public official spaces. Although singing in these languages was not strictly prohibited, song writers and singers, especially in the Catalan-speaking region, used this art form to highlight the imposed Castilian monolingualism in the music domain. Nova Cançó performers began translating and imitating French singer-songwriters (rather than employing traditional genres like *havaneres* or *rumbas*) but later developed their own distinctive style.

Translating popular hits is a strategy that continues to be followed by language activists. In 2015, Peruvian teenager Renata Flores Rivera became a social media sensation after posting a music video with a rendition of Michael Jackson's 'The Way You Make Me Feel' in the Quechua language, which has gathered more than 1.7 million views to date. Copyright disputes seem to have been prevented by acknowledging clearly the original source of inspiration and avoiding associations with commercial interests.

Language revitalisers have also 'invented' new singing traditions and given birth to mixed performance genres (song and dance), as the Māori action song, *waiata-ā-ringa*, exemplifies. This *waiata* (song) genre is an innovation from the early twentieth century and was associated with the activism of the Young Māori Party. Āpirana Ngata, a prominent party activist, devoted himself to compiling and publishing traditional songs and oratory examples during this period. *Waiata-ā-ringa* combines Western melodies with the performing of culturally prescribed movements which convey Māori narratives. The combination of dance and singing, and the collective, playful and aesthetic nature of these performances have proven to be a popular strategy to promote and celebrate the Māori language, *Te Reo*, in Aotearoa/New Zealand.

Singing in one's own language may be a mundane activity for many, but it can easily become an act of resistance, especially when its social dynamics change. The Yucatec Maya language, *maaya t'aan,* was widely used as the *de facto* lingua franca during the early twentieth century. Yucatec Maya people have preserved different forms of literature, written in Latin characters since the sixteenth century. Yucatecan *trova*, a local romantic song style which emerged in the early twentieth century, was initially a bilingual genre, but as the Indigenous language of Yucatan was gradually displaced by Spanish, Maya song composition became infrequent. In the early twenty-first century, however, young Maya speakers have started using global music genres like hip hop, reggae and rock to sing in their own language. The number of Indigenous-language hip hop singers in Mexico and other Latin American countries has grown significantly in the last two decades.

Music and song can converge in unexpected ways to help gain new audiences for displaced or minoritised languages. Sometimes this happens through the dynamisation of aged traditions in new genres and with new music technology, where old verses are remastered and re-recorded by young artists and put back into circulation. A good example of this is the work of the Comcaac or Seri rock band *Hamac Caziim* (Sacred Fire) who, in the 1990s, sought and obtained authorisation from their tribal government in northern Mexico to recreate festive and ceremonial chants in heavy metal form. A true literary tradition, Seri songs have contributed to maintaining a sense of community for this relatively isolated people in the Mexican Sonora state. Traditional songs follow harmonies based on a pentatonic scale, employ an arcane language style and explore landscape inspired themes. Hamac Caziim's experiment, which has become known as Seri Metal, was well received by Comcaac elders and, more importantly, by young people. Their work spearheaded the organisation of festivals and other public events to make the language more visible, a sort of Seri renaissance in the early twenty-first century.

Lyrical performance may not be a common practice in all language contexts. For example, few Tzutuhil, Kaqchikel or K'iche 'proper' songs are known around the Atitlan Lake of Guatemala. However, the poetic intonation and metaphoric figures maintained by *aj q'ijab'* (daykeepers, or religious specialists), which reflect literary traditions that go back to Maya Classic inscriptions, are a source of inspiration for some young musicians in the region. Combining this poetic heritage with his fondness for hip hop, René Dionisio, aka 'MC Tz'utu', has emerged in the popular music scene as an effective revitaliser of Guatemalan Maya languages. MC Tz'utu's compositions reclaim and make productive use of decidedly Indigenous aesthetic resources like alliteration (repetition), and the use of semantic pairings also known as 'parallelisms' (for example 'our language, our clothes', a pairing that evokes 'cultural tradition'). Although repetition of catch phrases from Western hip hop seems to mirror the parallelism of Maya poetic forms, the lesser importance of rhyming in MC Tz'utu's rapping provides his work with a distinct Indigenous aesthetic.

As we have seen in this section, song and literary traditions are employed in innovative ways by language and cultural promoters. An aspect which is definitely present but relatively downplayed in relation to revitalisation strategies is the way in which language is embodied and becomes present, not just in everyday life but, perhaps more significantly, in larger public spaces. I will touch briefly on this dimension in our next segment.

Embodying Language: Cinema, Video and TV

Audio-visual media has become the predominant form through which cultural and linguistic contents circulate nowadays. This is also true of music, especially since the 1990s, which saw the beginnings of the music video as the preferred self-marketing medium in North America and Western Europe. Collaboration between musicians and filmmakers has sometimes resulted in true masterpieces, with awards being offered annually worldwide to different aspects of music film production.

As with Hollywood musicals, the relation between song and cinema has also been strong in other, non-Western, contexts like the powerful film industry in South East Asia. Songs and movies always went hand in hand in this densely populated, multilingual part of the world. Today, hundreds of films are produced every year in Hindi (Bollywood), Tamil (Kollywood), Telugu (Tollywood), Kannada (Sandalwood), Bengali, Malayalam (Mollywood), Marathi and Bhojpuri. These represent only a handful of the 122 major, and more than 1,500 minor languages spoken in India. To deal with this hyper-diverse linguistic landscape, Indian cinema experimented in the 1930s with the production of trilingual or multilingual films. The approach consisted of shooting the same scene in three or more languages, to create different versions of the same story. With the development of film technology, dubbing became the preferred solution to deal with linguistic diversity in cinema, not just in India but in Western Europe, too. Here, the protection of national cultural industries instituted the dubbing of English-language films and TV programmes in the official language, a practice that has been maintained in France, Spain, Portugal, Italy and Germany, to name a few. This is also common in Latin America, both in Spanish and Portuguese. Dubbing in minority or Indigenous languages has, however, been historically less common. We will examine two significant examples of this later in the chapter.

With greater availability and affordability of video recording equipment, the production of film and television in endangered languages is today seen as a good way of capitalising on the ubiquity and popularity of this medium. The number of video productions in minoritised languages is, however, still insignificant in comparison with the number of movies and programs released in English, Hindi, Mandarin, Taiwanese, Arabic, Japanese, Spanish, Portuguese and Yoruba. While the quantity of films in minoritised languages might not be significant, occasionally their cultural and political impact can prove more decisive.

This is the case of the film *Atanarjuat: The Fast Runner*, released in 2002 and directed by Inuit filmmaker Zacharias Kunuk. This movie is one of many videos released by Igloolik Isuma Productions, a loose association and production company which began making films in the 1990s in the Nunavut territory of Canada. Early productions by Isuma ('To Think') attempted to capture the daily lives and struggles of Inuit people, and often employed a voice-over narration in Inuktitut language. *Atanarjuat* was Isuma's first full-length feature and the first ever fiction film in Inuktitut. The story was based on the legend of the fast runner, the title character, and takes place in a time before contact with White settlers. Paul Apak Angilirq was the one who thought about compiling the different versions of the traditional story and turning it into an approximately three-hour long movie.

The relevance of *Atarnajuat* is clear to see: it was voted the best Canadian movie of all time by a poll of experts at the Toronto International Film Festival in 2015. The critical recognition and commercial success of this work has inspired other First Nations directors to create more material in their own languages. The production company has also created an online platform called Isuma.tv that aims to 'honour oral languages' and that currently hosts video content in more than eighty Indigenous languages.

A similar experience in South America, although without the same critical reception by the international film circuits, is the project 'Video in the Villages' (VIV). It was founded by a non-indigenous Brazilian, Vincent Carelli, in 1986, a time of political effervescence and instability in the region. Since then the project has provided financial and technical support to several Amazonian Indigenous people to create their own media in their own languages. VIV productions cover various political, spiritual and territorial aspects of the lives of approximately forty Indigenous peoples. Patricia Ferreira (Mbya-Guarani), Ariel Duarte Ortega (Mbya-Guarani) and Divino Tserewahú (Xavante) are some of the most prolific and talented Indigenous filmmakers to have emerged from this collaborative project. VIV productions travel from village to village by boat, retelling mythical and historical events, inviting the reinterpretation of Indigenous identities and galvanising the political energy of different peoples to defend their territories and ways of life.

As with Indigenous literature, one of the most important challenges of Isuma and VIV is the distribution of film materials. Although the Internet has facilitated access to their video production, consumption remains limited to movie connoisseurs, cultural activists and academics. Social media platforms like Facebook, YouTube and Vimeo offer the possibility of increasing their audiences. However, a lot still needs to happen for Indigenous films to have the power to make young people interested in learning real, endangered languages instead of made-up ones from global franchises, like Klingon (Star Trek), Elvish (Lord of the Rings) or Dothraki (Game of Thrones).

Before this can happen, perhaps the second-best thing may be what Diné or Navajo language activists decided to do in New Mexico. In 2013, the Navajo Nation Museum and Lucasfilm Ltd teamed up to dub *Star Wars Episode IV: A New Hope* in the Diné language. The project was thirteen years in the making, the brainchild of Manuelito Wheeler, director of the Navajo museum. Searching for ways to preserve Diné, he first asked his wife Jennifer to help him translate ten pages of the movie script. He decided to use this film given its popularity among members of his reservation and because it is still considered one of the best films of all times. In addition to raising enough funds to pay for translators, dubbing actors in Diné and recording studios, time was one of the main challenges.

The Diné dubbed version of the Episode IV was released on DVD as a limited edition the same year and can now be ordered online. The second full feature to be dubbed in Diné was the animated children's film *Finding Nemo*, which was also made available as a DVD in 2016.

In 2013, two young Paraguayans, Pablo Javier and Víctor Fabián Báez, from Santa Rosa, Misiones, became a sensation on the Internet when they started posting homemade 'parodies' in the form of Guaraní dubbed video clips of popular TV programs, like the Mexican comedy program *El Chavo del 8*, and Japanese animated series 'Pokemon' and 'Dragon Ball Z'. They began their dubbing with the most basic technology: a microphone, and hacking software. What inspired them was not a preoccupation for the preservation of the language (Guaraní is the most spoken Indigenous language in the Americas with an estimated eight million speakers, and the only Indigenous official language of the Mercosur trade region) but the thrill of hearing their mother language spoken in a global TV series. Despite the social media success they achieved, this did not result in a more professional and extensive project. They have nonetheless continued posting their 'parodies' on YouTube, hoping to monetise the thousands of clicks they get for their work.

The Art of Revitalising Languages

From the presentation of the previous cases (which are but a tiny sample of the myriad efforts that exist worldwide), some general principles and guidelines for working with arts, music and other cultural activities can be sketched.

Displacement and loss are strongly linked to the stigmatisation and lack of visibility of languages. To counteract these processes, language activists could:

(a) Reclaim forsaken written, performative and verbal art forms; a strategy that has the double effect of restoring forgotten or censured aesthetic traditions while, at the same time, strengthening the sense of worth in cultural and linguistic communities.

(b) Adapt traditional genres (chants, storytelling or dance), renew their artistic repertoire and/or create hybrid aesthetic forms for younger or new audiences.

(c) Use current technologies and social media to reach new audiences, inspire the younger generation, and increase the presence of their linguistic and cultural identities in the national and global scenes.

(d) Take advantage of the success, influence and familiarity that certain artistic products enjoy, like songs, films or TV series, and use these as templates and inspiration for linguistic and cultural reinterpretation.

Although reinventing their own narratives and experiences through new media is a good base for revitalisation, not everything has to be created from scratch.

There are significant challenges to implementing these strategies. Some of the more apparent obstacles are presented here:

- Audience creation: the low numbers of literate people in minoritised languages usually means that written publications and textual media only circulate in reduced social spaces. Language activists sometimes combine oral and written forms of communication, like radio programs and online podcasts, where those who are literate read out new poetry and narrative to those who have not been taught. The creation of audiences for other forms of art, like song and cinema, is also important given the disproportionate competition of cultural products in dominant languages and the stigmatisation of minoritised languages art forms.
- Audience reach (circulation): in addition to the need to create new audiences, circulation is another important obstacle to deal with. While literature, music and films in dominant languages have well established marketplaces, minoritised language productions struggle to have even a symbolic presence in mass media. Radio stations won't program their music, commercial cinema theatres won't list their movies, and big TV channels won't broadcast their videos. Endangered language cultural productions, like their speakers, are kept in the margins, in small government-sponsored music or art film festivals, or in specialised circuits of enlightened cultural consumers. The challenge here is not just to put minoritised languages in global circulation platforms (anyone can have a YouTube channel) but to do so in a way that creates a cultural shift and new attitudes towards them. A few globally watched TV series, and even big Hollywood productions, have signalled a new appreciation for linguistic diversity, but perhaps only for their self-interest. This is exemplified by the inclusion of dialogues in Scottish Gaelic in the series *Outlander*, or by the full-length feature *Apocalypto*, entirely in Yucatec Maya (which presented, on the other hand, historical and cultural distortions that were the topic of a heated debate in Mexico and Guatemala). But, while it seems that Netflix does not have a problem offering worldwide Klingon subtitling for the new Star Trek series (*Discovery*), it seems unlikely that it will similarly offer subtitles in Nahuatl, Quechua or Guarani to its subscribers in the Americas anytime soon.

In spite of these limitations, the success stories reported here seem to have benefitted from a core set of principles. The following are some of the more easily identifiable: a strong commitment to the language and culture, long-term grassroots collaboration and engagement, reflexive and extensive research, social inventiveness, technological curiosity and creativity, cultural audacity and experimentation in close dialogue with the keepers of tradition (so as to prevent community divisions), and strategic alliances with a wide range of stakeholders, including governments and cultural industries, to highlight but a few.

We are still a long way from being able to solve the seemingly unstoppable loss of linguistic diversity in the world with a handful of steps and recipes. But, as some of these examples have shown, even the smallest of actions can contribute to the increase in the presence and dynamism of minoritised and endangered languages.

FURTHER READING

Aggabao Thelen, C. (2008). Our ancestors danced like this: Maya youth respond to genocide through the ancestral arts. In R. Solinger, M. Fox, and K. Irani, eds., *Telling Stories to Change the World: Global Voices on the Power of Narrative to Build Community and Make Social Justice Claims*. New York: Routledge, pp. 39–54.

Aufderheide, P. (2008). 'You See the World of the Other and You Look at Your Own': The Evolution of the Video in the Villages Project. *Journal of Film and Video* 60 (2), 26–34.

Barrett, R. (2016). Mayan language revitalization, hip hop, and ethnic identity in Guatemala. *Language & Communication* 47, 144–53. www.sciencedirect.com/science/article/pii/S0271530915000701.

Cru, J. (2015). Bilingual rapping in Yucatán, Mexico: Strategic choices for Maya language legitimation and revitalisation. *International Journal of Bilingual Education and Bilingualism* 2(5), 481–96. http://dx.doi.org/10.1080/13670050.2015.1051945.

Evans, M. R. (2010). *The Fast Runner: Filming the Legend of Atanarjuat*. Lincoln: University of Nebraska Press.

Floyd, S. (2008). The pirate media economy and the emergence of Quichua language media spaces in Ecuador. *Anthropology of Work Review* 29(2), 34–41.

Trinick, R. and Dale, H. (2015). Head, heart, hand: Embodying Māori language through song. *Australian Journal of Music Education* 3, 84–92.

INTERESTING LINKS AND EXAMPLES

Ancient Manx Gaelic given revival boost with weather animations, www.bbc.com/news/world-europe-isle-of-man-41747474.

Guaraní dubbing, www.abc.com.py/edicion-impresa/suplementos/abc-revista/doblado-al-guarani-por-tres-rosenos-624812.html.

Kapa haka: Māori performing arts; 20th century innovations; Te Ara, the encyclopedia of New Zealand, http://teara.govt.nz/en/kapa-haka-Māori-performing-arts/page-3.

Michael Jackson en quechua, la niña que revaloriza la lengua de los incas, www.elespectador.com/noticias/actualidad/michael-jackson-quechua-nina-revaloriza-lengua-de-los-i-articulo-582154.

Navajo Dubbing of Star Wars, http://navajotimes.com/news/2013/0413/042513sta.php; www.navajotimes.com/news/2013/1213/121213starwars.php; www.wsj.com/articles/navajo-version-of-finding-nemo-aims-to-promote-native-language-1419033583.

Rekedal, J. (2014). Hip-hop Mapuche on the Araucanian Frontera. *Alternativas* 2, 1–35. https://alternativas.osu.edu/en/issues/spring-2014/essays1/rekedal.html.

Renata Flores Rivera – Michael Jackson's 'The Way You Make Me Feel' (Quechua Version), www.youtube.com/watch?v=BvT9y0HqItE.

16.1 Art, Music and Cultural Activities in the Revitalisation of Wymysiöeryś

Justyna Majerska-Sznajder

The revitalisation of Wymysiöeryś wouldn't be so advanced today if we hadn't taken up the task of revitalising not only the culture, but also the inhabitants of Wilamowice. We started this when we were only teenagers, together with Tymoteusz Król. Back in the 1990s, a person who encountered our town would only be presented with colourful costumes and old cottages – just the view that journalists would use when they wanted to show the last speakers of Wymysiöeryś. The regional ensembles of dance and singing presented only the costume and folklore.

I began my personal engagement with language revitalisation as an adventure with the regional ensemble as a young child. Back then I had no clue how complicated the problem of revitalising Wymysiöeryś culture was. Having joined the children's ensemble 'Cepelia-Fil' I still didn't feel engaged in Wilamowice itself. Nobody could explain to me the phonetically transcribed lyrics of songs (luckily, even back then I spoke with Tymoteusz and my great-grandmother in Wymysiöeryś). Nobody made that sure the costumes people wore reflected faithfully a specific local dress code – even though it is an important marker of identity.

Luckily, in 2007, Tymoteusz and I both joined the Song and Dance Ensemble 'Wilamowice'. It might seem that the actions of such ensembles are folkloric in nature and destined only for the stage, i.e. that they form a mixture of 'the nicest looking', most pleasing elements of culture for the audience, yet are completely deprived of deeper reflection. Nothing could be further from the truth.

The ensemble was founded in 1948, only three years after the Wymysiöeryś language and culture had been banned by local officials collaborating with the communist authorities. For many years it functioned as a 'time capsule' as members collected costumes, their names and meanings, old songs and poems, and – above all – embraced the eldest inhabitants of the town who passed on their knowledge to the younger members and also their language, when they had the courage to do so. Thanks to the ensemble we could reach a greater number of inhabitants.

Through the ensemble we got engaged with the activities of the Association 'Wilamowianie', a NGO that has enabled us to start a more conscious revitalisation program. In the framework provided by the Association we have organised many cultural events which were strongly oriented towards promoting Wymysiöeryś in the community and changing linguistic attitudes, which still view Wymysiöeryś as 'something negative' (see Chapter 7). We tried to keep every meeting relaxed – some topics weren't at all connected with revitalisation. However, we have always tried to 'smuggle in' Wymysiöeryś themes – like during a family fair which included a movie created by our youths about the 'Pierzowiec' (feather plucking) tradition. We attempted to make our activities more attractive by including excursions, meetings and workshops that could reach the biggest possible number of inhabitants.

Thanks to our collaboration with the Faculty of 'Artes Liberales' of the University of Warsaw, we organised several international events which made the community members aware of the huge external interest in the revitalisation efforts taking place in Wilamowice. Showing the inhabitants how much their cultural heritage is appreciated in academia made it more important to them too. We have also understood the need to 'de-folklorise' our activities, while keeping respect for traditions. Thus, Wymysiöeryś also became a medium for modern culture. In 2014, a theatre group was formed, called 'Ufa fisa', literally 'On the feet' (referring to a metaphor of making Wymysiöeryś culture able to stand again on its own feet). The actions of this group allowed more people to engage in cultural revitalisation and to learn the language, including those people who simply wouldn't like to or couldn't attend regular classes. Moreover, the exclusive use of Wymysiöeryś on stage fosters the creation of new intergenerational bonds: to understand the plot, spectators have to ask the eldest speakers and the teenagers who have learned the language and this makes them feel empowered. Staging our performances both in the town and neighbouring villages as well as in the Polish Theatre in Warsaw (see Figures 16.1.1 and 16.1.2) is an additional way of raising the prestige of the language and the awareness of its value as an important asset, both locally and more widely.

The next step was the creation of a band comprised of the members of the Majerski (fum Biöetuł) family (see Figure 16.1.3). They perform covers of modern songs translated by us and our students, thus proving to the skeptics that Wymysiöeryś is not only suited to old local songs. The new songs are real earworms – even those who don't learn Wymysiöeryś sing them. We also make sure that Wymysiöeryś is always present in the local landscape – not only on various information boards but also during events that are not directly related to revitalisation itself, such as during street fairs and festivals where we promote Wymysiöeryś using merchandise such as t-shirts, bags, badges, mugs and banners.

Luckily, the last few years have proved that the effort put into the revitalisation of language, culture and community members has been fruitful. Language attitudes

286 *Justyna Majerska-Sznajder*

Figure 16.1.1 Performance in Wymysiöeryś, *Uf jer welt*, Polish Theatre in Warsaw. © Engaged Humanities Project, University of Warsaw

Figure 16.1.2 Performance in Wymysiöeryś, *Ymertihła*, Polish Theatre in Warsaw. Photo by Krzysztof Kędracki, Polish Theatre in Warsaw

Figure 16.1.3 Concert in Wymysiöeryś, the Majerski family. Photo by Marcin Musiał

have changed. Many activities initiated by us now have a life of their own – the inhabitants introduce Wymysiöeryś into their environment and the youth organise their own initiatives, like the first Wymysiöeryś Day or location-based games in Wymysiöeryś. This makes us enormously happy.

16.2 *Fest-noz* and Revitalisation of the Breton Language

Nicole Dołowy-Rybińska

The Breton language, one of languages of Brittany, France, is an endangered language with about 200,000 speakers, mainly from the oldest generation. There are also a few dozens of thousands of new speakers. One of the most significant Breton cultural activities is a *fest-noz* (plural *festoù-noz*), the 'night festival' during which people get together, dance (not only) traditional Breton dances, enjoy themselves, and create a unique community connected by participation in Breton culture and – in some cases – by the use of Breton language. Nowadays these events are held throughout Brittany at all times of the year, in every possible location, with participants of all generations. They reaffirm that Breton culture is still alive. The music at a *fest-noz* is usually performed live, in most cases in Breton, although the range of possible accompaniments is broad. The most typical is the *kan an discan* ('call and response') song style, which involves singing without instrumental accompaniment by two or three individuals, whose voices overlap distinctively. The bagpipe-bombard, a traditional woodwind instrument pairing, also appears, playing a similar type of music. Yet very often there are whole bands on stage with 'modern' instruments.

The type of music, the place of performance and the participants differ according to when and by whom the *fest-noz* is organised. The functions of *fest-noz* have changed, just like the function of the Breton language. When daily life in the Breton language was concentrated in the rural areas in Lower and Central Brittany, traditional dances and festivities were related to the agricultural year: *fest-noz* developed from celebrations after collective community work was completed. These customs could not have survived the changes that took place in Brittany during the 1920s and 1930s: the appearance of new technologies moved the Bretons towards French culture and France's conscious centralist policies targeted minority cultures and languages. These policies ridiculed and humiliated Bretons and their language. During the first half of the twentieth century, the Bretons abandoned their language and traditional dances.

The revival of the Breton language and *fest-noz* started in the 1970s. Speaking and singing in Breton came to be regarded as a moral duty of young people whose parents had rejected it. The struggle for a Breton way of life became part of the social movement of the 1970s. It was when young people began contesting official culture and expressing their revolt in a festive, musical way. The concept of *fest-noz* as a rural festival became widely accepted and it perfectly matched the social attitudes of young Breton activists who were searching for their roots. As a result, *fest-noz* provided a link between the worlds of the 'young' and the 'old', between 'modernity' and 'authenticity'. *Fest-noz* events were no longer seen as pure entertainment or even a manifestation of pro-Breton attitudes; they became a way of life. The 1970s were successful in bringing forward the question of the Breton language as an important element of Breton culture, as well as re-evaluating Breton identity. Breton music, literature, theatre, and audiovisual arts bloomed. In 1977, the first Diwan community-run immersion school was formed. Since Diwan schools received no subsidies, money required to run them was collected during *fest-noz* organised by school collectives, activists and friends. After that period *fest-noz* lost some impetus. The late 1990s saw the arrival of a new style of *fest-noz*, closely linked to the Bretons' fast-changing lifestyles and matching the progressing urbanisation as well as the advent of new, digital media. There are now Cyber Fest Noz events with several dozens of dancers live-streamed and transmitted through the Internet and accessible all around the world. The format is appealing to young people and makes participation in a minority culture attractive. Over time, *fest-noz* became an integral part of Breton culture. It did change style and function, but it has always been connected with Breton identity. It has also been a tool for Breton language revitalisation as many young people open themselves to the Breton language thanks to participation in these events. With its festival character, it is easily accessible to people; it allows those who want to use Breton to meet and develop closer relationships; it is also a place where most Breton activist movements and ideas come into life.

16.3 Modern Music Genres for Language Revitalisation
Josep Cru

The arts, and musical production in particular, are becoming ever more central domains in grassroots efforts for language revitalisation in Latin America. Modern music genres such as rock, reggae, rap among others have been appropriated by Indigenous youths all over the continent. In Mexico, for instance, a growing number of bands are using Indigenous languages as a vehicle for artistic expression: Sak Tzevul (rock in Tzotzil), La Sexta Vocal (ska in Zoque) or El Rapero de Tlapa (rap in Mixtec) are examples of cultural activism among youths who look to expand their languages into new domains of use. Rappers from other Latin American countries, such as B'alam Ajpu in Guatemala, Luanko and the band Wechekeke ñi trawun in Chile, or Liberato Kani in Peru (to name but a few), are some outstanding examples of artists who have an already extensive career singing in Indigenous languages (Tzutujil, Mapudungun and Quechua, respectively). In the Yucatan Peninsula of Mexico, hip hop as a cultural movement has become particularly prominent, and a sizeable number of Mayan rappers use now Yucatec Maya in their performances. If we consider the number of online views of songs such as *Ki'imak in wóol* by Tihorappers Crew (over 450,000 views in two years on YouTube) and the overwhelmingly positive comments to performances in Indigenous languages, the impact that these songs can have in changing negative attitudes towards Indigenous languages is noteworthy.

Some central aspects of rap make it a particularly productive genre for language revitalisation purposes. On the one hand, the central place that verbal fluency and creativity play in rapping aligns with Indigenous cultures that often favour oral ways of cultural expression, and, on the other, the local adaptation and recreation of hip hop as a global popular movement associated with modernity and 'coolness'. As is well known, one of the ideological pillars of contempt for Indigenous languages is the alleged inability of these languages to express modernity and their unjustified association with cultural backwardness. Lastly, hip hop performances may incorporate a political element and provide a platform for the expression of marginalised voices. Some highly politicised Mapuche rappers, for instance, use hip hop as a platform for broader social struggles that include demands for language rights and political recognition.

Several video clips of Indigenous rappers are available on YouTube; try searching for the groups mentioned. Their music can also be found on other online platforms such as Soundcloud, Hulkshare and even Spotify.

16.4 The Jersey Song Project
Kit Ashton

Most people understand that songs can be a great way to help learn a language and perhaps remember some important phrases or patterns, but in fact the value of music for language revitalisation goes much deeper than that. Music is of course one of the most powerful ways to keep a language alive in our hearts and imaginations, and music can be profoundly connected to identity. Through music we can create inspiring and memorable collective experiences that can really help boost the status and public image of a language. When used in a culturally sensitive way, music can be a very versatile and useful tool in the linguistic toolbox.

One successful example of this from my own experience is The Jersey Song Project (which I have to say is an idea I stole from some friends in Guernsey!). The small British island of Jersey, in the Channel Islands, is home to the endangered language Jèrriais (a local version of Norman). As a local musician and activist I've been finding out how music can help in the revitalisation process. The central concept of The Jersey Song Project was to facilitate and curate collaborative songwriting between local musicians (who didn't speak much Jèrriais, if any) and Jèrriais speakers, towards a final performance of songs that could be on any theme and in any genre, but would include *at least one word of Jèrriais in the lyrics*. Over the course of a few months in 2018, I advertised the project and organised for twelve local bands and solo artists to work with Jèrriais speakers and come up with something for the final gig. This took place at a professional performance venue as part of a local festival in the autumn.

The project was a real success, not just in terms of the final gig going well, but for the deeper connections that the musicians and audience made with the language, and also for the excellent publicity the whole project generated over those few months. I'd highly recommend running a similar project wherever there is enough of a local music scene for it to be appropriate (like I said – I stole the idea, so please do steal it from me).

Just a few practical pointers ... I'd say there are three main ways of getting the collaborations going:

(1) The ideal way: musicians could meet up with native speakers and write something entirely new together (you'd need to organise this carefully to make it go as well as possible).
(2) Musicians could set an existing endangered language text (e.g. a poem) to music, with the support of native speakers or teachers.
(3) Musicians could work with native speakers/teachers to translate some of their own lyrics of a non-endangered language song they've already written.

Cover versions are OK, and the right song could be very popular, but you might run into copyright issues; and anyway, participants will probably engage more deeply if they use their own songs. Also, I'd say allow plenty of time for the process to unfold and try to make as much of a public 'splash' as you can with whatever you might do for the final performance, or recording, or both! Finally if you do run your own version of this, please get in touch as I'd love to hear all about it ... Bouonne chance m's anmîns! [Good luck my friends!]

16.5 One Song, Many Voices: Revitalising Ainu through Music

Georgette Nummelin

The Ainu are an Indigenous group native to the northern Japanese island of Hokkaido, the island of Sakhalin and the Kurils. Their language is critically endangered, although there are ongoing efforts to improve its profile, and increase the take-up of the language. Those of Ainu descent are also electing to become more visible, both within Japan, and as part of the global Indigenous community. One of the ways that some Ainu are demonstrating and transmitting their cultural and linguistic identity is through music.

Traditional Ainu music relies on singing, *rekuhara* (throat singing), *mukkuri* (mouth harp), and in the Sakhalin tradition, the *tonkori* (a plucked string instrument). *Upopo* (domestic work songs) tend to be simple in structure, with many songs sung in rounds. *Yukar* (sung epics) are formed of a short repetitive melody, and a *sakehe* (refrain) unique to each *yukar*. Contemporary Ainu music draws on many of these elements, but there is still diversity in how the music is expressed, although the use of the Ainu language, in titles or lyrics, remains the defining element.

Artists such as Oki Kano and ToyToy demonstrate the breadth of contemporary approaches to Ainu Music, but it is perhaps the group Marewrew who are most prominently weaving discussions *about* the language, and audience interaction *with* the language into their performances.

Marewrew is a group comprised of four female singers of Ainu heritage, who originally formed in 2002 to work with Oki Kano, the most well-known Ainu musician in Japan, and who later began performing as an independent ensemble. They perform *upopo*, some of which they have learned directly from family members, either acapella (unaccompanied singing) or accompanied by clapping or the *mukkuri*. All their material is performed in the Ainu language, and during performances they wear traditional clothing, and sometimes recreate the facial tattooing that Ainu women wore traditionally. Their music is based on simple foundations, repeated rhythmic and vocal patterns, and the use of nonsense syllables; but it is hypnotic and compelling. As a listener, understanding of the language is an additional benefit but not a crucial requirement for enjoyment. However, Marewrew enjoy enabling their listeners to interact more with the music, and actively encourage participation and understanding of the songs' contexts.

Marewrew not only explain the meanings of songs, they also teach a number of songs during their sets, creating a shared space where the audience become active participants in a performance that uses the Ainu language. These 'educational segments' are almost delivered as mini-workshops, inviting further questions and queries from their audience. At a 2018 concert in east Tokyo that I attended (see Figure 16.5.1), this collaborative approach went even further, with a number of audience members not only knowing some of the songs performed, but offering translations of Ainu terms if one of the singers was unsure of the most accurate

Figure 16.5.1 Concert poster

Japanese term. From singer to audience and back again, a teaching and expansion of vocabulary and context: everyone present engaged in learning and disseminating Ainu. Leaving a concert, or coming to the end of recording, may of course be the end of the process: we generally listen to enjoy music, not to learn. However, the potential is there for a listener to seek out more recordings, to want to understand, to actively *experience* more, and part of that experience can be learning more of the language. Hearing Ainu music for the first time as an undergraduate in the early 2000s certainly set me on that path, that just over fifteen years later, sees me researching the impact of Ainu language music on the language and actively learning Ainu myself.

Thus, a single song, Umeko Ando singing *Saranpe* as it happens, was enough to make me want to move from being a passive admirer of Ainu music and the Ainu language, to becoming an active participant: to learn and disseminate, not merely appreciate.

SUGGESTED LISTENING

Umeko Ando. (2011). *Ihunke*. [CD] Sapporo: Chikar Studio/Tuff Beats.
Marewrew. (2016). *Cikapuni*. [CD] Sapporo: Chikar Studio/Tuff Beats.
Marewrew. (2012). *Mottoite, hissorine*. [CD] Sapporo: Chikar Studio/Tuff Beats.
Oki Dub Ainu Band. (2016). *Utarhythm*. [CD] Sapporo: Chikar Studio/Tuff Beats.
ToyToy. (2016). *Ramu*. [CD] Sapporo: FIST/sambafree.inc.

EXAMPLES

Umeko Ando. *Pekambe Uk* https://youtu.be/dCD6SDyTlck.
Marewrew. *Sonkayno* https://youtu.be/WokvUb-SQo0.
Oki Dub Ainu Band. *Suma Mukar* https://youtu.be/W6ntowW-Aos.
ToyToy. *Senjin* https://youtu.be/Qb1wXsFPMj4.

16.6 The Language Revitalization, Maintenance and Development Project

José Antonio Flores Farfán

The Language Revitalization, Maintenance and Development Project (PRMDLC) in Mexico has been active for over three decades. Based on the idea of direct collaboration between speakers and researchers, the PRMDLC runs collaborative workshops to encourage a high level of participation. The PRMDLC starts from the recovery of peoples' own language and culture, producing oral and image-based culturally appropriate materials, recreating them in prestigious media such as a TV screen, where Indigenous children rarely see their languages. Therefore the basic goal of the PRMDLC is to establish a (re)vitalising corpus; among others, a collection of printed, audio-visual and multimedia materials in Indigenous languages, produced and consumed by speakers themselves, while at the same time aiming to impact a broader audience (see Figures 16.6.1 and 16.6.2).

Figure 16.6.1 *Los sueños del tlacuache.* © PRMDLC Project

Figure 16.6.2 'Carrusel'. *Los sueños del tlacuache.* © PRMDLC Project

The PRMDLC holds revitalisation workshops aimed at encouraging and/or reinforcing permanent revitalisation through self-developed activities such as language games and music, from the bottom-up. Speakers are credited as the first and principal (multi)authors of multimedia products, including local tales as *The Mermaid and the Opossum*, riddles and tongue twisters, books, documentary films, games, and different musical genres (for example rap, rock, *jarocho* music). Participation of speakers is highly valued and incentivised, dignifying their languages and cultures. For instance, we have worked, among others, with a native artist and two Maya-speaking linguists and one anthropologist, leaders of the Maya team. They have seen their work published and available at major bookstores around the country and beyond, as well as included in multimedia products (Maya riddles, tongue twisters, tales) circulating on the Internet and even on public television. They are committed to disseminate the products within their own communities – their primary audience.

The PRMDLC workshops are organised as follows. Participants are summoned in events such as local patron saint festivities. These festivals are favourable occasions for bringing together many people, including migrants who have moved to big cities or even the USA, and visitors from several other local towns. Children attend workshops with their siblings, parents or grandparents, promoting links between generations. Children are invited to watch an animated movie: after showing the riddle(s) or the Mermaid/Opossum movie(s), the floor is thrown open to participation. Local champions leading the workshops invite the audience to repeat a tongue twister, or ask if someone knows another similar version of the stories, opening up the possibility of children's spontaneous participation and even other emergent dynamics. Participants can express themselves freely. In principle there is no time limit (most sessions last from two to five hours). This allows for a relaxed atmosphere, unlike typical school dynamics. For example, animated riddles are shown, a genre that engages audience participation. This motivates strong participation by children, who suggest diverse, not conceived as 'correct' or 'incorrect' answers to the riddles (for instance the reply to the Nahuatl riddle *Maaske mas tikwaalantok pero tikpiipiitsos* ('No matter how angry you are, you are going to kiss it anyhow') can vary, ranging from a bottle to an *aatekoomatl*, 'drinking water gourd', or even other possible emergent answers. Riddles, tales, and tongue twisters are bastions of linguistic and cultural retention. Riddles, for example, are a powerful genre that calls on interaction and verbal play, not to mention tongue twisters that are culturally powerful language games stimulating interaction and cultural continuity.

In this way the PRMDLC develops a method of indirect revitalisation. This means that participation is open to spontaneous, not forced participation, in 'natural', cultural sensitive ways. It stimulates intergenerational transmission of the endangered language. In this sense, it is up to children whether or not to participate. It is very different from formalised ways of participation typical of school contexts that work as inhibitors of Indigenous knowledge and tongues, and therefore favour assimilation.

SOME MATERIALS PRODUCED BY THE PRMDLC

www.youtube.com/watch?v=n0WPB6dZOSE (In Nahuatl, with translations to Spanish, English and Catalan).
www.youtube.com/watch?v=riASdGAsbYc (Nahua riddles)
www.youtube.com/watch?v=fwmgIaUg0J0 (Maya riddles)
https://ciesasdocencia.academia.edu/JoséAntonioFloresFarfán/Books.
www.academia.edu/28686161/Tsintsiinkirianteenpitskontsiin_Trabalenguas_nahuas (Nahuatl tongue twisters)
www.academia.edu/28686145/kankaltaanoob_pdf (Maya tongue twisters)

17 Technology in Language Revitalization

Robert Elliott

A Principled Approach

Working with technology in any kind of language setting is imperative in today's world. The number of potential technological tools that are available to help us work more efficiently and effectively as language revitalizers, teachers, materials developers, language documenters, language advocates, administrators, and learners is quite impressive, even overwhelming. This chapter will attempt to weave together some of the main considerations that many of us encounter when dealing with technology in our day-to-day professional activities. We will look at the set of skills necessary for working with technology, talk about how to get started when incorporating technology, cover some of the domains of technology use, discuss the creation of materials, and finally look at special considerations when working with technology in language revitalization. But before we begin, let's start by discussing a principled approach for incorporating new technology into the language learning environment.

Principles, Not Tools

Perhaps it is best to start with a counter example, one that too many technology consumers and language teachers use as a default strategy when incorporating new technology. It goes something like this: I found this great new app online for my phone/tablet/computer; it can do this amazing thing; now I want to see how I can find a way to use it in my upcoming lesson next week.

This approach can be called 'app driven' or 'tool driven'. An app-driven approach prioritizes technology while moving learning needs into the background. Although in some cases this approach may lead to a successful use of technology for learning, more often than not it is gimmicky and has limited pedagogical success. You might say it is putting the cart before the horse: a solution looking for a problem.

A more sound approach would reverse the roles of learning and technology, and place the learning in the foreground, something that might be called a 'needs-based' approach. To give a real-life example, Rosanne, an Ichishkíin language teacher who is not very confident in using technology, had just introduced a unit on using conversations at the breakfast table. She would like her learners to create, practice, and then record a dialogue so she can listen to their speech and give feedback on their pronunciation and vocabulary use, but she is not sure how best to go about this. Once the need has been identified, the search for the best technology solution can begin. So, in looking for an audio recording option, from talking with other people, Roseanne is considering: (1) the free recording program Audacity, with students uploading a file to a shared folder online such as One drive, Dropbox, or Google Drive; (2) an online recording program called Vocaroo that learners can use to record, save, and send audio files to the teacher; or (3) a preloaded app on the students' cell phones (there are numerous apps for Android or iPhone, such as Voice Recorder or Voice Memos that come preinstalled) so that they can send the teacher their audio file in an email or text from their phone.

Now that the options have been identified, Roseanne can decide which one works best for her learning context, weighing the pros and cons of each potential tool. From the three options above, perhaps the students have access to only one class computer, which would rule out option one. Vocaroo for phones requires a download and a little training, and Roseanne decides that there isn't enough time for that in her already busy curriculum, so option two is ruled out. All of Roseanne's students have cell phones that already have audio recording apps, so after considering various factors Roseanne feels option three is the best choice. By using this needs-based approach, Roseanne is more likely to find the best tool for her particular purpose and context.

To take another example, Paulo, a language program manager and someone generally skilled in using technology, wants to build a short, online course for people interested in learning Tolowa-Dee-Ni'. He wants to have many audio files of common phrases included in the website and has a very modest budget, but he is not sure which is the best website builder to use. Now that he has defined his need he looks for a solution. One option he is considering is Google Sites. He knows it is free, easy to use and that he can invite people to view the website so he can control who is able to use it. However, it would require maintaining the user permissions list of people as well as adding and deleting people. He has heard about Wix and thinks their websites look particularly nice and easy to build, but the free plan uses a 'wix' domain name; he could try the starter plan at roughly US $4.00 per month, but it still contains ads on the site, which he doesn't want. He also considers WordPress. The only cost he can see is for hosting, which also runs at about US $4.00 per month, but he thinks he might be able to host the site on his department server. He can password protect the website with a single password, thus avoiding maintaining a user list. While some people complain that WordPress is not powerful, it can easily host audio with a player, which is the main technical goal he has for this website. After weighing the advantages and disadvantages, he chooses WordPress for his project.

A Necessary Skill Set

So what does a language revitalizer need to be able to do in order to complete her job effectively in today's technology-dependent world? Is there a set of basic standards or a specified skill set for those working with endangered languages? For English language teachers, for example, a set of standards have been developed by Healey and her colleagues at TESOL, most of which are also applicable to language revitalization. Some of the standards for teachers they have identified include:

(1) knowledge of various essential tools and how to use them;
(2) ability to integrate technology into the curriculum;
(3) incorporation of technology into assessment such as feedback and record keeping; and
(4) use of technology to improve opportunities for communication and collaboration.

Each of these areas will be discussed separately.

Knowledge of Various Essential Tools

Neither Roseanne nor Paulo were experts in all technological areas; no one can be. Yet, is there an ideal skill set that would help them perform their jobs better? A definitive list of essential tools is difficult to specify because of the wide variety of tasks that a language revitalizer is required to perform. Yet any list would likely include the following as a start: word processing programs (e.g. Word, Google Docs, or Open Office); presentation programs (Powerpoint, Keynote, or Prezi); spreadsheet programs (Excel, Open Office Calc, or Google Sheets); video and audio playback programs (Quicktime, Windows Media Player, or Vlc); and search engines (Chrome, Firefox, or Safari). Language workers should ideally feel comfortable using these programs and in creating language materials and classroom supplements. They should also feel confident in training learners to use such programs or in troubleshooting students' issues.

To someone new to technology, like Roseanne, a list of skills and tools like the above could feel daunting. More important than being 'good at X'

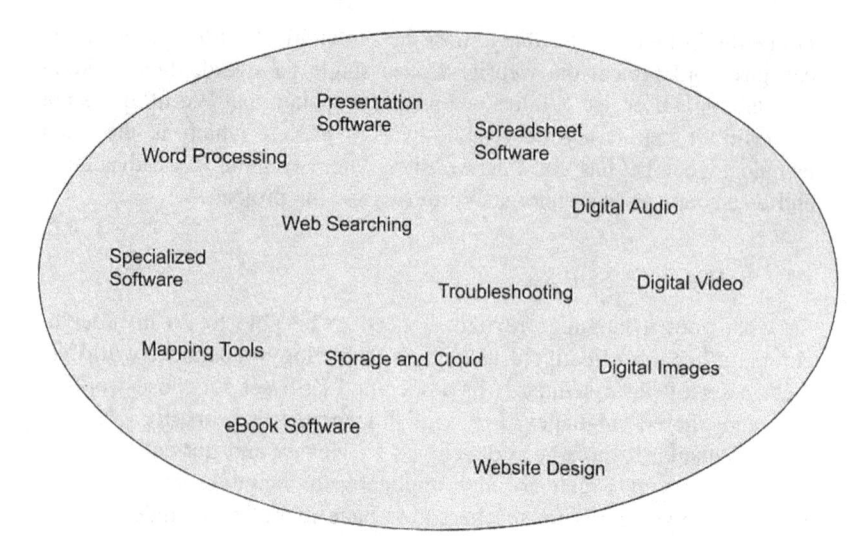

Figure 17.1 The Wide World of Apps. A possible sea of uncharted 'Apps' relevant to language revitalization workers. Developing expertise in all areas is daunting, perhaps even an impossible task

program or expertly knowing specific tools, however, is the ability to feel comfortable with technology generally. Feeling comfortable with trying out and adapting to new technology will go a long way as tools are in a constant state of change. For example, software developers often add new features, change the location of menus and options, or even remove features altogether after updates. Not only are existing tools in flux, but new tools keep being developed while old tools become obsolete or unsupported. One example of this constant change is MS Word. Since its release in 1989 Word has undergone at least fourteen different major versions, with additional minor versions released in-between. While ten years ago you may have been an expert at version 12.0 of Word, many features have changed with the latest release.

While it would be ideal to have language revitalization workers competent in all essential technological skills and confident in their abilities to troubleshoot and help others, the reality is that the 'World of Apps' and related necessary skills are vast (see Figure 17.1). One way to handle this daunting task is to start small with current needs, and then build out into what some have called 'islands of competence'. That is, someone desiring to increase their skill set can begin with what they already know, or start with a small area that is most in need, learning only a few new things at a time. Over time, they can slowly build their skills and expand their knowledge into new or related areas (see Figures 17.2 and 17.3). In Roseanne's

Technology in Language Revitalization 301

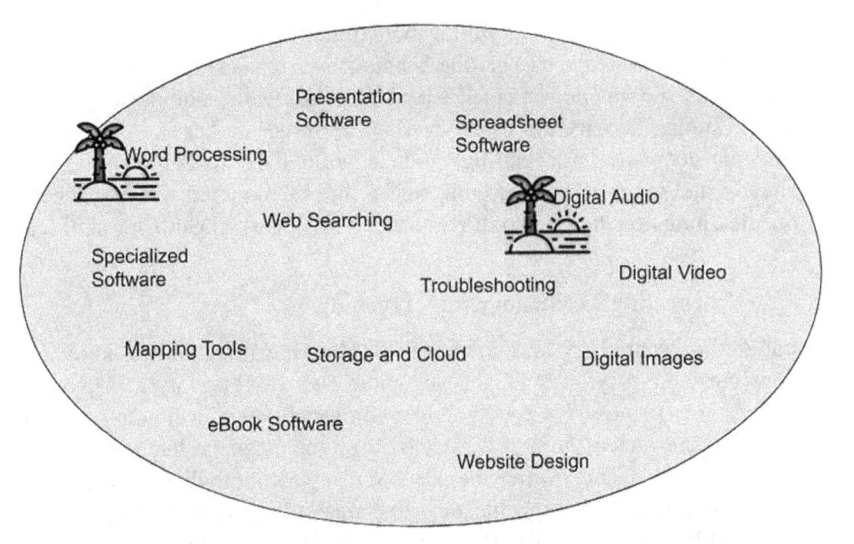

Figure 17.2 Islands of Competence. Rather than feel overwhelmed by the vast number of areas that need to be learned, users can start small, building 'islands of competence' in a few specific skill sets

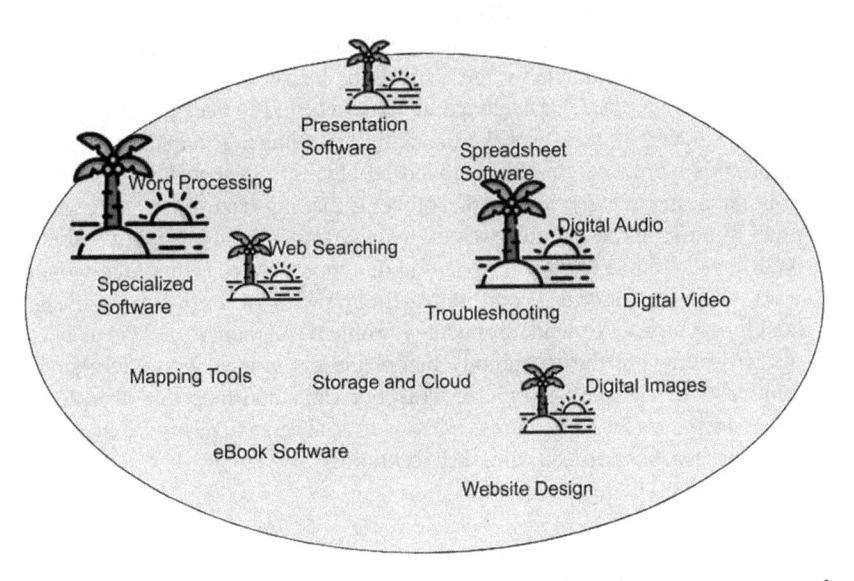

Figure 17.3 Expanding Islands of Competence. Over time, a user can expand their islands of competence, forming larger islands, chains of islands or even turning islands into entire continents

case, she originally knew very little about digital audio, but has now learned a bit after her experience of getting her students to make recordings on their phones, so she has built a small island of competence. The next time she does a similar activity she might even build further on her skills and have students do some basic editing of their audio files. In Paulo's case, he already had many islands of competence, but he ventured out into a new one, learning how to use WordPress and adding a new island to his skill set.

Integrating Technology into Teaching

Integrating technology into your work or class means intimately knowing your curriculum, your students, and your own teaching style. Although increasingly younger learners are more comfortable with technology, often they are unaware of how to use technology for language learning. While many of today's students may be adept at using technology generally, their use often falls into very specific areas that are not language-learning related; a skilled language revitalization worker will know how to use technology specifically to foster language learning, and know how to share that knowledge.

When integrating technology into language teaching, it is important to be aware of the curriculum, learning goals, and objectives. For example, if the objective is to have students talk about what they did yesterday in the past tense in the language, this will dictate what types of tools the teacher would consider. In addition, teachers should know whether the equipment and space available is suitable for the goals of the lesson or class. A class based project, for example, that included audio would likely necessitate instructing the students in how to make the audio recordings. The quality of these recordings would be greatly improved by having access to headphones to limit the ambient noise of the other students making recordings at the same time. In turn, this might influence the type of recording technology chosen. Additionally, a teacher leading a lesson that incorporates technology would want to be sure that she is comfortable enough with the software so that she could troubleshoot or work around any problems encountered. This usually means testing out the technology before the class; even if the teacher is familiar with the tool, testing can work out kinks and help to successfully integrate the technology into the lesson. As an added resource, in many cases the teacher can call upon her technologically savvy students to help those that are having trouble.

Assessment

A final way to use technology is during assessments. Assessments can be formative or summative, and technology can be used to enhance assessment and feedback for any of the four common skills: listening, speaking, reading, or writing. In addition, there are numerous ways to create interactive tasks, activities, and quizzes, which can be used to assess learning and will be discussed later in this chapter. Finally computers offer a way to keep track of attendance and grades, sometimes through the use of a Learning Management System (e.g. Canvas www.canvaslms.com/), or grading software (e.g. Thinkwave www.thinkwave.com/), or, when these are not available, in teacher created spreadsheets (e.g. Excel or Google Sheets).

Evaluating Potential Technology

Before selecting a particular technological tool it is useful to go through an intentional evaluation process. Listing your priorities or relevant issues is a good place to start and requires knowledge of the strengths and the constraints of your particular context.

There are two types of issues that you might find on your list: general issues and context-specific issues. General issues that are likely to be important in nearly all language contexts include cost, ease of use, powerfulness of the tool, and availability. Specific items unique to your context might include ease of use, appropriateness to the age of users, appropriateness to the culture of users, and compatibility of fonts to the orthography of your language.

Free and Open Source Tools

Nearly all language revitalization contexts operate on a tight budget. Free tools, or tools with free versions, are most likely to be valuable in such situations. Luckily there are numerous suitable resources to consider, though one may need to be a bit creative in adapting the tool to the local context. Also, caution should be taken when evaluating 'free' apps; they may limit the length of time you can use it, stop you using it after a set number of times, contain watermarking or advertising on the product, or other deal-breaking problems.

To take one example, MS Word is standard for most computers, but costs money. Free and open source alternatives to Word include WPS Office Free, Libre Office, and Google Docs among others. Specific adaptations, such as installing fonts from a source like 'Language Geek,' may be required to get your word processor to work for your language. In another example, while some computers may include built-in audio editors as part of a bundle, Audacity is a free, open source audio editor that has some surprisingly powerful features. To export your files as smaller MP3 files, an extension (LAME encoder) may need to be installed as an adaption.

Iterative Process of Incorporating Technology

Incorporating technology into your work should be seen as an ongoing process; rather than finding a definitive, immediate solution, incorporating technology is better viewed as something that happens over time. In most cases, a proposed technology solution has some glitches, tradeoffs, or downsides, or it doesn't work as smoothly as we want it to. Sometimes these issues are severe enough that we search for another tool entirely. More often glitches mean that we need to 'tweak' the tool, the way we introduce it to learners, or the support we give to users.

To do this, it can be beneficial to look at incorporating technology as an iterative process. After introducing a new technology, take some time to stop and reflect. Jot down a few notes about what worked, what didn't work, and how it might work better in the future. The next time you use the technology, make any necessary adjustments and afterward reflect again. Don't be afraid to keep an eye out for new technology that might do the job better. Finding the right tool for the right job, and knowing the right way to use it, takes time.

Safety, Privacy, and Ownership

A final consideration when using technology, particularly in language revitalization contexts, is safety, privacy, and ownership concerns. For those working with children, special care needs to be taken to protect them from some of the seedier sides of the Internet. For example, while many social media tools such as Facebook can be a useful learning and communication tool, extra precautions should be taken when using them with children. Sometimes it is better to use an education specific tool, such as Edmodo. Drafting a set of general guidelines and policies for social media use is something many language departments and schools have done. An example policy could include: making all student communications public; separating professional from personal accounts; using official or school district equipment for communication; and refraining from posting any personal information about students.[1]

Issues around ownership and control of data and information have historically affected Indigenous and minority communities disproportionately. When using proprietary software, for example, care needs to be taken that ownership of the material remains with the community, and that producers of information can control distribution and who is

---

[1] www.edutopia.org/sites/default/files/pdfs/edutopia-anderson-social-media-guidelines.pdf

able to view the products. For example, iBooks Author is a program that can easily create professional looking eBooks, but there are some limitations. Since it is a proprietary program, the fine print states that books created with iBooks Author cannot be sold except through iTunes. This is not a problem if a community wishes to give away books through its own method of distribution (email, website, jumpdrive), but in some cases it might not be what a community wants to do with the content they have developed.

Domains of Technology Use

In this next section, we will consider both where technology will be used, and what types of language it can support.

Technology within the Classroom

Decisions about what technology to use in the classroom are largely limited by availability and what we have access to. For example, whether we have access to classroom computers, computer labs, laptops, tablets, smartboards, and cell phones will shape what options we have and the choices we make. Classroom teachers, again, should take care that they are using the technology with a clear language purpose in mind.

In some settings, the 'classroom' is nontraditional, sometimes even without walls. Many communities in the USA have an annual culture or language camp, where groups of community members gather, sometimes far away from 'the grid,' which affects what kinds of technology can be used there. In one case, a community that was holding their camp in the mountains at a traditional gathering spot wanted to have access to audio and interactive activities. The community had access to a set of tablets, so an eBook was developed and preloaded onto these. When the children at the camp went to the language tent, they were able to interact with this multimedia material without any Internet connection. At night, the language camp leaders simply had to remember to charge the batteries.

Technology outside the Classroom

Learning Management Systems (LMSs) offer many options for extending the learning beyond the classroom. However the big ones, such as Blackboard, Canvas, and Moodle, are typically tied to schools or departments that have significant budgets and, in the case of Moodle, technology support services. There are free versions of the larger LMSs: For example, Blackboard has Coursesites, and Canvas has Free For Teachers, both of which are stripped down versions of the full systems. Another option for smaller budgets are LMSs that are free and self-contained, such as Google Classroom, ANVILL, or Obaverse. ANVILL, for example, is designed specifically for emphasis on spoken language, is free to teachers and students, and allows administrators to add students and guests as needed.

As in the case of Paolo, discussed earlier in this chapter, website development can be an important way to host or share information about language with a community. Several free sources have already been mentioned (Google Sites, Wix, WordPress), but numerous alternatives exist, with new ones popping up constantly. In choosing a website editor, factors that Paolo took into consideration were cost (is it free or, if not, does it fit my budget), ease of use (how long will it take to be proficient), and powerfulness (can it do what I want it to do). In addition, stability of the platform – whether it will be around in a few years and whether the free option will change if the business model changes – should be a top consideration. Other types of communication platforms, such as blogs (EduBlogs, Tumblr) or discussion forms (phpBB, MyBB), can also be valuable communication tools.

As well as extending learning time for individuals, technology outside the classroom has the potential to include whole families in the language revitalization process. When possible, learners can include siblings, parents, grandparents, or even extended relatives into language assignments or projects. In one example of intergenerational learning, High School students were tasked with building audio materials about common phrases in the language, to be hosted on SoundCloud. The students tapped into the knowledge of older family members to help with vocabulary and pronunciation, and they helped teach phrases to younger siblings who knew little of the language. In another example, one language revitalization learner/teacher carried around a dedicated audio recorder. When new phrases or words came up when interacting with fluent speakers in his family or in community gatherings, he asked to capture them on his recorder so that he could continue working on improving his own fluency. This could also be done easily on a phone.

Listening and Speaking

For many communities, the language is traditionally used for spoken communication. At the same time, if the language is highly endangered, there can be few opportunities to hear or speak the language. This is one problem that technology can easily help address. Technology can offer learners another purpose for using the language, and materials developed can be used to increase the profile of the language and people's exposure to it. For recording and organizing audio files there are several options, including Vocaroo, Padlet, and VoiceThread. Padlet, for example, can be used for group pages where students record an audio or video file on a specific topic and then ask other learners to listen and respond to it. Individual Padlet pages can also be used for solo work, such as keeping audio journals.

Animation is another option that sometimes drives up learners' motivation. Volki, SockPuppets, and GoAnimate all offer easy platforms for building animations that audio can be layered onto. Volki, for example, allows learners to create an avatar and then record the spoken language, so that the avatar appears to be doing the talking. Learners can create an avatar that represents and speaks for them, or they can create animal avatars, and work on the language the animal might be using. SockPuppets allows users to create up to four characters that can interact in a language, and it can be quite fun for younger learners at the same time as developing their confidence in the language.

Creating videos is perhaps the most powerful tool, but it takes some time for users to be trained on how to do this. Windows Movie Maker on PC and iMovie on Mac are both good initial movie editors. Another option is movie editing in the cloud, with an app like WeVideo or YouTube Video Editor. Both are good free options. Adobe Spark is a free app that can be downloaded or used in the cloud, and it can be a good all-in-one editor for younger learners or for those who can't afford to take the time to learn how to use a more powerful tool. Finally, even Powerpoint can incorporate audio into slides and be turned into a movie.

Reading, Writing, and Vocabulary

Reading materials in endangered languages can be scarce. While some endangered and minority languages have a robust written history, many do not. If written materials exist, online databases can offer language workers easy access to collections. For example the 'Ulukau: Hawaiian Electronic Library' catalogues newspapers in the Hawaiian language from 1834 to 1948. For languages with little or no written resources, materials designers will need to be more creative. For example, by using tools like Google Forms, Survey Monkey, or Qualtrics, teachers can create surveys that include simple questions for beginner students or reading sections for more advanced students, or a general comprehension test using a multiple choice format.

Writing with technology offers many possibilities beyond simple word processing. Collaborative writing 'in the cloud' allows for creative pair, group, and even whole class writing activities using Google Docs. An activity can be scaled up or down depending on the proficiency of your learners. Survey tools mentioned above can be open ended, requiring students to respond to questions in writing. WordClouds can be used with tools like PollEverywhere, where students are asked a question, such as 'what's your favorite animal'. Students then respond on their phones, and their answers are displayed in real time in a word cloud.

Vocabulary options are many. Quizlet, Anki, and Memrise allow both learners and teachers to build their own flashcards. There are numerous crossword puzzle makers and word search makers. Cloze test makers, such as Learn Click or Cloze Test Creator, allow you to easily make fill in the blank type activities where learners are required to use all of their language skills to complete the task.

Another option for vocabulary is the use of databases. The Miami-Illinois Digital Archive (MIDA) is one example (http://ilaatawaakani.org/). Developed by the Myaamia Center in collaboration with the Miami Tribe of Oklahoma, the goal of this database is to assemble all the various resources in the Miami-Illinois language into a single searchable space that can be useful for both researchers and learners. It currently has over 50,000 entries and there are plans to open up the resource to other language communities with a sister project called the Indigenous Language Digital Archive (https://ildarchive.org/). This new site is being used now by the South West Oregon Dene Research project to build the Nuu-da' Mv-ne' digital archive. Online dictionaries, such as the Siletz Dee-ni' dictionary (http://siletz.swarthmore.edu/), are another option. Such dictionaries often have audio associated with the written entries to aid learners in the pronunciation of words and phrases. While the resources listed in this paragraph typically require training and support, these can be among the most powerful tools available to language revitalization workers.

Considerations for Language Revitalization Contexts

The Low Tech Environment

In some language revitalization contexts there is little access to technology or computers. Nevertheless, there are still powerful ways that technology can be creatively utilized. A single computer classroom can be a valuable tool, especially if teachers have access to a projector and speakers. Teacher-controlled activities, such as a Powerpoint presentation of a story in the language, can incorporate audio, images, and even video. The single computer can be used for students' presentations, as a workstation in part of a rotating station in the classroom, or as a spot for students to write a short story together, either led by the teacher or where each student comes up and continues the story in a chain activity.

Even in environments lacking computers, most students now have smartphones. Many younger students use social media on a regular basis, and teachers can set up spaces to use the language such as an Instagram or Twitter feed. More simply, teachers can encourage students to text with each other in language using their phones, or tap into texting tools such as Facebook Messenger or Whatsapp. An additional option for cell phone use is Kahoot. A teacher can set up a language quiz or poll, sharing the address with students so that they can answer the questions and see the results immediately from the computer projected at the front of the class. Smartphones in general are becoming more common, but challenges remain in terms of unequal access, variation in platforms and apps, and the ability of learners to use their phones effectively for learning and not get distracted.

Creating Materials

One of the biggest challenges facing small and minority languages is a lack of materials. Producing materials is a specialist area for publishers working on learning materials for major languages, yet small profit margins rarely allow for any collaboration with Indigenous communities. Tribal and community language programs are often short on capacity and funding, which leaves the bulk of materials creation up to individual language departments and teachers. Where possible, language programs should have a technology expert who can help create materials and coach teachers who want to create their own materials but need support. Training personnel at conferences, workshops, or institutes not only increases capacity, but often results in the creation of materials that can be taken back to the community and directly used for learning. Creating e-books, electronic dictionaries, or other digital materials avoids the additional costs of printing materials.

Documenting with an Eye toward Everyday Language

Since many 'smaller' languages are still being documented, it is important for community members to work with linguists or documenters to make sure that the type of everyday language needed for communication and conversation is captured. Instead of word lists dictated by linguists looking for minimal pairs, documentation should be done on natural, everyday communication. When possible, it is preferable to have two or more speakers interacting in a realistic situation so that documentation can capture the nuances of the language, such as greetings, turn taking, changing of topics, agreement, joking, or closing. Using video offers further opportunities for capturing paralinguistic communication that is vital to effective cultural competence in the target language, such as facial expressions, proxemics, and gesture. Language workers can then more easily repurpose documentation materials into pedagogical materials. The 'sweet spot' is when documentation is useful to a community of teachers and learners and not just linguists.

Including Learners in the Process of Materials Creation

Another option is to include students and learners in addressing the need for materials. Project Based Learning (PBL) offers many options for both increasing the amount of material available in a target language, but can also extend the reasons for using the language, encouraging students to get involved. Projects can be teacher led or student led, but are often negotiated so students have some input in deciding the direction of the project. Creating maps, videos, books, e-books, posters, audio material, and websites are all examples of products that students can help create. When these materials have an authentic use outside of the classroom, it enhances the project. For example, in one situation, high school language students created language materials to be used in a preschool immersion classroom. They were trained in how to capture and edit audio, video, and images, and how to turn these into an e-book. They then produced a small library of e-books that featured images and recordings of themselves speaking in their language, as well as recordings from the wider community, and even of the preschool children who were to receive the materials.

A Healthy Skepticism toward Technology

While technology certainly offers language teachers opportunities that did not exist before, it is important not to look at technology as a silver bullet for endangered languages. There are limitations and pitfalls associated with using technology, time and money being perhaps the most important ones. Given the reality of limited budgets, technology can be a heavy drain on language programs where equipment and applications need to be kept up to date. There is often a learning curve associated with new programs as well as the time commitment required to produce materials, and teachers are often short on precious time. A language revitalization effort has to look at where their time and money would best be spent, and in many cases technology will not be the best answer. Finally, much of what can be accomplished with technology is best described as an extension of learning. That is, initial teaching of new language features is usually best done in person, with technology acting as a way to reinforce or extend the learning, offering more opportunities for practicing the language or reviewing language skills.

'Train the Trainers' Model for Workshops

How can knowledge of best practices in using technology be shared most effectively? One model that has proven useful in many teaching contexts is the 'train the trainers', or 'train the leaders' approach. An example of this is the Costa Rican workshop: 'Primer Taller de Formación de Maestros de Lenguas Indígenas Costarricenses: Estrategias Didácticas y Uso de Herramientas Tecnológicas' held at the University of Costa Rica in April of 2018. Fifteen members from seven Indigenous language groups from around the country were selected to come to the capital to take part in the two-week workshop. Participants were carefully chosen on the basis of being language leaders or important teachers in their communities, who would not only benefit from the workshop themselves, but who would then be able to return home and share what they had learned with others. After learning about pedagogy and technology, participants developed an action plan for how to share their ideas once back home, effectively becoming trainers themselves. This model, when implemented successfully, allows for the quick dissemination of useful techniques and ideas about language teaching and technology use, which can then benefit as many people as possible.

Technology as a Resource for Teacher Support

Teachers and people working in language revitalization situations often feel isolated and alone. With few others in the tribe or community concerning themselves with the same issues, many teachers are in need of support. Some support can come in the form of moral support, just having a place to 'vent' or share problems that are hard to understand unless you are doing similar work. Support can also be in the form of asking questions about problems and getting feedback on possible solutions. Support also comes in the form of learning about what people are doing in one context that can potentially be useful for other contexts. While traditionally conferences and workshops have been outstanding sources of such support, time limitations and the expense of travel can create obstacles to getting this type of support.

Technology serves an important role in addressing this problem. Social media, emailing or skyping others with expertise offers us an ability to receive such support anytime, anywhere. Facebook groups and email lists, such as the ILAT list, are a place for public sharing and discussion of ideas unique to this specialized community. Similarly resource centers such as the NILI Resources Center (http://nilirc.com/) offer a place for teachers to browse materials for ideas, search templates that can be turned into their own language, or use ready-made materials if the language they are working with is represented.

17.1 How about Just Shifting Back? How One Passamaquoddy Speaker Led Her Community to Language Documentation and Revitalization

Ben Levine

Margaret Apt, a middle-aged Passamaquoddy woman from Eastern Maine, USA, had grown up away from the Reservation and was doing everything she could to improve her Passamaquoddy language skills, but now the Elders were no longer speaking in public. She noticed that when they needed a new word to discuss a contemporary topic they would shift to, and then remain speaking in, English. Passamaquoddy, an Algonquian language of the Eastern USA and Canada, was becoming invisible. I asked Margaret if we could try an experiment using video. She agreed and began to convene a group of speakers who also agreed to be filmed. Whenever the talk drifted into English, Margaret would gently remind the speaker to switch back to Passamaquoddy. It worked, and soon speakers were having long conversations about contemporary experiences totally in Passamaquoddy. This speaker-facilitated, nonintrusive, documentary style videotaping soon became an accepted method for Passamaquoddy language documentation. Subsequent presentation of the video back to the participants and community, referred to as Video Feedback, stimulated more deeply contextualized conversation and sometimes motivated new language initiatives (see Figure 17.1.1). Margaret became the first Facilitator of the method that came to be called Natural Group Conversation and Activity Documentation. So just by acting on her wish to speak Passamaquoddy with her friends without English intruding, and with a little help from the video, Margaret launched an active process of language revitalization in her community that is also being replicated elsewhere.

As Facilitator, Margaret would create a safe space for speaking. She might start the conversation off with a question and then ask for contextualizing information. Speakers gained confidence and soon were telling stories, laughing, or commiserating – creating speaker-driven language in natural, real-life ways. Playing the video back gave the speakers new awareness and the emotional strength to take on the topics that concerned them and activities they wanted filmed. More speakers became involved, and a new confidence to address language endangerment emerged as Passamaquoddy became more visible again.

This practice of video feedback triggers new and often deeper conversations, creating rich content for teaching and learning as well as linguistic analysis. Recording these conversations and playing them back has proven to be helpful in addressing historic community trauma and its effects in suppressing language use. It has also resulted in the emergence of new leaders advocating for revitalization.

Margaret and other participants next learned to log, transcribe, translate, and subtitle over 100 videos, first available as DVDs that later became part of the Passamaquoddy-Maliseet online dictionary and audio archive which can be seen at www.PMPortal.org. Margaret taught her daughter Plansowes and some friends who had tried to learn Passamaquoddy and understood the language but couldn't speak it,

Figure 17.1.1 Ben Levine and Julia Schulz documenting Passamaquoddy-Maliseet natural conversation as developed with Margaret (Dolly) Apt. Photo by Ian Larson

how to record dictionary entries and example sentences with Elders and then post them on the Portal. The recording process immediately helped these tech-savvy, 30-something fluent comprehenders improve their language skills and increased their interest in learning and using the language. Excited at this breakthrough, they shared Portal links to words and videos on social media. Soon there was heightened visibility of the language, increased respect for speakers, and an expanding new constituency for Passamaquoddy language, especially among those living in the diaspora who could now be connected to the language. The Elders, in turn, became acquainted, in a non-threatening way, with the Passamaquoddy-Maliseet writing system.

The participants in Margaret's conversations subsequently initiated new language revival projects: two immersion preschools; a video-based program for fluent comprehenders and language classes for adults. One man engaged in graduate studies so that he could become a linguist for the tribe. Two others became language teachers. What started with one person, Margaret, looking for ways to get her own Passamaquoddy language back, grew into language revitalization with many different components. Today there are new speakers of Passamaquoddy for the first time in forty years, and the model has inspired other groups. Language activists in an Ayöök-speaking Mixe community in Southern Mexico saw Passamaquoddy videos and invited Speaking Place to start the documentation and revitalization process in their town. The Mixe have used the same methods. They have also had training from our team on linguist-guided community self-documentation. Like the Passamaquoddy who inspired them, they have started immersion schools and are building a Mixe radio station. Now other towns in Oaxaca are starting to adopt these methods as well. While each community shapes the methods and process to their own circumstances, starting with video documentation of facilitated natural group conversation and activity can be a potent launching pad for revitalization.

17.2 Online Language Learning Materials Development

Jennifer Needs

Welsh is relatively fortunate among the world's lesser-used languages, with its official status, government support, rich literary tradition, dedicated radio and television channels, and important role in the education system in Wales. Welsh-medium education is available from nursery right through to university-level, whilst those attending English-medium schools learn Welsh as a second language. It is also possible to learn Welsh as an adult, and around 18,000 learners attend adult Welsh classes in Wales each year.

One course provider, Nant Gwrtheyrn, specializes in week-long residential courses, which particularly attract learners from abroad or whose lifestyles don't suit weekly classes. However these learners sometimes find it tricky to maintain the 'buzz' and keep using their Welsh once they've returned home. Through the KESS[2] programme, a partnership was established between Nant Gwrtheyrn and myself, a PhD student at Cardiff University, in order to develop a research-based set of online learning materials that would complement the beginners' level residential course and allow learners to maintain regular contact with the Welsh language.

Despite the very specific context of the project, the lessons I learned should be applicable to online materials development in many environments.

- Try to plan a manageable project based on available human/financial resources. Do you need to create an entire curriculum or just supplementary materials?
- Don't expect the planning and writing process to follow linear stages – decisions made part-way through the process, or new information about learners' needs/expectations, will mean you need to revise earlier work.
- If online learning resources are already available for your target language, try to collaborate with the authors rather than competing with them. Don't reinvent something that has already been produced for your language – focus on creating new resources which will complement existing ones.

---

[2] Knowledge Economy Skills Scholarships (KESS) is a pan-Wales higher-level skills initiative led by Bangor University on behalf of the HE sector in Wales. It is part-funded by the Welsh Government's European Social Fund (ESF) convergence programme for West Wales and the Valleys.

- In terms of the language content of materials, consider the domains in which you hope learners will use their language skills. For example, you could select vocabulary and phrases used in the home, in the workplace, in ceremonies, or in the wider community.
- Also keep in mind why you are creating *digital* learning materials as opposed to paper materials. To reach a geographically dispersed audience? To encourage learners to practise frequently? To facilitate independent learning? Electronic learning materials should not simply be digitised versions of paper materials (e.g. PDFs of worksheets). Instead they should offer something over and above the 'offline' experience, making use of what technology can uniquely offer – e.g. interactivity even without classmates/tutors, or instant personalised feedback, or helping make input comprehensible by offering hyperlinks and images.
- Don't allow technological developments to dictate the resources you create without reference to language learning theories/principles. In other words, don't create something just because it's technically possible – always reflect on the benefits a resource will bring to the learning experience.
- For audio/video resources, consider including recordings of 'new speakers' as well as 'native speakers'. In some language contexts this would be an appropriate way of demonstrating that learners are valued members of the linguistic community.
- Plan for future sustainability! I failed at this one, as the online platform hosting my resources has disappeared, taking my content with it! So think about long-term plans for your materials – e.g. how they might be migrated to new platforms, or how they might be adapted for mobile devices as opposed to computers.

17.3 Rising Voices

Eddie Avila

The Internet provides a special opportunity for communities that speak Indigenous, endangered, and minority languages to attract and involve younger generations in language preservation and revitalization – an involvement that is crucial for the survival of these languages and cultures.

Supporting such communities, especially Indigenous communities across Latin America, in this work has been a primary focus of Rising Voices (RV), the digital inclusion initiative of the organization Global Voices. RV works to promote equity and diversity online through training, mentoring, and the creation of peer-learning networks. With the increased accessibility of devices such as smartphones and tablets, and the spread of Internet connectivity (including through community-owned networks) Indigenous communities are increasingly accessing information online. However, they rarely do so in their native language. That is changing. Communities' access to information and digital tools is making it easier to create multilingual content themselves. Creating content online by uploading videos to YouTube, translating free software, or writing on blogs and social media platforms is a positive step that Indigenous communities can take toward ensuring that their language is present in all facets of life, especially in the digital realm.

Rising Voices' support takes many different forms, including organizing workshops and gatherings. In recent times, we have held events in Mexico, Colombia, Peru, Ecuador, Guatemala, Bolivia, and Chile, in collaboration with a range of local partners. In these meetings, participants run hands-on workshops and engage in peer-led discussions addressing the linguistic, technical, and socio-cultural obstacles they face promoting their languages online. These events also include a public component designed to showcase the work and its possibilities. A direct result of these gatherings has been the creation of local, national, and international networks of mutual support and solidarity.

Rising Voices has also created the *Activismo Lenguas* (Language Activism) portal to map projects across the region and to highlight the important role that technology is playing in language revitalization, as well as to inspire other communities wanting to do similar types of initiatives. Visitors to the portal can search by country, language, and the type of digital tool that they utilize in their revitalization activities. We are also working to research and analyze the opportunities and challenges for sharing knowledge through Wikipedia in Indigenous languages. This work has given us valuable access to the perspectives of practitioners on the ground, and allowed them to share their stories.

Finally, our social media campaigns encourage engagement with minority languages in a fun way, such as tweeting and creating memes. In observance of the International Year of Indigenous Languages 2019, Rising Voices created a rotating Twitter account (@ActLenguas) where each week a different Indigenous language digital activist manages the account, tweeting about their personal experiences of using technology in support of language revitalization. Our work in Rising Voices has shown the possibilities provided by technology. But it is important to stress that the Internet and digital media are only tools, and that the real driving force behind this work is the hundreds of young people who have stepped forward and demonstrated their commitment to ensuring that their language and culture are reflected in all facets of society, including the Internet.

Afterword

Julia Sallabank and Justyna Olko

We have learnt a lot from preparing this book (and from the Engaged Humanities collaborative project that motivated it). It has been inspiring to work with so many people from all over the world, and to hear their stories and their approaches to solving problems that arise. Sometimes these problems and solutions are quite specific to their cases, but often we see similar issues in different communities and language contexts. We hope that this book will inspire you too, and that the solutions and ideas discussed will help you to develop and test your own strategies.

This book has tried to focus on positive aspects of language revitalization and its complexity, in order to encourage participation. Its goal has also been to help you to deal with different facets of revitalization, which sometimes can only be done step by step, though keeping in mind other important challenges and tasks that need to follow. It is important, however, to recognize that the road may not be smooth and that problems may arise. Here we offer some tips on how to minimize their impact.

Firstly, it may not be easy. Language revitalization can take a long time – even generations. Activists can get discouraged and 'burn out'. It helps if you can gather a group of keen people who support each other, and who share both the work and the joy of speaking their language again. It also helps to make contacts with other communities and support networks, to avoid feeling isolated. Links with academics can provide access to literature on how others have addressed problems.

Secondly, language revitalization is complex. It is not only about language: it may include many areas of life such as culture, education, politics, healthcare, environment, social and broadcast media. You will need allies with a range of expertise, e.g. project planning, fundraising and accounting, computer programming, public relations, teacher training, syllabus design, art and crafts, museum and archive curation, care for senior citizens. Not all of these people may speak or learn the language, but their support is vital and they share a commitment to supporting language revitalization.

Thirdly, disagreements are common (almost inevitable); individuals and groups may disagree on strategy and on what the language should be like. It is important to remember that **language links people; we should not let it become a barrier**. Remember you all have the same broad goal, and that an integrated plan needs different parts. Most importantly, you can't afford to put anybody off – especially young people, who are the future.

Fourthly, we should keep in mind that language revitalization is – in a great majority of cases – a **never-ending process**. We should always plan at least one step ahead and make sure there are followers to take over the task. Even very successful language revitalization projects meet with serious challenges after generational turnover. They require constant effort to keep their languages spoken and used by the youngest generations. This is, for example, the case of the Manx language that was brought back on the Isle of Man back in the 1980s, and the revolutionary self-determination movement of the Diné/Navajo that resulted in the creation of the famous immersive community-controlled school in Rough Rock in 1966. To keep the language in use across generations, these new generations need to be attracted to and engaged in the process. Fortunately, new tools, approaches and solutions develop along the way, often through collaboration and reading books like this.

Fifthly, we have observed that language revitalization movements can get distracted by activities which are attractive and fun, but which don't have a lot of language content. You are likely to have limited resources, both human and financial. Weigh up the usefulness and relevance of ideas, and prioritize them accordingly. Awareness raising is important, but you may be losing speakers in the meantime. It can be easier to campaign for someone else to do something, e.g. for the government to recognize your language, or for it to be taught in schools, than to change your own language practices. The heart of language revitalization is using our languages in the community, with our family and friends. If we don't have a core of fluent speakers, we can't provide the language needed for other activities.

Successful language revitalization therefore needs courage, perseverance and openness to new ideas. But the most important thing is: speak your language!

Index

Abkhazian, 229
acquisition
 by adults, 40, 97, 240, 242
 by children, 1, 4, 40, 89, 93, 95, 115, 137, 156, 163, 172, 209, 249, 260, 295
 of majority language, 20–1
 by second language learners, 97, 162, 171, 188, 237, 314
 theories of, 42, 172, 235, 237–8, 242, 244
 through education, 114, 223, 226, 235, 269
activities
 artistic, 151, 182, 252
 community, 12, 29, 117, 147, 177, 209
 cultural, 102, 117, 145, 193, 285
 at home, 246–8, 250
 naming, 272
 symbolic, 39
 for tourists, 145–7, 149, 151
 traditional, 142, 144, 158, 253
advocacy, 135, 141, 177
Afar, 224
Ainu, 168, 185, 229, 291
Albanian, 118
Algonquian languages, 187
Alznerish, 217
ancestors, 10, 12, 29–30, 32, 94, 156, 160, 263, 270
Anishinaabemowin, 271
announcements, public, 38, 117, 142
anonymity, 77
 ideology of, 107
apps, 63, 103, 303
 for language learning, 241, 297
 for recording, 298, 307
Arabic, 229–30, 279
Aranda, Western, 224
Arawakan, 80
Arbanasi, 117
archives, 30, 59, 204, 206, 317
 access to, 77, 207
 community-based, 209, 308, 312
 and community knowledge, 208
 interface language of, 207

 and training, 205, 207–8
 use of, 38, 43, 201, 207, 226, 242
archiving, 77, 200, 207, 216
Argentina, 91, 180–1, 184
Armenian, 229
Arrernte, Eastern, 224
arts, 182, 192, 271, 273
assimilation, 14–15, 23, 41, 91, 93, 99, 135, 143, 174, 231, 288, 295
Asturian, 173, 188
attitudes, 5, 86
 changing, 51, 102, 110, 112–13, 115, 117, 119, 121, 131–2, 135, 152, 169, 209, 251, 282, 285, 289
 of government, 28, 71, 133
 to language learning, 251
 negative, 27, 94, 100, 104, 110–13, 118, 199
 of nonspeakers, 114
 of older speakers, 28, 202
 positive, 18, 26, 104, 106, 110, 113, 116, 120, 132, 147, 288
 of wider community, 104, 135, 151, 169
 within community, 89, 104, 169
 of young people, 120
audiences
 for archive materials, 205
 for films, 280, 282
 for literature, 274, 282
 for music, 277, 282, 290–1
 online, 281
 participation of, 291
 for projects, 63, 66–7, 152, 293
Australia, 18, 23, 88, 91, 203, 210, 224, 226
Australian languages, 188
authenticity, 33, 42, 89–90, 107–8, 116, 141, 146, *See also* purism
 ideology of, 107
 and modernity, 122, 288
 and tourism, 145–6
awareness
 of attitudes and ideologies, 104, 116–17, 129, 168

319

awareness (cont.)
    of endangerment, 49
    of history, 29
    of projects, 75
    public, 63, 109
    raising, 38–9, 51, 102, 135–6, 147, 154, 182, 285, 318
Ayuuk (Ayöök), 193–4, 313

Bangladesh, 74
Barngarla, 23
Basque (Euskara), 56, 88, 110, 142, 173, 178–84, 186–9, 193, 231, 276
behaviour
    and attitudes, 110
    changing, 45, 50, 112, 124, 130, 135
    in language learning, 235
Belarusian, 172
benefits (of revitalization), 9, 11, 15, 18, 22, 141
    cognitive, 10, 115, 141
    for community, 19, 26, 153, 265
    economic, 11, 29, 141–2, 153
    educational, 19, 222, 257, 265
    for identity, 12
    for wider community, 9, 154
Bengali, 279
Bhojpuri, 279
bilingualism. *See* multilingualism
Black Tai (Lao Song), 24–6
Bolivia, 316
borrowing, 32, 41–3, 48, 89, 97, 119, 139, 202, 209, 232
    and purism, 48
Botswana, 224
Brazil, 163, 168, 207
Breath of Life programme, 38, 208
Breton, 13, 36, 108, 111, 172, 183, 287
budget, 61, 67, 72, 75–6, 78–9, *See also* costs
Buryat, 193
business, minority languages in, 141, 152, 166

campaigning, 44, 113, 117, 136, 151, 170, 173, 179, 231, 289, 318
Canada, 18, 20, 60, 88, 156, 180, 184, 189, 212, 271, 280, 312
    funding, 73
Catalan, 56, 88, 173, 183, 186–7, 193, 276
Celtic languages, 182, 184, 231, 241
change, language, 34, 202, 242, 260
    acceptance of, 40
    as growth, 40
    challenges of, 42
change, social, 11, 23, 32, 126, 135, 144, 157, 205, 288

Cherokee, 21, 269
children, involvement of, 295
    removal of, 14
    speaking to, 17, 34–5, 203, 210
    and technology, 304, 307
Chile, 91, 180–1, 185, 189–90, 289, 316
China, 88, 168
Chinese, 92, 229
Chinuk Wawa, 254, 264
cinema, 279, 282
classrooms
    for adults, 240
    Indigenous, 236, 266
    language for use in, 240, 249, 255
    learning outside of, 254, 263, 267, 270, 305–6
clothing, traditional, 46, 57, 100, 125, 128, 133–4, 284, 291
coauthorship, 57
code-mixing, 41, 47, 96–7, 118–19, 139, 202, 209, 218
Cognitive Behavioral Therapy, 19
collaborations, 67, 93, 131
    among learners, 103
    between communities, 179, 187, 192, 194
    between community members and researchers, 38, 51–2, 77, 177, 216, 285, 293, 309
    between teachers, 314
    and films, 278, 280, 283
    and funding, 73, 179, 190
    intergenerational, 13, 103, 132, 138, 211, 240, 258, 260, 263, 265, 284–5, 306, 313
    reluctance for, 50, 186
    and shared experience, 70, 187
    and songwriting, 290
    and technology, 299
Colombia, 92, 189, 316
colonialism, 14, 87, 93, 101, 161, 180, 186–7, 217, 238, 240, 258
colonization, 18, 22, 91, 146, 186, 189, 199, 237, 257, 274
Comcaac (Seri), 277
commercialization, 30, 57, 141–2, 146, 149, 151, 280–1
commitment, 127, 133, 164, 283
    of activists, 18, 70–1, 90, 136
    of community, 132, 152
    of learners, 250, 271
    of teachers, 97, 255, 261
    of youth, 316
commodification, 108, 147
communities, types of
    ancestral, 87, 89
    diaspora, 101–2, 177, 313

exiled, 91–2, 100, 218
migrant, 92, 166, 295
new, 100–1, 103, 218, 259, 287, 313
of practice, 88, 93, 102–3, 195
community
  consultation with, 51–2, 58, 200, 205, 211, 283
  decision making and control, 56, 165, 168, 209, 211, 228
  defining, 33, 85, 100
  engagement, 20, 50, 116, 147, 151, 172, 285
  initiatives, 56, 119, 131, 168, 172, 216, 230, 259, 264, 284, 312–14
  joining, 44, 115, 270
  leaders, 25, 160, 177, 248, 263, 312
  needs of, 51, 54, 61, 63–5, 87, 160, 168, 183, 216, 230, 238
  organizations, 101–2, 167, 225, 285
  relations within, 24, 87, 156–7, 218, 263
  sense of, 38, 70, 147, 278
  strengthening, 10, 13, 15, 18, 25, 99, 102–3, 116, 135, 156, 162, 209, 259, 263, 288
community members
  as activists, 31, 50, 52–3, 57, 77, 94, 126, 131, 137, 159–60, 248, 259, 270, 280, 312
  as researchers, 15, 25, 50, 73, 78, 139, 156, 163, 177, 200, 209, 224, 232–3, 263, 313
  training of, 52, 77, 94, 151, 177, 182, 209, 216
community, wider, 25, 33, 75, 81, 94, 104, 109, 114, 120, 152, 154, 160, 169, 259
  support of, 260, 275, 285, 317
conferences, 180, 192, 233, 309, 311
conflict ethnolinguistic, 228
  handling, 34, 131, 158, 317
  and researchers, 52, 54, 164
  within community, 50, 53, 88, 90, 157, 225, 228
connections, emotional, 123, 138, 161, 261, 263, 290
  to community, 264, 266
consent
  informed, 58, 76–7, 200
  conversation, 5, 39, 192, 209, 266
  clubs, 70, 74, 121
  and debate, 275, 282
  documentation of, 202, 224, 312, 314
  with elders, 12, 29, 193, 211, 218–19, 248, 269, 312
  for language learning, 39, 116, 152, 203, 251, 298
  skills for, 16, 242, 244, 250, 270
  via social media, 102, 185
  withdrawal of, 58
copyright, 277, 290

corpus, 200–2, 208, 244
  contents of, 209, 232, 244, 309
Corsica, 37
Corsican, 188
Costa Rica, 311
costs, 68, 72, 75, 147
  of publications, 78, 81, 260, 309
  reduction of, 192, 259
  of technology, 303, 305, 310
  travel, 78, 189
  of websites, 298
counting, 41, 255
courses, cultural, 144
courses, field methods, 177, 216
courses, language, 15, 23, 29, 114, 131, 144
  for adults, 66, 121, 258, 269, 313–14
  for children, 259
  community, 75, 119, 216, 249–50, 259
  distance-learning and online, 103, 236, 244, 298, 314
  residential, 314
  in schools, 65, 151, 163, 250, 260
  summer schools, 102, 193, 261, 305
  in universities, 133, 136, 139, 144, 177, 257, 261
courses, literacy, 177
Cree, 188
critics, 4, 35, 274
Croatia, 118
Croatian, 118
Cuba, 91
culture. *See also* heritage, cultural
  appropriation of, 57
  disruption of, 22, 101
  curriculum, 5, 73, 139, 171, 192, 211, 233, 241, 245, 247, 253, 266
  culture-based, 172, 263–4, 267
  development of, 235, 252, 257–8, 264, 314, 317
  reclaiming, 12, 15, 25, 38, 41, 44, 156, 245, 273, 278, 281, 284, 288
  revitalization of, 12, 14, 86, 144
  and technology, 299, 302
Czech, 40, 105

dance, 28, 57, 145, 232, 248, 273, 275–7, 281, 284, 287–8
Danish, 86
decolonization, 2, 4, 14, 58, 180
dementia, 21–3, 29, 153
description, language, 159, 201, 208
development, economic, 30, 143–4, 147, 149, 151–2, 156
dialects, 36, 48, 56, 86, 90, 105, 109, 113, 118–19, 166, 169

dictionaries, 221, 223–4, 244, 259
  creation of, 46, 72, 177
  for learning, 244, 252, 308
  monolingual, 233
  online, 59, 63, 65, 103, 308–9, 312
Diné (Navajo), 1, 21, 91, 280, 318
disadvantage
  economic, 87, 93, 101, 113, 141, 199
  social, 112, 125, 129
discrimination, 24, 27, 55, 87, 90, 92–3, 101, 111–13, 125, 131, 141, 153, 191, 222
displacement, linguistic, 87–8, 273–4, 281
diversity
  biological, 143
  cultural, 141, 175
  linguistic, 33, 99, 142, 151, 165, 169, 173–4, 177, 183, 224, 274, 279, 282
  within communities, 102
Diyari, 204
Djibouti, 224
documentation, language, 34
  community-driven, 30, 177, 189, 194, 232, 260, 314
  of everyday communication, 35, 200, 209, 309
  historical, 12, 29–30, 43, 58–9, 64, 94, 156, 203, 230, 307
  of language change, 41
  and language learners, 201, 210
  and metadata, 200–1, 205, 208, 210–11
  planning, 64, 76, 209
  for revitalization, 94, 158, 199, 211, 293, 310, 312, 314
  of traumatic memories, 29
  use of, 38, 46, 200–1, 203, 208
documents, legal, 183–4
domains, 34, 96, 114, 124, 174, 200
  expanding, 9, 11, 152, 169, 177, 199, 211, 289
  in the home, 246, 259
  for learning, 165, 249–51, 315
  and policies, 10
  public, 38, 88, 108, 173–4, 261–2, 275–6, 278
  reclaiming, 236, 240, 245–6, 249
  restricted, 92, 97, 125–6, 219, 242
  and technology, 305

Ecuador, 316
education
  access to, 101
  bilingual, 188, 233
  formal, 26, 30, 116–17, 139, 224, 258
  Indigenous, 253, 257, 266
  informal, 116–17, 263
  in majority language, 24, 126, 251, 269
  meeting mainstream standards, 41, 257, 265
  mother-tongue, 19, 200, 221, 235
  primary, 121, 152, 236, 252–3, 261, 264
  special needs, 20
  through Indigenous language, 115, 251, 253, 257, 264, 314
  university-level, 133, 136, 139, 144, 257, 261, 314
El Salvador, 81, 91, 127, 194
elders, 264
  involvement of, 39, 53, 103, 112, 131, 203, 209, 240, 254, 258, 260, 263–4, 267, 269–71, 285, 312
  and ownership, 120, 158
  and purism, 42, 53, 119, 202
  speaking to, 36, 138, 210, 312
elicitation, 218
emotions, expressing, 123–4, 262
employment, 23–4, 101, 109, 111, 113, 115, 126, 137–8, 140–1, 143, 153–4, 161
  using minority language in, 114, 141, 149, 151, 154
empowerment, 4, 11, 31, 56, 91, 93, 135, 139–40, 157, 161, 173, 193, 216, 227, 285
Endangered Language Alliance, 181, 187
Endangered Language Fund (ELF), 73
endangerment, 2, 4, 49, 86–7, 98, 178, 187–8
  biological, 142
Engaged Humanities project, 2, 46, 94, 134, 149, 192, 218, 317
English, 40–1, 96, 102, 115, 119, 126, 149, 163, 185, 187, 207, 223, 231–2, 279, 312
  First Nations English, 89
environment
  Indigenous management of, 143–4, 147, 152–3, 221, 254, 264–5, 268, 272
  relationships with, 144, 248, 266, 317
equipment, technical, 54, 72, 78–9, 212, 279, 302, 310
Eritrea, 224
Estonia, 231
ethics, 77–8, 131, 215–16
Ethiopia, 224
ethnobotany, 143, 248
European Charter for Regional or Minority Languages, 169–70, 175, 184
Euskara, See Basque
evaluation, 25, 62, 66–70, 157, 182, 211
  external, 68
  of plans, 45
  of technology, 303–4
Evenki, 16
events, community, 15, 132, 135, 266, *See also* activities & festivals
expertise, 160–1, 164, 189, 317
expressions, formulaic, 41, 209–10

Index

families, language choice in, 114, 126, 135–7, 140, 165, 177, 246, 249, 251, 258, 306
features, typological, 201, 210
festivals, 38, 276, 278, 282, 290
  language, 131, 136, 259, 287
  online, 288
  traditional, 287–8, 295
fieldwork, 193, 200, 216, 218
  training for, 194
filmmakers, Indigenous, 279–80
films, 94, 177, 182–3, 195, 259, 274, 278–81, 285, 295
  distribution of, 280, 282
  dubbing, 273, 279–80
  multilingual, 279
  subtitling, 184, 282, 312
Finland, 144, 235, 253
Finnish, 105
First Nations (Canada), 12, 19, 181–2, 280
fluency, 9, 38–9, 97, 249, 255, 289, 306
folklorization, 24, 146, 231, 284–5
fonts, 205, 228–30, 303
Foundation for Endangered Languages (FEL), 73, 180
France, 13, 92, 111, 119, 167, 172, 180, 186, 228, 279, 287
French, 108, 119, 167, 190
  Acadian French, 180, 184–6
  in Africa, 190
French Guyana, 190
funding, 33, 51, 67, 280, 317
  academic, 72–3, 260
  agencies, 51, 57–8, 75, 141, 160, 162, 190
  and evaluation, 68
  applications, 65, 67, 75–6
  community initiatives, 25, 61, 259
  crowd funding, 67, 73–4
  government, 169, 185, 274
  informal fundraising, 73–4, 288
  lack of, 69, 163, 259
  local, 67, 72, 81, 120, 147
  through tourism, 146–7

Gaelic, 147, 180, 184–6, 231
  Scottish Gaelic, 142, 184, 187, 282
  Irish Gaelic See *Irish*, See also *Manx*
Galician, 173, 276
games
  for children, 35–6, 70, 203
  interactive, 147, 149, 209, 259, 305, 309
  language, 94, 149, 259, 295
  for learning, 177, 216, 250, 252, 259
  for tourists, 151, 287
gender, 54, 158, 275
genocide, 87, 91, 128

Georgia, 229
Georgian, 229
German, 87, 217–18, 232
  Low German, 170
Germany, 91–2, 170, 279
Ghana, 230
globalization, 86–7, 145
goals, 9, 11, 50, 62, 76, 87, 160
  achievable, 39, 45, 162, 257
  of community members, 51, 89, 161–2, 216–17
  defining, 63
  of language documentation, 208
  long-term, 37, 65
  short-term, 64–5
government
  local, 25, 50, 55–6, 67, 151, 163, 261
  national, 11, 50, 67, 151, 160, 162, 174–5, 224, 230, 263, 274, 283
  tribal, 65, 78, 156, 277
grammar, 167, 200, 216
  simplification of, 41–2
  teaching of, 36, 240, 244, 249
grammars, 63, 221, 224
  and purism, 159
Greenland, 16
greetings, 16, 18, 35, 41–2, 45, 94, 142, 209, 232, 245, 255, 309
Greko, 102, 138, 193
Guarani, 207, 281–2
  Mbya-Guarani, 280
Guatemala, 80, 86, 274–5, 278, 282, 289, 316
Guernesiais, 35, 39–41, 119, 188, 193
Guernsey, 4, 35, 39, 119
Guyana, 163

Haitian, 185
Haudenosaunee, 271
Hawai'i, 226
Hawaiian, 20, 256
healing, 10, 13, 91, 132, 221
health, 264
  physical, 18, 21, 23, 29, 143, 153
  psychological, 15, 17, 23, 25, 127–8, 131–2, 138, 153
healthcare, 81, 101, 143, 153, 317
Hebrew, 17, 92, 188, 229
heritage, cultural, 4, 10, 16, 118, 138, 163, 223, 317
  documentation of, 206, 218, 285
  learning about, 26, 263, 266
  and tourism, 58, 142, 145, 151
  and youth, 29, 120
Hindi, 40, 279
homeschooling, 236, 249, 251

Ichishkíin, 298
identity
  for adults, 240
  changing, 108, 133, 169, 218
  and community, 60, 85, 109, 161, 275
  of community, 51, 89, 104, 106, 108–9
  connecting with past, 32, 36, 263
  and goals, 39–40
  ideologies, 86–7, 104
  immersion, 12, 20–1, 115, 172, 221, 240, 242, 255, 261
  individual, 136, 153
  of language learners, 238, 242, 271, 315
  local, 24, 284
  and migration, 93, 96
  modern, 100, 107–8
  multiple, 100, 102
  negative, 25, 100
  negative, 94, 100, 113, 125, 154
  positive, 47, 114
  racist, 90, 125
  reclaiming, 4, 9, 11, 13, 15, 29, 31, 44, 100, 121, 258, 280, 288
  of standard language, 105, 173
  and stereotypes, 13, 105
  symbolic, 45
  of youth, 177, 288, See also language nests & master-apprentice programmes
  camps, 61, 181
  pre-schools, 35, 121, 136, 152, 256–7, 264, 269, 310, 313–14
  schools, 41, 121, 136, 152, 240, 251, 256–7, 264, 288, 314, 318
implementation (of projects), 62, 68, 157
India, 74, 279
inequality, 23, 101, 112, 146
influence
  from Indigenous language, 89, 96
  from majority language, 40, 46, 85, 89–90, 98, 118, 139, 188, 242
  of traditional usage, 40, 119
institutions, academic, 56, 58, 75, 180, 261, 271, 274, 285
  and community members, 74, 133, 216
  and Indigenous researchers, 234, 257
institutions, language, 169, 181
institutions, local, 67, 78, 81, 115, 131, 143–4, 177
Instituto de docencia e investigación etnológica de Zacatecas (IDIEZ), 139, 191, 233
intelligibility, mutual, 86, 101, 191, 217
Internet, 15, 122, 185, 190, 224, 275, 280, 288, 295, 304–5, 315–16

intimacy, 24, 36, 123
Inuit, 187–8, 279
Inuktitut, 181, 188, 279
Ireland, 106, 148, 231
Irish, 43, 106–7, 142, 152, 187, 231
Isle of Man, 41, 120, 148
ISO codes, 171
Italian, 118
Italy, 102–3, 170, 194, 279
Itzá, 86
Izọn, 193

Japan, 23, 88, 168, 170, 185, 229, 291
Japanese, 24, 229, 279
Jejudommal, 123–4
Jèrriais, 36, 290
Jersey, 36, 290
jokes, 16, 203, 209, 276, 309
Juǀ'hoan, 221
Judaism, 17, 100, 229
Judeo-Persian, 229

K'iche Maya, 80
Kalaallisut (Greenlandic), 16
Kāi Tahu. See *Māori (Southern)*
Kannada, 279
Kaqchikel Maya, 80–1, 275, 278
Karaim, 229
Kashubian, 113, 170–1, 193, 231
Kaurna, 204
Khoekhoegowab, 224
Khwe, 220
Kiliwa, 85
knowledge
  cultural, 10, 16, 210, 234, 249, 263, 266, 269, 276
  documentation of, 16, 41, 64, 143–4, 203, 221, 268
  Indigenous ways of knowing, 234, 237, 244, 254, 272
  local, 25, 143, 146–7, 164, 266
  traditional, 53–4, 128, 142–4, 156, 172, 221, 253, 266, 268
Korean, 123, 223, 229
Kristang, 258
Kurdish, 231

Ladino, 229
landscape, linguistic, 38, 116–17, 146, 149, 152, 154, 218, 231, 285
language
  as secret code, 92
  banned, 38, 141, 276, 284
  choice of, 90, 93–4, 97, 106, 108, 112, 124, 135, 165, 183

Index

dead or dormant, 40, 86, 90, 93, 120, 156, 158, 226
formal, 34, 36
national, 86, 88–90, 95, 98, 105, 118, 123, 126, 174–5
ritualistic, 44, 210, 274, 276
sacred, 12, 17, 203, 255
standard, 11, 36, 105, 107, 173, 224
symbolic use of, 18, 38, 89, 94, 98, 142, 146, 166, 210, 271
taking back, 14, 130
of wider communication, 4, 80, 200
Latgalian, 170, 231
Latvia, 170, 231
learners, 95, 103, 209
assessment of, 235, 250, 259, 270, 299, 302–3
and authenticity, 108
and daily language use, 209, 246–7, 249, 251, 254–6, 259, 261–2, 315, 318
errors of, 102, 237
goals for, 15, 241–2, 245, 249–50, 253, 255, 267, 302
and historical trauma, 238, 242
responsibility for learning, 251–2
as teachers, 306
and technology, 299
and written materials, 223, 227, 240–2, 307
Lemko/Łemko, 91, 193, 261
Lenca, 80
lifestyle, 18, 23
tourist experiences of, 145
traditional, 18, 23, 122, 135, 143, 145, 280, 288
Limburgian, 170
links
between activists, 94, 192, 194
between communities, 71, 94, 134, 144, 159, 161, 178–9, 181–2, 184, 188, 193, 291, 314, 316–17
between projects, 70, 73, 76, 178, 251
between teachers, 244, 311
within community, 13, 39, 85, 209, 219, 288
listening, 29, 60, 104
literacy, 63, 222, 224, 226–7, 230–1, 274–5, 282
and Christianity, 221
literature, 140, 232, 259, 273, 288
new styles of, 273–5
oral, 275–6, 278, 281–2
traditional, 43, 277–8, 314
Lithuania, 229
Lithuanian, 231
livelihoods, traditional, 264, 266
agriculture, 64, 107, 143, 234
fishing, 144, 250
reindeer herding, 16, 144, 254, 267

loanwords. *See* borrowing
logotherapy, 128–9
Lombardese, 228
loss, language, 22–3, 92, 97, 153, 281
lullabies, 203, 210
Lushootseed, 236, 245

Maasai, 57
Maaya t'aan. See Yucatec Maya
Makushi, 163, 193
Malawi, 224
Malayalam, 279
Malaysia, 258
Maliseet (Wolastoqi), 12, 312–13, *See also Passamaquoddy*
Mam Maya, 80
Mandarin, 279
Manx, 39, 41, 90, 120, 148, 193, 318
Māori, 20, 35–6, 38, 40, 44, 88, 136, 148, 152, 179, 187, 240, 251, 277
Southern (*Kāi Tahu*), 88, 179
Māori Language Commission, 43, 152
Mapuche, 178, 180–1, 184–5, 190
Mapudungun, 289
Marathi, 279
marginalization, 4, 24, 55, 101, 125, 162, 222, 273–4
marketing
and funding, 152
of heritage, 146
of languages, 151–2, 154
of products, 149
of projects, 67
of revitalization, 142, 144, 147, 152
master-apprentice programs, 13, 39, 62, 74, 236, 240, 245, 248; *See also* mentor-apprentice
Masurian, 193
creation of, 38, 62, 94, 103, 161, 167, 177, 183, 211, 216, 293, 297, 299, 307, 309–10, 314–15
distribution of, 59, 170, 193, 274, 282, 295, 304, 312
for language learning and teaching, 64, 72, 76, 94, 163, 177, 193–4, 209, 222, 226, 232–3, 235, 239, 241, 246, 249, 261, 264–5, 274, 299, 307, 309, 312
legacy, 201, 205, 226
materials for children, 64, 144, 310
multimedia, 177, 273, 293, 305
for online learning, 177, 268, 314–15
and variation, 159, 224
written, 36, 221, 261, 268, 307
Mayan languages, 80, 274

media
  interest of, 25, 56, 219
  news, 121, 273
  role of, 116, 151, 166, 261, 317
media, social, 11, 70, 103, 114, 172, 185, 209, 225, 273, 277, 281, 288, 309, 317
  for awareness raising, 115, 313
  blogs, 268, 306, 315
  for campaigning, 166, 316
  for changing attitudes, 289
  communities, 101
  Facebook, 103, 185, 250, 261, 280, 304, 309, 311
  Instagram, 250, 309
  policies, 304
  for teachers, 311
  Twitter, 309, 316
  WhatsApp, 102, 309
  YouTube, 15, 280–2, 289, 307, 315
medicine, traditional, 16, 143–4, 249, 270
Megrelian, 229
Mennonites, 92
mentor-apprentice programmes, *See also* master-apprentice programs
methodology (for revitalization), 76, 78, 94, 177, 179, 211, 218–19, 233
Mexico, 30, 57, 85–6, 92, 94–5, 101, 124, 143, 178, 194, 274, 277, 282, 289, 293, 313, 316
Mi'kmaq, 12, 20
Mi'kmaw, 180, 184–6
Miami-Illinois. *See myaaamia*
Miami Tribe, 74, 156, 308, *See also* myaamia
migration, 89, 92, 96–7, 101, 126, 137, 187
  economic, 101
  forced, 22, 143
Minderico, 184
minoritization, 55, 128, 273
Mirandese, 169
Mississauga, 271
Mixe, 314
Mixtec, 101, 177, 193–4, 274, 289
Mixteco/Indígena Community Organizing Project (MICOP), 101, 177, 216
modernity, 23, 45, 114, 122, 126, 202, 258, 285, 288–9
Mohawk, 188
  in Indigenous language, 125
  monolingualism, 10, 20, 119, 166
  in national language, 88
  and nationalist ideologies, 113, 165, 173, 276, 288
  within projects, 103, 139, 191, 233
Mopan, 86
  economic, 10, 88, 97, 109, 114

motivationsof activists, 4, 12, 38, 44–5, 112, 138, 280
  of researchers, 50, 293
  for revitalization, 9–11, 22, 39, 49, 104
  of speakers, 10, 87, 89, 114, 136–7, 288
  of teachers, 253, 260
movements, grassroots, 87, 141, 168, 258–9, 275, 283, 289
multilingualism, 40, 86, 93, 96–7, 109, 115, 120, 154, 166, 169, 171, 238, 266
  benefits of, 4, 10, 20–2, 29, 115, 153, 266
  concerns about, 20, 113, 115, 119, 242
  replacive bilingualism, 88
  of younger speakers, 89
museums, 29, 46, 67, 74, 81, 193, 280, 317
  folk, 28–9, 121, 284
  hip hop, 277–8, 289
  and identity, 278, 290
  learning through, 261, 291, 295
  living, 147, 149, 151
  music, 276, 282, 287–8, 290
  new styles of, 277–8, 281, 288–9, 291, 295
  online, 147
  rap, 90, 278, 289, 295
  reggae, 277, 289
  rock, 277, 289, 295
  traditional, 268, 273
myaamia, 15, 156, 158–9, 163, 252, 308

N'ko, 230
Nahuatl, 30, 40, 47, 94–6, 98, 124, 139–40, 143, 154, 191–2, 194, 233, 282, 295
names
  language, 171, 207
  personal, 128, 133, 208, 231, 253, 262
Namibia, 220–1
Naro, 224
nationalism, 88, 100, 113, 173
Native American nations, 91
Navajo. *See Diné*
Nawat (Pipil), 91, 103, 127, 130, 193
neocolonialism, 46
nests, language, 63, 65, 88, 152, 172, 179, 236, 240, 246, *See also* immersion
  at home, 240, 245–6, 249, 251
Netherlands, 92, 170
networks (for revitalization), 93–4, 178, 185, 192–4, 316–17, *See also* links
New Zealand, 20, 35–6, 44, 148, 152, 277
non-governmental organizations (NGOs), 80, 144, 163, 166, 181
  and communities, 81
  and funding, 73–4, 78, 147
  local, 81, 285
normalization, 173, 274

Norway, 16, 18, 21, 144
Norwegian, 86
nostalgia, 4, 45, 146, 202
nursery rhymes, 35–6, 203

Ojibwa (Anishanabeeg), 20, 240
Okanagan Salish, 74
Okinawan, 23
orthography, 165, 202, 228
　development of, 38, 207, 211, 220–1, 223, 226, 228, 230
　and identity, 224, 227, 229–30
　and ideologies, 228–30
　non-standardized, 205, 232
　and phonology, 223, 230
　and technology, 11, 303
Ossetian, 229
outcomes, 77, 138
　educational, 11, 257
　measurable, 63, 66, 70, 76, 162
ownership, 90, 225, 259
　and authenticity, 33, 42, 48, 107–8, 116
　of data, 57, 304
　and learners, 108, 122

Pahka'anil, 236, 244–5
Paraguay, 281
Passamaquoddy, 212, 312
　and difficult issues, 55
　influence of, 42
　and language learners, 45, 240, 245, 291
　new styles of, 273, 276–7, 281, 285, 289, 291
　pastconnecting with, 4, 12–13, 31–2, 40–1, 134, 156, 161, 202, 218
　performances, 38, 288, 290
　traditional, 146, 199, 273, 276, 278, 284,
　See also Maliseet
permissions, 56, 75, 78, 164, 204, 207
persecution, 28–9, 55, 100, 111–12, 125, 133, 141, 148, 218
Peru, 181, 277, 289, 316
phonology, 177, 201
Piedmontese, 170, 228
Pipil. See Nawat
place, 18, 142, 160, 254, 263, 266
placenames, 63, 221, 228, 255, 271
planning
　activities, 5, 15, 32, 34, 37, 62, 64
　and community members, 51, 53, 211
　and funding, 75
　projects, 52, 62, 68, 157
　strategic, 45, 62–3, 65, 68, 105, 258, 318
　for teaching, 172–3

planning, language, 167, 173
　acquisition, 171–2
　bottom-up, 39, 168
　corpus, 167, 173
　prestige, 169
　status, 167, 173
　top-down, 169–70
plants, 16, 64, 142–3, 248–9, 266, 270
poetry, 43, 45–6, 177, 232, 261, 273, 284, 290
Poland, 56, 86, 88, 91–2, 99, 113, 170–2, 176, 193–4, 217, 229, 231
policies
　of archives, 206–7
　bottom-up, 110, 112, 165
　community, 90, 117, 165, 181–2
　educational, 10, 88, 94, 117, 125, 141, 165, 171–2, 175
　influencing, 173, 182
　national, 33, 89, 136, 141, 143, 165–6, 174, 176, 224–5, 274
　top-down, 112, 114, 165, 168, 170
　and writing systems, 224, 226, 229–31
policy-makers, 135, 143, 153, 165, 167–8, 172, 177
　language institutions as, 164, 172
Polish, 29, 40, 47, 133, 149, 218, 232
politeness, 36, 41
politicians, 50, 71, 141, 143, 167
Portugal, 169, 279
Portuguese, 184, 207, 279
post-vernacular, 37, 94
Potawatomi, 236, 244
poverty, 86, 111, 137
power, social, 159, 162
pragmatics, 109, 201–2
prayers, 12, 38, 200, 221, 265, 274
prestige, 10, 96, 105, 111, 133, 154, 169–70, 174
　low, 113–14, 120
　raising, 28, 31, 35, 112, 218, 285
　reclaiming, 119
　of traditional speakers, 107
pride, 20, 26, 109, 114, 118–19, 162, 177, 221, 257
privacy, 77, 203, 304
　language use in, 108
products, 142, 145
　handicrafts, 144–6, 149, 264, 268
　souvenirs, 149, 151, 285
proficiency, 87, 95, 120
　and employment, 151
　of learners, 162, 210, 238, 241, 245, 307
　of teachers, 242, 255
　of youth, 95, 158

projects
  design of, 66–7, 76
  impact of, 75–6, 153, 200, 220, 226, 262, 279, 289, 293
  timelines for, 63, 68, 76
  urban, 259
pronunciation
  correct, 159, 241
  of new speakers, 41–2, 298, 306, 308
protests, 112, 135–6, 167, 182, 276
  through music, 276–7, 288–9
Provençal/Occitan, 228
publication, 274
  academic, 52, 57, 161
  of books, 94, 221, 274, 276, 282, 295
  of Christian materials, 221
  and consent, 58
  of digital materials, 309–10
  in newspapers, 261
  of storybooks, 74, 177, 232
purism, 32, 42, 46, 48, 90, 96, 108, 118, 139, 159
  as positive, 90
  and teaching materials, 202

Q'eqchi' Maya, 80, 278
Quebecois, 190
Quechua, 43, 185, 207, 277, 282, 289

racism, 87, 90, 93, 125, 154, 205, 259
radio, 77, 117, 121, 273, 282, 314
recognition
  of endangerment, 49
  as language, 37, 47, 56, 90, 109, 118–19, 154, 170
  lack of, 92, 101, 113, 135–6, 169, 175–6, 273
  official, 88, 113, 136, 170–1, 266, 281, 314
  seeking, 86, 110, 112, 167, 170, 182, 188, 289, 318
  symbolic, 118
reconstruction, language, 33, 35
recordings
  creating, 200, 211–13, 216, 232, 260, 313
  ethical issues with, 57, 204
  historical, 59, 203, 205, 244
  for language learning, 298, 302, 306, 313, 315
  storage of, 215
  use of, 221, 244
registers, 35, 38, 40, 48
research
  benefits for community, 61
  Indigenous, 60, 233–4
  planning, 25, 61

researchers
  knowledge of community, 51, 54, 70, 116
  negative views of, 55, 260
  positionality of, 56, 61
  relations with community, 51, 61, 70, 75, 78, 131, 160, 168
  and status, 159, 218
  and time constraints, 50–1
resilience, 11, 15, 88
resistance, 15, 88, 114, 116, 277
resources
  assessing, 5, 34, 37, 63, 67–8, 164, 168, 264, 314
  lack of, 132, 318
  mobilizing, 93, 131
  sharing, 101, 179, 185, 189
respect
  for community, 50, 54, 56, 60
  for language, 221
  for researchers, 59, 218
  for speakers, 96, 210, 313
  for stakeholders, 70, 160, 163–4, 263
revival, language, 4, 92–3, 173, 223, 313
riddles, 210, 295
rights
  human, 135, 141, 166, 174
  intellectual property, 57, 204, 304
  land, 221
  linguistic, 11, 92, 112, 135–6, 141, 166, 174–5, 182, 184, 222, 289
rituals, 44–5, 88, 136, 214, 221, 266
  in school, 267
Rom/Romani, 92, 100
Russia, 88, 100, 229
Rusyn, 176
Ryūkyūan, 170, 229

salaries, 68, 72, 78, 161
Sámi, 16, 18, 21, 144, 193, 236, 253, 266
Sámi University of Applied Sciences (*Sámi allaskuvla*), 144, 172
San Martín Peras Mixtec, 177
Sandawe, 221
Saxon, Low, 170
schools, field, 46, 149, 192–3, 195, 218–19
schools, language teaching in, 91, 171, 211, 248–9
  concerns about, 36, 40, 113
  mainstream, 4, 121, 172
Scotland, 148, 184
Scots, 170
Scots, Ulster, 170
scripts, 188, 224, 228–30
self-determination
  personal, 9, 14–15, 18, 22, 129–30
  political, 11, 15, 31, 188, 318

self-esteem, 18, 26, 31–2, 70, 139, 153, 220, 226, 255
sensitivity, cultural, 57, 60, 94, 253, 266, 295
shamans, 12, 17, 95
shame, 85, 97, 109–11, 125, 141, 154, 271
shift, language, 14–15, 23, 48, 90, 101, 112, 119, 126, 171, 202, 230, 312
   reversing, 88, 93, 110
Siberia, 12, 16–17
Sicilian, 170
signage, 11, 38, 44, 63, 116, 121, 152, 155, 221, 228
SIL, 133, 171, 221
Silesian, 47, 171, 176, 193
Siletz Dee-ni', 308
Singapore, 258
Skwxwú7mesh (Squamish), 180
smartphones, 103, 212, 298, 308–9, 315
socialization, language, 87, 97, 109, 158
software, 76, 79, 179, 205, 207, 211, 281, 300, 302–4, 315
solidarity, 38, 109, 144, 178, 180, 184, 191
songs, 28, 38, 57, 62, 210, 232, 273, 282
   for language learning, 255, 289
   new, 261, 273, 276–7, 285
   online, 289
   traditional, 12, 18, 45, 94, 103, 205, 248, 265, 267, 273–4, 276–7, 284, 287, 291
Sorbian, 168
South Africa, 145–6, 203
South West Oregon Dene, 308
space, monolingual, 139, 191, 240, 246, 257, 269, 285
Spain, 56, 88, 92, 180, 183, 186, 194, 276, 279
Spanish, 32, 47, 80, 96, 98, 101–2, 125–7, 139, 184, 191, 207, 233, 274, 279
   Indo-American Spanish, 89
speakers
   fluent, 95–6, 203, 218, 240, 248, 257, 318
   and language documentation, 200
   last, 90–1, 120, 257, 260, 284
   needs of, 161
   new, 9, 34, 39, 42, 98, 115, 122, 136, 148, 151–2, 168, 209, 262, 270, 287, 313, 315
   non-, 45, 95, 108–9, 163
   potential, 104, 115–16, 135, 137, 152
   semi-, 39, 93, 95, 97, 312
   silent, 19
   traditional, 34, 90, 103, 107, 315
   urban, 37, 60, 85, 93, 108, 124, 146, 254
   young, 43, 90, 96, 103, 119, 154

speaking
   fear of, 19
   opportunities for, 114, 116, 119, 135, 138–9, 169, 187, 192, 209, 219, 239, 242, 246, 251, 306, 312
   spontaneous, 97, 242
spirits, communicating with, 12, 160
spirituality, 12, 136, 162, 221
stakeholders, 33, 86, 94, 160, 163, 283
   relations between, 163–4
standardization, 11, 33, 37, 105, 167, 225, 274
   lack of, 118, 202
   and language planning, 173
   of orthography, 36, 191–2
status, 36, 109, 171
   raising, 38, 152, 170, 200, 266, 290
stories, 12, 25, 60, 103, 133, 205, 208, 240, 255, 265, 272, 275, 295
   and contemporary storytelling, 275, 281
   and dance, 275, 277
   and films, 279–80
   and learning, 245, 264–8, 270
   and storytelling, 271, 273–4, 276, 312
success, 127, 187, 211, 257, 282, 285, 290
suicide, 18, 153
surveys
   of attitudes, 5, 115, 177, 193, 218, 250
   of community, 145, 163
   environmental, 142–4, 168, 266, 268
   Guatemala, 80
   Guernesiais, 120
   Irish, 106
   of languages, 62, 211
   of learners, 250
   of projects, 52, 161, 184, 315, 318
   sustainability of archive resources, 206
   tools for, 308
   of vitality, 70, 174
Svan, 229
Swedish, 86
Sylheti, 74, 193

Tai, 193
Taino, 91
Taiwanese, 279
Tamazight, 187
Tamil, 279
Tanzania, 221
Tasmania, 91
teachers, 97
   as learners, 235, 241, 252, 255, 269
   fluency of, 236, 255
   lack of, 5, 274
   recruiting, 94, 220, 239, 270, 313

teachers (cont.)
  and technology, 299
  training of, 177, 181, 244, 253, 261, 309, 311, 317
teaching methods, 183, 192, 216, 235, See also language nests & immersion
  Accelerated Second Language Acquisition (ASLA), 236, 249, 252
  Can-Do statements, 236, 245
  choices of, 172, 238, 242, 245, 252, 298
  communicative, 241–2, 244, 258, 263
  culture-based learning, 250, 253–5, 263–4, 266, 268, 270
  direct, 241–2
  grammar-translation, 240, 242, 244
  home learning, 251, 256, 259
  immersive, 248, 252, 254–5, 261
  kinetic activities, 241, 249–50, 252, 255
  project based learning, 310
  radically input-based, 241–2, 244
  reclaiming domains, 236, 240, 245, 249
  and technology, 297, 307–8, 311
teams, 26, 69, 93, 103, 131, 138, 200, 259, 263, 295, 317
technology
  access to, 221, 227, 275, 298, 303, 305, 308, 315
  creative use of, 283
  digital, 147, 225, 288
  file formats, 205, 213
  for language learning, 297, 302, 305, 307, 309–10, 315
  and language use, 306, 309–10, 315
  for recording, 79, 212, 298, 302–3
  for revitalization, 224, 316
  skills for, 297, 300
Tehuelche, 184
television, 117, 273, 279, 282, 293, 314
Telugu, 279
texting, 11, 103, 118, 225, 309
Thailand, 24
theatre, 28, 38, 55, 103, 133, 151, 261, 275, 285, 288
  for language learning, 285
Tolowa Dee-ni', 236, 248–51, 298
tourism, 30, 145, 153
  community initiatives, 145, 149, 221
  and local languages, 147, 152
  and tourist information, 149
transcription, 31, 200–2, 207, 211, 216, 312
translation, 31, 200–1, 205, 207, 211, 216, 232, 290–1, 312
transmission, 171, 211
  broken, 13, 24, 88, 95, 97, 102, 111–12, 114, 119, 123–4, 128, 182, 199, 222, 226, 258

  cultural, 17, 162
  intergenerational, 25, 35, 87, 96, 108, 137, 141, 152, 158, 239, 258, 262, 295
  reestablishing, 103, 240, 246, 269, 306
  responsibility for, 4, 138
trauma, 18, 22, 85, 91, 111–12, 153, 238
  addressing, 14, 28–9, 53, 312
  and consent, 55, 58
  in schools, 88, 111, 113, 125, 139, 271
Tu'un Savi (Mixtec), 177, See also Mixtec
Tübatulabal, 244, 245, See also Pahka'anil
Tumbuka, 224
Turkish, 230–1
Tzotzil, 289
Tzutuhil Maya, 278, 289

Ukraine, 91, 176
Ukrainian, 231
UNESCO, 19, 70, 118, 120, 133, 174
United Kingdom, 92, 119, 148, 170, 194
United Nations Declaration on the Rights of Indigenous Peoples, 15, 58, 174
University of California, Santa Barbara (UCSB), 177, 216
University of Hawai'i College of Hawaiian Language, 172, 257
urbanization, 124, 142, 288
Uruguay, 91
Uruk, 193
USA, 21, 38, 88, 91–3, 96, 101, 126, 143, 156, 194, 203, 235, 264, 312
  funding, 73–4
use, language
  actual, 46, 113, 200, 209
  encouraging, 116, 135–7, 148, 222
  and identity, 238
usefulness (of language), 106, 108, 116, 140, 148, 154
Uto-Aztecan languages, 233

value (of language), 108, 126, 132, 140, 154, 162
  economic, 90, 138, 140, 142, 151, 154, 166
  emotional, 138, 146, 162
values, community, 44, 156–8, 253, 266–8
values, emotional, 124, 281
Vanuatu, 78
variation, 118, 173, 224
  by age, 41, 89, 105, 202
  in proficiency, 89, 92, 95, 97–8
varieties
  acceptance of, 90, 170, 224, 251
  choice of, 33, 37, 89, 124
  in diaspora, 92
  differences between, 89, 105, 192
  regional, 191, 244

Index

Venetian, 118, 170, 228
Veneto, 92
video, 94, 274
  for language documentation, 309, 314
  for language learning, 250, 265, 313
  music, 277–8
  online, 177, 277, 280–1, 315
  recording of, 214, 279, 307, 310
  for revitalization, 280, 312
Vietnamese, 230
Vilamovian. See Wymysiöeryś
visibility of community, 54–5, 291
  of languages, 38, 70, 114, 131, 142, 148, 152, 177, 278, 281, 283, 285, 312–13
  of projects, 103, 149
vitality, linguistic, 9–10, 14, 70, 80, 86, 88, 98, 141, 147
vocabulary, 16, 32, 43, 48, 167, 233
  documentation of, 176, 216
  grammatical, 35, 192, 233
  learning, 64, 223, 240, 248–50, 252, 254–5, 270–1, 293, 308
  new, 32, 36, 43–4, 167, 204, 232, 250
  reconstruction of, 40
  reduced, 41, 97, 118
  for schools, 33, 43, 233, 240, 264
  for technology, 33, 43
  traditional, 16, 48, 107
Võro (Southern Estonian), 231

Wales, 35, 151, 187–8, 228, 314
Wallmapu, 180
Wampanoag, 15
websites, 72, 151, 170, 250, 261, 280, 316
  development of, 76, 298, 306, 310
welfare linguistics, 23
well-being, 10–11, 22, 25, 153
  of community, 19, 22, 26, 44, 60, 157, 179
  of learners, 138, 238, 266–7
  of researchers, 59
  of speakers, 136, 226
  of teachers, 311
Welsh, 36, 136, 142, 148, 151, 184, 187–8, 314
Wilamowice, 4, 50, 55, 57, 99, 148–9, 193, 218–19, 260, 284, *See also* Wymysiöeryś
workplace, language in, 80–1, 142, 149, 151, 154, 209
workshops, 193
  craft, 264–5
  educational, 61, 149, 151, 193, 295
  on historical texts, 30, 94
  language documentation, 177, 194, 209
  language learning, 94
  literacy, 220
  music, 261
  orthography, 220
  revitalization, 76, 180, 182–3, 191, 293
  teacher training, 309, 311
  technology, 316
  for tourists, 147, 151
worldview, Indigenous, 17, 137, 172, 233, 242, 253, 257
  choices in, 223, 225
  development of, 36, 62, 173, 200, 222, 228
  educational factors in, 230
  and education, 126, 158, 221
  and identity, 231
  and language use, 165, 221
  obsolete, 205, 274
  and orality, 158, 192, 220–1, 226
  and policies, 167, 188
  and religion, 221, 224, 229–30
  standardization of, 37, 167, 229–31, 274
  symbolic use of, 220, 228, 231
  and technology, 307
  traditions of, 30, 118
  writing systems, 118, 193, 229, 313
  writing creative, 94, 233, 275, 308
Wymysiöeryś, 27, 59, 86, 99–100, 133, 140, 148, 155, 171, 176, 193, 231–2, 260, 284, *See also* Wilamowice

Xavante, 280

Yanesha, 181
Yiddish, 229
Yoruba, 279
youth, 28, 126
  disconnection of, 101
  initiatives of, 100, 102, 151, 258, 276–7, 287, 289
  involvement of, 26, 39, 42, 56, 63, 102, 151, 172, 180, 209, 259–61, 276, 278, 280–1, 285, 288, 315–16, 318
Yucatec Maya, 85–6, 90, 93, 96, 188, 194, 275, 277, 282, 289

Zaiwa, 193
Zoque, 289
Zulu, 145